THE MAKING OF THE
SUPER BOWL

THE MAKING OF THE SUPER BOWL

THE INSIDE STORY OF THE WORLD'S GREATEST SPORTING EVENT

DON WEISS WITH CHUCK DAY

Contemporary Books

Chicago   New York   San Francisco   Lisbon   London   Madrid   Mexico City
Milan   New Delhi   San Juan   Seoul   Singapore   Sydney   Toronto

Library of Congress Cataloging-in-Publication Data

Weiss, Don, 1926–
    The making of the Super Bowl : the inside story of the world's greatest sporting event /
Don Weiss with Chuck Day.
        p.   cm.
    Includes index.
    ISBN 0-07-139505-9
    1. Super Bowl.   2. Weiss, Don, 1926–   I. Day, Chuck.   II. Title.

GV956.2.S8 W45   2002
796.332'648—dc21   2002073685

1 2 3 4 5 6 7 8 9 0   AGM/AGM   1 0 9 8 7 6 5 4 3 2

ISBN 0-07-139505-9

Interior design by Nick Panos

McGraw-Hill books are available at special quantity discounts to use as premiums and sales
promotions, or for use in corporate training programs. For more information, please write to
the Director of Special Sales, Professional Publishing, McGraw-Hill, Two Penn Plaza, New York,
NY 10121-2298. Or contact your local bookstore.

This book is printed on acid-free paper.

CONTENTS

Preface...vii

Acknowledgments..xiii

PART I THE MERGER

ONE My Path into Pro Football.....................3

TWO Seeds of Union: Baby-Sitting and
Body Snatching...17

THREE Anatomy of a Merger...........................33

FOUR Coming from Behind on Capitol Hill...................47

FIVE Even the Football Was Different..........................61

SIX The "Royal Order of Realignment Recorders":
Fashioning One League from Two......................75

PART II THE SUPER BOWL

SEVEN Finding the Venue: It Had to Be Warm and
It Had to Be Big...95

EIGHT Uptight and Out of Sight...................................109

NINE January 1967: Year One: Not So Super..............121

TEN   On to Miami with a Mission............................133

ELEVEN   Joe Willie and the Jets.............................149

TWELVE   Murphy's Law and Stram's Chiefs....................165

THIRTEEN   Halftime..183

FOURTEEN   Celebrities, Motorcades, Coaches . . . and
Black Sunday.....................................201

FIFTEEN   My Favorite Years..................................219

SIXTEEN   What You Probably Didn't See.......................233

SEVENTEEN   Game Day: What You Still Don't See...............251

EIGHTEEN   What Really Made It Super.........................265

PART III PRIME TIME

NINETEEN   Sticking Our Toes in the Water....................273

TWENTY   Are You Ready for Some Football?....................281

TWENTY-ONE   The Blackout Battles............................291

PART IV MEN WHO MADE A DIFFERENCE

TWENTY-TWO   Pete Rozelle: A Man for His Time................303

TWENTY-THREE   Jim Kensil: A Tough Act to Follow............309

TWENTY-FOUR   Tex Schramm: One Brilliant "Bullmoose".......315

TWENTY-FIVE   George Halas: A Picture of Irascibility......321

TWENTY-SIX   Jim Finks: "Football Man".....................325

TWENTY-SEVEN   Don Shula and Paul Brown: Master and
"Wily Mentor".................................331

TWENTY-EIGHT   Bill Granholm: Unsung Super Bowl Hero........337

TWENTY-NINE   Eddie LeBaron: A Big Little Man..............343

THIRTY   Mara, Rooney, Hunt, and Modell:
A Historic Quartet.................................347

Appendix A: Super Bowl Data.........................351

Appendix B: Bulls, Bears, and Super Bowls.........389

Index...391

PREFACE

The late Dr. Norman Vincent Peale once said: "If Jesus were alive today, he'd probably be at the Super Bowl." Presumably, Dr. Peale felt that He would want to be among the masses.

The Super Bowl draws the masses. After 36 years it clearly has established itself as the most important single-day sporting event in the United States, if not in the world. Of the most-watched television shows in U.S. history, the first 10 are Super Bowls ranging in audience from 138,488,000 viewers for Super Bowl XXX in 1996 to 127,055,000 viewers for Super Bowl XX in 1986. Of the all-time top 75 sports events ranked according to Nielsen ratings, 9 of the top 10 are Super Bowls. Only the Wednesday evening telecast of the 1994 Winter Olympics (remember Tonya Harding and Nancy Kerrigan?) breaks into the Super Bowl's dominance. That telecast, by CBS, drew a 48.5 rating and a 64 share to place third among all-time sports events. The leader (and likely to remain that way) is CBS's telecast of Super Bowl XVI, which matched the San Francisco 49ers and the Cincinnati Bengals on January 24, 1982. Played in the Silverdome in Pontiac, Michigan, on a day when most of North America was locked in an icy deep freeze, the game had a 49.1 rating and a 73 share. It's been ranked number one from that day forward (see Tables 1 and 2).

TABLE 1: MOST-WATCHED SHOWS IN TV HISTORY

Rank	Program	Opponents, Year	Network	Total Viewers	Rating	Share
1.	Super Bowl XXX	Dallas–Pittsburgh, 1996	NBC	138,488,000	46.0	68
2.	Super Bowl XXVIII	Dallas–Buffalo, 1994	NBC	134,800,000	45.5	66
3.	Super Bowl XXXII	Denver–Green Bay, 1998	NBC	133,400,000	44.5	67
3.	Super Bowl XXVII	Dallas–Buffalo, 1993	NBC	133,400,000	45.1	66
5.	Super Bowl XXXVI	New England–St. Louis, 2002	FOX	131,700,000	40.4	61
6.	Super Bowl XXXV	Baltimore–New York Giants, 2001	CBS	131,200,000	40.4	61
7.	Super Bowl XXXIV	St. Louis–Tennessee, 2000	ABC	130,700,000	43.3	63
8.	Super Bowl XXXI	Green Bay–New England, 1997	FOX	128,900,000	43.3	65
9.	Super Bowl XXXIII	Denver–Atlanta, 1999	FOX	127,500,000	40.2	61
10.	Super Bowl XX	Chicago–New England, 1986	NBC	127,055,000	48.3	70

Data courtesy of Nielsen Media Research.

TABLE 2: ALL-TIME TOP 10 TELEVISION SPORTS EVENTS (January 1961–May 2002)

Rank	Program	Opponents	Network	Telecast Date	Rating	Share
1.	Super Bowl XVI	San Francisco–Cincinnati	CBS	Jan. 24, 1982	49.1	73
2.	Super Bowl XVII	Washington–Miami	NBC	Jan. 30, 1983	48.6	69
3.	XVII Winter Olympics	Figure skating competition	CBS	Feb. 23, 1994	48.5	64
4.	Super Bowl XX	Chicago–New England	NBC	Jan. 26, 1986	48.3	70
5.	Super Bowl XII	Dallas–Denver	CBS	Jan. 15, 1978	47.2	67
6.	Super Bowl XIII	Pittsburgh–Dallas	NBC	Jan. 21, 1979	47.1	74
7.	Super Bowl XVIII	L.A. Raiders–Washington	CBS	Jan. 22, 1984	46.4	71
8.	Super Bowl XIX	San Francisco–Miami	ABC	Jan. 20, 1985	46.4	63
9.	Super Bowl XIV	Pittsburgh–L.A. Rams	CBS	Jan. 20, 1980	46.3	67
10.	Super Bowl XXX	Dallas–Pittsburgh	NBC	Jan. 28, 1996	46.0	68

Data courtesy of Nielsen Media Research

Those of us who have been directly involved in the creation and growth of the National Football League's championship game are often asked three questions: How did it happen, how did it get so big, and did anyone ever imagine it would get like this? Typically, the answers are usually: I don't know; I have no idea; and no, I didn't. And each one of those answers is dead wrong.

Saying the Super Bowl got to be what it is by accident, luck, or happenstance fails to recognize the amount of planning, preparation, and pure sweat that has gone into it for 36 years. It's the same planning, preparation, and sweat that has gone into building the National Football League into the premier league of professional sports. That's not just my opinion but the conclusion reached from every sampling that's ever been taken in the past three decades. Both achievements have been the work of the same people—dedicated, driven, relentless persons who wouldn't let anything short of success satisfy them.

Ask Gina Henry, a former secretary in the NFL public relations office who was at her desk in our headquarters office in Newport Beach, California, at 5:00 A.M. every day for nearly two weeks before Super Bowl VII in Los Angeles. Why did she arrive at such an ungodly hour? Because her "hard-ass" boss decided we ought to be up and running by 8:00 A.M. New York time so that we could handle the phone traffic that was sure to begin shortly thereafter. She would still be there at 7:00 P.M., some 14 hours later, because the California and West Coast phoners didn't stop until that time. Of course, we gave Gina plenty of time to rest up for her ordeal of 14-hour days. Just before one Super Bowl, she was clipped by a cab a half block from the NFL office on Park Avenue in New York. Since she was unable to get to the office for a few days, we sent her electric typewriter over to her apartment by cab so that she could continue to process the armloads of media credential requests that needed to be answered.

We ran the Super Bowl out of the NFL's public relations department in those days, so what Gina did was special but not unusual. We asked the same of Kay O'Reilly, Connie Sisler, Nancy Behar, Susan McCann Minogue, Astrid Smith, Helen Chadakoff, and Maxine Isenberg, among others, in those early days as the game came of age. Working just as hard were Stu Kirkpatrick and heavy hitters like Joe Browne, Bill Granholm, Jim Heffernan, Val Pinchbeck, Jack Hand, Harold Rosenthal, Dick Maxwell, Pete Abitante, and Peter Hadhazy, along with the security duo of Pete Kranske and Damon Zumwalt.

How did it happen? Hard work, for one thing, and lots of thought. Every game had to be better than the last one. Media criticism? Sure, from some. But usually their complaint was that we were doing too much and were too often going one step beyond what the most dependent among the writers thought they needed.

As the Super Bowl grew and grew, we had one major concern: *Don't forget the game!* As Pete Rozelle once said: "Our purpose still is to match two teams who will play a game for the championship of the National Football League."

Of course, the games. And, of course, the players. As we recount in the pages that follow, the wins by the Jets and the Chiefs in games III and IV came dramatically on the heels of two Green Bay victories that had launched the series and put to rest real fears that this new NFL-versus-AFL rivalry might not be competitive enough to survive. Not every game since has been what the trade calls a "burner," but after 36 years, the NFC holds only a 20–16 margin, having lost the last two games to a pair of first-time winners, Baltimore and New England.

The Super Bowl has made monumental strides in the past two decades under the leadership of James Howe Steeg, who came aboard after Rozelle tapped me for broader league administration responsibilities. What *is* super today under Steeg was a long way from super then. Nevertheless, it was fun getting there and even more fun telling people about it.

I'd been wanting to write this book for quite a while, and friends and family were persistently bugging me. But it wasn't until I'd met Chuck Day that I decided the time was right. It was after I'd told a couple of Super Bowl anecdotes to the Ponte Vedra Rotary Club a couple years ago that Chuck and his wife, Judy, came up to me to talk about their pro football experiences in Cleveland that dated back to the first *Monday Night Football* game, in Cleveland Stadium, between the New York Jets and the old Cleveland Browns in 1970. One word led to another and Chuck said, "I'd like to write your book." A lunch or two later and we were ready to begin.

As I said, it's been fun. Now, I hope you'll enjoy reading about the making of the Super Bowl almost as much as I have enjoyed being part of its evolution.

—Don Weiss

ACKNOWLEDGMENTS

I'm known in the trade as a "saver," so when Chuck Day and I undertook this project a couple of years ago I was confident I had all the materials we would need to put it together. I was wrong.

As we went along, holes began to develop that needed to be filled. This is a meager effort to say thanks to a few people who were able to fill them.

Tex Schramm and Lamar Hunt gladly re-created their roles in the 1966 merger between the NFL and AFL that led to the game that became the Super Bowl. Art McNally, the NFL supervisor of officials for many years, and Jack Reader, his chief assistant, took us back to the days before the first AFL-NFL World Championship of Professional Football, as the game was called before it became the "Super Bowl." Susan McCann Minogue, formerly of the NFL office in New York, filled us in on some of the social functions I'd forgotten about, and Seymour Siwoff, of the Elias Sports Bureau, was his usual cooperative self.

I also am indebted to Jeff Pash and Vince Casey, of the NFL office, and to Bill Barron, John Wiebusch, and Paul Spinelli, of NFL Publishing, for their generous and frequent assistance. Both Chuck and I are grateful to Betsy Lancefield Lane and Julia Anderson, of McGraw-

Hill in Chicago, and to our agent, John Willig, of Literary Services Inc., in New Jersey, who were so encouraging from the beginning. Additional words of encouragement have come from Rick Catlett, president of the Gator Bowl Association in Jacksonville, Florida, and a longtime friend.

Finally, a special thank-you to George Lindner, of Warner, New Hampshire. On hearing of Pete Rozelle's death in December 1996, he wrote me a letter that told the story of how Oscar Riedener, the chief designer for Tiffany's, fashioned the prototype of the Super Bowl trophy from a cereal box. As they say, from humble beginnings great legends grow.

—Don Weiss

THE MAKING OF THE
SUPER BOWL

PART I

THE MERGER

ONE

MY PATH INTO PRO FOOTBALL

You might think that we'd start this story along the sidelines of a football field like the old Orange Bowl, where Joe Namath and his Jets made history, or at the Los Angeles Memorial Coliseum where it all began. But this is more than the story of 36 championship football games, so we need to start on the sidewalks of Manhattan, where one of my most vivid Super Bowl memories began to unfold in late October 1966.

On the kind of spectacular autumn day in New York that inspired a Frank Sinatra song, I strolled into the Dunhill tobacco and gift shop on Fifth Avenue, not far from the National Football League headquarters in Rockefeller Center. Yet, I scarcely had time to appreciate the weather. Whatever my calm demeanor may have suggested, I was a man on a mission during that lunch hour. And time was of the essence.

The preceding Friday, October 21, Congress finally had passed legislation containing an antitrust exemption that would allow pro football to proceed with the merger of the American Football League and the National Football League that it had announced the preceding June. It had been an arduous and contentious process. In fact, I doubt that more than a handful of people will remember that the merger had come precariously close to being scuttled altogether until some eleventh-hour sleight-of-hand tactics by two wily senators—Everett Dirksen, of Illinois, and Louisiana's Russell Long—who engineered what amounted to a legislative end run that got the deal done. So, in less than 90 days, the respective champions of the National Football League and American Football League would clash in a hastily organized affair, ambitiously being billed as the first "AFL-NFL World Championship of Professional Football."

Barely a year into my job as the NFL's director of information, I suddenly was confronting myriad tasks, many for the first time. This one, however, was familiar: finding an appropriate memento for the sports writers who were expected to cover a game whose date and location were still to be determined. These critical details weren't my concern. They were the responsibility of a newly formed committee of pro football owners. For the moment, my responsibility was picking out something sports writers would appreciate having. The Dunhill shop in midtown Manhattan seemed like a good source.

After looking over several items, I selected a small but attractive travel alarm clock. Beige, square shaped, and not much larger than a candy bar, it would fit nicely into any suitcase. In time, I hoped, the little clock might rekindle memories of a new pro football championship game that was steadily arousing more and more curiosity, at least among the mushrooming throngs of pro football fans.

"Is it possible to have an inscription put on this?" I asked the salesclerk. Certainly, he assured me. "OK, then, this will do just fine," I said, as he nodded approvingly. "And, by the way," I added casually, "I'll need 650 of them."

He was dumbfounded. His stare expressed a mixture of disbelief, wondrous amazement, and sale-of-the-century good fortune.

"I will need them all gift wrapped, too," I added.

In retrospect, the salesclerk couldn't have been any more surprised on that October day than many of the alarm clock recipients would be less than a decade later, for what sports writers chronicled on a sunny January 15 afternoon in 1967 offered scant evidence of what was being brought to life. The Los Angeles Memorial Coliseum, site of the inaugural world championship of professional football, was barely two-thirds filled, despite our having trimmed its seating capacity to 93,000. The gaffes and miscues we endured became nearly as legendary as the Green Bay Packers' 35–10 victory over the Kansas City Chiefs had been predictable.

For that matter, the Dunhill salesclerk couldn't have been any more stunned than I am today whenever I pause and ponder how the Super Bowl has mushroomed into . . . well, pick whatever words suit your fancy. *Time* magazine once called it the "Great American Time Out." The *Los Angeles Times* declared the Super Bowl to be "New Year's Eve, the Fourth of July, and Mardi Gras rolled into one." Pete Rozelle liked to describe our creation as "the last chapter of a hair-raising mystery. No one would miss it."

No, they wouldn't. And for more than three decades they haven't. But within pro football's hierarchy in that autumn of 1966, you could have described the Super Bowl with two words: *an afterthought.*

To be sure, Rozelle was already envisioning something special. In an interview with *Detroit News* sports columnist Jerry Green two weeks after announcing the merger, Pete commented about how he hoped that the game would grow into "the sporting event of the century." But that sounded awfully ambitious. Although the AFL had pretty much shed its "upstart" status and begun exhibiting some staying power, at least outwardly, fans regarded the NFL's own championship game as the football equivalent of baseball's World Series. Television ratings during the past half dozen years documented as much. So, until the merger's announcement in June, little public clamor had surfaced for the NFL champion to play the champion of what many dismissed as a decidedly inferior league, even if interest among fans and sports writers in a postseason pro football playoff was intensifying.

Among owners in both leagues, a world championship game was strictly incidental to their overriding concerns: the future of professional football and the need to regain control of their finances. By today's standards, of course, the bidding war for college talent looks downright miserly. By mid-1966 standards, however, it had grown obscenely expensive. Worse, this war was on the verge of spinning further out of control. Teams from both leagues were beginning to compete not only for college draft choices but also for established pro players. The strain had become evident, even among a growing number of smaller-market NFL franchises.

For pro football's owners, then, the merger was all about fixing their finances and preserving their brand of football. It was not about having their respective champions play each other. In fact, the Joint Committee of six owners (three from each league) that convened in late July 1966 to begin working out the merger's details didn't even begin discussing the new championship game until the second day of their first meeting. And they didn't select the date of the inaugural game until November 9, barely two months before its scheduled kickoff. Equally telling, the NFL's owners, who then numbered 15, took another three weeks to approve the contract with the Los Angeles Coliseum; the one-year rental agreement was signed on December 1, just 45 days before the game was to kick off.

Naturally, the prospect of the AFL and NFL settling bragging rights on the field was as intriguing a notion among the owners as it was among fans and writers. But it was nowhere near the owners' top concern. Besides, the outcome of such a game was hardly in doubt, not even among all but the most ardent AFL followers.

If such initial indifference toward the Super Bowl now looks astonishingly ironic, it was in keeping with the times. For, until the late 1950s, pro football itself hadn't been much more than an afterthought, relatively speaking. Baseball was entrenched as the national pastime, and once the dust settled from the World Series in early October, college football dominated the sports pages throughout the rest of the year. Although pro football had its loyalists and was enjoying steadily increasing popularity, it still was ranked no better than second in the eyes of most American sports fans.

But not in my eyes. I've been an avid pro football fan for as long as I can remember. Growing up in Aurora, Illinois, I followed George Halas's Chicago Bears, never once dreaming that someday I would be working alongside the team's legendary founder and coach.

By the time I graduated from East Aurora High School in 1943, sports had become an all-consuming passion for me. Whatever I was going to do in life, I decided, it would have to have something to do with sports. I had participated in basketball and golf, and for a time even aspired to play golf professionally. But my aspirations to write were even stronger. I not only had been managing editor of our high school newspaper but also had sampled my first taste of the professional world by joining the sports staff of Aurora's *Beacon-News*, at the ripe old age of 16. For all I know, we may have had the youngest staff of any newspaper sports section ever. George Eisenhuth, the paper's sports editor, was only 19. We both went into public relations, with George going on to enjoy a rewarding career in Chicago.

Those early experiences helped me set my sights on writing for a wire service. I would get to cover a variety of sports, I reasoned (correctly, as it turned out), and working under deadline pressures struck me as an exciting writing environment.

Next, however, was college. I spent a year at Cornell College in Mt. Vernon, Iowa, before enlisting in the Navy for two years. The Navy molded me into a radar and radio operator, then put me on submarines patrolling the Atlantic Ocean, mostly after the war ended. I never saw any action, but operating in tight quarters was great training for learning to work under pressure and, perhaps, for learning to spot nuances that later would serve me well while inspecting Super Bowl venues.

I returned to Cornell College for another year after I left the service, then transferred to the University of Missouri, where I earned my journalism degree in 1949. Between my second and third year of college, I married my high school sweetheart, Charlene Thomas. We had grown up together in Aurora and were married on August 23, 1947, the day after my 21st birthday. It wasn't just a coincidence either: My mother had insisted I had to be 21 before I married. Maybe it was her way of helping me make sure I found the right girl. If so, Mom's insistence paid off. Charlene and I have been married for more than 55 glorious and meaningful years.

After college, I landed a job with the Associated Press. It blossomed into a 14-year career with the wire service. I was hired over the phone by a guy looking for a radio news writer in its small bureau in Huntington, West Virginia. At the time, I didn't even know where Huntington was. It didn't matter. When the offer came over the phone, I jumped at the opportunity. After working two years in Huntington as a general newsman, the job I had dreamed about in my youth beckoned in 1951: a position writing sports for radio with AP in New York. My four years there and eight more on the AP sports desk would turn out to be everything I had hoped they would be, and then some. Once in New York, it didn't take long for my love of pro football to intensify into a fierce passion. In time, that passion would reshape my career.

New York's AP sports desk in the early 1950s operated at Fifty Rockefeller Plaza, in the heart of Manhattan. It was home to about a dozen writers and editors who each covered a variety of beats. The AP desk also was home to hardened attitudes worth reviewing, for they offer a sense of perspective about how the media looked on pro football until the early 1960s.

Like most newspaper sports staffs of that era, particularly those in New York, the AP desk operated strictly on a seniority basis. Guys in their forties and fifties had a hell of a lot more opportunities than guys in their twenties. I was 28, so initially I worked the desk and occasionally covered golf and basketball. The AP veterans, meanwhile, helped themselves to the top beats: baseball, college football, and boxing. Pro football, notably, was not among them. Indeed, more often than not, NFL games were assigned to the least-experienced and least-talented writers.

Much of this mind-set had been shaped by Ted Smits, the AP sports editor. Don't misunderstand; Ted was a successful journalist. It's just that his priorities had been cast in stone for years: First and foremost were the Olympics. College sports—college football in particular—came next. Then, finally, came pro sports. Other than major league baseball, though, the pros were a weak third, and Ted held New York's football Giants and the entire National Football League in utter disregard. Not even the Giants' resounding 47–7 pounding of the Chicago Bears in the 1956 league championship game did much to alter his thinking.

Ted was hardly alone, either. The sports-writing world was dominated by guys who were his mirror images, except that some ranked college sports ahead of the Olympics.

In 1956, however, I met one other writer who shared my enthusiasm for pro football, Jim Kensil. We felt that the NFL possessed the potential to explode in popularity and that it deserved far more attention than it was getting, and both of us were growing increasingly frustrated by AP's ongoing neglect of its coverage. These mutual feelings brought us together and forged a personal and professional friendship that lasted until Jim's death in early 1997. Had we not met, I might never have joined the NFL.

Working together, beginning in the mid-1950s, Jim and I steadily began to acquire more control of the AP's behind-the-scenes activities. And, whether or not Ted Smits wanted it, the NFL started getting some decent play, at least on occasion. By then I had become a night supervisor—essentially the night editor—running the sports desk during the most hectic, fast-paced hours of an around-the-clock operation. I never once minded working at night because that's where the action was.

Working nights offered another benefit. I could attend NFL games during the afternoons on autumn Sundays at the Polo Grounds or Yankee Stadium, wherever the Giants happened to be playing. I'd be in my seat for the kickoff, then leave in the fourth quarter and head for the office. On returning to AP, I'd occasionally dash off sidebar stories about things that had happened during the game or personality pieces on the players who had figured prominently in the outcomes. During the week, Jim and I routinely made phone calls, created ideas, and wrote pro football features. Much of AP's advance copy for NFL championship games in 1958 and 1959, in fact, originated from our strategy, with help from Gabby Bowen, a writer from AP's Baltimore bureau.

We hadn't necessarily been assigned to do any of this, mind you, but we didn't care. Jim and I were living vicariously outside of our assignment lanes in an effort to get closer to our passion. All the while, we kept pressing Ted Smits to give pro football far more space and attention than it was getting.

We may as well have been talking to a football; it was that tough a sell. The AP's coverage—if you want to call it that—of the NFL's 1958 championship game illustrates Smits's disdain.

To this day, legions of veteran fans still insist that the Baltimore Colts' 23–17 overtime victory over the Giants in Yankee Stadium was one of the best pro football games ever played. With more than 80 years of pro football games—including 36 Super Bowls—it's a hefty claim but a valid one, nonetheless. In a performance that launched his legendary status, quarterback Johnny Unitas drove the Colts down the field to set up a game-tying field goal, with 12 seconds left to play. In overtime and with night descending on Yankee Stadium on a cold Sunday after Christmas, Colts fullback Alan Ameche charged through a gaping hole in the Giants' line to score the deciding touchdown.

The second half, in particular, had been an absolute thriller in every respect. Televised nationwide by NBC, it captured the fancy of fans everywhere and is heralded as a seminal moment in pro football history. Yet, Joe Reichler, the AP writer who covered the game, didn't file his lead until nearly 40 minutes after Ameche had crossed the goal line!

Jim and I were almost beside ourselves. In fact, *we* finally wrote the bulletin for AP after watching the game on television in the office because 30 minutes had gone by and we hadn't received so much as a syllable. We were competing tooth and nail with both United Press International and International News Service in those days, and often were up against top-notch writers whose names might be familiar: Oscar Fraley and Bob Considine, to name two. So we had to move. And we did.

We kept right on moving, too, all the way to NFL headquarters, thanks in large part to an ironic twist: a seemingly routine meeting that I had helped arrange in early 1961.

By January 1961, the Philadelphia Eagles had supplanted Baltimore as NFL champions, having beaten a scrappy team from Green Bay that had been rebuilt and reenergized by a heretofore little-known ex-Giants assistant named Vince Lombardi. Back in New York, it finally was beginning to dawn on Ted Smits that pro football had a future. That the public had starting flocking to NFL games no doubt helped spur his change of heart.

Whatever his motivation, Ted started assigning quality writers to cover significant NFL games. Late the following year, for example, Jack Hand would handle the night lead for the 1962 NFL title game between the Giants and the Packers in Yankee Stadium—a key assignment. I would have a key assignment of my own: game-running summaries and leads for afternoon papers. Two other AP writers would join us, a startling change from what had been the norm.

Jim, meanwhile, was busy nurturing his new fascination: an innovative column he had created on his own time a year or two earlier. Appearing weekly, the *Sports Dial* focused on sports coverage on television and radio. One of the very first of its kind, Jim's column was attracting some national attention and a few faithful readers, including the new young leader of the National Football League.

Alvin Ray "Pete" Rozelle had been elected NFL Commissioner in late January 1960, succeeding Bert Bell, who had suffered a sudden and fatal heart attack a few months earlier while attending a Philadelphia-Pittsburgh game. Rozelle had been a compromise choice, elected on the owners' 23rd ballot, at 10:30 on a Tuesday night, to break an eight-day stalemate. Indeed, had Marshall Leahy, the NFL's San Francisco–based legal counsel and one of the leading candidates, not insisted on moving the NFL offices from Philadelphia to the West Coast, Leahy likely would have been elected instead. Even Pete poked fun at his unexpected win: either the league couldn't afford to prolong its meeting further at the fashionable Kenilworth Hotel on Miami Beach, he'd quip, or "It was because nobody knew who I was."

Whatever the reason, Rozelle wasted no time proving that the league's owners had made a superb choice. During Rozelle's first year as Commissioner, for instance, the NFL generated more than $11.8 million in gross receipts from more than 3 million fans, the third straight year that attendance had surpassed the 3 million mark. Those numbers sparkled, yet also paled in comparison to the significance of an internal move he ordered.

Rozelle's first three-year contract authorized him to maintain the NFL offices "in a league city selected by him east of the Mississippi River," as official league minutes described the provision. I imagine it took Pete about 15 minutes to conclude that whatever future awaited the NFL would be far brighter with a headquarters in New York City than in Bala-Cynwyd, Pennnsylvania, the Philadelphia suburb where Bert Bell had run the league. Within six months, Rozelle had moved the NFL's office to Rockefeller Center, not far from the headquarters of AP and NBC. The address was no coincidence. From day one, one force guided Rozelle's leadership and influenced his thinking and planning: television.

Better than any other sports executive I have ever known or observed, Pete instantly recognized television's power and grasped how pro football could harness that power to drive its growth. Much of the very first owners' meeting that he chaired the morning after his election was devoted to television, even though the agenda included key expansion issues: Dallas was entering the league for the 1960 season, and Minnesota would be admitted during that same year and begin play in 1961. Even so, discussions about television continued well into that Wednesday night.

The cornerstone of Rozelle's television strategy was a leaguewide contract, and he began amassing support for it almost immediately. While portions of that strategy already were in place when he became Commissioner, it remained a novel idea, for television sports was still very scattered as the 1960s unfolded. A number of NFL clubs had contracts with CBS, but a few had their games televised by other networks, and a few others had private deals with independent promoters. The Cleveland Browns, for example, had sold their television rights to a local brewery.

Rozelle's emerging television strategy was a tailor-made topic for Jim Kensil's *Sports Dial* column, and Jim was giving it ample attention when NFL owners convened their annual postseason meeting at New York's Warwick Hotel, in January 1961. As I was about to discover, Rozelle had been reading Jim's column ever so intently.

Covering the meeting for AP, I was having a conversation with Pittsburgh owner Art Rooney when Rozelle walked out of the meeting room and approached the half dozen writers who were sitting there with me. I hadn't encountered Rozelle until that moment, and as he approached, I was struck by both how young he was and his engaging, yet forceful presence.

"Is anybody here from the AP?" Rozelle asked.

"Yes, I am," I replied, interrupting my chat with Rooney.

"Do you know this fellow Kensil?" Rozelle asked.

"I do," I said. "As a matter of fact, he's my best buddy."

I was starting to tell Rozelle more about my relationship with Jim, but Pete had only a moment to talk and simply asked me to have Jim call him.

Returning to the office later that afternoon, I relayed the information to Jim and didn't give it another thought until he came back from his appointment with Rozelle a day or two later.

"How'd it go?" I asked. "Fine," Jim said. "We had a nice talk, a really interesting time. In fact, he offered me a job." The revelation, of course, startled me. In retrospect, it shouldn't have.

Our "clandestine" coverage of pro football had introduced Jim and me to Joe Labrum, the NFL's public relations director—in name only, as far as we were concerned. Whenever we called Labrum for information, we got no real help at all. I'm told Joe was a nice man, and I have no reason to believe he wasn't. He had joined the league in 1947 to serve his longtime friend Bert Bell, who had become NFL Commissioner a year earlier. But Joe catered strictly to his cronies, primarily the sports writers at New York's half dozen daily newspapers and his buddies in Philadelphia. We always felt like a couple of young pests unworthy of his time.

It was hardly the kind of attitude and presence the NFL needed. But Rozelle already knew that. In evaluating the staff he had inherited, he quickly saw that a change was needed. Pete, after all, had come from a public relations background himself. He had written game programs for the Los Angeles Rams while he still was in school and had done public relations for the University of San Francisco and Compton Junior College before that. As a matter of fact, Pete's public relations prowess eventually led to his promotion to the Rams' general manager, the position he held before being elected NFL Commissioner.

Soon to turn 65, Labrum was ready to retire. So, at the conclusion of that January 1961 meeting in New York, Rozelle got league owners to approve a pension for Joe Labrum and set out to hire a new public relations director . . . who turned out to be Jim Kensil.

Jim did more than begin assembling the pieces that would become the NFL's renowned public relations machine. He became Pete's trusted right-hand man, a relationship that would continue for 16 years until June 1977, when Jim became president of the New York Jets.

Despite Jim's departure from the Associated Press in 1961, we remained extremely close. I continued covering the NFL and some league meetings, and barely a day went by without our talking on the phone. Practically speaking, in fact, I may have started working for the NFL almost as soon as Jim did. He loved to use me as a sounding board for ideas during our conversations, and he kept me informed of everything that was going on. So, when I finally did join the league, I was up to speed on key policy issues, league goals, personalities, strengths and weaknesses, and, certainly, the rationale that nurtured the growth of the NFL's relationship with the media. Equally important, Jim's conversations also afforded me insights into Pete Rozelle himself. I got to know Pete before I really got to know him, so to speak.

In a sense, I've come full circle. Although I officially retired in 1994, I'm still involved with the National Football League, primarily at the Super Bowl and in various committee activities, including 30 years with the influential Competition Committee.

I made an interim stop along my way to NFL headquarters, though. In late November 1963—the very week that John F. Kennedy was assassinated—I left the Associated Press for a public relations job with the U.S. Golf Association. I had always loved golf, of course, and thought I saw an opportunity. It proved to be a good decision. I worked for Joe Dey, a former Philadelphia newspaperman who went to the USGA as its executive director as a fairly young man. At the USGA, I gained invaluable public relations experience, writing for and managing the association's publications, helping run tournaments, and blending my basic journalism skills with those that the PR world required.

All things considered, it was a good life, and one I never really considered leaving—until Kensil called me one day in June 1965. This time, he wasn't after reactions but some recommendations. The NFL was going to "expand the public relations department," as he put it, and Jim was looking for candidates. As I was to learn, Rozelle was starting to set in motion a broader expansion of the league office and was relying more and more on Jim as an executive assistant and operations chief. In turn, they both were looking for someone who eventually could take over the public relations operation. My background and NFL knowledge were obvious strengths.

"I might be interested myself," I said, after Jim explained why he had called. I can't say that Jim's initial overture was a ruse, for he didn't come right out and say, "Would you be interested?" But once I did express interest, Jim said he'd speak with Rozelle. Sure enough, Pete soon called, and I had a job interview within a couple days. By the end of June, I was on board, although existing USGA commitments delayed my joining the NFL full-time until September.

Rozelle had a penchant for hiring newspapermen because they certainly knew what sports writers needed to cover games. But it wasn't without misgivings, as Pete admitted when he hired me. He was torn between being able to tap my brain full-time and my no longer being available as an ex officio sounding board. Rest assured, I had never been a shill for pro football. Rozelle simply had valued and respected my opinions as an interested outsider, just as he genuinely respected the views of sports writers in general.

Those feelings set the tone for my NFL career. Pete Rozelle was unwavering in his insistence that the league level with the press and help them do their job. Moreover, by our providing them with information that helped them better perform their jobs, he reasoned, writers would follow pro football more intently and naturally tend to look with favor on the NFL—or at least be less inclined to go out of their way to criticize us.

It's important to understand this relationship with the media, specifically with television, because it was a critical factor that we leveraged in building the Super Bowl's appeal.

Another factor, though, was more critical. All three of us—Pete Rozelle, Jim Kensil, and I—simply loved pro football and wanted to see it grow. That, it surely did, far surpassing even our wildest dreams.

But we couldn't spend much time dreaming in the fall of 1965. The business of pro football had grown infinitely more complex. And contentious. We had an escalating war to fight and win. The enemy, of course, was those despised competitors from a brash, upstart aggregation known as the American Football League.

TWO

SEEDS OF UNION

Baby-Sitting and Body Snatching

Pro football's bitter and intense war over college talent was well into its sixth year by the time I started my new job as the NFL's director of information in mid-1965. It wasn't until I came on board full-time in September that I could fully grasp how my colleagues' feelings toward the American Football League had hardened into raw hatred.

The NFL headquarters that Pete Rozelle had established in the summer of 1960 was a modest suite in the General Dynamics Building at One Rockefeller Plaza, essentially across the street from the Associated Press offices where my New York sports-writing career had begun. Only now I had an office on the 23rd floor overlooking Rockefeller Center's landmark skating rink, where noon-hour concerts offered pleasant sounds to complement my view of Manhattan's skyline. The music rose so clearly that it seemed to come from the next room . . . when I had time to listen.

Today, the NFL has a staff of 450 at its Park Avenue headquarters. We managed ours with less than a dozen, including the Commissioner. Officially, Jim Kensil directed public relations. But he was spending more and more of his day assisting Rozelle. As did Bert Rose. Bert, who had a public relations background, had been one of Pete's buddies on the West Coast. He also had served as the Minnesota Vikings' first general manager when the team entered the league in 1961 but had moved into the league office to handle assorted chores by the time I arrived.

Mark Duncan had arrived a year earlier as supervisor of officials, while Austin Gunsel, who had been a candidate for Commissioner in 1960 before Pete was elected, had stayed on to serve as league treasurer. Harry Standish, Bert Bell's brother-in-law, ran the personnel department, overseeing player records, waivers, and trades, with help from a capable woman named Mary Cavanaugh. We also had a couple of secretaries, including one for Kensil who became my secretary, plus Thelma Elkjer. Thelma had worked for Rozelle during his Los Angeles Rams years and came east to serve as his executive secretary until he retired—and remained for six more years after that. She also had been Tex Schramm's secretary when Tex was the Rams' general manager. Before her long career ended, Thelma would become a league legend herself, after playing a key role in the NFC's 1970 realignment saga.

Among us was a celebrity, too: Buddy Young handled player relations, suddenly an all-important task. Standing only 5-foot-4, Buddy had been an All-America at Illinois before becoming one of pro football's smallest runners ever. Also a great sprinter and a man I had known since my high school days, Buddy had been one of the first African Americans to play pro football, beginning in 1947, with the New York Yankees of the All-America Football Conference. He starred as a running back and kick returner for nine years in New York, Dallas, and Baltimore, where the Colts retired his jersey when he retired after the 1955 season.

About the time I arrived at league headquarters in 1965, NFL Films and NFL Properties also arrived as league entities, owned by the member clubs. Films had come to life a few years earlier in Philadelphia as Blair Productions, a family-run enterprise headed by Ed Sabol. Its breakthrough assignment had been the 1962 NFL championship game between the Giants and Packers in Yankee Stadium. That footage spawned many opportunities, and Rozelle wanted to take full advantage of them. Properties, meanwhile, had been an existing enterprise operating under a contract with Roy Rogers Enterprises in California. It was to remain on the West Coast for the time being, but Pete had hired Larry Kent and one other person to manage the business as part of the league itself.

Expansion notwithstanding, we still were modest in numbers, and our routines reflected it. Prompted by Pete himself suggesting, "How 'bout pizza today?" or words to that effect, we frequently lunched together as a staff in the conference room. Lunches, in fact, were among the few official meetings we conducted.

While Rozelle wasn't big on staff meetings, he was big on communications. He would just wander in and sit down. We'd talk a while, then carry out whatever we needed to do. Rozelle's enduring image is of a very polished and smooth breed of executive. In many respects, he was, and he could be extremely firm when he needed to be. Yet, a part of him consistently sought the help and opinions of others, or their confirmation. Pete always wanted to feel comfortable with a decision that he had worked out in his own mind.

Above all, Pete Rozelle had magnificent timing. Like his grasp of television, it was an innate sixth sense. He was unfailingly aware of the right time to do something—and the wrong time. Still fresh in my mind are occasions when we'd plead, "OK, Pete, now, now!" . . . but Pete would just smile and light another cigarette.

However, what dominated Rozelle's mind—and everyone else's—as 1965 faded was nothing to smile about: the battle with AFL clubs over college draft choices.

Evidence of the battle's intensity could be found just outside Pete Rozelle's office, which I first observed not long after being hired. It was an incredible sight. Piled high on a 10- to 12-foot-long worktable were more United Airlines tickets than I had ever seen in my life. There had to be hundreds of them, to every conceivable destination in the land. Hidden from most of the staff, this cache was guarded intently by Thelma Elkjer while she prepared them for mailing. Dependable and ever loyal, Thelma understood the gravity of her responsibility. Airline tickets were critical supplies for the soldiers carrying out a special mission along the front lines of our raging war.

"Operation Baby-Sit" was the brainstorm of Bert Rose. Almost from the moment they began competing for college football talent in 1960, both leagues had devised schemes to corral draft choices and keep them under lock and key until after they had signed contracts. Rose molded these plots into something approaching an art form. He had hatched Operation Baby-Sit for the Los Angeles Rams' 1964 draft, but once Rozelle caught wind of the idea, he wanted the entire NFL to employ it, which is what brought Bert to New York in the first place. Anything that could turn the tide in this long-running war was worth trying. By signing college players, the AFL was stealing parts of the NFL's future and grabbing headlines on the sports pages. Most alarming of all, it was gaining precious credibility.

The fledgling AFL had signaled its intent early on, signing nearly half of the established league's 1959 draft choices. The Baltimore Colts, on their way to repeating as NFL champs that year, initially dismissed the upstart league as an annoyance until they lost four of their top five 1959 choices. One of them was future Hall of Fame lineman Ron Mix, who signed with the then Los Angeles Chargers.

Once ignited, the war escalated quickly. At least once, the AFL was accused of conducting an illegal secret telephone draft weeks before the officially scheduled draft, to gain the upper hand. In such an atmosphere, skirmishes and ugly confrontations were inevitable and common.

As the 1964 Orange Bowl game concluded, for instance, Minnesota Vikings scout Joe Thomas, who had been tailing Nebraska lineman John Kirby for weeks in late 1963, supposedly watched in horror as a Chargers scout tried to sign Kirby to an AFL contract right on the field. Thomas leaped from the stands, charged onto the gridiron, and threw a punch at his AFL adversary.

Rose's elaborate scheme was designed to be subtler but no less effective. Two months in planning, Operation Baby-Sit called for NFL "representatives" to attach themselves to the collegians likely to be selected in the early rounds: They were to contact players before the draft (then conducted by both leagues in late November) and remain with them until the draft had concluded and the players were safely under binding contracts. In practice, representatives addled up to their targets long before the draft began. Some tales suggest that in 1965, the second and final year of Operation Baby-Sit, a host of college stars were contacted before their seasons even kicked off!

Representatives weren't authorized to negotiate contracts per se but were expected to get a general idea of what players anticipated, what perks would interest them (cars, for example), and how much contact they had had with the AFL. At the moment a player was selected, a deal was to be struck over the phone and the player signed immediately. The linchpin of the plan, of course, was keeping teams and the league informed of potential draft choices' whereabouts at all times. Those precious details were guarded at NFL draft headquarters in New York.

Naturally, we quickly dubbed our representatives *baby-sitters*. But *body snatchers* would have been just as appropriate.

At first, they were predominantly the college scouts of NFL teams, on temporary loan, so to speak. By 1965, however, the need for a more sophisticated breed was apparent, and the NFL recruited a veritable battalion of baby-sitters from among New York advertising agencies. Who better to promote the NFL than Madison Avenue mavens?

As part of his television strategy, Rozelle had befriended the ad world's leading lights as soon as he had come to town. They became invaluable relationships that we leaned on heavily, and they led us to additional contacts. This network literally burgeoned.

Jack Landry was a case in point. Perhaps Pete's closest friend in New York in those days, Jack was head of marketing for Philip Morris and the guy who more than anyone else put pro athletes in television commercials. It was Jack who was behind Giants quarterback Charlie Conerly's becoming the first Marlboro man, and Jack's wife, Virginia, was the namesake for Virginia Slims cigarettes. Jack also largely was responsible for that brand's promotion of women's tennis tournaments for so many years. He made one fine baby-sitter and recruited and supervised others, too.

Such assistance also reflected Rozelle's ability to establish strong ties with powerful people from various circles of influence. These same relationships, notably, would serve us well again in the early years of developing the Super Bowl's popularity.

In the fall of 1965, however, a Super Bowl wasn't even a figment of our imagination. We had a war on our hands and were deadly serious about winning it. We armed our baby-sitters with facts about how to sell the National Football League to college athletes: why it was superior to the AFL, its superior pension plan, the advantages afforded by the league's cities, and on and on. You could spend hours reading the stuff, which was dispatched to each baby-sitter, along with those airline tickets piled outside of Rozelle's office.

Understand, though, that only a portion of those tickets were earmarked for the baby-sitters themselves. The rest had been secured for use in emergency situations, such as spiriting celebrated draft prospects from one town to another on a moment's notice to escape the clutches of rival "hand-holders" hired by the AFL. Having United's resources at our disposal proved as invaluable as Rozelle's advertising pals.

A major sponsor of games televised on CBS and the official airline of most NFL teams, United was enterprising in its own right. Along with arranging for the tickets, it helped us devise an especially potent weapon: the Gold League pass. When flashed by a baby-sitter, the pass was supposed to whisk its holder into those "friendly skies" anytime, anywhere, with or without a ticket, no questions asked. It held that much clout.

Such clout was wielded often. To keep Verlon Biggs away from New York Jets personnel director George Sauer during the 1964 draft weekend, baby-sitters reportedly flew the promising Jackson State tackle from Mississippi to Detroit, took him to the Lions' game on Thanksgiving Day and a National Hockey League game that night, changed hotels twice, then took off again, this time to Washington, D.C. Sauer couldn't be shaken, however, so NFL baby-sitters moved into and out of three Washington hotels, never once registering Biggs under his own name. Alas, Sauer's dogged determination—with help from Biggs's Jackson State coach—ultimately won this fight, which proved to be worth it: Biggs helped the Jets win a Super Bowl and still ranks fourth among the team's all-time sack leaders.

I'm told that NFL baby-sitters had more luck with Clarence "Clancy" Williams, a Washington State defensive back. Learning he had been flown to San Diego by the Chargers, a baby-sitter was immediately dispatched to haul Williams back to Washington State's campus in Pullman. He succeeded, only to have Williams disappear a second time when he was left alone for no more than a few minutes: The player had been whisked to Toronto, this time by a Canadian Football League agent. In the blink of an eye, the NFL office itself dispatched an emergency baby-sitter to Toronto. Williams was located, contacted, talked into returning, and then rushed to Chicago, where, along with a growing collection of prospective draftees, he was registered at a hotel, again under another name. Hours later, Williams was drafted by the Rams, who signed him on the spot.

"You promised to call me back!" an AFL hand-holder later protested. "They didn't even let me call my mother!" Williams shot back. Of course they hadn't. Calling Mom might have compromised the war effort.

My own contribution to Operation Baby-Sit was limited to helping coordinate activities at the two New York hotels (one public, one secret) that we used for the 1966 draft, which was held over Thanksgiving weekend in 1965, the last time we fought the AFL for college players. My involvement could have been greater, though. I could have been a baby-sitter myself.

Kensil had tried to recruit me in 1964, when I was still working with the U.S. Golf Association. Jim really pleaded with me, too. Sorry, I replied apologetically, not a chance. Not that I wasn't interested. I was. But I had promised Charlene and my daughters that we would spend Thanksgiving weekend at Sturbridge Village in Massachusetts. Charlene made it abundantly clear that the only baby-sitting I would be doing that weekend would be in the Weiss family's behalf. It was the right decision, of course. Even so, having firsthand knowledge of what baby-sitters endured would have been mighty handy, given how my career turned the following autumn.

From all accounts collected over the years, baby-sitters endured plenty (listed in alphabetical order): blackmail, bribes, crapshooting, drinking, finagling of every magnitude, flashy cars and flashy women, kidnappings as necessary, a multitude of lying, and plenty of spying. Baby-sitters resorted to whatever was necessary. Some worked in teams. Others flew solo. All of them had wild stories. While I never had firsthand knowledge of any of these tales, none have ever been refuted.

Quite the contrary, in fact. During the first common draft held after the merger, Jack Landry dropped in to regale attendees about the days of yore. "Hey, I've got half a dozen guys from Michigan State stashed in a hotel in Yonkers," Landry laughed. "What do you want me to do with them?"

If the saga of Tom Nowatzke is any indication, he might well have heard, "Just don't let 'em out of your sight! And keep a low profile."

Nowatzke was a 235-pound Indiana fullback drafted in 1964 by the Detroit Lions and AFL New York Jets. Shea Stadium was brand new that year, and the Jets were eager to show it off to Nowatzke when he came to New York to attend an All-America dinner hosted by Eastman Kodak. Nowatzke seemed duly impressed with Shea but not as much as his buddy was, a chap named Dick Pollard. When Nowatzke and the Jets discussed contract terms, Pollard was again at his side and every bit as interested. Maybe more so, in fact, which aroused the suspicions of young Chuck Knox. Then an assistant coach for the Jets, Knox peppered Pollard with unfriendly questions in menacing tones. His suspicions were well founded: When Nowatzke signed a contract with the Lions, Pollard was still at his side in his role as an NFL baby-sitter. "I thought Knox was going to take a poke at me," Pollard later said. Ironically, Knox left the Jets three seasons later . . . to join the Lions.

A Colts baby-sitter rented the entire floor of a Rockville, Maryland, motel to secure prized Duke linebacker Mike Curtis. He also answered all incoming telephone calls but still was briefly outflanked by Don Klosterman, then a top scout for the Kansas City Chiefs. Klosterman knew Curtis was engaged, so he had his secretary call the motel and in a sweet voice claim to be the linebacker's fiancée desperately needing to speak with him. The ploy worked, and she handed the phone to Klosterman, who made a desperate plea of his own. Not desperate enough, though. Curtis spurned the Chiefs and signed with the Colts.

Buddy Young himself is credited with keeping the Chiefs from signing Gale Sayers, who of course was destined for stardom with the Chicago Bears. Buddy's theme was straightforward and well intentioned. He knew Sayers had become deeply committed to the civil rights movement during his college years at Kansas and convinced the running back that he would be far happier playing in Chicago than in Kansas City. Being from Chicago himself and having endured racial prejudice during his playing days, Young was convincing.

Other baby-sitters weren't nearly as high-minded. While details are sketchy and no one from either the NFL or AFL ever admitted to it, stories have endured of players occasionally being entertained by the pleasures of young ladies. As one account unfolded, two players—one married, one single—were stashed in a city hotel and growing restless as the 1964 draft crawled along. Their baby-sitter suggested that the pair go downstairs and have a drink in the hotel bar, complimentary, of course. They eagerly accepted such hospitality, raced to the lounge . . . and just happened to encounter two very friendly, very attractive, and very willing young ladies. The twosome turned into a foursome in no time and returned to the players' room, where they found a bounteous array of food and drink, also complimentary, of course. The impromptu party continued until the wee hours. Around 5:00 A.M., the phone rang. It was the baby-sitter, who asked to speak to the married player.

"One of our teams is going to draft you, but we want to make sure of you before we waste a pick," the baby-sitter said, sounding less cheery than he had the preceding evening. "You'd better tell us you're going to sign because it surely would be awful if what you've been doing got back to your wife, now, wouldn't it?"

Groggy from lack of sleep, the married player still recognized blackmail when he heard it. He signed for a paltry bonus, about one-sixth of what his single roommate later negotiated . . . with a team from the other league.

Unsavory and wicked? Absolutely. But it was war, and, like love, all was fair. In those days, Tex Schramm of the Dallas Cowboys used to point out that a team couldn't afford to gamble, especially on first choices. "They simply had to be sure things," he said. Baby-sitters' insights helped spot them. Their insights and tips also helped clubs spot situations where they'd be better off swapping rights to college players who they couldn't sign, to keep them from signing with the rival league.

For instance, word got around that Notre Dame All-America receiver Jack Snow had had enough of playing football in a freeze, wanted to play as a pro in his native California, and was ready to sign with the Chargers to ensure it. NFL draft rights to Snow belonged to the Vikings, who traded them to the Rams primarily to thwart the Chargers. The Rams then sent scout Jack Faulkner to baby-sit Snow, and Snow signed a Rams contract a few weeks later in New York. To celebrate, Faulkner took Snow to Toots Shor's, where the first person they ran into was Vikings coach Norm Van Brocklin. Never a diplomat, Van Brocklin glared at Snow before unleashing a torrent of curses. The newest Ram, the coach screamed, wouldn't catch a pass against Minnesota the next season. In another irony, Van Brocklin hired Faulkner nine months later as his defensive backfield coach. Whether Van Brocklin still remembered the incident isn't clear, but the Vikings did beat the Rams the next season. Twice, in fact.

Draft rights to Dick Butkus were swapped, too—by the AFL. They originally belonged to the Denver Broncos. The Broncos quickly concluded that they couldn't match the Chicago Bears' prestige or pocketbook but maybe Sonny Werblin could. Werblin was the Jets' new and free-spending owner and, sure enough, offered Butkus a bundle. More, in fact, than the $200,000 that Bears owner George Halas gave the celebrated Illinois linebacker. That deal triggered charges of tampering and illegal drafting, but nothing was ever proved.

Besides, Werblin fared far better with another swap. The Jets had drafted Tulsa quarterback Jerry Rhome in 1963 as a "future choice." Rhome had broken almost every college passing record on the books but still hadn't impressed New York's owner when the two met. Werblin, who had made his fortune in show business and fully understood "star quality" and its value, felt Rhome sorely lacked the box office appeal he had seen in another college quarterback he had met. Werblin, in turn, traded Rhome's draft rights to the Houston Oilers for the AFL draft rights to the quarterback he coveted: Alabama's Joe Namath.

Even the Oilers sensed they were getting the worst of that deal, club executive John Breen later admitted. But they made it anyway because they also sensed they had a better shot at signing Rhome, while the Jets had a better shot of signing Namath. Werblin confirmed the wisdom of such thinking by signing Namath to the reported $427,000 deal that stunned pro football. It had its effect on Rhome, too: He upped his demands to the point where the Oilers lost interest and dropped out. Rhome then signed with the NFL Cowboys.

The Oilers also lost Ralph Neely to the Cowboys, despite the fact that they had signed him to an undated AFL contract before he played his final college game for Oklahoma in the Gator Bowl. Yes, it was patently illegal. But it didn't matter. Indeed, Neely and teammate Lance Rentzel were among four Sooners who did so, along with who knows how many collegians from other teams. As reported by *SPORT* magazine in 1965, Neely evidently wanted to collect his $20,000 signing bonus from Houston in 1964, when he stood to make far less money than he expected to earn in 1965. But once Dallas acquired Neely's draft rights from Baltimore and began wooing him with gusto, the offensive tackle began rethinking his four-year, $20,000-a-year, no-cut deal (plus a car) with the Oilers. Irate, Houston tried wining and dining Neely and his family. When that failed, Houston leaked the existence of Neely's secret contract. It never kept Neely from playing for the Cowboys, of course, but it kept him out of the Gator Bowl. His college coach was irate, too, and threw both Neely and Rentzel off the team.

Of all the stories from the baby-sitter era, the respective chases for Otis Taylor and Harry Schuh may top them all.

Taylor, a star receiver from Prairie View College in Texas, was in the company of NFL baby-sitters somewhere in Dallas on the eve of the 1964 draft, along with his teammate Seth Cartwright. Lloyd Wells, a Chiefs scout/super sleuth and Taylor's boyhood chum, was intent on finding—and freeing—them both. Tips from sources traced the players to a nondescript motel, where Wells raced to size up the situation. Conversations with bellhops and kitchen workers led Wells to the suite where the players were staying. Wells put a camera around his neck, approached the motel suite, and knocked on the door.

A burly chap answered coldly. Wells told him he was a local newspaperman, which seemed to put the burly chap at ease. Invited inside, Wells was at last able to speak briefly with Taylor in private. Appearing intimidated and eager to leave, Taylor told Wells he had been taken from the Prairie View campus in a cab three days ago.

Let's slip out of here now, Wells urged. Taylor refused to go without Cartwright, who was out at the time. Wells said he'd wait in a motel dining room but soon realized he was being watched by two men, one of them the burly chap he had met at the door of Taylor's suite.

Wells left the motel dining room, but the sight of the two men in his rearview mirror told him he was being followed. By now it was almost midnight. Unable to shake the two, Wells returned to the motel and started walking the grounds behind the building, and nearly got arrested for prowling. Stymied, Wells retreated to his hotel in downtown Dallas, where at 3:30 A.M. he got a phone call from Taylor. The receiver explained how the NFL baby-sitters had provided ample food and drink, along with some sleeping pills, to knock out the players for the night and had since departed. Unbeknownst to the baby-sitters, though, the players hadn't taken the pills. Alone in their room, they were packed and ready to travel.

Wells didn't need to hear another word. He raced back to the motel parking lot, entering cautiously via a driveway at the rear of the property. Evading a patrolling plainclothes policeman, Wells sneaked to the window of Taylor's room and tapped on the glass. Taylor and Cartwright opened the window and slipped out. Safely in Wells's car by 4:45 A.M., the three rushed to the Dallas airport. But as they started to approach the Braniff Airlines counter, another hurdle appeared: From a distance, Wells spotted some suspicious characters, probably there to intercept his companions, he thought. Refusing to see his hard night's work wrecked, Wells did an about-face before he could be spotted and drove Taylor and Cartwright to Fort Worth's airport, where at 7:40 A.M. they boarded a flight to Kansas City.

Before the day was done, Otis Taylor had become gainfully employed by the Chiefs and Cartwright by the Jets.

The saga of Memphis State offensive tackle Harry Schuh is equally bizarre. Its characters include his wife, his infant son, his parents, Oakland Raiders head coach Al Davis, assistant coach John Rauch, Rauch's wife, Los Angeles Rams scout and NFL baby-sitter Hampton Pool, Raiders scouts and hand-holders Ron Wolf and Maury Schleicher, plus extras from the AFL team's front office and Las Vegas nightclubs.

Davis had taken command of the Raiders organization in 1963 and was out to avenge the embarrassing defeats the team had suffered in previous drafts. The 270-pound Schuh was acclaimed to be the top offensive line prospect among college seniors, and Davis was going to sign him, price be damned!

First, the Raiders flew Schuh to Las Vegas on the eve of the NFL draft, as a "goodwill gesture." To fully express their goodwill, the Raiders also flew Schuh's wife and infant son; Rauch and his wife, Jane; Wolf; Schleicher; and public relations director Scotty Stirling to Las Vegas, perhaps to chronicle it all.

Also bound for Las Vegas was Pool. With the Rams expecting to draft Schuh, Pool had been appointed his baby-sitter and had first established contact with the tackle in Memphis. Predictably, Pool was livid when he learned of the Las Vegas trip, so before he took off after his quarry, he convinced Schuh's parents to report that their son had been kidnapped. The Raiders responded by having Schuh's wife call authorities and assure them that all was well and that her husband most certainly had not been abducted. She cheerfully obliged. Just to be safe, the Raiders entourage began shuffling the Schuh family around Las Vegas hotels like pieces on a Monopoly board.

Pool finally caught up to Schuh in a casino. Without saying a word, Pool addled up to Schuh and handed him a card. Whether Pool had written "Meet me in the bar" or "Call me at this number" has never been made clear. But it doesn't matter because Schuh didn't do either. Instead, he showed the card to one of his Raiders hosts. Wolf quickly reported the incident to Davis back in Oakland. Davis ordered the entourage to change hotels immediately and get three rooms for the Schuh family, each under an assumed name: one for Harry, one for the wife and baby, and one to be left empty, as a ruse.

According to one account, Wolf and Schleicher also bundled Schuh into a car and spent four hours riding around Las Vegas, all the while watching to see if they were being tailed. They weren't, so the Raiders' party resumed at a stage show in the Riviera. The good times were short-lived: Stirling, ever vigilant, spotted the NFL's Pool in the back of the theater. Stirling alerted Wolf, who led Schuh into a utility room closet to hide. As the story goes, a janitor had the misfortune of opening the closet but closed it the instant he saw the towering Schuh give him a menacing glare. Moments later, Wolf cracked open the door. He gave a Riviera entertainer a description of Schleicher and $50 to find him and bring him to the closet. Once that mission was accomplished, another call was made to Davis, who set in motion another twist.

Schuh's wife and son would fly to Los Angeles and stay in an apartment as decoys, to draw the attention of Pool and his NFL chums . . . while the Raiders would squire Schuh to another locale. The ruse worked to perfection. Up to and throughout draft day, the NFL staked out the Los Angeles apartment, convinced that Schuh would show up. He never did. He and Schleicher passed themselves off as pro wrestlers and boarded a flight to Honolulu, where they remained until draft day. The Raiders drafted Schuh in the first round, and, with the sands of Waikiki Beach tickling his toes, the hulking tackle signed a contract. The Rams didn't even draft him.

How many college players did Operation Baby-Sit watch over? Dozens each year, at least. A magazine article appearing in 1965 alleged that the NFL had 25 college players stashed in Chicago, Detroit, and Washington, D.C., and on the West Coast. That same year, the 49ers made several calls to NFL draft headquarters in New York trying to locate their potential draftees, who were tucked a few blocks away in San Francisco's Mark Hopkins Hotel.

Although the era is remembered for outrageous bonuses, modest gestures could mean a bundle, too: a Pitt linebacker decided Buffalo was more sincere, since that AFL team had contacted him early in his senior year, long before Baltimore had. So, even though the NFL Colts drafted him in the fourth round, Buffalo still signed its seventh-round choice: future NFL coach Marty Schottenheimer. Buffalo also lost a pick when owner Ralph Wilson saw no reason to give a $3,000 bonus to a Utah defensive back he'd never heard of. His refusal prompted Larry Wilson to fashion his Hall of Fame career with the NFL Cardinals.

The skullduggery wasn't limited to players. AFL old-timers remain convinced that scout Fido Murphy was a double agent. He showed up at the new league's inaugural draft in late 1959 alongside Frank Leahy, the Chargers' first general manager. John Breen, who had worked for the Chicago Cardinals before Houston hired him away, was in charge of that AFL draft and was wary. As far as he knew, Fido still worked for the Chicago Bears. Breen confirmed his suspicions by slipping Murphy phony names of college players. Fido was foiled when he praised them as "terrific prospects."

Baby-sitting fashioned some solid friendships: Bert Rose's brother-in-law got so chummy with Oregon's Ron Medved that he was a member of Medved's wedding party. However, friendship didn't ensure victory. University of Massachusetts hulking tight end Milt Morin and his AFL hand-holder became such great pals that the hand-holder, also a Bay State native and one-time pro football player, even helped Morin get a summer job. Morin, though, never gave the AFL a commitment and signed with the Cleveland Browns. Evidently, the hand-holder learned from the defeat, for in 1978 Ed King was elected governor of Massachusetts.

One could say that the AFL mirrored King's rebound. While the NFL was signing more than three of every four draftees selected by both leagues (one set of statistics put the figure at nearly 78 percent), it nonetheless rang as a hollow victory because it wasn't achieving the objective: The AFL was still around. To us, its endurance was mind-boggling.

Lamar Hunt's original Dallas Texans had been forced to abandon Texas for Kansas City in 1963, where they recast themselves as the Chiefs. The Chargers had abandoned Los Angeles for San Diego after just one season. In Boston, Billy Sullivan was constantly running the Patriots on borrowed money, while Denver's Broncos were dismissed as a nonentity playing amid a Rocky Mountains "cow-burg," in those ghastly, vertically striped socks. Yes, Oakland had scored a coup by corralling Harry Schuh in 1964, yet losing most of its draft choices to NFL clubs had become a matter of routine, so much so that the league had allowed the Raiders to draft players from other AFL teams in 1963 to help restore some semblance of competitive balance. That same gesture was extended to New York because the Titans were utterly moribund. The team had to be taken over by the league in 1962 before being recast as the "Jets" a year later by Sonny Werblin, leader of a new ownership group. The change, though, didn't seem significant, nor did the team's move to Shea Stadium in 1964.

Even a January 1964 blockbuster television contract that the AFL had negotiated with NBC struck us as too little too late. Built largely on Werblin's entertainment world connections and savvy, with ample assistance from NBC sports executive Chet Simmons, the five-year deal that telecast AFL games, starting with the 1965 season, gave the league $36 million. Today, it's judged as a huge, lifesaving boost. When the deal was struck, however, large chunks of the dollars were being lavished on college players, which also fueled higher salary demands from established AFL veterans.

In turn, then, the NFL remained convinced that the upstart league was living on borrowed time. And all it needed to do was to keep fighting and await the inevitable. The inevitable arrived, the next spring, but not quite as we had expected.

THREE

ANATOMY OF A MERGER

Examined in the warm glow generated by 36 years of history and unparalleled success, the pro football merger of 1966 now looks so logical that it seems all but preordained: After more than a half dozen years of bitter warfare, owners came to their senses, stopped throwing around money like drunken sailors, sat down, fashioned an agreement that other pro leagues would strive to emulate, and have lived happily ever after.

Uniting the NFL and the AFL wasn't nearly that cut and dried, though. The merger's architects, principally Tex Schramm of the Cowboys, Kansas City owner Lamar Hunt, and Pete Rozelle, confronted unexpected hurdles and endured countless tense moments. They logged thousands of miles to spend hours convincing their peers of the merger's merits. A sea of bitterness had to be overcome, and in keeping with the cloak-and-dagger nature of the pursuit of college draft choices, the entire adventure was spiced with generous dashes of intrigue. Fitting, when you think about it.

A portion of a magazine article written some years after the merger implies that if NFL owners of the late 1950s had been more accommodating to Hunt or more amenable to expansion, a merger wouldn't have been necessary and war would have been avoided. Hunt, then a youthful 28 and a member of one of the nation's wealthiest families, originally sought an NFL franchise but was rebuffed, prompting him to organize the AFL in 1959 with the likes of oilman Bud Adams (Houston), hotel scion Barron Hilton (San Diego), and insurance executive Ralph Wilson (Buffalo).

The implication of the article is provocative but mostly wishful thinking. Like others at the time, Hunt did want an NFL franchise and saw an opportunity with the Chicago Cardinals, whose presence in the Windy City had grown precarious. The franchise traces its roots to 1899, but the Cardinals had won just one title, in 1947, and had stumbled into the shadow of the Bears. The Cardinals' presence also irritated CBS: It stymied the network's bid to mold Chicago into a regional market for the Bears. But instead of selling what it had owned since 1933, the Bidwill family moved the Cardinals to St. Louis for the 1960 season, with CBS picking up part of the tab.

Likewise, the notion that the NFL disdained expansion stretches the truth. While George Preston Marshall, crusty owner of the Washington Redskins, did throttle some proposals, the NFL still had been sports' most progressive pro league in the postwar era. In 1950, it added Cleveland, San Francisco, and Baltimore from the failed All-America Football Conference and in 1952 tried to establish a franchise in Dallas. After that first Dallas effort failed, Bert Bell handed the franchise's assets to Carroll Rosenbloom, who took them to Baltimore in 1953 and revived the Colts, who had folded after the 1950 season. Before his death in 1959, Bell also had laid the groundwork that brought the Dallas Cowboys into the NFL in early 1960, during the same meeting at which Pete Rozelle was elected Commissioner. Moreover, just two days earlier, Chicago's George Halas had convinced an ownership group in Minneapolis to withdraw as an original AFL franchise holder and join the NFL to begin play in 1961.

By comparison, major league baseball and pro basketball wouldn't begin expanding (cautiously, at that) until 1961, while the National Hockey League operated just six teams until 1967.

Yet, had the NFL expanded even more aggressively, it probably couldn't have satisfied those eager to climb onto the bandwagon. Pro football's popularity was exploding. Some gurus even insisted that football was supplanting baseball as the national pastime. So, even if Hunt had found a way into the NFL, odds are others would have formed a new league. The opportunities were that sparkling.

By the spring of 1966, however, the sparkle was tarnishing. The war for college players was growing more outrageous each year. In 1965, the two leagues may have spent as much as $25 million to sign collegians ($7 million on the top 20 players alone, according to one estimate), plus who knows how much more on the escapades that preceded the signings. Among those watching these dollars flow to rookies were veteran players in both leagues. Naturally, they didn't like what they saw.

"If Joe Namath is worth $400,000, then I'm worth $1 million," reasoned Frank Ryan, who had quarterbacked the Browns to the 1964 NFL championship. About to receive a Ph.D. in mathematics from Rice Institute, Ryan's grasp of numbers was impeccable. Yet, even ordinary intellect could grasp the implications of his quip.

Certainly pro football owners could, who shuddered to even consider the consequences of established pros demanding en masse what the rookies were pocketing or, worse, marketing their talents to teams in the rival league. Hints of that were on the horizon. For example, Charlie Hennigan, who caught 101 passes for Houston, publicly demanded a hefty pay raise when he saw what the Oilers paid rookie receiver Lawrence Elkins (whose lone distinction after four uneventful seasons would be having his name placed on the team's all-time roster).

Understandably, then, the intense quarreling over college talent didn't keep rumors of clandestine meetings among rival owners from surfacing. As early as 1963, Ralph Wilson, Buffalo's owner, for example, was said to have broached the topic with Art Modell, who headed the Browns' ownership group. In 1964, more pointed exchanges are said to have occurred between Carroll Rosenbloom and Wilson, and perhaps Sonny Werblin of the Jets. Additional discussions about a merger surfaced among NFL owners meeting at the Biltmore Hotel in Palm Beach, Florida, in late February 1966—the first meeting I attended as an NFL staff member.

None of these exchanges, however, had led to any substantive discussions or movement, due largely to the hostile feelings fueled by the college draft war. After all, most pro football owners were pretty headstrong guys. "I hated 'em [the AFL]. There are days when I still hate 'em!" Schramm will freely admit. Tex wasn't alone, especially as teams felt forced to draft players they knew they could sign rather than those whose skills were needed on the field. Dallas, for instance, declined to pick Illinois's celebrated fullback Jim Grabowski for that very reason, which is why he went to Green Bay.

Other factors helped stifle potential peace initiatives. An AFL antitrust suit was a lingering irritant and stiffened Rozelle's resolve. The AFL's inevitable and frequent proposals to play a championship game, which began arriving by 1962 and were unfailingly polite and humble, were unfailingly and crisply rebuffed; the simple act of putting an NFL team on the same field with an AFL team would hand the upstarts instant credibility at the very moment the NFL was waiting for the upstarts to fold their tents and disappear.

As 1966 wore on, that looked increasingly likely, as unrealistic as that opinion may appear today. Despite the infusion of NBC money, rumors of deteriorating AFL finances persisted, prompting NFL clubs to stay the course, painful as it was becoming for teams in such markets as Pittsburgh and St. Louis.

Moreover, the informal "gentlemen's agreement" to not raid each other's rosters that Rozelle had struck with AFL Commissioner Joe Foss helped mold overall NFL-AFL relations into a moderately peaceful coexistence. Competition for college players remained fierce, but each league's respective roster players were considered off limits. Willard Dewveall, a Bears end, had played out his option and signed with the Oilers in 1961, becoming the first player to move deliberately from one league to the other. But such shifts were rare, so, apart from the college draft, the pro football realm, while still tense, was almost tranquil. The tranquility was soon shattered.

In April 1966, AFL owners abruptly replaced Foss with Oakland's general manager and head coach, Al Davis, which I heard about while

I was attending the Masters golf tournament with club public relations directors as guests of Rankin Smith, the owner of Atlanta's new NFL team. A very likeable World War II Medal of Honor flier and former South Dakota governor, Foss had served the new league well in its early years and was well connected in Congress. He had his AFL office in Dallas but rarely used it. Joe, it seemed, had climbed into that plane in the war and never climbed out of it. He was always off someplace, ultimately convincing AFL owners that he wasn't suited for their kind of war.

Davis, on the other hand, was a bona fide, brass-knuckles, street-fightin' warrior. He wasn't about to continue the informal gentlemen's agreement governing established players and almost immediately launched secret raids to sign celebrated NFL quarterbacks such as the 49ers' John Brodie and the Rams' Roman Gabriel to what were dubbed "cocktail napkin contracts." The Raiders soon signed Gabriel to a deal, starting in 1967, with a reported $100,000 down payment. Houston's Bud Adams offered Brodie a five-year, $750,000 deal spread over 10 years and cut another deal with Bears tight end Mike Ditka. Reportedly, eight NFL starting quarterbacks were dickering with the AFL. None of these stars ever played for their AFL suitors, but what Davis set in motion was a fire bell in the night that clanged for years.

In truth, though, merger history has given Al Davis more credit than he deserves. In my opinion, he was not the catalyst he has long claimed to be but one of several. Undeniably, he stirred up lots of anger and accelerated discussions. But serious discussions had begun a good six weeks before he became AFL Commissioner. The trouble Davis triggered was a mere episode in an entire drama written and directed by Tex Schramm, Lamar Hunt, and certainly Pete Rozelle. Davis never participated in a single conversation. Moreover, he was unaware of the details of the merger agreement until the night before the announcement. Davis's ultimate legacy to the merger was the protracted legal scuffling prompted by his talent raids, which made the merger's consummation more litigious and costly. He might best be likened to a sniper firing from bushes while his generals negotiate a settlement nearby.

That's understandable, though, because the last thing Al Davis wanted was a merger. He wanted capitulation.

Pete Rozelle wasn't that interested in a merger, either. To say it was "the last thing" he wanted would be an overstatement, but having endured more than six years of acrimony, nasty accusations, and legal challenges, Rozelle certainly was *reluctant* to abandon this struggle. A competitor in his own right, Pete liked a good fight and in many respects had come to relish this one, while growing ever more confident that the NFL was about to win it.

In short, the man who personifies pro football's merger and would spend months lobbying strenuously in its behalf first had to be convinced of its merits. At times, that process was painful.

Serious negotiations were initiated by a late February telephone conversation between Tex Schramm and Los Angeles Rams owner Dan Reeves. As Tex would write in a detailed account for *Sports Illustrated* less than two weeks after the merger's announcement on June 8, 1966, the two "explored the possibilities" of a deal. Afterward, Schramm shared the ideas that had been discussed during a phone conversation with Rozelle. Pete offered encouragement and suggested that subsequent talks initially include only those owners who would be directly involved. He was referring to Wellington Mara, owner of the Giants, and Lou Spadia, president of the San Francisco 49ers, the two teams that competed head-to-head with the New York Jets and Oakland Raiders, respectively. The strategy was to assemble a plan that NFL owners would support, then present it to AFL owners. If they accepted, Schramm's account continues, ". . . fine. If not, we could settle down to an all-out war."

In early March, Schramm and Rozelle outlined a plan, which originally called for the Jets to leave New York and the Raiders to leave Oakland (Seattle, Portland, and Memphis were possible relocation locales), and for Rozelle to be Commissioner of the merged leagues. Next, they divulged this plan to Mara. The Giants' owner wasn't enthusiastic but indicated he wouldn't stand in the way of a merger as long as other NFL owners proved to be supportive. He even speculated there might be a way to solve the competitive problem facing the Giants. Spadia's initial reaction was similar; Lou felt the 49ers could live with the Raiders across the Bay, provided that only the 49ers would continue to play existing NFL teams.

By early April, Schramm had conferred with Covington & Burling, the NFL's attorneys in Washington, D.C. (and the firm from which Paul Tagliabue would emerge as Rozelle's successor 23 years later), about legal and political ramifications and had approached Lamar Hunt. Hunt had been singled out for several reasons: One of the AFL's principal founders, he was respected by his peers; he was tired of the war and wanted peace; he could devote time to the negotiations; he had no real axes to grind; and unlike many pro football owners, he could zip his lip to protect the confidentiality of any deal in progress. In addition, Hunt lived in Dallas, not far from Schramm. In their first conversation, conducted in Schramm's Oldsmobile parked at Dallas's Love Field on the evening of April 4, Tex assured Hunt that the peace overture, while unknown to all but two NFL owners, was sincere and had Rozelle's support.

Hunt listened carefully, took some notes, and asked a few questions. Before parting, they also agreed to be each other's lone contact in order to maintain confidentiality and keep negotiations from becoming unwieldy or spinning out of control. Then Hunt departed for an AFL meeting in Houston where, ironically, league owners would replace Joe Foss with Al Davis.

A few weeks later, potential problems surfaced: Sonny Werblin was rumored to be selling the Jets, and newspaper stories were reporting that Barron Hilton was about to sell the San Diego Chargers. With the Jets' status in New York having a bearing on the talks, Schramm alerted Hunt, who later concluded that neither situation would derail a deal. Spadia, though, was growing restless and needed face-to-face reassurances from Rozelle and Mara, who flew to San Francisco to deliver them later in April.

In early May, Hunt huddled secretly once again with Schramm, who for the first time outlined what peace might cost AFL club owners. The two also talked further about the special problems posed by New York and San Francisco. Eyeing Hunt carefully for signs of resistance, Schramm saw none. Quite the contrary, in fact, which Tex relayed to Rozelle. Feeling optimistic, Schramm looked forward to the spring meeting of NFL owners and was further encouraged when Rozelle suggested that he and Tex meet with Mara and Spadia in New York a few days before that mid-May meeting in Washington, D.C.

Schramm's good feelings wouldn't last long. The atmosphere of the New York meeting, convened around 9:00 P.M. at the Plaza Hotel, struck Tex as strained. Whatever enthusiasm Spadia had had clearly was fading, while Well Mara, too, wasn't as receptive as he had been. Over lunch the following day, Rozelle and Schramm concluded they should not disclose the possibility of a merger at the owners' meeting but rather confer with owners individually and build consensus quietly and gradually. Such a tactic, they further concluded, would help maintain all-important confidentiality.

The strategy became moot not long after NFL owners convened in Washington's Shoreham Hotel. To most in the room, what Mara said after rising to his feet was a bolt out of the blue: The Giants had scheduled a press conference later that afternoon in New York, where they would announce that Pete Gogolak had been signed as the team's new placekicker.

Mara couldn't have caused a bigger explosion if he had set off a bomb.

For the first time ever, an American Football League player was jumping to the National Football League. But Pete Gogolak, who had played out his option with the Buffalo Bills, was no ordinary player. He was a marquee performer. The first successful soccer-style kicker in pro football, Gogolak was still regarded as unorthodox and a veritable symbol of the AFL itself. That Wellington Mara—one of the NFL's true patriarchs—would bother to even consider someone from the "other" league was incredible, and the implications staggering: Were more defections in the wings, at prices owners could only imagine? An escalating all-out war looked inevitable.

More shocking, perhaps, was the fact that Pete Rozelle was approving it! Rozelle had concluded that, according to the NFL's own constitution, Gogolak was a free agent and the Giants had every legal right to employ him. Most alarming of all was what the signing revealed about Rozelle's attitude toward the AFL. Conciliation was not on his agenda.

Reactions among owners were tremendous and volatile. Sitting in the room with them, I still can remember how astonished I was by the outrage being expressed. Jim Kensil and I had been alerted by Rozelle that Mara was going to make his announcement, but I couldn't have anticipated the storm that erupted. Schisms among owners were apparent. Exchanges between old friends such as Mara and Vince Lombardi, who was representing Green Bay, were particularly heated. Lombardi was so furious that his face turned red. It really hit the fan.

Rozelle, in fact, had to adjourn the session almost immediately but not before he, too, became embroiled in the emotional outbursts. Amid these exchanges, the possibility of a merger became exposed— and so did hints of Rozelle's opposition to it!

Schramm couldn't believe what he was seeing and hearing. Pete felt in his heart that the AFL's failure was inevitable. He had no reason to compromise, he insisted. His words would soon prove to be more pivotal than anything Al Davis might have concocted.

Instead of going their separate ways to cool off after the session ended, a handful of influential owners huddled privately: Schramm, Mara, Spadia, Lombardi, Cleveland's Art Modell, Baltimore's Carroll Rosenbloom, and Stormy Bidwill, co-owner of St. Louis. This gathering affirmed that attitudes at the club level had changed and that the Gogolak bombshell was the last straw. Despite Rozelle's intense feelings, the existing competitive climate simply did not make financial sense. The talent war was eroding NFL franchises, too.

Rozelle, the master of persuasion, was embroiled in an argument he would not win. The assembled owners designated Schramm to meet privately with Rozelle in Pete's hotel suite and convey their position: The league would pursue the merger under Pete's direction. But if he chose not to lead it, then NFL owners would pursue the merger without him.

Rozelle was alone in his suite when Schramm arrived and explained why he had come. The events of the past few hours had not weakened Pete's resolve one bit. He wanted to continue the fight. Schramm and Rozelle discussed the situation in detail. Finally, though, Tex told Pete that he had no choice, that this special group of owners had drawn a very tough line: If Pete Rozelle wanted to continue as NFL Commissioner, he was going to have to stand front and center for something that he really didn't believe in.

According to Tex, Pete sat back, struggling with his thoughts. His face could not fully disguise the tremendous battle raging between his deeply entrenched emotions and his sound judgment process. His eyes began to tear. With a nod, he excused himself and went into the bathroom. The time had come for the emotions and conflicts deep inside him to pour out. And they did.

A few minutes later, the door opened and Rozelle stepped out. Schramm said he had never seen such an intense look about him. Pete's mouth and jaw were set. His eyes were narrowed and full of resolve. He looked Tex in the eye and said, "All right, let's go!"

Tex never revealed much of this until after Rozelle had died in late 1996. He sent his handwritten version of their meeting to me for editing prior to its being included in a tribute to Pete that was being published in an NFL magazine. It remains a startling revelation and probably remained hidden for so long because even a hint of Rozelle's true feelings might have undermined pro football's positions in critical meetings that were to follow later in the year.

As much as any event, that climactic meeting accelerated merger momentum. Owners left Washington the next day, but a handful reconvened in New York, apparently in Rozelle's apartment. Along with the seven owners who had forced the issue at the Shoreham, Pete undoubtedly conferred with Dan Reeves, his pro football mentor, and with Pittsburgh owners Art and Dan Rooney. By Memorial Day, NFL owners were all on board, although winning Lou Spadia's firm commitment required special care and attention.

Rozelle then went to Dallas to polish the final proposal that would be presented to Hunt and, in turn, the AFL. To guard against leaks and eavesdropping, Pete stayed in Schramm's home, where one of Tex's three daughters dubbed him "Sneaky Pete" when she learned the true reason for his visit. She was a typical teenager but, once sworn to secrecy, maintained her silence throughout. It couldn't have been easy, though, because both Rozelle and Schramm were on the phone constantly to owners and borrowed a typewriter for Pete to use to make additional notes.

The merger hinged on two critical issues besides the actual act of combining and the resulting legalese: what to do with the Jets and what to do with the Raiders. From day one, the Giants had been unhappy about the presence of the Jets, although after six years of competition, New York had more than proved it could support two pro football teams. The Giants' games were perpetual sellouts, and there was a long waiting list for season tickets. The Jets, with Werblin's touch and Namath's celestial presence, had amassed a solid fan base of their own. The San Francisco Bay Area was another matter, however. The 49ers played in aging Kezar Stadium, before faithful fans who resided on a comparatively small peninsula. The Raiders, by comparison, were surrounded by fast-growing Northern California locales and about to move into a new stadium. Resolving both situations would take delicate negotiations, conducted primarily by Rozelle working quietly behind the scenes. Ultimately, they were settled by AFL clubs' paying an $18 million indemnity over the next 20 years, the largest part of the $26 million that the merger ultimately cost the AFL.

On May 31, a day after Rozelle returned to New York, Schramm welcomed Hunt to his home, where they reviewed the final proposal—in the same amicable manner that had marked each one of their conversations. The deal, Schramm stressed, had been approved by all 15 NFL owners. If the AFL proposed too many changes, everything could come apart.

Hunt, in turn, flew to New York to confer with Buffalo's Wilson and Boston's Billy Sullivan, who unbeknownst to Schramm had been acting as a committee of sorts and were being kept apprised of the merger talks. The trio reviewed the proposal and developed a list of 26 changes and additions, which Hunt relayed to Schramm at the end of the week. In studying these, Schramm and Rozelle concluded that about a third were acceptable, a third were unacceptable, and a third probably could be resolved with additional conversations. Rozelle addressed the problems with the respective owners of the clubs affected and also conferred with Hunt. From time to time during these few days in early June, they were within a few blocks of each other in New York, but they still conferred solely by telephone.

Hunt sat down once more in Schramm's Dallas home on Sunday, June 5, to go over both the proposal and the AFL's 26 requested changes. As midnight approached, only a few items were left unresolved, principally future expansion. Each league was due to add a team before 1970, when the two leagues were to combine. At issue was who would provide the players for the new AFL team and who would receive payment for the new franchise. In the end, AFL clubs provided the players, while the NFL received the franchise fee.

Hunt left for New York early the next morning. By midnight on that Monday, after another hectic round of phone calls and clarifications, he and Schramm had wrapped up the tentative agreement. Schramm called Rozelle, who contacted NFL owners during the morning of June 7 to confirm their assent.

One last task remained: proclaiming that peace had come to pro football. We had to move much more quickly than had been planned because rumors were rampant. Our lawyers at Covington & Burling urged Pete to announce the merger as soon as possible but to first brief two key congressional leaders, Michigan senator Philip Hart and New York representative Emanuel Celler. Rozelle flew to Washington to meet with Hart. Kensil flew to Washington later in the day, to help Pete put the key points of the deal in "capsule" form and draft the press release.

Even this process was tinged with intrigue: Hunt was to join the group Tuesday night in a suite registered under a fictitious name ("Ralph Pittman") at Washington's Sheraton-Carlton Hotel, but no one had told Hunt what the name was. As luck would have it, Lamar walked into the hotel just as Rozelle, Schramm, and their colleagues were returning from their meeting with Senator Hart. They all adjourned to the "Pittman" suite and tinkered with the press release until 3:00 A.M. Wednesday. Later that morning, Rozelle spoke with Congressman Celler before flying back to New York for the formal announcement. We called a press conference at the Warwick Hotel, where I had first met Rozelle five years earlier. Just after 6:00 P.M. on June 8, 1966, flanked by Tex and Lamar, Pete announced the merger that would change the face of professional sports.

The news was especially startling to Al Davis. He had not been invited to participate in the press conference, nor did he attend. Through the years, my understanding has been that Davis was unaware that merger talks had progressed as far as they had because Hunt, with other AFL owners' support, simply bypassed him. Davis was still AFL Commissioner, to be sure, but kept his considerable energies focused on signing players—veteran NFL quarterbacks primarily—and on establishing a league office in New York. Finishing that task by the end of May, Davis began building an AFL public relations staff to compete with what Jim Kensil and I had built for the NFL and hired three veterans shortly before the merger announcement. One of them, Val Pinchbeck, attended the June 8 press conference just to see what Rozelle had to say. Val, who had just left Syracuse University as sports information director to move to New York, returned with the news that he and fellow new hires Mickey Herskowitz, from the *Houston Post*, and Irv Kaze, from CBS Sports, were about to be unemployed. For that matter, so was Davis. No position existed for him in the newly expanded National Football League.

Rozelle's serving as Commissioner of the combined league—point number one of the agreement—had always been a principal concern, both within our office and among the 15 existing NFL teams. Indeed, as far as we were concerned, the other six key points of the merger were secondary. But, of course, they mattered plenty:

- The leagues would play a world championship game following the 1966 season.
- All existing franchises would remain in their present locations.
- A common draft would be held.
- Interleague preseason games would be played beginning in 1967, and a single-league schedule would begin in 1970.

- Two franchises would be added by 1968, one in each league, with the monies from each new franchise paid to the 15 NFL teams.
- AFL clubs would pay an $18 million indemnity to the NFL over a 20-year period: $10 million going to the Giants, as compensation for sharing New York with the Jets, and $8 million going to the 49ers, as compensation for sharing the Bay Area with the Raiders.

Of prime legal importance to the attorneys involved in the negotiations was that no city would lose its franchise, as had been proposed early on. With memories of moves by the Dodgers, the baseball Giants, the Washington Senators, and the football Cardinals still fresh in the minds of both fans and politicians, the pledge to keep all franchises operating was deemed paramount by the lawyers and more noteworthy than it might appear today. So, too, was the promise to expand, to New Orleans and Cincinnati, as it turned out.

The merger's last two points—particularly the $18 million in indemnities—still irritated some AFL owners and occasionally contributed to the strained atmosphere that marked early meetings of owners of both leagues.

Yet, apart from Al Davis, who never liked the deal and eventually returned to Oakland's front office in late July as an operating executive and part owner, the rest of the country uniformly praised it—sports writers, college sports officials, and, notably, players from both leagues. Sanity had been restored to pro football, they all said. Now the game could continue to march unimpeded to its glorious future and only smooth sailing lay ahead.

Of course, that's what we thought, too. We thought wrong.

FOUR

COMING FROM BEHIND ON CAPITOL HILL

Whatever euphoria the June 8, 1966, merger announcement had sparked was short-lived. Supplanting it was the sober realization that consummating the AFL-NFL merger would require every ounce of resolve Pete Rozelle had shown at the end of his fateful meeting in Washington with Tex Schramm and throughout subsequent negotiations.

There was an agreement, of course, and plans for a common draft that would end the loony shenanigans that added a bizarre twist to the annual college draft. There would be single-league play under the National Football League banner, beginning in 1970, and interleague preseason games, beginning in 1967. And, yes, the leagues' respective champions would meet in a postseason "world championship" game the following January, now seven months away.

In truth, these grand plans were all tentative. And, they almost collapsed in the fall of 1966.

Consummating the pro football merger hinged on resolving some murky antitrust questions. Rozelle had dutifully acknowledged as much on June 8, when the announcement of the merger was made, but this dash of reality was largely misunderstood, dismissed as irrelevant legalese, or ignored altogether. So was a modest Associated

Press story quoting Arthur Morse, a Chicago attorney and sports agent who relished creating headlines. Morse declared the merger was a blatant violation of antitrust laws.

His declaration was an omen, but no one paid attention, preferring instead to focus on the wisdom of what had occurred and the prospects of a world championship game, which were growing more intriguing by the day. Another Arthur, the much respected *New York Times* sports columnist Arthur Daley, observed that the merger promised stability "to the mutual benefits to all concerned." A *Washington Post* editorial concurred, praising the two leagues for their collective wisdom. Veteran players expressed relief, such as Aaron Brown of the Chiefs, who called it "the greatest news I've heard in years." Without a merger, "football would have been ruined," added Cardinals receiver Sonny Randle. College athletic directors, such as Michigan's Fritz Crisler, expressed thanks that baby-sitters and hand-holders would stop invading their campuses. So did college coaches. "Seven pro teams were represented when our spring practice began," Wisconsin's Milt Bruhn had stewed. And owners of well-heeled teams, such as Cleveland, Dallas, and Kansas City, admitted that even they could not have weathered the war indefinitely. "There would have been bodies scattered all over the landscape, and mine might have been on top of the hill," commented Cleveland's Art Modell.

That prospect had not entirely disappeared, for beneath these expressions of confidence floated a river full of potential deal breakers: unsettled tax and financial details, questions about television broadcasts, and more questions about how an expanded NFL would operate and be aligned, and when and where this new championship game would be contested. Floating along with them were leftover conflicts: The Giants remained wary about sharing New York with the Jets, while the San Francisco 49ers still fretted about the Raiders being across the Bay in Oakland. The $18 million indemnity certainly would help ease their suffering, but it was to be paid over 20 years, which continued to irritate AFL owners and to stoke Al Davis's wrath.

Yet, these uncertainties paled to insignificance when compared with the antitrust question. As much as avoiding the media, it had been the key reason for confidentiality and stealth during negotiations. Before he first contacted Lamar Hunt, in fact, Tex Schramm had been briefed about its ramifications by the NFL's attorneys at Covington & Burling. The attorneys briefed Schramm, Hunt, and Rozelle a second time on the afternoon preceding the merger's announcement. That's how important a concern it was.

Major league baseball had enjoyed its blanket exemption since a 1922 Supreme Court ruling, and it had been upheld in a 1953 decision. But that exemption applied only to baseball, and the court's 1953 affirmation had expressed misgivings and contained a suggestion that Congress tie up the lingering legal loose ends with new legislation. Furthermore, the court had specifically ruled against extending baseball's exemption to other professional sports in a 1957 decision, while conflicting opinions issued by two Wisconsin courts in 1966, following the baseball Braves' move from Milwaukee to Atlanta, had muddied the waters even more.

It wasn't entirely a new dilemma for football, however. Rozelle had successfully confronted it in 1961 in winning approval from Congress for the leaguewide television contract he struck with CBS the following January. The NFL also had spent the better part of two and a half years fending off the AFL's claim of monopolistic practices. Those charges had been dismissed in May 1962 by a district federal court judge, whose ruling had been affirmed by an appellate court two years later.

Despite these successes, there was no way of knowing how the courts or Congress might now appraise a pro football merger, however sensible and popular it might be. The Justice Department was in a position to at least offer guidance but declined to rush to any judgment. Football season, a Department official shrugged, was two months away.

Appraising all this uncertainty, Rozelle and the NFL's attorneys had quietly concluded that without some kind of legislative protection from Congress the merger could unravel.

Appropriately, then, the antitrust issue was atop the agenda of pro football's Joint Committee when it first convened on the morning of July 20 at the Plaza Hotel in New York. Established by Pete Rozelle, who served as its chairman, it was composed of six owners, three from each league. Hunt of Kansas City, Billy Sullivan of Boston, and Ralph Wilson of Buffalo represented the AFL. Dan Reeves of Los Angeles, Tex Schramm of Dallas, and Carroll Rosenbloom of Baltimore represented the NFL. Once assembled, they heard a briefing delivered by Covington & Burling attorney Hamilton Carothers. He told them that the merger's approval hinged on the personal attention of all team owners and ranking executives working with congressmen and senators.

The Joint Committee's initial strategy had been to get behind the "sports bill" that Michigan senator Philip Hart had introduced in early 1964. Hart's bill proposed extending baseball's exemption to other sports, as the Supreme Court had implied in 1957. It certainly afforded pro football the antitrust protection it needed to unite the two leagues, conduct a common draft, administer and assign players' contracts, and carry out expansion plans. Unfortunately, the bill had languished in the House Judiciary Committee, following its orderly approval by the Senate. Proponents hoped the pro football merger would give the Hart bill fresh momentum, but by late June it was clear it wouldn't be considered before Congress adjourned in late October, just ahead of the fall elections. So, at Carothers's recommendation, the Joint Committee's focus—and pro football's, too—shifted to seeking a specific antitrust exemption for the "expansion plan," as the merger was called in legislative circles.

As helpful as team owners could be, the lobbying campaign's chief crusader would be Rozelle himself. Pete had started well before he formed the Joint Committee. In fact, he had started before the merger was even announced.

Along with Senator Hart, one of the last persons Rozelle had consulted before returning to New York on June 8 was Brooklyn congressman Emanuel Celler, the crafty and crusty 78-year-old who had served his fellow New Yorkers in the House since 1923. Pete's telephone conversation that morning had been no mere courtesy call. As the powerful chairman of the House Judiciary Committee, Celler's support of the merger was essential. But everyone had reason to be optimistic about securing it, for Celler not only had supported

Rozelle's efforts to put together the leaguewide television contract in 1961 but also had introduced the very bill that made it possible.

This time around, unfortunately, the honorable Mr. Celler wasn't nearly as helpful. From our vantage point, in fact, he turned out to be a complete horse's ass.

The root cause of his opposition, many observers felt, had nothing to do with pro football and everything to do with baseball. Celler remained irate over the departure of the Brooklyn Dodgers to Los Angeles and, to a lesser degree, the baseball Giants to San Francisco. An acknowledged antitrust expert, Celler similarly despised the baseball exemption and wasn't about to extend its privileges to anyone else. If his stance brought pain and suffering to pro football, well, so be it.

None of these feelings, nor the obstacles Celler was about to throw in the merger's path, were evident throughout much of the summer. The only development of note, other than the late-July meeting of the Joint Committee, had been the AFL's move to increase player rosters from 38 to the NFL standard of 40, in anticipation of the postseason championship game.

Behind the scenes, though, we kept busy, amassing ammunition for the lobbying campaign and to rally the public to our cause. For instance, we compiled articles from newspapers in the home states of House Judiciary Committee members. Another tactic was developing "talking points" that stressed the merger's benefits to both pro football players and pro football fans. Win the fans' support, we reasoned, and win approval from Congress for an antitrust exemption. With help from a Washington lobbying firm, we drafted a version of these points for Pete to include in a speech he was to deliver at the Football Writers of America meeting in Chicago in early August. Pro football players, we felt, would enjoy

- more job opportunities in pro football, since the merger would keep all existing teams intact; increase AFL rosters from 38 to 40 players; and allow for the addition of two more franchises before 1970, plus the likelihood of two more franchises after 1970;

- a more stable pro football environment that would bolster weaker franchises;
- increased minimum salaries, something that the AFL had never before had and that would be increased in the NFL (to $12,000);
- a more equitable distribution of available payroll funds on each team, which, in turn, offered prospects of dazzling rewards to outstanding players;
- an improved and more generous pension plan that would pay players with 5 years' experience nearly $450 a month at age 65, then steadily increase so that players with 15 years of service would receive more than $800 a month;
- greater opportunities for players to develop second careers after they left pro football, since the merger stood to dramatically expand the game's horizons and, with them, players' reputations.

Football fans, meanwhile, could count on

- all 24 pro franchises continuing to exist in their present locations (while continued war all but guaranteed that several franchises would fold or move);
- new teams in Atlanta and Miami, which were joining the NFL and AFL, respectively; two more expansion teams in new locations by 1970; and perhaps two more expansion teams thereafter, making pro football "more nationwide in scope than any other professional sport";
- new football attractions, such as the championship game between the two leagues; interleague preseason games, beginning in 1967; and interleague regular-season games, beginning in 1970;
- improved financial conditions among all teams and a more equitable distribution of television revenues, which, along with single-league play and interleague trades, promised more intense and more exciting competition;
- avoiding the ugly and unfortunate "rich-getting-richer, poor-getting-poorer" pattern that had plagued pro sports for decades, causing the demise of the All-America Football Conference, the

Federal Baseball League, and the Basketball Association of America, and leaving fans in many cities without any pro team at all;

- a much better and more competitive game to watch in the stands and on television, thanks to the benefits the merger would bring to the players.

Given the story that the 200 assembled writers walked away with on that Friday in Chicago, what we prepared for Pete hadn't been worth the wear and tear on a typewriter ribbon. He cited them, of course, but what the writers remembered was a warning most never expected.

The pro football merger was in jeopardy!

A few hints might have been dropped now and then earlier during the summer. A few sports columnists familiar with Hart's sports bill—and Celler's opposition to it—were perceptive enough to sense matters might not be marching along to their desired conclusion. But this was solid, crisp, and dramatic news right from the merger's principal champion.

If Congress didn't pass legislation resolving the murky antitrust statutes in pro football's favor, Rozelle said, both leagues would have to consult their Washington attorneys and reevaluate the merger. He quickly reaffirmed his optimism that help would arrive in time, based on visits earlier that week to Washington, where he had asked Celler and the Judiciary Committee to consider legislation specifically addressing pro football's situation. But Rozelle also reaffirmed his stand that the merger, a common draft, and a championship game were an "all-or-nothing" plan. And, time was becoming a problem.

Rozelle's revelation didn't match the bombshell Well Mara had dropped at the May NFL owners' meeting, but it still aroused mountains of comment, not all of it positive, either. Some of the writers who had applauded the merger now chided "greedy owners" for trying to grab more protection than they needed and wondered how much fans really would benefit. Others, such as Dallas sports columnist Blackie Sherrod, recognized Pete's comments as a calculated and clear signal that he had kicked off another game besides pro football:

a tough, no-holds-barred legislative joust, whose stakes were high and whose consequences were enormous. Blackie was as right as rain, although in early August neither he nor anyone else seriously envisioned the merger falling apart.

A month later, everyone had to. As Labor Day approached and a football season along with it, Rozelle's tone was much more ominous, prompting *Washington Star* sports writer Mo Siegel to declare, "Peace in pro football is on the brink of collapse." By now, Pete had to admit the situation was grave, and a very real prospect existed that the leagues "could be back where we started—nowhere," he said.

Completing the merger without some sort of antitrust protection in place would expose the NFL to untold lawsuits in the future, he contended. Ambitious litigants, Rozelle said, would have what amounted to "a hunting license." In turn, unless Congress acted, he would have no choice but to recommend to NFL team owners that the merger be abandoned. The trip to Washington that Rozelle had quickly scheduled for the next week underscored how desperate the situation had become. By now, time was starting to run out.

Pete charged up Capitol Hill on September 8 with a new proposal, designed to revive the spirit of congeniality he had struck with Celler five years earlier. One could liken it to a draw play: Instead of an entirely new bill, he asked the congressman to consider an amendment to the 1961 television bill, the same statute that Celler had authored. The amendment would extend the original law's antitrust protection to the AFL-NFL merger itself. In Pete's mind, it was an ideal solution. It would give football limited but sufficient protection, and it contained a provision affording high schools the same protection from Friday night pro football telecasts that Congress had previously granted the colleges on Saturday. Most important, Pete and his allies reasoned that Celler should feel better about supporting this amendment because he could do so without having to abandon his "principled" stand against the Hart bill and broad exemptions for baseball and other pro sports leagues.

Celler was unmoved and turned Rozelle down cold. There would be no new amendment and no new legislation of any kind (the Hart sports bill already had been effectively laid to rest). Perhaps in a bid to appear somewhat helpful, he also urged Pete to simply go ahead and merge. Nothing's standing in the way, Celler kept publicly insisting. "There hasn't been any suit filed or questions raised," he said.

As if on cue, a man named Bob Nussbaum surfaced the very next day in Chicago. He and two partners, he declared at a news conference, had been assured by Lamar Hunt that they would get an AFL franchise for the Windy City in 1967 and that the merger had wrecked his plans. Nussbaum claimed he had lined up a coach and had begun building an organization that included Bears legend and Hall of Famer Joe Stydahar and ex–Notre Dame coach Frank Leahy. So, he was suing the NFL and AFL for $12 million (the $4 million suit sought treble damages). How serious were these allegations? It was never clear. But Nussbaum exemplified precisely the threat Rozelle had warned against, and Celler's assurances suddenly looked naive. Pete held fast to his position. The stalemate was hardening.

By now, fans and writers and politicians were beginning to take sides. Just about everyone, of course, wanted to see the merger completed. But whether or not congressional action was needed began generating sports page debates. Pro football could surely schedule its heralded championship game without antitrust protection and continue to carry out expansion plans, one view argued, characterizing Rozelle as either shrewd or greedy. Writing in Rozelle's defense, *Atlanta Constitution* sports editor Jesse Outlar characterized Celler as the "self-appointed athletic director of Congress." Others suggested that, without antitrust protection, college draft choices could sue the NFL as easily as Bob Nussbaum had.

Ever resourceful and not about to concede defeat, Rozelle took his proposed amendment to the other side of Capitol Hill. The Senate was far more accommodating. Two congressional legends, Illinois Republican and minority leader Everett Dirksen and Louisiana Democrat Russell Long, introduced the amendment, along with Roman Hruska, a Nebraska Republican. The strategy also called for the amendment to be concurrently introduced in the House by Louisiana Democrat Hale Boggs and a rising Republican from Michigan, Gerald R. Ford.

Dirksen even spiced up the proceedings by showing up in a wheelchair and saying he was "coming off the injured reserve list" on behalf of football fans everywhere. Perhaps his theatrics helped. The bill raced through the Senate in the blink of an eye. The Judiciary Committee passed it unanimously, in what was called an extraordinary session. The full Senate did likewise, clearing it on its unanimous consent calendar.

The Senate's swift action gave the House almost a month to act, but it still seemed like an impenetrable hurdle. Any new measure—the Senate bill included—had to be first voted out of the Judiciary Committee, and Celler remained intractable. While he indicated he would arrange for an expeditious hearing, he nonetheless chided the Senate for its hasty action, which he used to justify wariness and caution. "I don't want to buy a pig in a poke," Celler groused.

It soon looked as if Celler didn't want to buy a pigskin under any circumstances. He did schedule hearings for October 6 but before an antitrust subcommittee, not the full Judiciary Committee itself. It mattered little, for as soon as the hearings convened, a quorum call from the House floor delayed them until the following Tuesday. The procedure looked arduous and exhaustive. Scheduled to testify along with Rozelle were Milt Woodard, who had become AFL president after Al Davis left as AFL Commissioner; 18 House members who supported the amendment; Justice Department officials; Federal Trade Commission officials; NFL and AFL player representatives; NCAA representatives; and representatives from high school sports federations and television networks.

By now, Rozelle and Celler were eyeball to eyeball. While it had become obvious that the full House would approve the amendment, Celler was confident he could "plumb the depths of the merger plan" and delay the committee's proceedings long enough for Congress to adjourn before the House had time to act. House Speaker John McCormick was empowered to bypass Celler's committee, but that wasn't likely. Pete, meanwhile, was feeling more pressure to at least confirm plans for the championship game but refused. It was legal but not practical, he said, in his usual calm demeanor, and reiterated his all-or-nothing position.

Reports of NFL teams making plans for a traditional league draft in late November aroused fresh visions of baby-sitting escapades and ratcheted tensions higher. So did a $25 million antitrust suit filed against the Washington Redskins by the president of a proposed

United States Football League, who also insisted on appearing before the antitrust subcommittee.

Celler's hearings finally got under way in earnest on October 11 with an amicable exchange. "When two men ride a horse, one must ride behind," Celler commented, making it clear he was in charge. "Just so the horse moves," quipped Florida's Robert Creamer, one of the bill's supporters.

The horse didn't move. Usually flanked by Woodard, Schramm, and Hunt, Rozelle answered a wealth of questions, stressing that, while the NFL could be challenged on numerous issues, it merely was seeking "legislation that will exempt the merger act itself from antitrust litigation," he said. Yet, he and NFL attorney Hamilton Carothers spent much of their time sparring with Celler over assorted legal issues. At one point in a subsequent session (one of three in all), a glimmer of hope surfaced: Celler asked lawyers for the two sides to try to rewrite amendment language that would be mutually acceptable. But Carothers subsequently said the version prepared by subcommittee counsel Kenneth Harkins was so narrow as to be meaningless, while Harkins accused Carothers of demanding a "blank check." Amid the hearings, newspaper editorials added their opinions to those of sports writers.

By mid-October the merger was declared all but dead. Rozelle could only describe himself as being "hopeful." Congress would adjourn in a week, but Celler announced plans to methodically continue his subcommittee hearings anyway, despite pleas and prodding from his committee members. He looked for all the world like a victorious quarterback taking a knee in the final seconds of a bitter, hard-fought battle.

But Celler underestimated Everett Dirksen and Russell Long. If there ever was a political maneuver worthy of being labeled an end run, it was the last-ditch legislative tactic orchestrated by the two wily senators. "Quarterback sneak" might be just as descriptive.

Just as Al Davis over the years has received too much credit for his role in the merger, Senators Dirksen and Long probably have received far too little. The lawmakers had doggedly hunted for a path to steer

Rozelle's amendment past Celler's roadblock. They finally found it in an investment tax credit bill that had been high on President Lyndon Johnson's "must pass" list. While Celler arrogantly plodded along in the House, Dirksen and Long attached the amendment to the tax bill, on the grounds that the amendment would provide special tax treatment for four charity professional football games. It was good enough for the Senate, which approved the amendment unanimously, even faster than it had approved it three weeks earlier. Since the House had already passed the tax bill, the only hurdle left was approval by a House-Senate conference committee, plus the formality of a final vote in each chamber. That already was assured. As chairman of the Senate Finance Committee, Long would lead the Senate's conferees, while Arkansas Democrat Wilbur Mills would serve as his counterpart from the House.

It was all over but the shouting and the voting. The Senate passed the tax bill—containing the amendment that exempted pro football's "act of merging" from antitrust statutes—on Friday, October 14. House and Senate conferees agreed on the legislation's final language the following Monday. The House approved it three days later, and the Senate followed suit on Friday, October 21. In a week's time, pro football's antitrust exemption had become the law of the land.

Even Celler had to smile at being outwitted. After expressing his opposition to House-Senate conferees, he told reporters, "They caught me bathing and sold my clothes."

In the final analysis, maybe Celler had underestimated Pete Rozelle, too. At age 40, Pete had demonstrated a remarkable grasp of the political process and a consummate ability to enlist the support of powerful men with differing views. It was a performance NFL owners would never forget. And I cannot recall even one instance when Pete showed signs of strain or lost his cool.

Celler forever maintained that the public had been defeated, but pro football's growth speaks for itself. Even if he had prevailed, a merger of some kind—no doubt forced by failing teams and related chaos—was inevitable. The negotiated merger that did result was infinitely better.

Pete also had demonstrated a grasp of knowing how to reward political favors. For instance, Senator Hiram Fong of Hawaii had weighed in with his support in September. So, it may have been more than coincidental that Rozelle soon thereafter announced that the 1967 NFL annual meeting in February would convene in Honolulu. Nor was it only coincidental that before 1966 ended, NFL owners decided to locate the league's newest franchise in New Orleans.

Naturally, we all breathed a sigh of relief. Not for long, however, because our attention had shifted almost immediately to planning the world championship game, along with tending to the week-to-week activities of the 1966 NFL regular season. But these were largely familiar challenges, and knowing that the merger would now be a reality restored the feeling that we were in command of our future.

In reality, of course, the merger's saga was far from complete. Three-plus years of working out countless details and reconciling differences in league practices and organizing a common draft would be necessary to bring the two leagues together. Plenty of adventure lay ahead.

FIVE

EVEN THE FOOTBALL WAS DIFFERENT

It had become clear that uniting pro football was going to take a while, even before the antitrust issue erupted. I confirmed that fact firsthand in the third week of July, on the eve of the Joint Committee's first session in New York.

"We've got a meeting tomorrow, and one of the issues on the agenda is reconciling the constitutions of the two leagues," Pete Rozelle told me when he walked into my office on that summer day. "I'd like you to do a comparison," he said. "You know, take an issue in the NFL and take the same issue in the AFL. What are the procedures here? What are the procedures there? Then compare the two and put together a summary."

It sounded routine enough, and it was. But I literally worked through the night studying the two constitutions and preparing the comparison Pete needed the next morning. As I labored, I drew my own conclusion: About the only thing the National Football League had in common with the American Football League was that they both played a game called football.

Beyond that, no matter what the activity, the NFL did it one way and the AFL did it another. At times, the details seemed endless. They created mountains of red tape, legal opinions that would put you to sleep, assorted complexities that devoured weeks of time . . . and one contentious issue that was to put yet another cloud over the entire merger.

When the merger was announced, for instance, NFL teams each had 40-man playing rosters and up to 60 players under contract. AFL teams had 38-man rosters and up to 65 players under contract. Anticipating the game against the NFL champion, the AFL quickly raised its roster limit to 40. Reconciling everything else wasn't that easy.

The NFL also had a minimum salary of $5,000 (that's right), provided a training camp per diem, and required the Commissioner to raise any objections about a player's contract within 10 days of receipt. The AFL had no such provisions and no minimum salary. NFL players reported to training camp nine weeks before the start of the regular season; AFL players reported eight weeks before the regular season began. The NFL trading deadline was five weeks after the regular season began; the AFL's was six weeks. Waiver rules and procedures differed, too—significantly in some cases. So did penalties for players caught gambling or trying to control the outcome of league games: The NFL constitution afforded Rozelle the prerogative to suspend Green Bay's Paul Hornung and Detroit's Alex Karras for gambling in 1963; had those star players been in the AFL, they would have been expelled outright because that's what its constitution dictated.

A minimum of 10 votes was needed to elect the NFL Commissioner, who also had the sole authority to select the location of the league office. The AFL elected its Commissioner by a three-fourths majority (seven votes at the time), while an executive committee determined the site of the office. NFL teams sent 2 percent of their gate receipts to the league office, the AFL 3 percent or a minimum of $2,000. AFL teams had players' names on the backs of their jerseys. NFL teams did not. AFL home teams always wore colored jerseys during games. NFL teams had their choice of home uniforms, white or color. The NFL pension plan covered its players and front office people; the AFL pension plan covered only players and coaches and didn't really compare in value to the NFL's.

Each league also used a different playoff system and different officials, guided by different factors, who enforced and interpreted slightly different playing rules. The most noted was the AFL rule allowing two-point conversions, something the college game had adopted a few years earlier and one that Lamar Hunt badly wanted to retain. Hunt got his wish . . . but not until some 28 years later, in time for the 1994 season. (In the 1968 preseason, both leagues experimented with what was called the "pressure point." The ball was placed at the two-yard line, and teams either ran or passed for a one-point conversion. But it was discontinued after the experiment due to lack of support.)

Almost everything needed to be discussed and was resolved without too much fuss, but it all needed ponderous review. Along with these nuances was a dizzying number of legal and tax issues, many of which had been further complicated by the tactics Al Davis and others had used in the three months he waged war on the NFL as AFL Commissioner. Attorneys had a field day from the get-go. For instance, it took several years and payments from every NFL club to settle one contract dispute that swirled around journeyman quarterback Jim Ninowski.

Last, but certainly not least, television contracts were different. NBC had exclusive rights to AFL games through the 1969 season. The NFL's deals with CBS generally covered two years. Television obligations had been the number one factor in not merging officially until February 1970 and launching single-league play the following September. As it turned out, we needed every minute of the three-plus years they provided to get our ducks in a row. In fact, the Joint Committee that first convened in mid-1966 continued meeting periodically well into 1969.

Since the NFL technically was expanding to include AFL teams, an immediate freeze was put on anything that the AFL could do internally without Rozelle's knowledge, to help everyone get their arms around these nettlesome and mundane matters. None of this work ever inspired anyone to arrange a testimonial dinner, but it all needed attention nonetheless. If I learned anything in 29 years, it was that administering the National Football League is a constant succession of tedious application of various rules and procedures.

One other detail needed attention, too. Each league played with a *different* football. The NFL football, made by Wilson, was dubbed the "Duke," which always showed up on the promotional film footage CBS used to begin its telecasts. Expressly designed for the NFL, it dated to the league's early years and was especially well suited for kicking. Spalding made the AFL football, essentially the same ball used by the colleges. Called the "J5-V," it was slightly more slender than the Duke and allegedly better suited for passing. What accounted for the difference was a technical measurement called the "ogive" (pronounced "OH-jive"). If you measured each ball at the same spot, you'd find the AFL ball wasn't quite as fat as the NFL ball. In addition, the laces on the AFL football were a quarter of an inch longer than the laces on the NFL football.

To fans and most officials, the differences were imperceptible, and most of them probably couldn't have cared less. But quarterbacks and centers could distinguish these differences in a heartbeat, and they cared plenty. To settle the matter initially, the Joint Committee ruled that each league would continue using its own ball until single-league play began in 1970, at which time Wilson would became the sole manufacturer of the official NFL football. The new model wasn't quite as fat as the Duke had been but still differed slightly from the J5-V.

One dilemma remained, however: Whose ball would be used for the world championship game, now due to kick off in two months that seemed to be flying by with frightening speed? And, what about interleague preseason games that were to begin in 1967? The answer was *both*. We borrowed a tried-and-true technique used for years in high school football games.

Each team would snap its own league's football while on offense. For the first championship game, then, Kansas City quarterback Len Dawson handed off or threw the AFL J5-V, while Green Bay's Bart Starr used the NFL Duke when the Packers had the football. As long as game officials, ball boys, and other fellows on the sidelines paid attention, the solution was dandy. On a few occasions, though, those along the sidelines of the Los Angeles Coliseum saw a team's center get set for the snap and then heard him bark to an official, "Hey, this isn't our ball!" The oversight was quickly rectified, and play resumed.

If only it had been that simple to resolve the redshirt draft. That it wasn't was due to the issue's principal combatants: Pete Rozelle in one corner, Vince Lombardi in the other.

The stalemate that began in late 1966 probably never matched the threat posed by antitrust concerns, but for nearly two months it hung over the merger like a waterlogged beach towel on a puppy. It stopped progress almost dead in its tracks and delayed the much anticipated first common draft by six weeks. Before hostilities ended, Rozelle and Lombardi stood eyeball to eyeball, when for an instant the merger *did* appear in jeopardy.

"Redshirt draft" defined a provision that became part of the regular NFL college draft in the late 1950s. While some restrictions applied, it amounted to using a draft choice to select a college junior and holding the rights to that player in the hopes he could be signed a year later, when he became eligible to sign a pro football contract. Officially, we called such players "futures," but "redshirts" became as common a term, especially after the AFL began drafting juniors, too. By the mid-1960s, the later rounds of the NFL draft were amply sprinkled with futures, to the point that the AFL initiated a second draft of nothing but redshirts a few weeks after its regular draft, in an attempt to keep pace in the escalating college talent war. In fact, it looked to us as if AFL teams used the NFL's selection of futures to guide their redshirt selections. Still, signing anyone before he completed his college eligibility wasn't even considered, let alone practiced.

No one wielded the redshirt draft provision better than Lombardi, whose adroit maneuvers helped him stock the roster of his powerful Green Bay Packers in the early 1960s. For Vince, it was tantamount to having extra draft choices year after year. Blessed with so much talent, he could afford to trade quality players for draft choices at roster cut-down times. He then used some of those extra choices to pick talented college juniors and waited for them to become eligible.

A classic example of a redshirt was Donny Anderson, a fabled Texas Tech running back and punter. Lombardi picked Anderson as a junior, watched him play his senior year in college, then signed him as he would any other selection.

Predictably, then, Vince was outraged by two ideas that surfaced as planning for the common draft progressed: One was a proposal to conduct a separate redshirt draft after the regular draft, as the AFL had been doing. The other was a proposal to discontinue drafting redshirts altogether. Lombardi fought any procedural change in the college draft tooth and nail, and with the Packers en route to winning five championships in seven seasons, his growls about being "penalized for success" were taken seriously by owners and by Rozelle himself.

Yet, college football coaches and athletic directors had grown just as irate as Lombardi. In their eyes, it was bad enough that pro football conducted its draft before the college football season ended, as was then the practice. Having some of their best players already committed to the pros before they had concluded their college careers made college coaches even angrier. It seriously disrupted their teams, they charged, and served no useful purpose. About the only purpose it did serve, in fact, was standing as another symbol of the escalating competitive threat posed by pro football in general.

Considering these feelings, along with the political brushfires the antitrust hearings had ignited, Rozelle concluded that drafting futures—or redshirts—had outlived its usefulness. It's my understanding, in fact, that, as he sought the antitrust exemption in 1966, Pete all but promised congressional leaders that he would persuade owners to end the practice. AFL owners agreed without hesitation. For the most part, they were so pleased to be joining the National Football League that they bent over backward to cooperate at virtually every turn.

The Joint Committee was similarly inclined to recommend ending redshirt drafts, provided that college teams granted pro scouts access to college practice sessions, helped the NFL develop more accurate data about players, and permitted college assistants to do scouting work for pro teams. Perhaps as an interim step, the committee first proposed holding a five-round redshirt draft the following May after college football teams had concluded their spring practice session—but for one year only. It also proposed a regular common draft of 11 rounds, to be held one week from the Tuesday following the world championship game.

By the time NFL owners convened for a special meeting in early December, however, Rozelle had managed to persuade every NFL team to discontinue drafting redshirts entirely, with one exception: Green Bay. Given the other issues swirling about the merger, Pete evidently felt unanimity was essential. Unfortunately, Lombardi wouldn't give an inch. A committee of one—San Francisco's Lou Spadia—was appointed to discuss the matter further with Green Bay, but Spadia wasn't any more persuasive than Rozelle had been.

Efforts to end the stalemate resumed at a second special owners' meeting that convened in Los Angeles on the morning after Green Bay's 35–10 victory over Kansas City in the first world championship game. The victory hadn't softened Vince one iota, forcing an exasperated Rozelle to announce at the end of another long day that the draft, now set for February 1, would be postponed indefinitely until sometime after the annual NFL owners' meeting in late February, when the issue would be tackled yet again.

As we sat down at that annual meeting in Hawaii on February 20, 1967, I wondered how long Pete could endure Lombardi's intransigence without responding in kind. Rozelle rarely got edgy. More important, he had an innate sense not to push an issue so hard that it fell apart, plus the ability to keep discussions going no matter what. But even Pete Rozelle could have his moments. One appeared late in the week.

"I've got these extra choices because I have picked this talent well!" Lombardi began on that Thursday afternoon. "I've got the best team in football," he added heatedly, "and I ought to be permitted to continue building it!"

After hearing Vince caustically express doubt about the issue's overall importance, Rozelle exploded. "Goddamn it, I'll tell you how important this is!" Rozelle thundered back before pointing to a meeting room wall. "There's a phone over there. Do you want me to go pick it up and tell the AFL to forget about the merger? That the whole thing's off?"

The room went dead silent. Even Lombardi was at a loss for words. And for the next several moments, it remained dead silent while those assembled pondered the time and effort spent on negotiating the merger; winning antitrust protection; staging a world championship game; and resolving AFL indemnification issues, tax issues, and legal issues. Now, at long last, the sought-after common draft was in sight, but it all hung in the balance because of Vince Lombardi's insistence on being able to keep grabbing redshirts.

While others pondered, Rozelle sat there in front of a microphone in the middle of the U-shaped meeting table, allowing the silence and the tension to fully envelop the room. It seemed like four or five minutes went by. In Pete's hand was a pencil. And out of the clear blue, he snapped the pencil in half a few inches in front of the live microphone.

It sounded like a rifle shot.

I mean, I jumped. And I'm sure everybody else in the room did, too. It was amazing and typical Pete Rozelle. He had waited and waited for precisely the right moment to demonstrate how this whole thing was going to come apart if the owners—and Vince Lombardi—didn't come together. His sense of timing was incredible.

Still more silence followed, then a recess. I don't know what was said or by whom. But within 30 minutes, an agreement was reached. Minutes of the next day's meeting reported that the Commissioner stated that "he would assume everyone was in favor of the proposal made at Thursday's meeting regarding the policy of no redshirt drafting." I also remember Pete adding quietly, "Unless there's some objection, of which I hear none."

And with that, it all faded away quietly, without any vote that might have poured salt into Lombardi's wounds. References to redshirts had been withdrawn without so much as a whisper. A single common draft of 17 rounds would be held.

We conducted the draft on March 14, 1967, at the Gotham Hotel in New York, right off of Fifth Avenue in midtown. The setting was as strange as I can remember, for the ballroom we used had what looked like a running track ringing its terrace level. But it came in handy. With 25 teams participating, almost twice as many people were on hand compared with other years, and they were scattered all over the place. After what we had experienced, we were thrilled to see each and every one of them. Michigan State defensive end Bubba Smith was the first selection, taken by Baltimore. The irony of it all, perhaps, was when the round was finished, Lombardi still had had two first-round picks. It figured.

Once the redshirt adventure was behind us, most of the other issues fell into place quickly or seemed to. Our to-do list was a veritable potpourri.

One task that required immediate attention was scheduling preseason games prior to the 1967 regular season. That had been one focus of the very first joint meeting of NFL and AFL owners on December 2, 1966, in New York's Waldorf-Astoria Hotel. In the 75 minutes they spent together, beginning at 2:30 P.M., owners settled on having just one interleague game per team, which wasn't to be scheduled before NFL teams scheduled four other NFL preseason opponents. It sounds a little haughty, but some reasoning was behind it.

On the one hand was some natural apprehension among NFL teams about playing AFL teams, especially since this decision was rendered six weeks before the first world championship game. On the other hand, a few NFL clubs might have been tempted to load their preseason schedules with presumably weaker AFL opponents to generate better gate receipts, build a little momentum, and arouse fans' interest.

For the record, Denver was the first AFL team to defeat an NFL team that preseason, beating Detroit 13–7 in a game that director of personnel Mark Duncan and I attended in Denver. The Broncos also called Alex Karras's bluff. If the Lions lost, the star tackle had boasted before the game, he would push a peanut with his nose all the way back to Detroit.

If Alex acted on his vow, we didn't notice. By then our eyes were focused on the venues where games were being played. Next to the common draft, stadium accommodations were most important and prompted a far-reaching recommendation by the Joint Committee that was written into the new NFL constitution. In April 1968, the committee agreed that—at a minimum—stadiums of all teams should have "seating capacities in the area of 50,000" by the time single-league play began in 1970. It's more than coincidental that between, say, 1966 and 1972, all-purpose "cookie-cutter" stadiums were built in cities such as Pittsburgh, Cincinnati, Atlanta, Oakland, and in time, San Diego. Stadiums that had opened earlier in Washington and St. Louis, plus Shea Stadium in New York, were of the same genre. Many had moveable stands to accommodate both baseball and football.

Scheduling and revenue considerations made this issue critical. Many AFL stadiums in those days were becoming inadequate. War Memorial Stadium in Buffalo didn't have room for more than 45,000, while the Boston Patriots would play just about anyplace owner Billy Sullivan could find to seat somebody: cozy Fenway Park, Boston College, Boston University, and, for one season, Harvard. San Diego's Balboa Stadium couldn't seat more than 35,000, while Oakland and Houston both had used high school stadiums on occasion.

Some NFL cities weren't much better off. Minnesota's Metropolitan Stadium, built for the baseball Twins and used by the Vikings, was patterned after Wrigley Field in Chicago and didn't seat more than about 45,000 for football. Wrigley, meanwhile, was the periodic home of the Bears and could squeeze in perhaps about that many for football. It didn't matter if the mighty Packers played in Milwaukee County Stadium or Lambeau Field in Green Bay. They both had less than 50,000 seats, and, before 1965, Lambeau's capacity had been less than 40,000.

At that time, the "multipurpose" stadium was ingrained in sports philosophy. It would be a few more years before new football-only facilities were built. Kansas City opened 78,000-seat Arrowhead Stadium in 1972, a year before the Buffalo Bills opened Rich Stadium, which seated 80,000. Arrowhead was the most ambitious, since a new baseball stadium went up right alongside it at the same time. Originally, a retractable roof was to move on a track between both stadiums to provide protection against the weather. But the feature's $20 million to $25 million price tag made it too costly to add.

At the league office, we were just as concerned about other stadium features, such as lighting for television. That attracted our attention because networks were starting to broadcast games in color as a matter of routine. Yet, numerous stadiums weren't equipped to provide the kind of lighting the color cameras required.

Within the stadiums, "presentation" details needed attention, too. Our objective was straightforward. No matter where someone attended or covered a pro football game, we wanted to ensure a consistent, first-class experience: uniform operations and services to help fans attending the game, and standards of excellence to help the writers and broadcasters covering the game perform their jobs as easily as possible. One of the advantages both Jim Kensil and I brought to the league was that we had been newspapermen and were aware of what a sports writer looks for when he gets to a facility—not only a comfortable working environment and easy access to locker rooms—but also the assurance of being able to get a cab at a darkened stadium a couple of hours after a game has ended.

Press box accommodations varied widely. Some AFL operations were first rate, but others needed our guidance, as did a few NFL operations. Almost immediately, I began working with the AFL clubs and familiarizing them with the NFL philosophy of what league public relations and club public relations people should do. One of the things I felt strongly about was standardization. I felt that you ought to be able to walk into a press box on a Sunday in any of the places we played and get the same level of service. San Diego, say, should be no different from Cleveland or New York. At the time, it was quite a mishmash. We felt the same way about game programs. In 1966, some were outstanding. In other cases, teams should have paid their fans to read them.

Our zeal for consistency attracted critics, but it helped drive our effort to present NFL football in the best possible light. The Rozelle image, if it was nothing else, was first class all the way. Fiscal restraints were always considerations, of course, but with a little thought and planning, franchises could come up with ideas that were pretty special for fans and writers alike.

Starting in 1967, I spent a great deal of time going to AFL games, just as an observer. Pete had asked me to get as close to the AFL people as I possibly could. In those days, many of us went to games and continued to do so for as long as Rozelle was Commissioner. We had a core group of people in the office who would spend every weekend out of the city, just to observe. We weren't spying. We were there to see the pluses and minuses, and to bring back both good ideas and recommendations for improvements. In seeing for myself what went on, I got to know people, who in face-to-face conversations told me things I wouldn't have heard over the telephone. The relationships proved invaluable because when we were putting together the combined NFL office we had a strong reservoir of talent that we had identified at the club level for positions in the league office. Later, as the Super Bowl grew as a media event, we could tap this same talent pool for various tasks.

These journeys also enabled me to see AFL teams up close. For instance, as the 1968 season moved along, I concluded that the New York Jets were a much better football team than many NFL veterans imagined.

Combining offices and personnel, establishing the Office of the Commissioner, and moving to a new headquarters at 410 Park Avenue in Manhattan were on our agenda in the late 1960s, too, as well as coordinating NFL and AFL meetings to allow for joint sessions of owners. Not terribly exciting tasks, either, but absolutely essential. Rozelle even sought outside advice from Booz, Allen & Hamilton, one of the nation's blue-chip management consulting firms. The Office of the Commissioner was one of its recommendations and was envisioned as an umbrella organization overseeing the respective operations of both leagues until the merger officially took effect in February 1970. More important, it would serve as a symbol of unity.

As part of the plan, the NFL would have not only a Commissioner until 1970 but also a president. The position, which existed for only about three and a half years, was largely ceremonial, created to conform to the AFL organizational structure and provide a counterpart for Milt Woodard in pro football's new hierarchy. Woodard was a veteran AFL executive who became AFL president soon after we agreed to merge. To follow suit, the NFL named Cleveland's Art Modell as its president.

My title changed, too. I joined the new Office of the Commissioner as its director of public relations, overseeing public relations activities in both leagues. Along with Rozelle, the office included executive director Jim Kensil, treasurer Bill Ray, director of personnel Mark Duncan (who also continued serving as supervisor of officials), broadcast coordinator Bob Cochran, and director of security Bill Hundley. From this platform, a new National Football League began to take shape, a theme we promoted diligently when single-league play began in 1970.

This new platform also allowed me to further expand the public relations operation that Jim Kensil had expertly designed when he joined the league in 1961. Joe Browne came out of the NFL mailroom to become my young assistant; he's now the NFL's executive vice president for communications and government affairs. Joe joined Jim Heffernan, who directed the NFL public relations program, and Harold Rosenthal, who ran the AFL public relations operations. With this fresh horsepower, our NFL public relations machine shifted into high gear and kept right on rolling.

The entire reorganization took the better part of two years. Ironically, it became effective on October 21, 1968, two years to the day after Congress had passed the antitrust exemption that enabled the merger to go forward.

Meanwhile, the Joint Committee continued to confront all the details, meeting periodically throughout 1967 and 1968 and into 1969. Much of its business could be described as mundane. But one last issue of importance remained: realigning 26 teams for single-league play. It was to be an adventure all its own.

SIX

THE "ROYAL ORDER OF REALIGNMENT RECORDERS"

Fashioning One League from Two

Mark Twain once compared crafting legislation to making sausage. He would have used the same analogy to describe pro football's realignment ordeal, just as surely as he would have smiled approvingly on the honorable society that it spawned, the "Royal Order of Realignment Recorders."

From start to finish, realignment stretched across the better part of 21 months. Marathon discussions became the norm, some lasting into the wee hours of the next morning. One, in fact, lasted 35 hours and 45 minutes. Mind-numbing sessions notwithstanding, realignment was concluded finally and abruptly by a twist worthy of Alfred Hitchcock himself.

Like the merger, the NFL playing structure that emerged at last in mid-January of 1970 looks very logical: one league with two conferences of three divisions each, with the divisions built on traditional rivalries, geographic considerations, and stadium accommodations. Season schedules were prepared to reflect this tidy arrangement, and it has all worked so well over the years and so ably accommodated the league's subsequent growth that a critical fact has been lost: Creating it defied all logic.

The task looked disarmingly easy in the beginning, especially after the battles we already had fought. The same Joint Committee formed in July 1966 to oversee the merger's other issues and details had league realignment on one of its meeting agendas as early as November 1967. But existing network television contracts obligated the NFL and AFL to play separate schedules through the 1969 season. So, the Joint Committee didn't begin addressing the matter in earnest until April 1968, with the help of the Commissioner's headquarters staff. Quiet discussions that focused on schedules and traditional rivalries resumed in December and again in February 1969 before the Joint Committee formally introduced realignment as an agenda topic at an occasion that over the years has launched numerous NFL adventures: the annual postseason owners' meeting.

Convened on St. Patrick's Day in 1969 at the El Mirador Hilton Hotel amid the magnificent vistas of Palm Springs, California, this mid-March gathering was a historic occasion in its own right. It marked the first time that NFL *and* AFL owners and working club executives—and their families—convened as one, with several joint sessions on the weeklong agenda, along with social functions throughout the week. In all, as many as 300 attended.

Realignment was one of the agenda items, but it was heralded with as boring a heading as I can recall reading: "A Summary of Basic Information Pertinent to a Study of Scheduling and Alignment in 1970 and Thereafter." If the deadly prose put owners to sleep, the words that followed immediately woke them up. The summary contained four points:

1. Further expansion to 28 teams in 1970 was not feasible.
2. Realignment based on an extension of the present 14-game schedule was not feasible.
3. Realignment in 1970 should retain as many of the smaller four- and five-team divisions as possible.
4. The leagues should retain their identity for purposes of public image, although legally they would become one league in 1970, with some interleague play.

In other words, the committee was recommending that the existing 16-team NFL and 10-team AFL structures be kept intact. The new franchises that the league anticipated would all enter the AFL until it, too, fielded 16 teams. The recommendation, which became known as the "16-and-10" document, even included the NFL and AFL's retaining their respective logos.

On hearing its presentation, Paul Brown exploded in an icy fury. He just about went berserk. Back in football as the coach and principal ownership force behind the Cincinnati Bengals, Brown didn't give a hoot that his franchise had been awarded by the AFL in September 1967 and had begun playing as an AFL team in the 1968 season.

"I agreed to come back into the *National Football League*," he insisted vehemently, and nothing but the National Football League. Speaking in the crisp, chilling tones that could strike fear into brutish linebackers, Brown made it crystal clear that the Bengals' designation as a member of the American Football League was only temporary. As I recall, he was every bit as adamant as irascible Emanuel Celler had been during the 1966 antitrust congressional hearings.

PB's fury and unwavering insistence quickly mustered the support of fellow AFL owners. They, too, felt snubbed, and their feelings contributed to the tense, uncertain atmosphere that was evident throughout the meeting. Nearly three years after the merger, some of the residue from seven years of assailing each other as archenemies lingered, while the $18 million indemnity that AFL members had to pay the NFL, along with the other millions, remained a sore and sensitive subject. Not everyone was contentious throughout, but the meeting was punctuated by plenty of uncomfortable moments. Joint sessions that dealt with tax and legal issues ripped open old wounds and exposed angry feelings. One exchange between Well Mara of the Giants and Arnold Grant, a representative of the new Jets ownership, was especially testy. That each group still convened for separate business sessions probably didn't help either, but it was necessary, since the legal act of merging wasn't to occur until February 1970, 11 months away.

Almost from the moment the merger had been announced, AFL owners had remained wary that some other shoe was about to drop. The 16-and-10 realignment proposal that virtually maintained the status quo was about the last thing most of them wanted to hear. It left them wondering what else they had to prove, especially since the New York Jets' stunning 16–7 victory over Baltimore in Super Bowl III remained fresh in everyone's mind.

Contentious as it was on occasion, the meeting still stands as the NFL's most significant since the meeting that had elected Rozelle Commissioner in 1960. It's where the true structure of postmerger pro football began taking shape. Fortunately, some of the tension was eased by a memorable party thrown by the Jets, as part of their Super Bowl celebration. In fact, the affair established a new tradition for this meeting. The Jets' owners had arranged an exquisite dinner party, after which Hoagy Carmichael entertained us all. Hoagy sang and played his piano into the wee hours of the morning, as if he knew we needed a good bash to start building new relationships.

But not even Hoagy's talents could lighten the atmosphere enough to make any headway on realignment. A week's worth of trying led only to the creation of two more committees to study what had mushroomed into yet another dilemma: In the AFL group were Brown, Oakland's Al Davis, San Diego's Gene Klein, and Lamar Hunt of Kansas City. Comprising the NFL committee were the Giants' Well Mara, Chicago's George Halas, Dallas's Tex Schramm, Baltimore's Carroll Rosenbloom, and Cleveland's Art Modell (who by now also was serving in the largely ceremonial role of NFL president, while Rozelle and the rest of us administered both leagues). The groups' contributions were modest at best, though, and the task of recasting 16 and 10 into 13 and 13—in a manner that every franchise could endorse—landed squarely on the shoulders of all 26 owners. It proved to be a Herculean struggle. I don't think anyone realizes how much agony was endured.

Both leagues' owners next headed to New York in late April 1969 for a series of meetings that included joint and concurrent sessions. Meeting separately at various times over a three-day period, owners considered three options:

1. Total and complete realignment into two 13-team conferences, without any regard for previous league affiliations.
2. What was termed "unit realignment," which called for transferring existing divisions from one league to the other, in a manner to be determined.
3. The transfer of three existing NFL teams to the AFL.

While initial discussions were fruitless, the first glimmer of progress peeked through the gloom the second afternoon when NFL owners unanimously voted to pursue the third option and adopted a resolution authorizing Rozelle to discuss with any interested NFL clubs a move to what would be called the American Football Conference. The action revived optimism. Sensing an opportunity, Pete immediately began shuffling between the AFL and NFL owners groups. He also met with individual owners, particularly Rosenbloom, Modell, and the Rooneys of Pittsburgh. Progress proved elusive, however, so both sets of owners agreed to go home, think things over, and return to New York the following week.

On Wednesday, May 7, 1969, NFL owners began anew, meeting for 11 hours, while AFL owners tended to their own affairs. Nothing was accomplished. The NFL tried again the next morning, Thursday, sitting down to what turned out to be virtually three days and nights of nonstop sessions, save for periodic recesses of a few hours. Some of those recesses were called to confer with AFL counterparts.

In the midst of it all, Modell had to be rushed to a New York hospital with a stomach ailment. No matter, we rigged a speakerphone in a conference room so that he could continue contributing his thoughts from his hospital bed. The episode also enabled Modell to become better acquainted with a young NFL staff member. Art had landed in the hospital without any pajamas. Hospital gowns being . . . well, hospital gowns, he asked if we could send someone out to buy him something more suitable and less drafty. We quickly dispatched our promising young staffer to Modell, who handed him a

$100 bill and told him to use his best judgment. Given our young staffer's background—he had escaped from Hungary with his mother—it may have been the first time he'd ever held a $100 bill in his hand. Within an hour, though, he returned to the hospital from exclusive New York clothier A. Sulka with as fine a pair of silk pajamas as ever had been purchased in Manhattan, plus a few coins in change. Although taken aback, Art still must have taken a fancy to his $99 pajamas because seven years later, in 1976, he would hire our "young staffer," Peter Hadhazy, as his general manager in Cleveland.

As Art recovered, the NFL convened and reconvened. Thursday's session began at 10:00 A.M., recessed at 11:00 A.M., reconvened at 2:30 P.M., recessed at 5:05 P.M., reconvened at 8:40 P.M., recessed at 9:40 P.M., then reconvened yet again at midnight and continued until 8:00 A.M. Friday! After a two-hour break, a joint session began at 10:00 A.M., concluding before noon. At about 2:30 P.M., NFL owners sat down again, while AFL owners met or simply hung around on whatever couches and chairs they could find. A few stretched out on the red carpet of the NFL office itself.

The scene during these sessions and the others that were to follow throughout 1969 and into the next year may have been as chaotic as anything ever hosted at NFL headquarters. Meetings that convened one morning didn't adjourn until early the next. Instead of breaking for meals, Rozelle had two of his special assistants, Bill "Granny" Granholm and Bob Cochran, periodically bring food and beverage into the meeting room, without bothering to take orders. Matters became so hectic that Granny and Bob just dashed over to P. J. Clarke's, ordered whatever they thought was appropriate, and hauled it back. During one midnight run, they nearly got locked out of not only our offices but also the building itself. Only by the grace of a security guard were they kept from spending the night on the street with the owners' provisions.

Inside the building, Rozelle began insisting that negotiations continue uninterrupted until realignment was completed. Had owners been turned loose in Manhattan, Pete reasoned, they might never have reconvened. By my count, we sequestered them at one point for more than 30 hours, and as those hours dragged on, some of them naturally became restless. How restless? Well, consider this one little episode.

Just when it occurred remains unclear, but it happened. It reveals just how determined Rozelle was. During one session, we noticed that a few owners were retreating to the men's room with unusual frequency. A little investigating revealed why: They had airline-size bottles of liquor in hand and were sneaking off to down a quick drink. Pete responded by locking the men's room door! The tactic achieved mixed results. One owner—who shall remain nameless—soon found himself in dire need of the men's room, but the door was still locked. Becoming desperate, he recalled that one of our offices had a wet bar in it. Off he went, no doubt stepping carefully. Evidently he was mighty tired, too, or mighty something, for while the sink in the wet bar was conspicuous and otherwise unoccupied, this AFL owner missed it entirely and watered the wall. For several years thereafter, the office was affectionately known by select NFL insiders as "[So-and-So]'s sandbox."

Complicating logistics was the need to hold some of the meetings in the Maisonnette Room of the St. Regis Hotel, located around the corner on East 55th Street. Although the NFL's 410 Park Avenue headquarters were fairly new, our conference room wasn't big enough to accommodate all 26 owners and the Commissioner, plus assorted league executives who needed to be on hand. Eyeing an opportunity to become a hotel of choice among the distinguished NFL owners, the St. Regis was delighted to provide assistance and the space.

The hotel was so delighted, in fact, that, as one round of meetings dragged on, it canceled a long-booked performance by Hildegarde, a popular singer and entertainer of the era, who was scheduled to perform in the Maisonnette Room. She was duly advised that football came first and that she needed to go elsewhere. I don't know if she did, but I do know she was one unhappy lady. Then again, the way things were going, Hildegarde might as well have hung around and stuck in her two cents' worth. It couldn't have hurt.

As if all this weren't enough, we had to tend to the care and feeding of sports writers who were hanging around anticipating some kind of announcement. As much as we appreciated the stories the writers penned, as a matter of policy we met with them away from headquarters unless a special need or occasion dictated otherwise. Besides, we weren't about to have sports writers wandering the halls chasing rumors and tidbits of news. The owners were troublesome enough by themselves. Goodness knows what might have unfolded had the owners rubbed elbows with the writers. So, along with meeting space, we booked three suites for the writers at the St. Regis, and several of our staff took turns tending to their needs.

Perhaps too diligently. On duty for one shift was Harold Rosenthal, a colleague whom we had inherited from the AFL league office. Harold caught wind of writers ordering choice steak sandwiches and such from room service and putting the bill on the NFL's master tab. A former New York sports writer himself, Harold abhorred people indiscriminately spending lavish sums of somebody else's money (except when he was the one doing the spending). In decidedly un-PR-like fashion, Harold took it on himself to call room service and cancel the orders. He replaced them with what became a steady diet of pastrami sandwiches adorned with dill pickles, obtained from an undistinguished Manhattan deli. Many of the writers on the scene never so much as looked at pastrami again.

Sports writers are notorious grousers, and they may have tired of steak sandwiches, too. But in covering the realignment proceedings, they had earned the opportunity to find out.

Shortly before 1:00 A.M. on Saturday, May 10, the writers finally had reason to focus not on pastrami but pro football. Rozelle rousted everyone from his slumber and then announced that three teams, Baltimore, Cleveland, and Pittsburgh, had agreed to become part of the new American Football Conference. No matter the hour, it was a dramatic breakthrough. More drama unfolded within no more than 60 minutes. The three franchises and their new AFC brethren had further aligned themselves into three divisions:

- Boston, Baltimore, Buffalo, Miami, and the New York Jets would compete in the AFC East.

- Cincinnati, Cleveland, Houston, and Pittsburgh would compete in the AFC Central.
- Denver, Kansas City, Oakland, and San Diego would compete in the AFC Coastal (West).

Each of the transferring NFL teams was to receive $3 million for its sacrifice. And *sacrifice* did indeed characterize what Pittsburgh's Art Rooney and Dan Rooney felt they were making. Back home, the Steelers' faithful couldn't understand it. Perhaps one could discern a certain logic driving the decisions of Cleveland's Modell and Baltimore's Rosenbloom. But the Rooneys? One of the NFL's legendary, family-owned franchises joining the very bunch they had fought so hard to eliminate for so long? Never! But it was fact.

As it turned out, fans in Baltimore were an aroused bunch, too, to the point that some of the Colts' faithful were ready to tar and feather Carroll Rosenbloom and ship him out of town on a rail. John Steadman, the *Baltimore Evening Sun* columnist who had incessantly thumbed his nose at the AFL, never forgave the Colts' owner. To Steadman, Baltimore was NFL red-white-and-blue.

The ire of Cleveland fans would begin to subside in time, for two reasons. First, the Browns' legendary rivalry with the Steelers would endure. Second, prospects of a new intrastate rivalry with Cincinnati were intriguing in their own right, sparked not so much by geography but by the bitter animosity between Art Modell and Paul Brown; in January 1963 Modell had fired Brown, a coaching legend for whom the team had been named and, until his dismissal, the only coach the Cleveland Browns had ever had.

Along with the hour and fans' anticipated reactions, another factor further subdued the enthusiasm over the creation of the AFC: While the 16 NFL owners had approved the AFC plan, it still was tentative because the AFL's 10 owners decided to withhold final acceptance of the 3 NFL clubs into their realm until alignment of the 13 remaining NFL teams into the National Football Conference was completed (a decision some trace to Al Davis of the Raiders). Not even a compromise NFC plan was in sight, let alone one that would win the owners' *unanimous* approval.

So, more NFL-only discussions dragged on into Saturday night, with Rozelle moving between the two groups of owners. As midnight approached, it became clear that the NFL owners had reached an impasse that couldn't be resolved without additional meetings. Before recessing, though, Rozelle was able to report that he had convinced AFL owners to accept once and for all the transfer of Baltimore, Cleveland, and Pittsburgh to the AFC. So, half of the battle had been won.

As for the other half, well, how many different combinations of 13 are there? I never did find out, but we must have tried them all as the months went along. Each proposed plan was given a number, and records I kept indicate that at least 119 plans were officially submitted. But dozens of other variations were kicked around, too.

NFL owners, who now numbered 13, tackled realignment again at a weeklong meeting in New York that began on June 2, 1969. The following day they examined nine specific plans that had been submitted during various stages of the discussions (see Table 3).

None of them was acceptable. The owners did consider—and resolve—several other merger-related issues, such as waiver procedures and the specific football to be used in single-league play in 1970 (a Wilson NFL ball, of course). But by the time Friday, June 6, had arrived, NFL owners were no closer to realigning than they had been on the preceding Monday. All they could agree to before adjourning was to meet again in October. But nothing was settled then, either. So, one more special session was scheduled in New Orleans during Super Bowl IV weekend in January 1970.

By this time, of course, everyone was growing impatient and irritated. For what seemed like the umpteenth time, the pro football merger was fast approaching a deadline, with no solution in sight.

To begin with, the league office had to begin drawing up the 1970 regular-season schedule. Fortunately, some work already had been accomplished because as the AFC was realigned, the league also had determined that one five-team division and two four-team divisions would be formed in the NFC, as well. It also had established a

TABLE 3: NINE PROPOSED PLANS FOR REALIGNMENT CONSIDERED BY THE NFC OWNERS

No. 12	No. 102	No. 104	No. 105	No. 106	No. 110	No. 114	No. 115	No. 119
Los Angeles	Los Angeles	Los Angeles	Los Angeles	Los Angeles	Los Angeles	Los Angeles	Los Angeles	Los Angeles
San Francisco	San Francisco	San Francisco	San Francisco	San Francisco	San Francisco	San Francisco	San Francisco	San Francisco
New Orleans	St. Louis	New Orleans	New Orleans	New Orleans	Philadelphia	Detroit	New Orleans	Green Bay
Atlanta	Atlanta	Atlanta	Atlanta	Atlanta	St. Louis	Philadelphia	Atlanta	Detroit
Chicago	Green Bay	Chicago	Green Bay	Chicago	Chicago	Green Bay	Detroit	Chicago
Green Bay	Chicago	Green Bay	Minnesota	Green Bay	Detroit	Chicago	Chicago	Minnesota
Detroit	Detroit	Detroit	Detroit	Detroit	Green Bay	Atlanta	Green Bay	New Orleans
Minnesota	Minnesota	St. Louis	St. Louis	Dallas	New Orleans	New Orleans	Philadelphia	Atlanta
	New Orleans				Atlanta			Dallas
New York	New York	New York	New York	New York	Dallas	Dallas	Dallas	New York
Philadelphia	Philadelphia	Philadelphia	Washington	Washington	Minnesota	New York	New York	Washington
Washington	Washington	Washington	Philadelphia	Philadelphia	New York	Washington	Washington	Philadelphia
St. Louis	Dallas	Minnesota	Chicago	St. Louis	Washington	St. Louis	St. Louis	St. Louis
Dallas		Dallas	Dallas	Minnesota		Minnesota	Minnesota	

14-game format, with home-and-home contests between division rivals and five games against teams in other divisions of the same conference, plus three interconference games. That basic format was modified slightly for the five-team divisions and also called for Denver to play a fourth interconference game for at least five years as long as it remained in the four-team AFC West.

Of course, this format didn't do anybody any good as long as the NFC alignment was unsettled. Complicating matters further was the fact that we needed to put the finishing touches on new television contracts not only with CBS and NBC but also with ABC, which had agreed in May 1969 to begin televising—in "living color"—a new 13-game *Monday Night Football* prime-time series, starting with the 1970 season.

To the uninitiated, it's probably beginning to sound as if pro football owners of that era either weren't nearly as bright as they were alleged to have been or were incredibly stubborn and headstrong, especially since the NFL appeared to realign with ease in 2001. Without question, those who own pro football teams rarely are wallflowers, and some are a rare breed. Yet, as the 1960s were drawing to a close, myriad factors had to be considered: scheduling challenges, stadium capacity, whether or not a stadium was also used for baseball and other events, geography, traditional rivalries, ticket prices, transportation, and even the weather. Overriding all these factors, of course, was the owners' ultimate concern: the impact on their bottom lines.

For example, a division rival who played in a 75,000- or 80,000-seat stadium and had a sound season ticket base was much more attractive than one playing in a 50,000-seat stadium because, by definition, the gate receipts were bound to be larger. That, in turn, made the schedule the most important component because it dictated how often one team would play various other teams and the amount of revenue an owner could anticipate.

Almost as important as the schedule was stadium size. In the late 1960s, the capacities of pro football stadiums varied dramatically. Some clubs (mostly in the AFL) were playing in places with fewer than 40,000 seats, while in the NFL the Los Angeles Coliseum seated up to 100,000; Cleveland Stadium and Dallas's Cotton Bowl about 80,000; and Yankee Stadium, home of the Giants, some 65,000. That's why the Joint Committee's April 1968 decision, requiring that stadium capacities of all teams be at least "in the area of 50,000" by 1970, was so important. It virtually assured the owners that their bottom lines would grow.

Another key factor was geographic location. It had a certain amount of significance because each division wanted at least one warm-weather site so that its teams didn't face the prospect of playing each week in the snow and cold weather once November and December arrived. One reason the NFC Central (which turned out to be Minnesota, Chicago, Green Bay, and Detroit) was dubbed the "black and blue division" was that its players were frozen half the time (that was the "blue" part, bruises being the "black" part), for during the late 1960s they all played outdoors. Accordingly, one year after it joined the league with Seattle for the 1976 season, Tampa Bay became a permanent member of the NFC Central, to give that division both a warm-weather site and a stadium with 70,000-plus seats.

Mix in the impact of rivalries, transportation issues, ticket prices, and so forth, and one can begin to appreciate the dilemma the owners confronted. Anytime and every time NFC realignment discussions approached crunch time, the economic factor reared its head. We were forever hearing, "We don't want to play so-and-so in these little stadiums." For that matter, similar complaints had surfaced during the AFC realignment discussion. I still remember Modell quipping, "Denver? That's that city that's out there somewhere." Art didn't score a lot of points with his new AFC colleagues.

Then again, neither did other owners who muttered words like, "You couldn't pay me enough to go out there and play those guys." Of course, a couple of years later "those guys" in Denver were suddenly sold out every week, had 75,000 screaming fans in the stands, and were generating the best visitors' gate you ever saw. All of a sudden, owners were salivating to go out there and get a share of that money.

NBC's inclusion in the new television mix was yet another factor. Because it would continue to televise AFC games, NBC was not getting as many large markets as CBS was to get. NBC did have New York, Boston, and Miami, plus the growing locales of Houston and Oakland. But it also had several smaller markets, such as Pittsburgh, San Diego, Buffalo, and Denver, while CBS retained Los Angeles, Chicago, Philadelphia, and Detroit, as well as New York.

With all these factors parading through their minds, the owners tried again in New Orleans during Super Bowl IV festivities. In a relatively brief meeting, Rozelle strenuously urged them to submit compromise plans that they "would be willing to live with," as he put it, even if they didn't meet each and every preference or desired objective. By the time they adjourned, Pete had nine plans in his hands, including some from the June 2 meeting.

He took all nine into still another meeting in New York, which convened on Wednesday, January 14, three days after Super Bowl IV. Five hours of discussion proved fruitless. Thursday morning arrived and, with it, four more hours of discussions but no progress. After a 45-minute break, owners sat down again. Save for one more 45-minute recess, they remained in the room until 8:00 P.M. and agreed to meet again the following morning. With not even a shred of an agreement in sight, Pete had had enough.

Before the 9:30 meeting began on Friday, he called me and Mark Duncan, by then director of personnel as well as supervisor of officials, into his office, where we reviewed the nine proposals and identified the ones that seemed to have amassed the most support. Five proposals were favored. At Pete's direction, I typed each one on a piece of paper, and we numbered them, as shown in Table 4.

The three of us then moved to our conference room, where the owners waited. Once the meeting began, Rozelle said, "We have to resolve this, and since we cannot get an agreement any other way, we're going to do it my way." Then he explained what his way would be.

First, a green chalkboard draped with a cloth would be rolled into the room. The cloth would be removed, and the five plans would be presented to the 13 assembled NFC owners. Each of the five plans would be written on a piece of paper. One of those pieces of paper would be drawn at random to settle the dilemma once and for all.

TABLE 4: THE FIVE NFC REALIGNMENT PROPOSALS FROM WHICH THE FINAL PLAN (NO. 3) WAS CHOSEN

No. 1	No. 2	No. 3	No. 4	No. 5
WESTERN DIVISION				
Los Angeles	Los Angeles	Los Angeles	Los Angeles	Los Angeles
San Francisco	San Francisco	San Francisco	San Francisco	San Francisco
Dallas	Chicago	Atlanta	Dallas	New Orleans
St. Louis	Green Bay	New Orleans	New Orleans	Atlanta
	Detroit			
CENTRAL DIVISION				
Chicago	Dallas	Chicago	Chicago	Chicago
Green Bay	New Orleans	Green Bay	Green Bay	Green Bay
Detroit	Atlanta	Detroit	Detroit	Dallas
New Orleans	St. Louis	Minnesota	Atlanta	St. Louis
EASTERN DIVISION				
New York	New York	New York	New York	New York
Washington	Washington	Washington	Washington	Washington
Philadelphia	Philadelphia	Philadelphia	Philadelphia	Philadelphia
Minnesota	Minnesota	Dallas	St. Louis	Detroit
Atlanta		St. Louis	Minnesota	Minnesota

Second, and extremely important, Rozelle also presented a procedure to equalize receipts from intraconference road games, as well as air travel expenses. Doing so, he pointed out, would minimize the economic impact of whatever realignment plan was drawn. This new procedure would take effect beginning with the 1970 season and continue until 11 of the 13 NFC clubs voted to terminate it.

Pete then recessed the meeting for about 20 minutes while we put the five plans on the portable chalkboard and moved it into the room. At 11:00 on the morning of January 16, 1970, Pete reconvened the meeting. The cloth was removed from the chalkboard so that the owners could study each plan. About 25 minutes later, Thelma Elkjer, Rozelle's secretary, joined the group, carrying the plans on the five pieces of paper that were now folded and sealed. She put the pieces of paper into a large cut-glass bowl. On Pete Rozelle's signal—after 64 hours and 41 minutes of officially recorded debate, and who knows how many more hours of unofficial talks that had begun almost two years earlier—Thelma stuck her hand in the bowl . . . and picked number three:

- NFC West: Los Angeles, San Francisco, Atlanta, and New Orleans
- NFC Central: Chicago, Green Bay, Detroit, and Minnesota
- NFC East: New York, Washington, Philadelphia, Dallas, and St. Louis

As I said at the outset, it defied all logic. Especially since this plan originally had been the number 12 plan that was submitted for review and was among those discussed again at length in June 1969! No matter, the deed was done.

The plan that Thelma had selected wasn't flawless, of course. But the alternative was no deal at all. And it was good enough to last for more than 30 years until the NFL realigned itself again for the 2002 season as a 32-team league. Notably, the new 32-team alignment is exactly what Rozelle and other league executives envisioned in 1967 and is built on the same four-teams-per-division foundation established that same year, after being suggested by Tex Schramm.

As one would expect, some negative reactions were expressed. New Orleans and Atlanta playing in the NFC West, for instance, provoked a smattering of grumbles. So did the NFC Central's being composed of four cold-weather sites (until Tampa Bay was added in the 1976 expansion).

However, these alleged flaws were well worth accepting if only to end the cruelties forced on the writers and league officials who, at a moment's notice, had to trudge into and out of meeting rooms or trek down to the street and around the corner at all hours of the night to the East 55th Street entrance of the St. Regis to chronicle the bizarre proceedings.

It would be difficult to find a hardier band of sports writers and league officials who covered (*survived* is more like it) the exhaustive negotiations required to realign NFL teams with AFL teams in an expanded National Football League. With all due respect to journalists and broadcasters who have toiled strenuously at Super Bowls or battled bone-chilling conditions on the frozen tundra of Green Bay's Lambeau Field in January, such duty doesn't hold a candle to the harsh labor that chronicling this struggle ultimately imposed.

To preserve the memories and honor this effort, we formed our honorable society and named it the Royal Order of Realignment Recorders. A true realignment recorder had to be incredibly patient, resourceful, perceptive, tenacious, and tireless, and in possession of a steel-trap memory, a cast-iron digestive track, a generous expense account, and a cheerful disposition. The ability to nap in a lumpy hotel chair was another asset. If one was schooled in all conceivable mathematical combinations of 13, so much the better.

In commemoration of the bizarre finale to the realignment saga and the rest of the madness that went along with it, I had a friend of mine prepare a scroll, which has become a collector's item of sorts among the people who still have them. My father, who was a commercial artist and a very good calligrapher, designed the graphics. We identified three principal sessions during which the major steps of realignment were accomplished. Those who covered one of the sessions earned a scroll with one star, those who covered two sessions earned a two-star scroll, and those who participated in all three sessions got a three-star scroll.

A photo at the top of the document depicts a trio of writers in one of the St. Regis Hotel suites, all lying in various states of repose across three chairs and a couch. One of them is the *Baltimore Sun*'s Cameron Snyder, a big bear of a man, who found sleeping in a chair in a rumpled coat and tie particularly challenging. Shown with him are Dave Klein of the *Newark Star-Ledger* and Dave Brady of the *Washington Post*. All three are doing pretty much what they did during the realignment negotiations: killing time as they waited for something to happen. Usually, it was a long wait, which the scroll's wording in part reflects:

Be it further resolved that those great tribulations that they endured, from Palm Springs' Capon to Fun City's Pastrami and Pickles, from the El Mirador's sunlit verandas to the St. Regis' carpeted floors, shall not have been in vain but only a memorable interlude in the artificial turf of time.

I affixed Pete Rozelle's name at the bottom, then sent these scrolls to my dad, who dutifully inscribed the names. Then we affixed the official seal and awarded them with appropriate flourishes during a formal presentation at one of the Super Bowls, where most of the order's members could be found in late January. Rozelle got a kick out of it and always thought it was one of my best ideas. I remained grateful but far more grateful that Pete had finally found a way to solve a wild stalemate. I can't imagine how it might have ended otherwise.

And it certainly needed to end, not only to prepare the inaugural single-league schedule for the 1970 season but also to seize the opportunities of the moment. The reality that modern pro football was about to truly become one league was fueling a real burst of excitement and enthusiasm around the country—the new look of professional football.

Over the years, people regularly asked Pete about the likelihood of the NFL realigning again. Without fail, he deftly concealed his memories with a wry smile and delivered a pleasant but crisp reply: "Not in my lifetime."

He had other matters to attend to, including what was growing into the sports world's number one annual event, the Super Bowl.

PART II

THE SUPER BOWL

SEVEN

FINDING THE VENUE

It Had to Be Warm and It Had to Be Big

If Pete Rozelle had had his way, the first AFL-NFL World Championship of Professional Football would have kicked off not in the Los Angeles Memorial Coliseum but in the Rose Bowl.

Pete didn't have his way, of course, at least not in the autumn of 1966. So, over the years an assumption has persisted that the Coliseum was the only site seriously considered. Years later, Rozelle himself suggested as much in a *Los Angeles Times* article written by Bob Oates. That's not quite the way it was.

Almost from the moment he announced the merger, Rozelle seemed to have the world championship game framed in his mind. And perhaps he did. The vision he shared with a few of us, once the antitrust hearings concluded in late October, was crisp, dramatic, and ambitious: He wanted to play the game in a warm-weather locale at a neutral setting before as large a crowd as we could possibly attract.

What never dawned on any of us as we listened was that Rozelle's vision was a concept never before attempted in professional sports. To this day, most fans still don't give it a thought. Until the NFL and AFL champions collided, leagues always had decided their championships on the gridiron, the diamond, the court, or the ice of one of the participants. A neutral site was unheard of.

The only remotely comparable sporting events that we might have used to guide our planning were the postseason college basketball championships and college football's bowl games. Yet, the NCAA basketball finals, which I had covered during my Associated Press days, didn't begin to resemble the "Final Four" extravaganza played today and drew crowds of no more than 15,000 fans. In fact, the NCAA finals were just starting to eclipse the appeal of the NIT (National Invitational Tournament), strictly a Madison Square Garden basketball tournament in New York that benefited from nationwide NBC coverage and an eastern time zone start.

The New Year's Day bowl games, meanwhile, were steeped in decades-old tradition, cherished as civic treasures, and operated by well-established committees of movers and shakers. Linked to major college football conferences and large local bases of support, these committees generated the bulk of ticket sales. The bowls also had the luxury of knowing nearly two months in advance who would be playing.

We would have two weeks. But in late October 1966, we didn't even know that because no date for the new championship game had been set, nor a site chosen. As for tradition, well, there was the six-year war with our new partner and little else. Certainly, we counted on the natural excitement of the regular NFL and AFL seasons to promote the game, plus a rapidly growing curiosity about its "David versus Goliath" nature. Still, we knew whatever we might plan was bound to be saddled with a razor-thin margin of error.

Daunting task notwithstanding, we firmly embraced Rozelle's vision, which included one other critical component: For this new championship of professional football to grow into "the sporting event of the century" that Pete described in interviews, it would have to be first class in every respect and exacting detail. No compromising whatsoever.

So, where should a game of such stature, promise, drama, and challenge be contested? Why, in the Rose Bowl, of course! Where else?

It was the obvious site of choice, hands down. The renowned stadium in Pasadena, California, had it all: delightful weather, a breathtaking setting beneath the majestic San Gabriel Mountains, as many as 105,000 seats, a rich history of big football games, and—perhaps just as important—incomparable prestige and tradition. After all, this was *the* Rose Bowl, the fabled "granddaddy of 'em all," as sportscasters liked to proclaim.

The six-man Joint Committee of NFL and AFL owners that Rozelle worked with to oversee the merger's details embraced the idea. Minutes of an early-summer AFL owners' meeting indicate they, too, thought the Rose Bowl was ideal. Naturally, the world championship game was on the Joint Committee's opening agenda when it first met on July 20, 1966, in New York's Plaza Hotel, but it took a backseat to other issues and wasn't considered until the second morning of that initial meeting. Even then, members devoted only a modest amount of time to the game, concluding discussions by authorizing Rozelle to contact the Rose Bowl about pro football's interest and, presumably, to start discussing arrangements.

With the antitrust issue boiling over in Washington that summer, that's about all the attention the championship game got until our huddle with Pete in late October. The Joint Committee convened a second time about two weeks later in early November to review our progress and start planning in earnest. When it did, it learned of a startling state of affairs.

The Rose Bowl's powers that be were, at best, taking a dim view of hosting this long-anticipated football battle. The renowned stadium was owned and operated by the City of Pasadena, and two members of the Rose Bowl's board of directors opposed the idea outright, as if their hallowed turf would be sullied irreparably by the cleats of professional football players. Then, as now, these directors literally personified the Tournament of Roses: conservative souls bound by tradition and pedigree, in their white suits and red ties, with red roses in their lapels. That they controlled the biggest attraction going in college football—if not in all football—was self-evident. And the idea of playing any other football game *after* the annual Rose Bowl game on New Year's Day apparently struck them as something just short of scandalous.

But even conservative, tradition-bound souls in white suits had their price. Rozelle told the Joint Committee that the Rose Bowl's directors "were willing to pursue the matter further if they received a strong indication of interest" by the two leagues—"strong indication" being best expressed by agreeing to pay the Rose Bowl its usual 15 percent of the gate as a rental fee, *plus* 15 percent of all television and radio rights. Based on the first game's actual revenues, that would have amounted to at least $480,000. It was a hefty sum and one that left the Joint Committee thinking it would be appropriate for Rose Bowl directors to appear at official functions wearing black masks and toting loaded pistols. The precise reactions of committee members varied, but what they all amounted to was "Those starch-shirted bastards don't want us and they're telling us to get lost."

Similar messages had been dispatched from the Big Ten Conference and the Association of Western Universities, as the PAC-10 was then called. Bill Reed and Tom Hamilton, the conferences' respective Commissioners, both expressed "their concern" in letters to Rozelle, implying that pro football had no business traipsing across what was exclusively the grand stage of college football.

Able to discern "no" when they saw it, Rozelle and the Joint Committee concluded they would take their first AFL-NFL World Championship of Professional Football someplace else, where they would feel more welcome.

Besides, it was now November 9, and there was no time for haggling, especially since several attractive alternatives beckoned. They all met Pete's parameters, too. Eager representatives from Miami's Orange Bowl had approached Buffalo owner and committee member Ralph Wilson early on. Rice Stadium in Houston was also mentioned, while at one point Lamar Hunt, another committee member, suggested Tulane Stadium in New Orleans, home of the Sugar Bowl. Even Rozelle had a sentimental alternative. Having attended the University of San Francisco, he fancied playing in Stanford University's stadium in Palo Alto. Of all the other sites considered, though, the Los Angeles Coliseum emerged as the most advantageous.

It struck everyone as a solid choice. Not too far from the Rose Bowl, accessed by a major Los Angeles freeway, and located right on the edge of the University of Southern California campus, the Coliseum could seat almost as many fans as the Rose Bowl and had a sparkling history of packing in 100,000-plus throngs to watch the Rams play the San Francisco 49ers and other NFL teams, and Southern Cal battle both UCLA and Notre Dame. Built for the 1932 Olympics, the Coliseum offered a tradition of its own and, of course, balmy California weather. Since it was both the Rams' home field and the site of the annual NFL Pro Bowl, a solid working relationship among Coliseum general manager Bill Nicholas, Rams owner Dan Reeves, and the NFL itself was well established. So solid, in fact, that Reeves, who sat on the Joint Committee, too, had already spoken with Nicholas about the game and was assured that the rental charge wouldn't exceed $50,000—a mere tenth of what the gentlemen in Pasadena had requested.

With the site selected and Rozelle authorized to work out facility details with the Coliseum, the committee then pulled out a calendar. After some more discussion, it circled Sunday, January 15, 1967. League championship games would be played on New Year's Day, which that year fell on a Sunday, providing two weeks for pro football's first two world championship combatants to prepare and the media to build up the first meeting between two hated rivals. In the meantime, we now had 67 days to arrange what they'd do when they showed up.

The Joint Committee's task that November afternoon was far from complete, however. The unprecedented nature of the contest left members confronting a veritable laundry list of details, a number of which they'd never had to ponder before, such as who would officiate the game and under whose rules it would be played.

The NFL and AFL put six officials on the field in those days, and in anticipation of the question, we had surveyed a whole bunch of people—coaches, players, and officials—to rate the positions. Their collective opinion ranked the referee number one, followed in order by the umpire, field judge, back judge, head linesman, and line judge. Officially, there was to be a coin flip to determine which league would furnish the referee, with the remaining positions selected in order from each league on an alternating basis (in other words, 1-3-5 and

2-4-6). League administrators would then be responsible for naming the persons to fill the respective positions, in whatever manner they chose. Whatever alignment resulted from the coin flip was to be reversed each year thereafter until the leagues merged for the 1970 season.

I'll confess here and now that we "influenced" that first flip. We were determined that an NFL official was going to referee the first game. The other two NFL positions according to the formula, then, became the field judge and head linesman, which explains why, after one official's call went against the Packers during play in Los Angeles, Green Bay's Bart Starr instantly bemoaned to referee Norm Schachter, "Hey, Norm! Isn't he one of ours?"

Starr would have been referring either to field judge Mike Lisetski or head linesman Bernie Ulman, the NFL officials who joined Schachter for the first game. Referee Art McNally, field judge Herman Rohrig, and head linesman Burt Toler were the NFL alternates. The AFL officials selected for the first game were umpire George Young, back judge Jack Reader, and line judge Al Sabato. Umpire Paul Trepinski, back judge Charlie Musser, and line judge Harry Kessel were the AFL alternates.

We resorted to a little more subterfuge again sometime later to ensure that Green Bay wore its patented green and gold home uniforms, with Kansas City wearing white. We simply thought they looked better, especially with the game's being televised in color. The leagues and conferences have alternated jersey colors ever since. If the AFL was ever suspicious of either decision, no questions were asked.

Having this blend of officials, so to speak, gave the Joint Committee another issue to wrestle with: Just what should the men in stripes wear? With black-and-white television coverage being the usual order of the day in that era, people may be unaware that AFL officials wore red-and-white striped shirts, instead of the NFL's black and white. Mark Duncan, our supervisor of officials, used to call them "candy stripers" because they reminded him of hospital volunteers. Rather than have officials running around in two different colors, we had Wilson Sporting Goods design a special uniform. The jerseys resembled the NFL's but had solid black short sleeves, with the official's number and position in white, and a black collar. The caps were white, with a black bill, and Converse provided the shoes. These championship game uniforms were used only for the first two games, after which the game officials suited up in standard NFL issue. The uniform Schachter wore now hangs in the Pro Football Hall of Fame in Canton, Ohio.

We brought all 12 officials to Los Angeles two days prior to the game for a special clinic conducted by Mark Duncan. Due to league differences, their respective positions on the field during games varied slightly, as did mechanics and a few rules interpretations. Mark went out of his way to be gracious and conciliatory, and began by suggesting that there be some give-and-take on the mechanics. But after hearing in detail how the AFL officiated its games and after watching some game films, Duncan saw some glaring shortcomings. In certain situations, for example, no AFL official was watching the line of scrimmage on pass plays, which could allow quarterbacks to throw passes from beyond the line without being detected. Before the clinic ended, Mark found himself declaring, "I think we'll do this the NFL way."

We did something else the NFL way. Lamar Hunt strongly campaigned for the two-point conversion rule used by the AFL (and the colleges), and the Joint Committee weighed his contention heavily, in light of Rozelle's desire to make the game as special as possible. But in the face of strenuous lobbying from NFL coaches, the two-point conversion was shot down. Even though it looks like a simple goal-line play that starts on the two-yard line, NFL coaches had no experience with it following a touchdown and fought it from the start.

Also considered was rewarding the players $15,000 "winner-take-all." This, too, sparked a lengthy discussion, and at one point, winner-take-all appeared to be winning the day, at least in the conversations that took place in the office with Rozelle. Evidently, though, the Joint Committee concluded it wouldn't be fair. Green Bay's mystique was at its zenith at that time, and with the defending NFL champs having won three titles in five years and on their way to a 12–2 season and a fourth NFL title in 1966, I suspect most members anticipated it would be just like giving Green Bay players—or whatever power represented the NFL—$15,000 apiece.

Instead, the committee decided to award each player on the winning team $15,000 and each player on the losing team $7,500. With the average NFL salary hovering around $18,000 in those days, a prize of $15,000 was a princely sum in itself and aroused more than sufficient attention.

Collectively, players, coaches, and locker room staff on both teams would pocket $1.17 million of the $2.5 million in net income we anticipated earning from the game. The remaining $1.33 million was to be divided among the two competing clubs, the two league offices, and player benefit plans; in all, some 70 percent of the first game's revenues was earmarked for the players and their benefit plans. The committee budgeted $300,000 for staging the championship game itself: $200,000 for travel and training expenses, $50,000 for stadium rental, and $50,000 for halftime and ticket-selling expenses. All of these figures put the game's total budget at $2.8 million, or less than what one minute of Super Bowl television commercial time is worth today.

Myriad other game details had to be sorted out, too: The two competing clubs were to receive five thousand game tickets each to sell to their fans, and each of the other NFL and AFL teams would get two hundred. The rest of the tickets were to be sold to the host-city Rams and to the general public. Travel squads were limited to 65 players, coaches, trainers, equipment managers, and management personnel, and had to be approved by Rozelle. It was also during these discussions that committee members agreed to let each team use its league's respective football when it was on offense. Before it was done, committee members even had devised a formula for exchanging game films (either the last five games or any five games an opposing team might wish to select), and selected a neutral crew to handle the down marker and to move the first-down chains.

I shudder to think how long it might take today's breed of owners to agree on all these details. But the Joint Committee buttoned them up in two sessions on November 9 and 10 that together consumed less than half a day. Good thing, too, because the two leagues still had to sign off on both the plans and the lease for the Coliseum, and they didn't get around to doing it until December 1. Wrapping up television plans consumed a few more days, so it wasn't until December 13, 1966, that Pete Rozelle at last could announce that the AFL-NFL World Championship of Professional Football would be played in the Los Angeles Coliseum at 1:05 P.M. Pacific standard time on January 15, 1967—less than five weeks away.

A few blocks away at league headquarters in Manhattan, we were hard at work attending to our own laundry list of details. We had swung into action in late October, just as soon as Congress had given the merger antitrust protection. Even so, we began with less than 90 days to identify and tie up hundreds of loose ends.

It was on the Monday after Congress acted that I walked into the Dunhill shop on Fifth Avenue to buy those 650 travel alarm clocks I described as our story began. Giving sports writers modest mementos of the championship games that they covered was in keeping with the precedent we had established for NFL title games, and, of course, Rozelle's insistence that this game be first rate in every detail was always uppermost in my mind.

Along with something for the writers, we needed a championship trophy to give the winning team. Pete personally took charge of this requirement and never hesitated, going directly to Tiffany's. It was the only firm he contacted, and Tiffany's created a masterpiece—from unconventional inspiration. It may be the only $20,000 sterling silver trophy in history that sprang to life from a cereal box.

The remarkable story of its creation found its way to me 30 years later in 1996, in a letter written by a close friend of Oscar Riedener, who designed what we later named the Lombardi Trophy. After talking with Rozelle about his special request, Tiffany's president quickly called Riedener, the head of the firm's design department, to his office. A Swiss native, Riedener had misgivings about accepting the assignment. He knew next to nothing about American football. But this amounted to a command performance, of course. So, Riedener accepted with a smile, and on his way home he strolled two or three blocks up Fifth Avenue to FAO Schwartz, the famous New York toy store, where he bought a football. If he was going to design a football trophy, he reasoned, he first ought to familiarize himself with something he had never before owned and probably had never even gripped.

He carried the football home, but not feeling sufficiently inspired that evening, Riedener left it on the kitchen table, simply telling his wife it was for another design project he had to complete fairly quickly. The next morning, Riedener pulled out a nearly empty box of cornflakes, poured its contents into a bowl, and started munching . . . and thinking, all the while staring at the football. Once Riedener finished breakfast, he pulled out a pair of scissors and Scotch tape, then started cutting the empty cereal box. Five minutes later, after folding, cutting, and taping, he had transformed the box into a trophy base so that the football could be perched on top. Pleased with his effort, Riedener brought his cardboard base and the football to his office at Tiffany's to gather opinions from selected peers, one of whom was the man who sent me the letter in late 1996.

Over a typical Manhattan lunch a day or so later, Pete met with the Tiffany's delegation. It included Riedener, who drew a sketch of his design on a cocktail napkin. There may have been an adjustment or two, but essentially it was what everyone had in mind.

From the beginning, we all said we didn't want one of those garish types of sports trophies but rather something simple. You can't design anything much simpler than what Tiffany's produced: a sterling silver football on a three-sided base with each league's logo on either side. Other than replacing the league logos with conference logos following the merger, the trophy's design remains unchanged. I still think it's one of the most elegant of all sports trophies. When I look at it, I think of Pete Rozelle.

Rozelle also personally oversaw what were by far the single most important negotiations of the championship game: television coverage. That was by design because diplomacy was going to be essential. With the date and site of the game not selected until barely 60 days before kickoff, television coverage was another eleventh-hour decision, especially compared to today when such arrangements are buttoned down years in advance.

The negotiations could have taken an unusual twist, too. At the Joint Committee's first meeting in July, Bills owner Ralph Wilson had suggested the leagues could amass broadcast revenues of between $25 million and $30 million by ignoring the over-the-air networks and showing the championship game exclusively on closed-circuit television. Wilson's idea may sound outrageous today, but a precedent for it had been established. Heavyweight boxing championships were routinely beamed via closed-circuit television to theaters around the country, which sold seats to eager customers.

It's hard to say just how serious Wilson was or what the other Joint Committee members thought of his idea. However, it never resurfaced in future meetings. Once Wilson advanced it, Rozelle—who forever remained an ardent advocate of televising NFL games over the air—deftly tabled the idea by saying that television arrangements "could be discussed later." Undoubtedly, Pete had already had some preliminary discussions with the networks—at least CBS—but wasn't yet prepared to share their outcome or his own ideas with the Joint Committee.

Complicating the arrangements were two factors: First, both leagues had multiyear agreements with two different networks that had been signed, sealed, and delivered long before an AFL-NFL championship had been envisioned. The NFL's decade-long ties with CBS had grown so strong that the succession of two- and three-year deals was almost becoming routine. Meanwhile, NBC was in the second season of the landmark $36 million, five-year contract that enabled the AFL to live to see the pro football merger. Whatever was to be worked out, it was essential for the television arrangements to take both of these network relationships into account.

Second, and more vexing, selecting Los Angeles as the site meant the championship game would not be seen on television in the nation's second-largest market. The NFL's television blackout policy then in force prohibited televising any game within a 75-mile radius of the stadium in which it was being played—under any circumstances. From the day Rozelle had negotiated the leaguewide package with

CBS in 1961, and even before that, not a single exception had been made, not even for NFL championship games.

Rozelle solved the first issue in straightforward fashion, even if it came at a price. Cleveland Browns owner Art Modell, whose television background and expertise had made him a Rozelle confidante, brought a proposal from CBS to a special owners' meeting in late November 1966, called in part to review and ratify the championship game arrangements. CBS had put a $10 million offer on the table for exclusive television rights to the first four championship games, at $2.5 million per year. (Perhaps sensing what lay ahead, the network separately was seeking a $500,000 reduction in the per-year price it previously had agreed to pay for rights to the NFL title game.) Attractive as the offer was, an exclusive television deal with the NFL's pals at CBS would leave NBC out in the cold, and the AFL kept insisting that was unacceptable.

The solution turned out to be exactly what New York Jets owner Sonny Werblin had suggested—almost as an afterthought—to fellow AFL owners in early July. Werblin, the man who had signed Joe Namath and who also had television and entertainment world ties, had casually pointed out that the networks could pool coverage of the game. That would allow each network to use its own announcing team and sell its own advertising time on its own broadcast of the television feed. Which, of course, is exactly what happened.

At one point in the negotiations, Rozelle had considered open bidding, complete with sealed envelopes. Ultimately, however, Pete and the owners concluded that, as long as the game was going to be unprecedented, so would its television coverage. Both CBS and NBC would air the game, on television and radio. It hadn't happened before and hasn't since, a fact that's stuck with me all these years because I wrote the press release that announced these arrangements. The total contract was worth $9.5 million for the first four games, $500,000 less than what CBS had offered. Each network paid $1 million for the first game, for a total of $2 million. After the first year, the networks would alternate: CBS would televise the second and fourth years, and NBC the third, with each network paying $2.5 million for the opportunity. That $2.5 million sum, of course, also is considerably less than what one minute of Super Bowl television advertising time now costs.

In 1966, however, paying even $42,500 to run a 30-second commercial was unheard of. Yet, that's what the networks charged for the first telecast, or $85,000 per minute. The deal gave Rozelle the opportunity to declare that the championship game was expected to be the first pro football game to gross $3 million. And it set a pattern that continues to this day with the three networks currently involved: CBS, ABC, and FOX.

Unfortunately, no such solution existed for the second television-related complication—the blackout in Los Angeles. No one felt sufficiently comfortable about lifting it, although the idea did spark conversations. When the Rose Bowl was being considered as a game site, for instance, Rozelle discreetly sounded out Los Angeles writers about both the game's being played in Pasadena and how Southern Californians might react to the inevitable blackout that would result. Later, Rozelle also floated ideas about making the game available in Los Angeles on closed-circuit television, as well as to veterans hospitals in the area, on an experimental basis. But nothing was ever attempted.

The blackout would prove to have serious repercussions on attendance at the Coliseum (the Los Angeles media never accepted it). Attendance, in turn, would affect a decision to return to the Coliseum for the next three games, which the contract included as one-year options. In presenting game plans in mid-December, however, Rozelle had neither the time nor the inclination to worry about whatever problems a blackout in Los Angeles might provoke. With other post-merger issues swirling about him, Pete could at last be excited—and be relieved—that the championship game had been set. Now all we needed were a couple of football teams to play it.

EIGHT

UPTIGHT AND OUT OF SIGHT

Few self-respecting journalists and broadcasters, it seems, can resist the temptation to file cynical reports about Super Bowl Media Day. It's as if their barbs were some sports writers' rites of passage. Now held on the Tuesday morning preceding the game, Media Day assembles players from both teams at one convenient location for interviews and photographs. The noble intent is to give writers blanket access to the participants so that the participants can then resume their all-important preparation relatively free from weeklong disruptions. But the cynics lambaste this noble intention, which kicks off three days of controlled media access, as a colossal waste of time. Calling Media Day conversations "interviews," they complain in shrill voices, is an act of charity that stretches the definition of "interview" to the fullest.

For those looking for the culprit who started it all, it's time to step forward and shoulder responsibility. Media Day was basically my and Jim Kensil's creation, fashioned out of necessity in January 1967 with the best of intentions. As the world championship game approached, what pro football owners had initially dismissed as an afterthought was swelling into a giant curiosity but also a chaotic, disorganized nightmare. We merely were trying to establish a little order, nothing more. Besides, we had an accomplice. So, while it's appropriate to point fingers at me and Kensil, point another finger at Vince Lombardi.

At some point in arranging the game's details, my colleagues and I confronted the reality that the Joint Committee had grappled with in November: Playing at a neutral site imposed new procedures on everybody. One of them was bringing the participating teams to Los Angeles almost a full week ahead of kickoff.

Kansas City took our request in stride. Then again, the Chiefs took everything in stride and with a smile. Had we asked, I think Hank Stram and his team would have left for Los Angeles right from the field, in full uniform, after defeating Buffalo, 31–7, for the AFL championship. If we wanted the Chiefs to do something, say, at 9:00 Monday morning, they'd reply, "Sure. But if Sunday would be better, we'll do it then if you like." That's how thrilled they were to be part of what the television networks were starting to label "Super Sunday."

However, an early arrival in Los Angeles wasn't fine with Lombardi. Not one bit. Vince didn't see any reason at all to alter the Packers' customary itinerary: stay at home and prepare in Green Bay, then come in a day or, at most, two days before the game, just as if he were playing any NFL opponent. Flying to Los Angeles any earlier, he felt, was totally unnecessary.

In a sense, Vince was right. In many minds, the pinnacle contest— the real championship of pro football—already had been settled a week earlier in the Cotton Bowl in Dallas, where Green Bay had defeated the Cowboys, 34–27, in a nail-biting thriller on New Year's Day. In the final minute, the Cowboys had marched to the Packers' one-yard line, and until Dallas lineman Jim Boeke got called for a false start, the contest seemed destined to become the NFL's second title game to be decided in overtime.

Inwardly, however, Lombardi had little time to celebrate. He was feeling unprecedented pressure. And *pressure* was the absolute word. It was tremendous. In all the years that I observed Vince Lombardi, I never saw him as nervous and uptight as he was just before that first championship game in Los Angeles. He admitted as much many times afterward.

Was the NFL superior to the AFL? We thought it was. But that little assertion still had to be proved on the field. And as this extra title game drew near, the pressure to convincingly affirm the NFL's muscle was squeezing tough, unflappable Vince like nothing before or since. Adding to the strain he felt within were the words from other league coaches and owners, who reminded him constantly of the sacred importance of upholding NFL honor. I doubt that anyone truly realized what Lombardi had to endure. True, any NFL champion would have been gripped by such a psychological vise. But Green Bay was extra-special: two-time defending league champion, winner of four NFL titles in six seasons, the overwhelming favorite, and coached by a living legend wrapped in a mystique of his own.

So, we could excuse Vince for being unduly irritable. But we still had interviews to arrange. Think about it, we urged him in conversations about our media relations plans, while appealing to reason and common sense: We're trying to make this into a special event. Do you want us to tell all the writers who want to talk to you and your players that they have to go to Green Bay? In January? Where you and your one-man public relations department will have to handle them as best you can? And deal with the disruptions that come with it? Why not consider the plan we've put together?

It was a hard sell. Vince was very reluctant and gave us all kinds of grief. At last, though, he said he'd come to California . . . but not to Los Angeles. Instead, Lombardi declared, he would quarter his Packers at Rickey's Hyatt House in Palo Alto, then the favorite stomping ground of all the NFL teams when they traveled to the West Coast. If not the namesake hotel itself, Rickey's was one of the very first in the Hyatt chain. Residential in design, it rested in what then was the middle of nowhere. Rickey, whoever he was, took such great care of his special guests that teams stayed there religiously, which the NFL schedule accommodated. To defray travel costs, teams from the East typically played the San Francisco 49ers and the Los Angeles Rams on successive Sundays. So, a team first playing the Rams would go to Rickey's, then fly to Los Angeles for the game in the Coliseum, then fly back to Rickey's and work out nearby during the week before it played the 49ers the following Sunday at Kezar Stadium. A team scheduled to meet the 49ers first would reverse the itinerary.

But, Vince, we replied in frustration, Palo Alto is almost 500 miles from Los Angeles! You may as well be in Green Bay; we've got to have you in Los Angeles. After additional pleas, spiced by an occasional threat, Lombardi was convinced to abandon his Palo Alto plan. But the closest we could get him to Los Angeles was Santa Barbara, still 80 some miles away from inquiring sports writers.

Our solution to this logistical challenge was a chartered bus, except when it pulled away from the hotel and headed to Santa Barbara on that first Tuesday, the only soul aboard besides me was my former Associated Press colleague and pal Jack Hand. Still with AP, Jack was its star football and boxing writer in those years. I was delighted to have his company.

Other writers did make their way to Santa Barbara but in their own cars. They didn't go happily, in part because this was all new to them, too. But they had no choice because we had announced that the Packers were going to be available only during a certain time.

Vince was waiting with sheets of paper that listed room assignments, which his public relations man, Chuck Lane, then distributed to the writers on arrival. So, if you wanted to talk to Bart Starr in room 336, you took the elevator to the third floor, walked to room 336, and knocked on the door, and if Bart was there the interview would commence—usually with everyone sitting on the edge of one of the beds in the room. If Bart wasn't there, you went to see someone else. Except Bart would be there. So would every other Packer be where he belonged because Vince had told his players to be in their rooms at the appointed hour, or else. Say one thing for Vince. When he issued an order, it was obeyed. The interviews lasted almost as long as a writer wanted, and if another writer came along in the meantime, he came in and sat down on the edge of the bed, too.

Still, it was not exactly the most auspicious debut of our grand media relations plan. We heard plenty of complaints because it was so hit and miss. There were lots of instances where writers would go in to talk with, say, defensive end Willie Davis but didn't necessarily want to speak with Willie's roommate, which left the roommate sitting there cooling his heels while everyone listened to Willie.

We arranged for interviews with the Chiefs, headquartered just south of Los Angeles in Long Beach, in much the same way. The difference was that a smiling, engaging Hank Stram would personally meet each bevy of arriving writers and shake hands with them before helping direct them to his players.

And from these humble origins, the media week came to life. As it matured into a standing act of Super Bowl repertoire, Media Day was moved into a central location, usually the stadium where the game was to be played. On Wednesday and Thursday, the media horde would spend an hour or so with the players and coaches of each team where the teams were headquartered, then the head coaches would have wrap-up press conferences Friday morning at the media hotel.

That two-person bus Jack Hand and I rode to Santa Barbara in 1967 became in time a caravan of overcrowded buses traveling from base to one team's site, then to the other team's site, then back to base, with breakfast or brunch served at each site. The count now is in excess of two thousand writers, photographers, and sportscasters per day. Maybe the cynics would prefer the way Vince wanted it. But I doubt it.

Compared with the other arrangements made in Los Angeles in 1967, our makeshift media operation was a model of sparkling precision and efficiency.

My role in Los Angeles was limited to assisting the sports writers as an "information guy" and then running game operations on game day. Overall game arrangements were coordinated by Bert Rose, my colleague from the league office in New York who had devised the "baby-sitting" program during the war with the AFL, and Mickey Herskowitz, late of the AFL office. At Pete's request, Bert and Mickey flew to Los Angeles to start getting things in order and to select the hotel and workout sites and such. Assisting them was Jack Teele, who worked in the Rams' front office, and Kensil's secretary, Maxine Isenberg.

Bert eventually designated the Statler-Hilton Hotel as press headquarters. That was fine, except that we were so far down the pecking order that writers had to check the hotel activities board daily to find out where the pressroom was. Before too many mornings went by, we were putting up a sign in the lobby. If there were 11 groups convened at the Hilton that January, we had to have been the 11th. It was really chaotic. We didn't know from one day to the next where we were going to be. It depended solely on the various needs of other groups and functions taking place in the hotel. We were moved into a different room nearly every day. In fact, we were bounced just about everywhere, except into a different hotel, an option we felt forced to consider now and then.

By the end of 1966, we had grown accustomed to the standard procedure that Jim Kensil and I had established for the NFL championship games. The first thing we'd do was find a typewriter rental outlet and get as many manual typewriters as we could—100 to 200—as many as we thought we'd comfortably need. Next, we'd make arrangements with Western Union and then the telephone company and other office supply sources, all to create a first-rate, fully equipped working pressroom for the writers to compose and file their stories. In the Hilton, however, none of these arrangements could be made on anything but a temporary basis because our pressroom was being shifted around like a floating crap game.

Writers would leave the pressroom late one night and return the next morning to find it being set up for some civic luncheon that had priority over our operation. In turn, we were constantly arranging for people to take down, move, and then rearrange our equipment. To speed up the procedure, we set the manual typewriters on banquet tables in long rows, like you'd see under a tent at a golf tournament.

The writers, bless 'em, were pretty understanding, even those who were accustomed to what we typically provided for an NFL championship game. If there was a lot of criticism, I don't remember it, just plenty of laughter about it and good-natured barbs like "Well, where are we meeting today?" or "Might we have a clue about where we'll be working tomorrow?"

What may have helped us overcome these deficiencies with only minor strife was the fact that the press contingent that descended on Los Angeles was relatively modest. Strange as it may sound today, not all the NFL franchise cities sent media representatives to the first game. New Orleans, for example, had just been awarded the 16th NFL team and had had at least some consideration as the game site. Yet, neither of the city's papers found our championship game in the Coliseum worth its personal time and attention. It was no isolated exception. Bigger papers than those in New Orleans skipped the game, too. We estimated that, collectively, the AFL and NFL championship games attracted about 20 percent more sports writers than the battle between the Packers and the Chiefs, a further reflection of the expected outcome.

Still, by midweek we had what we thought was a pretty good turnout of people in Los Angeles, probably 40 to 50 out-of-town writers, which grew quickly as the week went along. By kickoff Sunday, we had issued some 650 credentials, including photographers but not including ancillary guys who worked for television and such. An impressive throng, of course. But it wasn't anywhere near what we would be drawing starting in two or three years. As it was, writers from suburban Los Angeles media outlets represented a good portion of that total.

Collectively, these members of the vaunted fourth estate probably were far more at ease than we were because we took considerable pride in being recognized for running one of the better press operations in all of sports. Too, we were well aware that this new championship game and everything surrounding it were the first visible results of the merger. For all the world, we wanted to put our best foot and football forward. Our accommodations at the Hilton made it a challenge. It was the most unsophisticated operation imaginable under the circumstances.

Perhaps it was apropos, then, that the cover of the press guide that we produced contained a small, but nonetheless, glaring and embarrassing mistake. From the day Kensil became public relations director, the NFL always provided a media guide for all of our championship games and later our divisional playoffs. You name it, we had a little pocket-sized guide for it. We filled it with team rosters, depth charts, a facts and figures page, previous records, and all kinds of notes. Naturally, we produced an AFL-NFL World Championship of Professional Football press guide, delegating the responsibility to Al Ward. A sports public relations veteran, Ward had worked in the Southwest Conference office and for the AFL office before joining the Cowboys' public relations staff. The guides arrived in Los Angeles shortly after I did, in the large volume we'd ordered. Just as we were about ready to put them into the briefcases we used as press kits for the media (where the travel alarm I had bought in New York also wound up), I took a quick look at the cover of the guide for the first time.

What I read was horrifying. There it was on the very last line: "Sunday, January 27, 1967, Los Angeles Coliseum." The actual date, of course, was January 15, 1967.

As meager as the mistake may appear to outsiders, Rozelle was more than a bit irritated. He was a stickler for accuracy. In fact, Pete was a stickler's stickler, although he usually was good-natured about it. If at any time during the 25 years we worked together I ever let a typo or similar mistake slip into anything I wrote, Rozelle would find it. I guess it was the old newspaperman in him. As important as the information in a press release was, it was equally important to him that it be well written, polished, and *accurate*. It was a sign of professionalism. You *didn't* make an error.

Now and then, of course, we did make an error. And it prompted a little ritual. Rozelle would circle something and send it back to me. I'd fix what he'd found and send it back to him, along with a disclaimer: "Pete, first mistake I ever made." From that point on, if there was ever any miscue that I had even partial responsibility for, it would come back to me with a note: "Here's another of your first mistakes."

This first mistake by Al Ward had us in fits. It also would prove to be an omen, but we didn't know it then. It was way too late to correct the error. Had we been able to reprint all those guides to correct that one little error, I guarantee you we would have done it. But we just didn't have time. All we did have time for was to acknowledge our mistake with a wry smile. When the game concluded, I moved over to the press box microphone and in a pleasant tone said, "And thank you for coming on January 15, instead of January 27."

For my money, at least, that guide has become a valuable collector's item. Because, at some point somewhere in the future, somebody's going to get his hands on one of those things and say, "Hey, I thought this game was played on January 15!"

Ward was part of a game staff so small that anyone who's observed the legions of NFL and team public relations officials overseeing the mammoth media operations of a modern Super Bowl would double over in laugher. It couldn't even be defined as "spartan." Along with me, Kensil, and Ward were public relations directors Chuck Lane of Green Bay, Jim Schaaf of Kansas City, and Jerry Wynn of San Diego, plus the three public relations men who had been part of Al Davis's short-lived staff when he was AFL Commissioner: Mickey Herskowitz, Irv Kaze, and Val Pinchbeck. Most of them arrived a few days before the game. Once they were in Los Angeles, the team publicists devoted most of their attention to their own local media unless we had some special needs.

One other staff member imported to lend us a hand was Rozelle's secretary, Thelma Elkjer. To my recollection, it was the only Super Bowl she attended but was distinctive for a second reason: We placed a Xerox copier in Thelma's hotel room to use as the "official" copier for reproducing press conference reports and other materials we prepared during the week.

Bert Rose's gang was no bigger. Much of his makeshift staff was recruited from outside the league office, especially for skills requiring distinctive talent, such as, for instance, selling tickets.

Putting tickets to a football game in the hands of the fans was yet another task the National Football League office had never had to worry much about. It did oversee distribution of NFL championship game tickets, but most of those always went to season ticket holders of the team hosting the game. Otherwise, individual teams always took care of selling tickets. The local Rams office was a big help, but Rozelle went looking for the NFL's best ticket operation and found it in Dallas, where the Cowboys had what we felt was a model organization. Pete also knew Dallas Cowboys ticket manager Kay Lang, so he brought her to Los Angeles and put her in charge of ticket distribution under Jim Kensil's direction.

It was a memorable assignment, to say the least. Kay didn't even have an office. She had what amounted to a suite in the Statler-Hilton Hotel and kept the tickets in a box underneath her bed, which was alongside another Xerox copier that we had rented for her to use. Honestly, that's how she worked, right from her room. So, as we needed tickets, we'd step across the hall and knock politely on the door. When it opened, we'd say, "Kay, I need eight tickets (or whatever the number was), and here's the money for them." Kay would take the money, get the box from underneath the bed, and pull out the eight tickets.

There were, of course, other outlets, especially since there were some 78,600 seats to sell to the general public. If you were a Rams season ticket holder, for instance, you could buy the same number of tickets to the championship game as you held season tickets. It stands to reason, then, that other tickets could be obtained from the Rams' office, too.

Apart from ticket operations, much of Bert Rose's talent was on loan, so to speak, from the Rams. Along with Jack Teele, the principal talents were Bill John, who served as the Rams' business manager, and equipment manager Bill "Granny" Granholm, who became my closest Super Bowl associate over the years. Granny really was much more than that, however. For as long as he walked this earth, he was a fun-loving friend who was forever near and dear to my heart.

Gaining Granny's talents was a stroke of incredibly good fortune if not divine intervention. A pal of Rams owner Dan Reeves, he had been with the NFL team since 1950. Our paths had even crossed once while I was still with the Associated Press. Being an equipment manager, Granny had solid working relationships with trainers, other equipment managers around the league, field maintenance guys . . . just about every behind-the-scenes function you could name. In short, he was precisely the man we needed to arrange training sites, hotels, and countless other game details and loose ends that we now needed to tie up. We were so impressed with him that Rozelle brought him to the league office late in 1967 as a "special assistant" to the Commissioner. The title was apt. Granny was special in every respect, and we never once had to worry about whatever we asked him to tackle.

Granny's versatility proved mighty beneficial to our diminutive staff. Yet we still thought we had sufficient numbers to handle a championship game that some had regarded from the beginning as an afterthought.

It always startles people to hear that, but that's what it was. Rozelle and I didn't arrive in Los Angeles until late on the Sunday night of the week approaching the new game. We flew in from Miami after attending the NFL Playoff Bowl, an annual NFL postseason game in the Orange Bowl that matched the runners-up in each conference. Lombardi always dismissed it as the "Loser's Bowl." Maybe so, but it produced the revenue for the players' pension fund, and we thought it worth our attendance. Besides, what Green Bay and Kansas City would play the following week in Los Angeles was simply "the game that we played after the NFL championship game." Not much more.

Notwithstanding that mind-set, we still never lost sight of Rozelle's directive to make this game special. For an instant, our zeal to promote the game and generate some newspaper headlines prompted a devilish suggestion: *Arrange* to have the new Tiffany trophy "stolen" en route to Los Angeles.

It was a tempting notion and aroused serious, albeit good-natured, discussion. In the end, however, wiser heads prevailed. It would be too much, we concluded, and if anyone ever found out we had contrived the alleged theft, the championship game would bring unwanted attention. The ruse also blatantly contradicted Rozelle's overriding insistence that our public relations activities always be built on honesty and fact.

But we did do the next best thing: When we unveiled the trophy for the first time at a party that we threw for all of the writers on the Friday night before the game, we hired two uniformed policemen to stand guard on either side of it the entire night, just to make sure it *would not* be stolen.

Hosted by Rozelle himself, that Friday night affair started an enduring Super Bowl tradition, interrupted only twice—the year of

Desert Storm and Super Bowl XXXVI following the September 11, 2001, terrorist attacks. Our guest list that first night totaled about 600, 95 percent of whom were writers in town to cover the game. Evidently, they not only had a great time but also told others because an invitation to what swelled into the annual Commissioner's party quickly became more cherished than a ticket to the game itself. Many of the now dwindling band of writers who have attended all Super Bowl Commissioner's parties to date still say the best ever was that first one held in the Hilton ballroom. Along with the trophy's unveiling, the evening featured a buffet dinner and classy entertainment by Les Brown and his Band of Renown.

A second party was held that year that people would just as soon forget. It served as a reminder that pro football owners had competitive streaks of their own. AFL owners hosted it in Beverly Hills a few nights before the game. As a gesture to the merger, they graciously invited NFL owners and their spouses to attend, too. It didn't turn out to be such a good idea. As the evening wore on, words were exchanged, tempers rose, and the party ended much earlier than planned. As often is the case, the owners' wives were as combative as the owners themselves. Maybe more so.

While others partied, we kept planning and preparing the Coliseum for the historic combat everyone had come to see. As part of our planning, we had scaled down the stadium seating from 100,000 to 93,000. We could have scaled it down much further.

NINE

JANUARY 1967: YEAR ONE

Not So Super

As years go by, a curious phenomenon occurs. Attendance figures at legendary sports events tend to swell. Ardent fans can't resist telling their buddies, "I was there for . . ." even if they weren't within 200 miles of the legendary event they're describing.

But the opposite has been true for the first AFL-NFL World Championship of Professional Football. As the years slip by, the crowd on hand at the Los Angeles Memorial Coliseum on that January Sunday in 1967 keeps shrinking, and the truth keeps getting stretched further and further out of shape.

Interviewed for a television special that appeared the night before one recent Super Bowl, Steve Sabol, of NFL Films, said that the Coliseum on that first Super Bowl Sunday looked like it was empty. So empty, in fact, that it also has been claimed on other occasions that the fans who were there were asked to move to seats opposite the television cameras, to make their numbers appear larger.

Like Steve's recollection, that vignette makes for a nice story. But the claim is bogus. No such request was made because about 62,000 of the Coliseum's 93,000 available seats were filled: 61,946 to be exact. That's the number we sold. Because we had not intended to sell any seats in the peristyle end of the Coliseum, capacity was trimmed by about 7,000 seats from its total of 100,000.

Those who were there weren't surprised by the game's outcome. Green Bay performed about as expected, trouncing Kansas City, 35–10, affirming the NFL's superiority over the AFL and setting Vince Lombardi's mind at ease, at least momentarily.

On television, the game was solidly successful. The combined ratings of the two networks that carried the game, CBS and NBC, were strong. The rating points for each network were around the 20s, with CBS ahead. So, the "share" of the television audience (those with their television sets turned on at the time of the game) would have been high, probably close to 50 percent. After the game, Western Union later reported that sports writers filed 582,334 words describing it, at the time the most words ever filed from one event.

Moreover, the game's revenues just about matched the $2.8 million that had been budgeted: $2 million from television; approximately $710,000 from ticket sales; $50,000 from film rights; and $20,000 from program sales, plus almost $20,000 from other sources. And the $15,000 and $7,500 players' shares were the largest in the history of team sports at that time.

Then again, we had been hoping for—and now and then quietly predicting—a $3 million gate, which would have been a first for a football game. And launching a new world championship game in a stadium filled to only two-thirds of its capacity was hardly what Pete Rozelle had in mind. If "Super Sunday," as the networks were calling it, was to be the grand celebration of the football season, it was making an inauspicious debut. In spite of the Super Bowl's meteoric growth over the next three years, I'm not sure Pete ever completely got over his disappointment at the size of the crowd in the Coliseum.

Why wasn't the game a sellout? Take your pick of reasons: the prices of tickets; the television blackout in Los Angeles; the nature of Los Angeles sports fans in general and their lack of interest in the AFL in particular; the lack of time we had to plan and promote to arouse more interest; the predictable outcome, given the Packers' unquestioned superiority; or all of the above. Whenever I look back on that first championship game, the last is the conclusion I always draw.

For years, Rozelle often wondered if we had overpriced the tickets. Seriously. The range we set for that first game was—don't laugh, now!—$6, $10, and $12. In early 1967, those prices may have been a little high because $10 was pretty much the price ceiling for a seat to a major sports event.

At least in my mind, though, the television blackout affected ticket sales far more than what they cost. From the moment Rozelle announced the Coliseum as the game site, reports began surfacing that we would break our long-standing policy of not televising any pro football game within a 75-mile radius of the stadium hosting it. No matter which newspaper you read—the *Los Angeles Times*, the *Examiner*, or any of the many others being circulated in the city in those days—to a man, their writers were convinced that Pete planned to lift the blackout. Surely, this consensus opinion insisted, the National Football League's Commissioner would want the historic first meeting between the two champions of pro football to be seen in the country's second-largest market. After all, wouldn't he want to ensure as big an audience as possible?

Of course, he would. But Rozelle never had any intention of lifting the blackout and made that clear whenever he was asked about it. Not even NFL championship games had ever been exempt, whether or nor they were sold out well in advance, and they almost always were. It simply was standing NFL policy, established to protect the ticket buyers and the hometown gate. Several lawsuits had challenged championship blackouts, but courts had upheld us every time. With the policy's never having been compromised before, then, Rozelle wasn't about to compromise it now, not even in a city the size of Los Angeles and despite having known from the outset what the impact on ticket sales would be. Being a former Rams general manager, Pete also likely still remembered the team's experiment with televising home games locally in 1950. The impact on attendance that season had been disastrous, to the point that television advertisers reimbursed the Rams to the tune of more than $300,000 for the resulting decline in ticket sales.

The papers remained adamant, though, and that assumption created a very reluctant local buyer and perhaps a backlash. Los Angeles fans' reputation for not buying in advance is well established. They wait to see how the day's going to turn out because there are so many other things to do in and around Southern California. Even during their heyday in Los Angeles, the Rams never had a huge season ticket base because fans knew they could walk up to the Coliseum on game day and find a reasonable number of its 100,000 seats still available. Whether fans had better things to do on the morning of January 15 or were registering a protest against the blackout, precious few felt moved to see the Packers tussle with the Chiefs.

More fans might have been drawn at the last minute had there not been such disdain for AFL football in Los Angeles. That was a factor, too. The City of Angels just did not believe the league had yet established itself as an equal. The Chargers had played in Los Angeles for one season in 1960 but failed miserably and promptly moved to San Diego. So, why pay even $6—let alone $10 or $12—to see a game whose outcome wasn't in doubt? Moreover, Los Angeles fans had had numerous chances in the past six years to see the mighty Packers because they played the Rams in the Coliseum once each season.

Whether a well-orchestrated promotion plan could have rousted more spectators out of their lethargy is anyone's guess, of course. But we never had time for such strategy. And practically no group marketing existed for the first game. We made tickets available to the teams, the networks, Rams season ticket holders, and the public at large. But that was about it.

Whatever the reasons, some 31,000 seats were empty when the Chiefs kicked off to the Packers. In one respect, maybe it was a blessing. Along with sports history, the 61,946 fans who were at the Coliseum witnessed two events I'd just as soon nobody had ever seen.

Having one of the hands fall off the scoreboard clock during the opening kickoff is no way to begin the World Championship of Professional Football. But that's what happened. For all I know, some writer may have started a story with the words "Hickory, dickory, dock. The hand fell off the clock."

This little episode began in Dallas, where an engineer friend of Cowboys owner Clint Murchison had approached Clint about a remote-control system that could be connected to the clock on the stadium scoreboard. Scoreboards in late 1966 weren't the sophisticated electronic marvels they are today, and while they all had game clocks, the time appearing on them was never "official." In NFL games, the time kept by the field judge down on the field was the official time. As we used to say, the scoreboard clock was merely a *memorandum* of the game. If you saw 3:30 on the clock, 3:30 might be left; but more likely 3:28 was really left, or 3:32. Fans, in turn, never knew exactly how much time was left in each quarter or the game itself.

The AFL had begun using the scoreboard clock as official, but that meant the official time of a game was controlled entirely by a clock operator along the sideline or in the press box, a person who was responsible to the home team. In our view, that wasn't very official, was too imprecise, and at the end of close games offered opportunities for mischief that might be too tempting to ignore.

On the other hand, a remote-control system like the one being demonstrated in Dallas was promising. One of its components was attached to the hands of the scoreboard clock and a remote-control unit, which used radio signals to start and stop the clock, was placed in the hands of the field judge, thereby making the scoreboard both official and precise instead of the judge's having to rely on a stopwatch on the field that no one could see from the stands.

The Cowboys first tested the system under game conditions on Thanksgiving Day in the Cotton Bowl against the Browns, using it only as a backup. But it worked flawlessly, and Dallas used it a second time in the NFL championship game, as a backup again and just as successfully. The tests were so flawless and the Cowboys so impressed that Murchison and, probably, Tex Schramm, too, recommended the system be used—this time for real—at the AFL-NFL championship game in the Coliseum. Rozelle pretty much left the decision to Mark Duncan, Jim Kensil, and me. We decided to go for it.

It would add one more new twist to the game: The first AFL-NFL battle also would be the first occasion where the official time was kept on the scoreboard clock so that everyone in the stands and everyone watching on television would know precisely how much time was left. Rozelle warmed to the idea immediately. So did Tex—it gave him another Dallas "thing" to crow about.

Just to be safe, though, we brought the system's creator and his son to Los Angeles for extensive testing in the Coliseum. First, he attached a component to the hands of the big wrought-iron clock that hung high above the seats at the peristyle end of the Coliseum. Then we began experimenting with it, hours at a time for several days, to ensure its reliability and to ensure that Norm Schachter, the game referee, and other officials knew how to use it. Everyone worked tirelessly, while the system moved the hands of the old clock as flawlessly as it had performed in Dallas. We had our final test on Saturday afternoon. At one point, the system's proud creator was even shooting the remote control unit between his legs to show off its capabilities. No matter how he stood or where, the hands on the clock moved to his every command. Forward and backward, backward and forward.

Everyone was thoroughly satisfied. Our press guide pointed out that the scoreboard clock would be official, and we made a special point of announcing the breakthrough to the media, as part of the big new era of professional football that was about to begin. Then we tested the system one last time on Sunday morning before the game. Once again, it was flawless.

When the Chiefs kicked off a few hours later, the field judge pushed the button in his hand to start the clock . . . and watched in disbelief as one of the wrought iron hands promptly fell off and plunged toward the stands below. It must have fallen 50 or 60 feet. I can still see it. It looked like a giant spear.

To our everlasting good fortune, no one was underneath, and no one was injured. Had there been people sitting in those stands, someone might have been killed.

People who hear this story ask me what I was thinking. I didn't get much chance to think. While the hand was still in the air, the phone next to me rang. I picked it up on the first ring to hear Rozelle asking, "What the hell happened to the goddamn clock?"

As we would learn, it was metal fatigue. We had tested everything so much that we simply wore the old clock out. So, instead of the time on the scoreboard clock being official, no time was showing on the scoreboard at all, and no other clock was in the Coliseum. Throughout most of the first half, the field judge had to use hand signals to tell the Packers and Chiefs how much time remained. But the fans had no idea how much time was left until the end of the quarters or until the two-minute warning was issued near the end of the half.

No such calamity began the second half. All we did was start the half twice, for the sake of a television commercial. Somebody might regard that as an omen, too.

When the Packers kicked off to begin the second half, NBC's telecast hadn't returned to the game, so the first play wasn't televised by NBC, prompting the referee to blow it dead. CBS's cameras were used to capture the action on the field, and its picture was fed to both networks. But CBS and NBC each used its own announcing team—Ray Scott and Jack Whitaker for CBS and Curt Gowdy and Paul Christman for NBC—and its own production crew, and sold its own advertising time. The CBS team finished its halftime report, aired its commercials, and returned to the game right on schedule. Unaccustomed as everyone was to having two television networks involved in the same game, nobody was monitoring the NBC broadcast, which wasn't quite on schedule. The signal was given to the field that all was ready, the referee called for the second-half kickoff, and Green Bay kicker Don Chandler promptly obliged. But while CBS viewers saw the kick, NBC viewers saw a commercial, leaving NBC yelling, "Hey, wait for us!" or words to that effect.

Referee Norm Schachter immediately realized what had happened and blew his whistle while the ball was still in the air. By the time everyone lined up again, NBC was ready and the half started anew. No harm came of it, but it could have been very embarrassing. Green Bay was leading Kansas City by a narrow 14–10 margin, and one shudders to think of the hue and cry that would have erupted had the Chiefs run that first kickoff back for a touchdown.

At that point, heroics by the Chiefs didn't seem beyond the realm of possibility. *Sports Illustrated*'s Tex Maule, a huge NFL supporter, was in shock, and lots of NFL folks were feeling quite uncomfortable at halftime, including me. We had presumed Green Bay's lead would be much larger. Kansas City was crisp and had moved the ball on the Packers, thanks to some wrinkles in its game plan that seemed to give the NFL champs some problems. Len Dawson, the Chiefs' quarterback, was always very mobile, and when you combine that with the talents of running back Mike Garrett, you even might say that the Packers were rocked back on their heels a bit. As the score suggested, it was a competitive and well-played first half. Green Bay scored first, but the game was tied, 7–7, at one point in the second quarter.

Yet, whatever dreams Kansas City may have been entertaining at halftime came crashing down when the second half got under way for real. Green Bay began to show its dominance as soon as the third quarter unfolded and in the final 30 minutes overwhelmed the Chiefs en route to a 35–10 victory.

A couple of key plays ignited the inevitable. An interception by the Packers' Willie Wood took the ball to the Kansas City five-yard line, where Elijah Pitts then scored on a five-yard run. Pitts scored a second touchdown in the fourth quarter. Green Bay receiver Max McGee also scored a pair of touchdowns on receptions from Bart Starr, who was named the game's most valuable player. Afterward, a jovial McGee admitted that he had been carousing the night before. Then in the twilight of his career, Max hadn't expected to play much and likely wouldn't have if Boyd Dowler hadn't reinjured a shoulder hurt two weeks earlier in Dallas.

The contest was pretty much decided by the time the fourth quarter began, but one last episode is worth recounting. Packer Backers would call it poetic justice.

Throughout the two weeks approaching the game, a Kansas City defensive back, Fred Williamson—alias "The Hammer"—had boasted about how he was going to really pound Green Bay. The consensus among football people was that the best part of The Hammer's game was his pearls of wisdom rather than his gridiron prowess, an opinion that gained strength when Williamson left football to pursue an acting career after a couple more seasons. Yet, from a promotional standpoint, we just loved it, for The Hammer was pounding out headlines across the country.

Williamson should have quit while he was ahead. Toward the end of the game, The Hammer tried to tackle Packers running back Donny Anderson but smacked into Anderson's knee, instead, and was knocked out cold. He was really stretched out. The Packers, of course, roared with delight along the sidelines, all of which was captured by NFL Films and summed up by Willie Wood, who exclaimed, "The Hammer got nailed!"

To a lesser degree, so did the Chiefs. As the final minutes wound down (the time coming courtesy of the field judge), a colleague and I led the writers out of the Coliseum press box and down along the sidelines toward one of the end zones. The trek was customary: to enable the writers to make their way to the locker room for interviews without getting hung up in the crowd exiting the stadium. We had reached the sidelines when the Packers scored their final touchdown, and had seen up close the play that exposed how really defeated the Chiefs were. The impression they left was that they were devastated. That Kansas City team had some outstanding players. Essentially, it was the same corps that would win Super Bowl IV three years later, and a number of them are in the Hall of Fame. But in the second half of the game in Los Angeles, they had simply been worn down and battered by Green Bay's depth and talent.

Even so, Vince Lombardi went out of his way to be as gracious a victor as he could possibly be. In accepting the trophy from Pete Rozelle (captured in that famous photograph shown in the insert), he uttered all the words expected of the coach of pro football's just crowned champions—except the words the writers wanted to hear: Just how good were the Chiefs, compared with NFL powers such as Dallas and Baltimore? Vince ducked the question as best he could, but the writers were relentless and kept pressing him. Once and for all, they wanted Lombardi to pronounce the NFL as being the superior league.

Remaining in good humor, Vince finally relented and said, "You want me to say we're better? OK, we're better."

Still, he was very reluctant to say it, although he did add, "There are several teams in our league that are better than the Chiefs."

It wasn't much, but it was enough to satisfy the sports-writing world, which had been crammed and jostled into one of the strangest locker room settings I can remember. The championship trophy is presented on the field now, but up until just the last few years it was presented in the locker room. The players' cubicles in the Coliseum locker rooms had doors—like you'd find in a washroom. Our first reaction when we saw them was that they would make interviews difficult, since guys could go into those things and disappear if they wanted to. We wanted to remove the cubicle doors, but the Coliseum refused, about the only detail we had trouble with. Then again, the Packers had no reason to hide.

Stuffed with cameras and camera platforms, and people all over the place, the locker room scene was pretty hectic, especially because no stage was set up for the actual presentation, as was done in subsequent years. In fact, I was suspended along a rafter with what seemed like a dozen photographers, so that I could listen to Rozelle and Lombardi standing on the floor below. It was the only place I could find within earshot. The setup for the presentation of the trophy created all kinds of confusion, and as I hung there I made a mental note to design something better in the future.

Amid all this humanity, it's a wonder the trophy itself wasn't crushed. But it escaped without a scratch . . . until it got to Green Bay, where a second Tiffany trophy story unfolded.

Tiffany's suggested taking its work of art back to New York for engraving after the game. Then the trophy would be sent to Green Bay for the Packers to display permanently. Not on your life, Vince insisted. He was taking the trophy directly to Green Bay so that it could receive the acclaim it deserved from Packer Backers here, there, and everywhere. *Then* he would have it sent to New York for engraving. Tiffany's acceded to Lombardi's wishes and didn't think a thing of it. But when the Packers' front office finally shipped the trophy to

New York, it was packed in an ordinary cardboard box and mailed via parcel post. When it arrived, the trophy had been crushed. Tiffany's had to create another one to replace it. I don't know who paid for it. After all the mishaps that surrounded this game, you could say it was a fitting finale.

Crushed as they may have been, several members of the Chiefs later came into the Green Bay locker room to offer their congratulations to the Packers. The Kansas City locker room wasn't far from the Packers', just down the one tunnel that led onto the field. So it was a quick jaunt, and one that could be made without attracting a great deal of attention or fanfare. I took the Chiefs' classy gesture as one more indication of how glad these guys were to be part of all this, even though they had been defeated.

The Packers, by the way, won this game without the services of one of Lombardi's favorites, Green Bay's golden boy, Paul Hornung. He had been the Packers' MVP many times, but a pinched nerve in his neck kept him out of the game against the Chiefs. The topic arises on sports talk shows now and then, and for some reason it bugs the hell out of me because people who should know better insist that Hornung was in the game. He wasn't. In fact, Hornung never appeared in another NFL game. Before the next season, he was selected by the New Orleans Saints in the expansion allocation draft but retired before playing for them.

But at this point in 1967, Hornung was still golden, and so was Green Bay. Even if their world championship had been expected, the Packers' resounding victory was no less satisfying. And never mind that Rozelle was handing Lombardi the Tiffany trophy during the very period that the two were feuding bitterly over the redshirt draft. For the moment, that was forgotten. On this Sunday, Green Bay had been super (perhaps the only thing that had been).

The glow of the Packers' accomplishment had warmed the hearts of NFL partisans, too, to be sure. Yet, we didn't feel super. Relieved was more like it, for the game had been anything but an artistic success (it also eroded interest in the Pro Bowl game the following week in the Coliseum). The embarrassing adventure with the scoreboard clock, the second-half kickoff, the fuss over the television blackout, even the gaffe on the press guide, weren't exactly the substance of the "sporting event of the century." I suppose, though, that it could have been worse. We concluded our pregame show by releasing four thousand pigeons to the heavens, and no incidents had been reported.

Departing Los Angeles, we knew our work was cut out for us if the World Championship of Professional Football was to become the event that Rozelle envisioned. If we needed a reminder, there was always the vision of those 31,000 empty seats in the Coliseum.

ON TO MIAMI WITH A MISSION

It never was meant to be a threat and certainly wasn't spoken as one. That was not Pete Rozelle's style. Yet, as Jim Kensil and I listened to his words during our flight home from Los Angeles after Green Bay's victory over Kansas City in the first championship game, there was no mistaking his resolve. "Never again is there going to be a championship game that isn't a sellout," Pete said, above the drone of the jet engines.

There wasn't the slightest trace of anger in his voice or any intent to affix blame. Just conviction. The planning wheels may have started turning in behalf of pro football's second world championship game right then and there.

Rozelle had plenty to think about on that flight home: myriad loose ends and unsettled issues swirling about the merger, the stalemate that was delaying the first common draft, and assorted NFL and AFL matters to attend to. Despite his focus on such matters, Rozelle's disappointment over the Coliseum crowd festered. And before he put the game behind him, he wanted to make clear that the next time around there wouldn't be any empty seats. There weren't, and there haven't been any since.

Pro football's second world championship game, played in Miami's Orange Bowl on January 14, 1968, may be dismissed as uneventful to those who even remember it, except for its being Vince Lombardi's final game as coach of the Green Bay Packers. Yet, as one-sided as Green Bay's 33–14 victory over Oakland was, the game deserves far more credit than it's ever received. The foundation of all that we did to build the AFL-NFL World Championship of Professional Football into the celebration that would earn the name Super Bowl—the strategy, the planning, the organizing, and many of the individual tactics—was laid in Miami. It was the first year we had the opportunity to do any serious planning. We weren't about to waste it.

Miami's unabashed enthusiasm to host the second game bubbled to the surface within weeks after the first game ended (of course, the city had already promoted the Orange Bowl as a possible site for the first game, too). The Joint Committee selected January 14, 1968, as the game date when it next met in March 1967—in Miami, no less. Yet, it waited until late May before recommending the Orange Bowl as the game site. The idea of a city's making a formal offer to host a pro football game was still at least two years away, but Sugar Bowl officials in New Orleans had conveyed their "interest." The option also existed to return to the Coliseum. Given the television blackout and attendance problems, however, Los Angeles got no support. When NFL owners affirmed Miami as the game site during their spring meeting on May 25, not even Rams owner Dan Reeves voted for Los Angeles; he merely abstained.

Having a good six months to plan the game almost seemed like an eternity, compared with the 75-odd days we had had the preceding autumn. We had a rallying cry, too: *Sell out the Orange Bowl!* It's a cry that became infinitely more meaningful shortly thereafter, when Rozelle asked me to serve as coordinator for all the game arrangements.

I had joined the National Football League in part to respond to sports writers' questions. Rozelle's goal to sell out the championship game prompted a question that I faced for the first time: *How do we fill the Orange Bowl?*

The answer emerged as a group of us simply put our heads together, in typical Rozelle fashion, to examine concepts that practically all of us were confronting for the first time: target audiences, group sales, and marketing. Playing the NFL championship game in the city of one of the participating teams had allowed us to take it for granted that it would sell out. Heavy group marketing had never been necessary. But it was now.

Three of our target audiences were obvious: fans in the cities of the two teams playing in the game and pro football fans in Miami. But at the time, none of these audiences boasted big numbers.

From our perspective, we didn't think a team in Green Bay, say, could sell more than a few thousand tickets to a game it didn't know it was going to be in until, at most, two weeks beforehand. Initially, then, participating teams didn't receive any more than 5 percent of available tickets. In retrospect, we badly underestimated what the championship game was about to become. Three years later, for example, Kansas City received 5,000 tickets for its trip to Super Bowl IV in 1970 but could have sold 10 times that many.

The Miami Dolphins' season ticket base also was modest, certainly no more than 20,000 or so, because pro football hadn't come to southern Florida until 1966, and the Dolphins didn't start winning until Don Shula arrived in 1970. Still, we gave these fans the same courtesy we had extended to the Rams' season ticket holders: They could buy tickets to the championship game on a one-for-one basis. The tactic would pay off. Both Miami and New Orleans leveraged this privilege to build their season ticket bases as the Super Bowl began to glitter.

In mid-1967, though, this game had barely begun to flicker, so we kept hunting for additional targets. We found them in a familiar realm.

While unfamiliar with the ticket-selling business, the NFL league office was up to its eyeballs in the television business. That put television advertisers and sponsors smack-dab in the middle of our crosshairs, along with media organizations, sporting goods manufacturers, and anyone else with business ties to pro football. Moti-

vated by the declaration Rozelle voiced on that flight home after the
first game, we marketed the game to these groups with a vengeance,
built on a strategy that endures to this day.

Because we never could know in advance who was going to play,
we promoted the game as a big, midwinter, "must-attend" media
event. This was more than a championship football game. It was a
gala celebration lasting for an entire weekend.

"We want to make our new championship game something extra-
special," we declared, then added the clincher, "and we want *you* to
be part of it."

It was an offer that television partners couldn't refuse. Companies
such as Ford Motor, Chrysler, and Coca-Cola found it especially
appealing because it gave them an opportunity to build the game and
the weekend into an attractive incentive program (in this case a free
bonus trip to Miami) for their sales forces, other deserving employees, and, of course, their own key customers and clients. Moreover,
it strengthened their identity with pro football. Securing that kind of
corporate support guaranteed critical ticket sales in advance to people who relished being on hand to see professional football crown its
world champion but didn't care that much about who would be on
the field. It was a true win-win partnership.

Ford and Chrysler were two of pro football's principal sponsors in
those days, so their participation in the game in Miami was a natural. Ford was the originator of the pass, punt, and kick competition
and was spending tremendous amounts of money on the NFL, which
is why most of us were driving Fords in those years. I had Fords in
my future for a long time. Accordingly, the Super Bowl became a fix-
ture in Ford's future. Chrysler, meanwhile, was the "car of the AFL"
for many years, and while its participation didn't quite match Ford's
it was still significant.

Along with auto companies, we approached marketing executives
at Eastern Airlines and National Airlines, the two big carriers into
and out of Miami. National, in fact, was based there. But instead of
asking, "Would you like some tickets?" we asked, "How many tickets would you like?" and encouraged them to put together packages

for the game. They were delighted to join us. As I recall, National's allocation was around 600 tickets, but had they come back and asked for another 500, we would have said absolutely.

The airlines' support gave us momentum to initiate still more conversations, this time with hotel chains. We discussed blocks of tickets that ranged anywhere from 600 to 1,000. The hotel chains started weaving championship game tickets into their promotional packages, also. Other blocks of tickets went to media organizations such as *Sports Illustrated*, which used them to entertain its advertisers. A few charitable organizations bought limited numbers of tickets, too, to auction off in conjunction with fund-raisers. And, since NASA had such a presence in Florida, we got the space agency involved, and it became a big supporter for many years.

Next, we turned to the advertising agencies and marketing contacts we worked with in New York City, in many cases the very same contacts we had recruited for our "baby-sitter" program at the height of the AFL war. Pete's close friend Jack Landry, the ranking Philip Morris marketing executive who had been such a great baby-sitter, proved equally adept at helping promote our game. We leaned on Jack and his peers heavily, and they, too, rallied to our support with gusto.

We had one more weapon in our arsenal: Rapidly growing NFL Properties had its own bevy of clients, sponsors, and prospects to tap, such as Wilson Sporting Goods, other sports equipment makers, Frito-Lay . . . and the list goes on. Relationships of every description were sprouting from the deals this still-young organization was putting together. Then swelling into one of the top marketing and licensing enterprises in the country, if not the world, NFL Properties leveraged its ticket allocation with the skills of an artist on canvas. It became an enormously critical source and also was responsible for a big magazine insert that promoted the championship game in Sunday supplements distributed all over the country. Before too long, NFL Properties was responsible for about 10 percent of the stadium capacity. I still run into people who used to come to the Super Bowl as its guests, including a couple of guys I occasionally play golf with. NFL

Properties became so successful, in fact, that it soon began competing with us for hotel space in host cities.

Perhaps most helpful of all, however, was Rozelle himself. He made some of the initial contacts and worked as hard as anybody to help muster momentum, in spite of everything else he had on his plate. Then again, Pete was a master at public relations and, through his circle of influential friends in New York, was able to establish tremendous relationships. He also had the vision of being able to *build*, although at this point not even Pete Rozelle's vision could anticipate what the championship game was destined to become. Nobody's could. All we were trying to do was sell out a stadium for a game in mid-January 1968.

I don't mean to suggest we were standing on Manhattan street corners grabbing people as they walked by. And not all of these initiatives jelled at once. But we were making a concerted effort to get people involved, and slowly but surely we could see the Orange Bowl starting to fill up. Our public sale was much larger and more active than we had envisioned initially, too.

Before we were done, we had marketed the bejabbers out of this game, working our fannies off and calling in every chit we had. So, about a week before Green Bay and Oakland collided, we were able to declare the Orange Bowl a sellout.

And make no mistake. We *sold* the tickets. We never gave them away. Pete felt that padding the house was false advertising and cheapened the product. What organizations did with their tickets once they bought them from us was their own business. However they distributed them, though, they found that their participation was such a success that many of them have been doing it ever since.

We also adjusted the ticket prices slightly for this second game, retaining the $12 and $6 prices but trimming the middle tier from $10 to $8. These prices were in place until we adopted a single $15 price for Super Bowl IV in New Orleans. Despite Pete's concern, $12 was considered reasonable. If you were buying 1,000 tickets, you were only spending $12,000 to get them—money well spent in the eyes of corporate marketers who anticipated long-term payoffs. The same pricing policy applies today, except that a premium has been added for "club-level" seats. And, of course, tickets don't cost what they did in Miami. Tickets to Super Bowl XXXVI were $400 each, face value.

Neither our strategy nor our tactics had been remotely possible for the first game in Los Angeles, of course. We didn't have time other than to make available some blocks of tickets to the networks and the Rams' season ticket holders. Whenever the Packers, Chiefs, or anybody else had called asking for 50 tickets, say, we were inclined to reply, "How 'bout 60?"

We had other factors in our favor in Miami, as well. The city itself was all but jubilant from the beginning, in sharp contrast to the relative indifference we faced in Los Angeles. The enthusiasm was infectious. Miami officials even came up with a little memento for the writers and media. Miami Beach in mid-January was a draw all its own, of course, and helped establish our concept of a championship football game being played in a big stadium in a neutral warm-weather site.

In essence, we were taking a page out of the college bowl game book. We were selling the warm weather, the beaches, the golf courses, the restaurants, and the entertainment in the host city. No matter who the combatants are and no matter who wins, we assured, it will be a gala weekend to remember.

While none of this enthusiasm mushroomed overnight, those with even a casual interest in football started to grasp the new AFL-NFL championship game as a great midwinter event culminating a long season. Moreover, it was played at a time when not much else was going on. The college football season had ended by early December, with the playing of Army-Navy. Postseason bowl games had been played, too. That allowed our game to take center stage. If we looked carefully, we could see it was starting to grow. In Miami, too, the Packers were themselves a great draw, with the Lombardi legend at its peak. Even the weather was gorgeous, just tremendous.

Yet, as important as the weather in Miami was the weather in Green Bay, Wisconsin.

You can't talk about the first pro football championship game in Miami without first talking about the "Ice Bowl"—the NFL championship game played between Green Bay and Dallas two weeks earlier in Green Bay, on December 31, 1967. My telephone conversations about the weather began around 2:00 on that Sunday morning.

Joe Cronin (no relation to the baseball great) was a statistics nut and a sports collector who worked for the Green Bay weather bureau. His passion for sports and my role as the league's director of information had turned us into phone pals, so I knew immediately who he was when I answered the phone in the suite Jim Kensil and I were sharing at the Northland Hotel, just about the *only* hotel in Green Bay.

"I don't want to alarm you," Cronin said, "but I thought you'd want to know it could be 16 degrees below, or worse, today, with unbelievable windchill." Even for Green Bay in the dead of winter, it was going to be damn cold.

Both the Packers and the Cowboys had anticipated cold weather but nothing like what was blowing in from the north. The Cowboys, who were staying about 30 miles from Green Bay in Appleton, had arrived late Friday, participated in a routine workout Saturday, and assumed that game-day conditions and temperatures would be more of the same.

After ending my conversation with Cronin, I quickly dialed the Cowboys' Al Ward, Tex Schramm's assistant. "You'd better let Tom know we have a new forecast, and it's going to be damn cold, with a minus windchill," I said, referring to Dallas's head coach, Tom Landry. In those days, windchill didn't get the attention it does now, but I remember that it hovered between 35 and 40 degrees below zero.

While I called Ward, Kensil called Rozelle, who was in Oakland (where temperatures were in the mid-50s) for the AFL championship game, to be played later on that same Sunday. Pete's initial reaction was a burst of laughter, but he, too, instantly recognized the gravity of the situation.

We seriously considered postponing the game and might have, except the weather forecast for Monday and Tuesday was even worse than what was expected on Sunday. The bitter cold front rolling into Wisconsin from Canada wouldn't leave the area until midweek. I confirmed that with a second call to Joe Cronin after I hung up from alerting a sleepy Al Ward. By around 4:00 A.M., both teams had been alerted, as had Mark Duncan and the officials who were to work the game.

Kensil talked with Lombardi, who was astonished to hear that we were even thinking about a postponement. But he did understand our concern, to the point that someone in the Packers' front office managed to get a local sporting goods store to open so that we could buy gloves, ski masks, thermal underwear, and the like for the game officials and for ourselves. The teams were mostly on their own, but in subsequent conversations with the Cowboys later that morning, we gave them the names of a few people who could supply additional equipment if they wanted it.

My personal needs had included a new overcoat, to replace the one that had disappeared Friday night in a restaurant coatroom, along with a pair of cashmere earmuffs that had been in one of the pockets. The only thing left when I went to retrieve it after dinner was a cashmere scarf that my daughters had bought me for Christmas.

Part of Lombardi's astonishment was grounded in more than his rugged, play-no-matter-what reputation. Under the new sod at Lambeau Field, electric heating grids had been installed. During workouts on Saturday, Lombardi had been upbeat in showing off the new system to the Cowboys' Tom Landry and Tex Schramm, and was confident that the field wouldn't be affected by the weather, come what may.

In truth, the heating grids actually backfired and made conditions worse. The field was covered by a tarp, which was elevated slightly to keep it from freezing to the ground. With the heating grids turned on, the system created moisture underneath. As soon as the tarp came off, the moisture froze, almost in an instant. (No wonder. The official temperature when the game started was minus 16 degrees.) The heating grids melted the ice, all right, but just enough to allow it to refreeze on the surface throughout the game. As the game wore on and the temperature dropped, footing became more and more treacherous.

Along the sidelines, a number of NFL Films cameras were useless. They froze, too. Believe all you hear about the 1967 NFL championship game in Green Bay. It truly was a day to remember . . . or forget. The press box was enclosed but not heated, and the windows were constantly fogging over. We tried to clear them with deicer— after moving some writers out of their front-row positions. Success was limited, however. We finally brought up a heater, like the ones then used along the sidelines. It probably was a fire hazard, but we had to take some of the chill off simply so people could work. You could see your breath in there.

And yet, I never saw an empty seat in the stands. Every time I glanced at the crowd, I'd see this tremendous amount of what looked like exhaust rising into the air. It was as if I were looking at a huge herd of elk in a meadow. But these were Packer Backers, 50,861 strong, and this was Title Town USA. Anyone lucky enough to have a ticket wasn't going to let cold weather, not even bone-chilling temperatures, keep him from cheering on his beloved champions. Nor did the weather keep fans from tearing down the goalposts after the Packers' victory. The irony was, it really was a beautiful sunny day in Green Bay, just incredibly cold.

On the Cowboys' side of the ball, lightning-fast Dallas receiver Bob Hayes was a sad sight to behold. On this Sunday, he was anything but lightning fast. Landry didn't want his receivers wearing gloves, and Hayes played the entire game with his hands stuck in his pants. He was considered the world's fastest human and was the reigning Olympic sprint champion at the time. But Bob was a nonfactor against Green Bay because he was freezing, pure and simple.

Hayes was hardly alone, of course. Countless players suffered frostbite, especially the offensive linemen, a consequence of the three-point stances they all took before each play. Lombardi, meanwhile, was on the sideline looking like a Russian general, with a camel hair coat and fur cap.

Despite all this, it was really a pretty good game: the Packers taking an early lead, then coming from behind on that famous late-game drive capped by Bart Starr's one-yard sneak with 13 seconds left to play. With 4:50 showing on the clock, Green Bay drove 68 yards in 12 plays, and won, 21–17. From what I heard afterward, Starr thought about handing off to Donny Anderson. But Anderson had had a terrible time with his footing all day and had slipped a few times. So, Starr decided to keep the ball. It wasn't a broken play, but I don't think even his teammates knew that he planned to keep the ball and follow Jerry Kramer and Ken Bowman, who wedged out the Cowboys' Bob Lilly and Jethro Pugh, Pugh slipping back slightly as the two lines surged at the snap. Positioned at the back of the end zone, Ed Sabol, of NFL Films, captured the memorable play because his camera was one of the few that were working.

The Cowboys claimed afterward that the Packers' line moved just slightly before the snap. If it did, it wasn't discernable. One Packer was slightly miffed, too. To this day, Bowman thinks he should have gotten more credit for his blocking on that play. But Kramer was a very popular guy, and, along with Starr, he got all the attention in the locker room.

How the players performed at all is beyond my comprehension. Afterward, I couldn't move. As the Packers started their late-game drive, I left the press box and walked through the stands with a few writers. My task was to get some postgame quotes, then carry them back up to the press box for distribution to writers who chose not to wind through the stands and into the locker room. By the time I returned, I was so cold that I didn't think I could do my job. I was out of breath, I couldn't speak, and I sure as hell couldn't type. It was that cold. So, you can imagine what the players had to endure.

Kensil, who had stayed in the press box, took bottles of Canadian Club and Old Grand Dad after the game ended and went from seat to seat pouring "antifreeze" for the guys who wanted it, to help them warm up. Even guys who didn't drink took some. That's another memory I won't forget.

This time, we didn't have trouble convincing Vince to bring the Packers to Miami a week early.

Compared to subzero Wisconsin, Miami was a tropical paradise, as the media duly reported. Cleveland *Plain Dealer* writer Chuck Heaton was among those flying directly from Green Bay to Miami. Considering the windchill, he later noted, he experienced literally a 100-degree swing in temperature in a matter of hours. He landed in

Miami, where it was 80 degrees, wearing wool underwear, toe to neck. Heaton was a sight to behold when he checked into the headquarters hotel on Miami Beach.

On arrival, everyone found vastly improved championship game arrangements. The hotel was one of the best, the Doral-on-Beach. And, we truly got into a planning mode for the first time. We had a good grasp of what we had to do, had the people on hand to do it, and, perhaps most important, had time to prepare. As coordinator, I was responsible for the general organization. But I had plenty of help.

Kensil handled most of the tickets, other than the media requests, which I took care of. Jim did what we call the ticket "layout" and decided how many tickets the networks were going to get, how many NFL Properties was going to get, and so forth. We also brought back Dallas ticket manager Kay Lang, as our on-the-scene ticket manager. Joining Kay were more club public relations people to work with us in the media room and at the game. After all, this was largely a *media event*. As many as 10 public relations directors started to work for us on a regular basis each year.

Bill Granholm and Mark Duncan took charge of the workout facilities, as we tried to create a home away from home for the participating teams. During the regular season, visiting teams usually arrive on Saturday, go through a light workout, play the game on Sunday, and return home. This was completely new. If we were going to bring teams in a week in advance, we couldn't expect them to operate with whatever equipment was nearby. Bill Granholm made arrangements to have special blocking sleds available and took care of other needs. Each team had its own way of preparing for games, so we went out of our way to accommodate them. Bill, of course, did a masterful job and didn't miss a detail. He even drew up alternate travel routes for team buses, just in case.

The Packers, for example, came in the Sunday before the game, and while Vince was still his challenging self, he didn't complain about the facilities. We housed the Packers at the Galt Ocean Mile Hotel in Ft. Lauderdale, not far from their workout facilities: the field used by one of the New York Yankees' minor league baseball teams.

The Oakland Raiders, the AFL representative, stayed in Boca Raton, an hour away, and trained at a nearby boys' school once used by the Miami Dolphins as their preseason camp.

One of the first decisions we made was to turn the halftime show and all the pageantry over to Earnie Seiler. Despite being in his seventies at that time, Earnie was *the* undisputed impresario of the Orange Bowl pageantry and on loan, so to speak, from the Orange Bowl committee. He put together the halftime show and continued to do so whenever we played the championship game in Miami. We selected the talent, in case we wanted to arrange a special attraction. But Earnie was the coordinator.

Along with starting a ritual of going to the championship game site almost immediately from the NFL or AFL championship game, whichever one I was attending, I also had become the hotel coordinator. Special challenges came with it, at first, prompted by our success at selling out the Orange Bowl.

All these fans needed places to stay. Initially, the demand for hotel rooms sparked a problem because many hotel properties wanted to inflate their prices, often considerably. To stop it, we got them to sign an antigouging pledge. Otherwise, some of these places might have doubled or tripled their rack rates. We also convinced the hotels, and the city, too, to make a specific number of rooms available to us. This commitment, in turn, enabled us to create a master work sheet that listed every property in the Miami area that we were interested in. So, instead of letting corporate groups grab whatever hotel space they could, *we* held all those rooms and coordinated their distribution. Ironically, at the beginning, one of our biggest competitors for hotel rooms was our own subsidiary company, NFL Properties. Sometimes they drove us nuts, bless their hearts.

Ford, for instance, used its game tickets to create an incentive program that rewarded its top dealers throughout the country and planned functions of its own, along with participating in some of our events. And, in addition to hotel rooms, Ford and others needed space in ballrooms and other locations. This necessitated event coordination, too, further expanding our planning role.

All of this was prompted by nothing more than sound organization, to avoid chaos. At the same time, though, we now had several constituencies to serve, not just the media.

As the game approached, speculation started to build that this was going to be Lombardi's last game as the Packers' coach, which proved accurate. Vince didn't announce it officially until several weeks after the game, but his players treated it like it was his last game, after nine seasons, five NFL championships, and the first two championship game victories over the AFL.

At halftime, Jerry Kramer exhorted his teammates to play the last 30 minutes for Vince. Later he said, "We all felt it was the old man's last game."

As much as anything, this feeling motivated the Packers after their exhausting experience in the "Ice Bowl." Green Bay was heavily favored—by almost two touchdowns—but our concern at the NFL office was whether the league championship game had taken too much out of the team to justify its role as favorite over the Raiders, who had walloped Houston, 40–7, in the AFL championship game. By now, many of the Packers were in their early thirties and feeling their years of gridiron battle. Their bodies simply weren't responding as quickly as they had in the players' younger years. In fact, many of the Packers later admitted that, if they had had only a week to prepare to play the Raiders, their bodies wouldn't have been able to handle it.

Yet, Green Bay won easily, 33–14. It jumped to a 13–0 lead early in the second quarter and never looked back. The game was characterized by the Packers' first touchdown, on a play that Oakland managing partner Al Davis recognized almost as soon as the ball was snapped.

Our control booth in the Orange Bowl (where I sat as game coordinator) was located in the stadium's old mezzanine press box. Right next to us, in one of the team booths, was Davis, and you could pretty much hear everything that was being said. Davis is a consummate football guy, who sees things very quickly and often reacts noisily. What he saw was Green Bay's quarterback, Bart Starr, about to exploit the Raiders' defensive back Howie Williams. Starr had gained a reputation for being an exceptional third-and-one quarterback. Because his play faking was so outstanding, Bart often completed long passes on third-and-one situations, when everybody expected the Packers to run. Sure enough, on this third-and-one situation, with the Packers leading 6–0, Starr faked a running play. At that instant, I heard Davis yelling, "Howie! Howie!"

As Starr faked the handoff, Green Bay receiver Boyd Dowler rushed past Williams, whose job was to stay with Dowler deep. But Williams went for the fake, and Davis knew it immediately. Dowler flew right past Williams, Starr zipped the ball to Dowler, and Dowler raced to the end zone to complete a 62-yard touchdown play. Just like that it was 13–0 . . . and Davis was banging his hands on the wall.

Starr took advantage of another third-and-one situation later in the game, hitting Max McGee with a 35-yard pass. By this time, though, all Davis could say was, "Aw, jeez!" or something like that. It wasn't a touchdown, but the play led to one.

The game concluded with an unusual sight: Kramer and his teammates picked up Lombardi and carried him off the field—unusual because Vince was not a "carriable" guy.

If the game wasn't an artistic success on the field, it had been a smashing commercial success. CBS televised it and enjoyed very strong ratings, somewhere in the high thirties. Along with favorable media comments, the television ratings reflected a budding phenomenon.

Across the country, people were paying attention to this game. Not only that, a great many of them were concluding that they wanted to be a part of it, too.

No wonder. The CBS cameras had captured a sellout crowd on a warm and absolutely gorgeous day, spectacular and colorful pageantry that included a U.S. Air Force flyover, a gala halftime show that featured a rousing performance by the Grambling University band, a crowning achievement by a legendary team, and perhaps the final moments of glory for its renowned coach.

Staging the game in Miami proved to be a great decision. For one thing, it was much closer to the country's major metropolitan centers than California, and media attention was much better than it had been for the first game. The sports writers relished coming to Miami in mid-January and flocked to the Orange Bowl in droves. Joining them were many members of the New York advertising community, plus assorted high rollers and celebrities. Like moths lured to a bright light, they sensed that this was an event they needed to be part of, adding to the glitter. It was just a whole different ball game than it had been the first year and left us with a certain comfort level of having done a much better job of accomplishing what Pete Rozelle envisioned.

Our postmortem turned up only one concern: the game itself. The Raiders brought a 13–1 regular-season record to Miami and were the class of the AFL. Yet, Oakland was no match for Green Bay, even though the Packers' team then was not considered as powerful as the one that had defeated Kansas City a year earlier.

The NFL's apparent superiority after two consecutive, convincing victories by Green Bay, in fact, left many of us wondering about the game's future. Next year that would change.

ELEVEN

JOE WILLIE AND THE JETS

Smitty was nervous. You knew that just by looking at him. In fact, as he sat next to me in our control booth in the Orange Bowl, awaiting the kickoff for Super Bowl III on that January 1969 Sunday afternoon, I had never seen him look so nervous. "Just a feeling is all," he said in an uncertain tone.

A premonition? Coming from almost anyone else, I would have dismissed it. Coming from Smitty, it was a notion to be reckoned with. More than three decades later, it remains a vivid memory of what might be the most significant football game ever played.

Don Smith was the longtime public relations director of the New York Giants and an astute football man. For the second straight year, he was serving as our press box public address announcer for what even the NFL finally was beginning to call the Super Bowl, albeit unofficially and somewhat grudgingly.

The source of Smitty's anxiety was Baltimore Colts quarterback Earl Morrall. Acquired by the Colts from the Giants the preceding August, Earl had been pressed into action when the legendary Johnny Unitas injured his shoulder early in the 1968 season. Morrall promptly spun a legend of his own. His 26 touchdown passes and 2,909 passing yards transformed a 12-year journeyman into the toast of pro football. He was the league's leading passer, its most valuable player, and a stellar performer on a 13–1 team that clearly was the league's most talented and powerful. Baltimore's only defeat had come in the sixth week of regular-season play, and the Colts had avenged that 30–20 loss to Cleveland with almost frightening precision when the teams collided again in the NFL championship game, punishing the Browns, 34–0.

Yet, as celebrated a season as Earl was enjoying, it couldn't erase Smitty's recollections of the three preceding seasons Morrall had spent with the Giants. His passing had been erratic, his performances often undistinguished. "When Earl has a bad day," Smitty would say, "he really has a bad day."

What Earl was about to have in Miami was his worst nightmare: just six completions for 71 yards and three first-half interceptions that squandered one scoring opportunity after another, all the while stoking the momentum and the confidence of the underdog New York Jets. Would the outcome have been altered and the NFL's supremacy and honor been preserved for at least one more year had Earl not suffered his dreadfully bad day? We can only imagine.

It's said that professional football came of age in the 1958 NFL championship game when the Baltimore Colts rallied for a dramatic overtime victory against a team from New York, the Giants. The Super Bowl came of age almost exactly a decade later when the Baltimore Colts suffered one of the most improbable defeats in sports, at the hands of another team from New York, the Jets. It is an ironic reversal of fortune that every Super Bowl aficionado should savor.

The notion is well known but no less correct. The Jets' astounding 16–7 victory on January 12, 1969, did more than any other event in the history of the Super Bowl to establish the game's credibility . . . or save it, even if NFL blue bloods didn't feel that way at the time. Had Baltimore won—as virtually everyone was predicting—the history of pro football's championship game very likely would have unfolded much differently. Questions, conversations, and speculation about its future had followed the Colts and Jets to Miami, and were becoming hard to ignore.

To be sure, the rapidly growing popularity of the game and its festivities was undeniable, as were the eye-popping television ratings it had generated in its first two years. People simply wanted to be part of it, while those who couldn't be there wanted to watch it on television. And as much as Pete Rozelle disliked the idea, the name "Super Bowl" was catching on, too, to the point that these very words graced the cover of the programs we printed for the third championship game.

The game's credibility was another matter entirely, however, leaving its long-term success in doubt. That NFL championship games were far more competitive than the Super Bowl game was equally undeniable, while the NFL's overall superiority over the AFL was difficult to dispute. Had the Colts defeated the Jets with anything approaching the ease with which the Packers had routed Kansas City and Oakland in the first two games, the Super Bowl's viability would have come under a dark cloud and prompted serious discussions about how much longer this apparent mismatch could continue beyond the 1970 expiration date of the original television contract with NBC and CBS. League realignment (about to be hotly debated by team owners) might well have unfolded much differently, too, had the Colts prevailed.

How the championship game might have been restructured is anyone's guess. Yet, such thoughts had to be lurking somewhere in Pete Rozelle's mind because Baltimore looked so invincible.

After compiling their 13–1 regular-season record, the Colts had disposed of postseason opponents Minnesota and Cleveland in workmanlike fashion as they rolled to the NFL title. To this day, Don Shula says that the Colts' 34–0 drubbing of the Browns in Cleveland Stadium might have been as good a game played by any team he ever coached—and the teams Shula coached included the undefeated Miami Dolphins in 1972. It was a thoroughly dominating performance on both sides of the football.

Oddsmakers made Baltimore a prohibitive, 18-point favorite over the AFL champion New York Jets. No Super Bowl team in history has ever been a more lopsided favorite, not even mighty Green Bay: the Packers were favored by 14 and 13½ points, respectively, in their first two games. In fact, the Colts' 18-point spread has been equaled only once, in 1995, when San Francisco, led by Steve Young, met San Diego in Super Bowl XXIX, also played in Miami (the 49ers justified the odds, winning 49–26).

No less an authority than Vince Lombardi dismissed the Jets' chances as "infinitesimal." Of the 55 pro football writers polled the day before the game, 49 concurred with Lombardi and predicted final scores that ranged as high as 27–0, 38–0, and 47–0. *Sports Illustrated*'s Tex Maule saw the Colts winning 43–0. Three- and four-touchdown margins of victory were commonplace, and all but five of the writers expected Baltimore's winning margin to be in double digits.

The Colts themselves were so confident that owner Carroll Rosenbloom threw what looked for all the world like a victory party for his coaching staff eight days before the game was played. The Colts arrived triumphantly in southern Florida unduly early, during the preceding weekend. Whether Shula wanted to practice longer in better weather or simply wanted to reward his players for a great season isn't clear. In any event, the arrival inspired Rosenbloom to express his appreciation for his coaches' hard work by hosting an informal get-together around the large swimming pool at his lovely home on Golden Beach. An exclusive enclave of no more than a half dozen breathtaking, oceanfront homes, Golden Beach lies just north of Hollywood, Florida, 45 minutes north of Miami. It was off Golden Beach, in fact, where Rosenbloom was swimming when he drowned (somewhat mysteriously) just over a decade later. Knowing that we had been in town for nearly a week ourselves, Carroll also invited Jim Kensil and me to join the party.

It was meant to be only a prelude. The *real* party—the mother of all victory parties—was being planned for the following weekend, after the Colts had been crowned pro football's new champions. That was to be the elaborate celebration. And when I say elaborate, I mean *elaborate*. Rosenbloom was sparing no expense and already had lined up celebrated headliners to entertain his guest list of about 200 that included members of the Kennedy family and Maryland governor Spiro Agnew, then the vice president elect. A prelude though it may have been, the Saturday evening affair still was in keeping with the tremendous year the Colts had enjoyed and a gala occasion in its own right. Carroll was there in all his glory, of course, while Shula and his assistant coaches, equally full of confidence, were really unwinding and having a great time. It set the tone in the Colts' camp for the entire week.

It also reflected the ebullient mood and grand expectations of Carroll Rosenbloom himself. Always the flamboyant NFL owner, Carroll was the classic New York capitalist, with a great presence in Manhattan. Carroll also was the classic entrepreneur. He had earned his fortune buying and selling businesses and brokering numerous big deals. In addition to his home in Florida, he had a regal apartment on Central Park South and enjoyed a close relationship with the Kennedy family, among others. His club memberships included golf privileges at Deepdale, one of Long Island's most exclusive private courses, where he would periodically entertain some of us from the league office while his wife, Georgia, would entertain the ladies in the clubhouse. Rosenbloom's ties extended to Hollywood, California, where he served on the board of Warner Brothers.

His only real relationship with Baltimore, in fact, was as owner of the Colts. He had purchased the franchise when it lay moribund in Dallas in 1953, almost as a favor to his old friend Bert Bell, and then basked in the glow of the team's successes during the ensuing 15 years. During the regular season, it was his custom to assemble large and influential groups of friends at La Guardia or Kennedy airport and fly them to Baltimore and back for the Colts' games. On occasion, I joined them because it afforded me the chance to attend an NFL game outside of New York, get firsthand interviews, and still get back to my office in time to write and send out postgame press releases throughout the night.

Rosenbloom's team had won back-to-back NFL championships in the late 1950s, including the milestone 1958 title game in Yankee Stadium. Still, the Super Bowl in Miami was to be his crowning moment. Rosenbloom envisioned a new football dynasty, and who could blame him? Green Bay's decline had been swift and precipitous, following Vince Lombardi's retirement, and Baltimore loomed as the logical heir apparent. Guided by Shula, the most promising young head coach in all of pro football, a perennially strong team that had been a legitimate NFL contender for a decade now looked practically unbeatable. Its offense was potent and balanced, its defense ferocious, the blue horseshoes on its white helmets known nationwide. The luster of the Unitas name still glowed and struck fear in the hearts of pass defenders everywhere. The names of the quarterback's supporting cast might be changing, but the outcome on the field remained impressive and consistent. Truly, this was a team whose future was still ahead of it, whose owner was convinced that the Super Bowl trophy was destined to be in his grasp. That Don Shula was preparing the Colts for the very last time was beyond anyone's comprehension.

Rosenbloom was so ebullient, in fact, that we heard he had invited the Jets' head coach, Weeb Ewbank, to the postgame festivities he was planning at Golden Beach, for old-time's sake: Weeb had directed the Colts to their championships before taking over the Jets in 1963. He graciously declined, saying he hoped to be attending a victory party of his own. In the meantime, Weeb had a ruckus to react to: the "guarantee" heard 'round the world.

Joe Namath would have made headlines in Miami had he simply whispered, "We're going to win," on his way out the door. After all, he was Joe Namath, and he could whet the journalistic appetites of the ravenous New York media without saying a word. But Joe said quite a bit during that Thursday evening banquet at the Miami Springs Villas. And he wasn't whispering. Speaking at a long-established "quarterback club" sports function that had attracted as many reporters as local football fans, Joe's declaration was as forceful and crisp as it was dramatic:

"I *guarantee* you we're gonna win!" he asserted with typical Namath bravado. "I guarantee it!"

The words came like a bolt out of the blue. Those assembled heard more pearls of wisdom during that evening, including Broadway Joe's claim that the Jets were "the better team." Yet, even if Namath had zipped his lip the instant after he issued it, his now legendary guarantee still would have been splashed across the top of sports pages all over the country, in 72-point bold type, usually reserved for stunning elections, political scandals, and grisly murders.

They were the words that every coach dreads. Positively the last thing Weeb Ewbank wanted to hear coming out of the mouth of his quarterback were those boastful and challenging words. He was astonished. Always cooperative, but always conservative and never boastful, Weeb was sufficiently challenged by just preparing his team for its first playoff appearance without his mouthy, cocky quarterback firing up the powerful Colts even more. But as much as the low-key Weeb wanted Joe to keep his mouth shut, all he could do was shake his head in frustration and move on.

Outwardly, the Colts reacted in predictable fashion. Placekicker Lou Michaels was Baltimore's most visibly upset player. A rough-and-tumble guy to begin with, Lou took particular exception to Namath's comments, and because he, too, liked to move around a bit in the evening, stories circulated that Michaels and Namath ran into each other in a Miami watering hole and got into a heated argument. How close they really came to exchanging blows is a matter of opinion . . . and perhaps imagination.

Other instances of confrontations between players flared up late in the week approaching the game. Or so we were told. In general, Colts' players dismissed the Jets as reckless and boastful. "Just who is this brash young guy, anyway?" they were heard to ask. Responses sprinkled with "that Mickey Mouse league" were commonplace. Today, we'd simply label it trash talking.

In truth, Joe may have been more calculating than he's been given credit for over the years. As much as anything, I think his guarantee really shook up the Colts, while it strengthened the Jets' resolve. Moreover, the guarantee was not nearly as ludicrous as the reactions implied.

About to complete his fourth season with the Jets, Namath had the talent to back up his boasts. He had more than earned the accolades that fanned his fame, along with the full confidence of his teammates. Joe led the Jets to an 11–3 regular-season record in 1968, then delivered a memorable and clutch performance in the AFL championship game. People who saw it still marvel at the frozen-rope passes he threw across the field in the 27–23 upset of Oakland. He didn't complete that many of his throws on that cold, raw day in New York's Shea Stadium, just 19 of 46, including an interception. But Joe also threw for 266 yards and three touchdown passes in swirling winds that made passing difficult in itself. Namath's final touchdown toss was the second of two to Don Maynard and culminated a fourth-quarter drive that capped the dramatic come-from-behind victory over the Raiders, the defending AFL champions, whose 12–2 record was the best in their league.

Just as important as Namath's heroics, however, was the quarter-back's supporting cast. Always toiling in Joe's shadow, they had quietly grown into a quality unit by the 1968 season and were interesting in their own right. I had seen that for myself and gained plenty of respect for the Jets—and other AFL teams—because I was making it a point to watch them play, to become more familiar with our new pro football partners. Matt Snell and Emerson Boozer were capable running backs, while Maynard and George Sauer were equally capable receivers, blessed with great hands. Maynard was a long-stride guy and Sauer, a wonderful possession receiver. The offensive line, anchored by guard Dave Herman and tackle Winston Hill, was absolutely first rate, too. And, in Ewbank, the Jets had as solid a head coach as you could find.

Still, it was Namath who remained far and away the celebrity in Miami. He must have been media savvy from the day he was born, one reason why Jets owner Sonny Werblin spent $427,000 to sign him in 1965. Even without his guarantee that the Jets would win, Joe was wonderful copy, anything but aloof and always available for interviews, notwithstanding the many demands on his time. Ironically, at some point during that week, Joe incurred a fine after failing to show up for a media session. It was a pretty good sum for that era, too, around $500. Just why he was AWOL has been long forgotten. For all I know, he simply wasn't able to escape from all his fans at the pool.

When the Jets weren't working out, that's where you usually could find Joe, lounging around the pool of the Galt Ocean Mile, the team's headquarters hotel in Ft. Lauderdale. It was as if he were holding court there, with large throngs of people hanging on his every word. It was like that whenever we stopped at the hotel. You didn't have to ask where Namath was. Find the crowd and you'd find Joe. He was a sports writer's dream, always saying what the writers wanted him to say.

Joe was our dream, too. We loved every syllable, even if our NFL roots caused us to think he was a little misled. We couldn't have promoted the game better had we written our own script.

Literally overnight, Namath's guarantee of a Jets victory turned a colossal mismatch into a must-see event and twisted Baltimore's 18-point spread into a promotional advantage: A championship game that had been winning public acceptance ever so grudgingly was now a legitimate contest, pitting the AFL's green-and-white clad David against the NFL's blue-and-white clad Goliath. It was a theme Pete Rozelle embellished to the fullest when he opened what was becoming the Commissioner's annual "state of the NFL" press conference on the Friday morning preceding the game. Namath's guarantee even rekindled the strong feelings that still separated AFL owners from NFL owners, further fueling the momentum.

The game site was another plus. Returning to Miami never received much debate, given our success there the year before, although New Orleans again received some consideration before Miami was confirmed in the spring. The site worked, that's all, so why change? Southern Florida was a perennial venue of choice among many NFL owners. So much so, in fact, that some sentiment was building to make Miami the game's permanent home. Even today, a few owners—the Cardinals' Bill Bidwill, for instance—would just as soon play the game there every year.

Returning to the Orange Bowl proved especially fortuitous. Almost by definition, any New York team playing a postseason pro football game in Florida generates a healthy demand for tickets. Even so, the late surge in demand for tickets generated by the Jets' presence was startling, except there weren't many tickets to be had.

The auto companies, airlines, hotels, and other clients we had wooed to Miami the preceding year were more than eager to come back. Predictably, interest among the television networks and advertising community soared. The 55,000 tickets we sold to the general public, beginning in early September (priced once again at $12, $8, and $6) were gone by late October. The tickets allocated to Jets and Colts fans weren't nearly enough and prompted the need to conduct lotteries in order to ensure an equitable distribution. In barely 12 months, we had gone from asking, "How many tickets do you want?" to having to say as nicely as we could, "Here's how many tickets you can have."

The festivities we planned in the Orange Bowl were in keeping with the buildup that the game was getting, thanks in part to Rozelle's public relations wizardry. The national heroes of the day were the three Apollo 8 astronauts, who a few weeks earlier had piloted their spacecraft on the historic flight in orbit around the moon. As soon as he learned of their interest in the game, Pete issued them invitations. But we didn't stop there. We arranged for Frank Borman, James Lovell, and William Anders to lead the crowd in the Pledge of Allegiance, as part of the pregame ceremonies, after having them introduced by no less a celebrity than Bob Hope. In addition, we invited Borman's two sons to serve as ball boys during the game.

Earnie Seiler had arranged another rousing halftime show, titled "America Thanks" and featuring the Florida A&M marching band, among the very best college bands in the land. And adorning the 50-yard line of the Orange Bowl gridiron itself was a full-color rendition of the Tiffany championship trophy. Mix in the glamour of Miami Beach, its dazzling hotels and restaurants, plus our year-old organizational skills that we continued to fine-tune, and pro football was now blessed with a season finale that was worthy of what television broadcasters and everyone else were calling it: the "Super Bowl."

Much to Pete Rozelle's everlasting regret. "We're pretty well stuck with it," he acknowledged at his Friday press conference. From the moment "Super Bowl" drifted into his ears, Pete disliked the term and spent a good deal of energy resisting it while he searched in vain for something better. Never mind that "Super Bowl" had been weaving its way into the sports lexicon for three years, thanks mainly to television. It may have been the only facet of the NFL's rich relationship with broadcasting that Pete ever found objectionable.

Always meticulous when he spoke, Rozelle specifically disliked "Super." He thought it was a slang word, and he had no use for slang words. For instance, he never cared for the phrase "Is that right?" Anyone who uttered it would hear him reply, "I don't know whether it's *right* or not, but it's *correct*!"—a rejoinder that Bill Granholm learned to ape with aplomb, when he was out of Pete's earshot, that is.

"Super Bowl" was grossly incorrect to Rozelle. So, while those words graced the cover of the game program in Miami, the official title remained the "AFL-NFL World Championship of Professional Football." We would have liked to have used "Pro Bowl." But, of course, we already had one.

Pete's resistance was so enduring that he had us run a contest among writers in mid-1969 to find a better name. The prize was an all-expenses-paid trip to Honolulu for the 1970 NFL annual meetings, where we planned to announce the winning entry as the game's official title, with an appropriately grand flourish. Writers submitted numerous suggestions, but all of them were decidedly unremarkable. "Ultimate Bowl" and "Premier Bowl" were about the best of the lot. So, "Super Bowl"—the name first offered by Lamar Hunt after seeing his children frolic with a "super ball"—endured. It's been apt, too, for it's given both the championship game and pro football a pretty incredible bounce, just like Super Bowl III itself.

Of the 36 world championship games I've experienced to date, Super Bowl III is without a doubt the one I watched most intently. What took place in the Orange Bowl on that January afternoon was nothing short of bizarre. Right from the opening kickoff, it was a football game wrapped within a "this can't be happening" aura, and it captivated fans wherever they were watching. Sitting in the control booth, Don Smith and I were dumbfounded. We couldn't believe what we were seeing.

The Colts moved the ball fairly well at first and dominated the first quarter. They were inside New York's 20-yard line on three or four occasions but squandered one opportunity after another and had nothing to show for their efforts. Lou Michaels, Baltimore's standard-style, left-footed field goal kicker, who had gone toe-to-toe with Joe Namath, missed a chip-shot field goal, blunt shoe and all. Tom Matte ripped off a big run of 45 to 50 yards to set up another scoring opportunity, only to have Morrall throw an interception near the goal line. Baltimore seemed on the verge of seizing control of the game on several occasions but let it slip away every time.

No sequence better reflected the course of Super Bowl III than the unforgettable second-quarter flea-flicker pass play. Captured for the ages by NFL Films, it is one of the most famous clips in pro football history and showed the fateful play from several angles, in full motion and slow motion. Fans who have seen it a hundred times still scratch their heads.

The flea-flicker pass had become a staple in Earl Morrall's repertoire and was one that the quarterback had relied on in New York before joining the Colts. Smitty recognized it the instant Colts center Bill Curry snapped the football: Morrall handed off to a Colts running back, who then flipped the ball back to Morrall as the Jets' defense was drawn in. Meanwhile, Jimmy Orr, Baltimore's fleet bantam-sized receiver, streaked down the sideline without a soul around him. The play worked to perfection and was even reminiscent of the Green Bay touchdown pass that had incensed Oakland's Al Davis a year earlier. Orr not only had run free down the sideline, but he also was all alone in the end zone, practically doing jumping jacks and frantically waving his arms.

Sitting next to me in the control booth, Smitty began saying, "Orr! Orr! *Orr!*" In fact, I had to check to make sure his press box microphone was turned off. It was, but it wouldn't have mattered because practically every NFL supporter in the press box—if not the whole stadium—had to be muttering what Smitty was muttering, by now in impatient tones. Orr could have run to Key West with the football if only Earl Morrall had thrown it to him. But Morrall didn't see Orr. Instead, he tried to hit another receiver in the middle of the field. The ball hung in the air, and the Jets picked it off with eaglelike precision. It might have been the play that broke Baltimore's back.

What had been a frustrating afternoon for anyone with NFL loyalties was growing more ominous by the moment. Smitty and I had seen enough football to sense that the scoring chances the Colts had squandered would come back to haunt them. Joe Namath's guarantee and Smitty's worst fears were now unfolding before our very eyes. Neutrality flew out the window. Emotions honed by years of wielding our public relations skills to make the AFL look as bad as we possibly could consumed us. For this day, we were NFL fans. We didn't give a hoot about what a Jets victory might mean to the Super Bowl, to NBC's television future, to pro football's future . . . to anybody's future. What we were watching was an outrage!

That the Jets' first-half offense hadn't been especially productive was of little consolation. New York still took a 7–0 lead into the half, on the strength of a Matt Snell four-yard run at the six-minute mark of the second quarter. And it was enough to give the AFL champions an unbeatable head of steam in the second half. There would be no regrouping by Baltimore, no stirring second-half comeback, no launching of a new dynasty.

Namath still gets the credit for the historic victory and was named the game's most valuable player. But his teammates really won the game. It was a wonderfully mixed attack. Snell was as big a factor as anybody and finished with 121 yards running. He and Emerson Boozer just kept moving the ball on the ground, while Namath picked apart Baltimore's secondary with timely, clutch, pinpoint passes, eight to George Sauer alone. Jim Turner's three second-half field goals gave New York a comfortable margin of victory. For the most part, the Jets did exactly what they needed to do to beat the heavily favored Colts, holding the ball for a full 36 minutes. When Baltimore did have the ball, New York created clutch turnovers, grabbing four interceptions and recovering one fumble.

But it was along the line of scrimmage that the AFL upstarts were at their best. While the Jets' offensive line was smaller, it was quick and effective. Guard Dave Herman just *manhandled* Bubba Smith. The defense was equally sturdy, unforgiving and far better than it was given credit for. John Elliott, Verlon Biggs, and Paul Rochester anchored the line, while Randy Beverly picked off two passes, and

Jim Hudson and Johnny Sample—a vindictive, talkative ex-Colt—picked off one each. The Jets just weren't going to lose.

They marched to a 16–0 lead before Baltimore scored. Shula went to Unitas, who took the team to its only touchdown midway through the third quarter. The solid 80-yard drive enticed a few NFL fans to fancy the Colts rebounding and coming back to win. But while the Colts periodically strung together a few first downs, they were never in the game. Unitas, too, threw an interception that killed one last-gasp scoring drive. Whether they truly believed their prediction, the six writers who had picked the Jets' upset were vindicated: *Newsday*'s Stan Isaacs, Wells Twombly of the *Detroit Free Press*, Furman Bisher of the *Atlanta Constitution*, Murray Janoff of the *Long Island Press*, Jim Peters of the *Buffalo Courier-Express*, and Bob Halloran of WTVJ-TV in Miami.

Having seen the AFL in action, I had known its best teams were far better than many fans believed. And yet, I had a hard time believing that New York could do what it was doing to the mighty Colts. For NFL traditionalists, it was a black day indeed.

In the hectic aftermath, I made the mistake of saying so to NBC sports executives Chet Simmons and Carl Lindemann, who, of course, were as ecstatic as anyone in the AFL. I can't imagine Chet ever enjoying a greater day. He was 10 feet off the ground, absolutely floating on cloud nine. I brought him back to earth just long enough to incur his wrath. After hearing Chet describe—correctly—New York's victory as being the greatest moment in the history of pro football, I muttered what I was really thinking. Simmons—a really nice man—snarled something in reply, turned on his heels, and walked away in disgust. He was really upset. I can't recall exactly what I said, although the word *fiasco* may have tumbled off my tongue.

It had been that kind of day. Before the game had started, I noticed Spiro Agnew sitting on the Colts' bench, in violation of league policy. It was left to me to instruct the vice president elect of the United States of America to leave the field.

But nothing any of us felt could begin to match what Carroll Rosenbloom was suffering. Watching his vaunted team lose was crushing enough. Watching his vaunted team lose while sitting in the press box surrounded by writers was unimaginable agony. And that's where the Colts' owner sat.

It wasn't unusual at all. While these days we're more accustomed to seeing NFL owners surround themselves with close friends and colleagues in private suites, several of them over the years preferred to watch their teams from the press box. So, in addition to making an owner's box available, we routinely made two seats available to them in the Super Bowl press box. Carroll was acting on that courtesy. Presuming a victory, perhaps he wanted to be in position to accept congratulations. He surely wasn't prepared to accept what he saw.

Rosenbloom was a picture of complete and utter devastation. Once the game started, I don't recall his having much to say at all. And certainly no one was about to say anything to him. By the end of the game, Carroll was totally drained of color and just sat there in silence with his head in his hands.

The mother of all parties at Golden Beach was hastily canceled. It's been reported that Ted Kennedy went back to Golden Beach anyway and already was lounging in the hot tub when Rosenbloom finally returned. But Carroll didn't want to see Ted, nor anyone else, and told his wife, Georgia, to either extend his regrets or make up an excuse for his absence. He was a broken and bitter man.

More bitterness was to come, too. The impact of the stunning loss was far-reaching and altered the course of pro football history significantly beyond the Super Bowl.

Surely aware that Rosenbloom's relationship with Don Shula had soured, at least for the time being, Miami Dolphins owner Joe Robbie called Baltimore a few months later, seeking permission to speak with Shula about coaching the Dolphins. Rosenbloom was out of the country at the time, so Robbie talked with Rosenbloom's son Steve, who did not dissuade the Miami owner from talking to Shula and subsequently hiring him. The elder Rosenbloom thus returned home to find himself lacking both an NFL dynasty and a head coach.

What Rosenbloom would have told Robbie had he been available remains open to conjecture because he still brooded about the defeat, and Shula's contract was due to expire. Rosenbloom himself insisted that he would have denied the request and angrily accused Robbie of tampering. The nasty dispute ultimately cost the Dolphins a number one draft choice—well worth it, given Shula's success and Super Bowl years in Miami. It also prompted the league to rewrite its tampering rules with more precise language.

The Jets, of course, were as deliriously happy as the Colts were devastated. And even NFL loyalists had to extend best wishes to Weeb Ewbank, whose improbable victory represented another pro football milestone, the first coach to win a world championship in both the NFL and AFL.

The one irony amid the jubilant celebration was that the owner who was responsible for a good part of the victory was no longer on the scene. Before the 1968 season began, Sonny Werblin had sold the team, which his millions had built, to a new ownership group headed by Phil Iselin and Leon Hess. They accepted the trophy from Pete Rozelle with grace and offered the appropriate comments. Yet, like almost every act of distinction made in the Jets' behalf that year, the owners' speeches readily disappeared quietly into the shadows cast by the team's celestial quarterback.

The classic and enduring personification of pro football's new world champions remains Broadway Joe Namath jogging triumphantly off the field, surrounded by teammates and fans. As Joe makes his way to the joyous locker room, he is extending his golden right arm, raising his index finger, and gesturing unmistakably, "We're number one." Then again, he had guaranteed it, hadn't he?

A year later, another underdog would prove it wasn't a fluke.

TWELVE

MURPHY'S LAW AND
STRAM'S CHIEFS

It's a wonder Super Bowl IV was ever played. Dilemmas and assorted crises are part and parcel of any championship sports event. Yet, what plagued the Super Bowl the first time we brought it to New Orleans almost defies imagination. It got to the point where we could have been excused for looking to the heavens to see if we had wandered under the same black cloud that haunts forlorn Joe Btfsplk in the "Li'l Abner" comic strip. Whenever any of us looked skyward, our eyeballs were likely to be pelted by cold drops of incessant rain.

As wretched as the weather was, though, it turned out to be the least of our problems. For starters, there was Tulane Stadium itself. The first time I laid eyes on it I almost cried. The only time it looked good was when it was filled with 80,000 fans. It was a complete dump!

There was also a severe hotel shortage. The top floors of the hotel that was to be our headquarters—the Roosevelt—caught fire during my visit there the preceding August. While I lost personal belongings, what the NFL lost was worse: 200 or more hotel rooms at a time when the city didn't have enough hotel rooms to begin with.

Then, five days before the game, quarterback Len Dawson of the AFL-champion Kansas City Chiefs was linked to a federal investigation of organized gambling. Dawson was exonerated, but the distraction was enormous. Especially in 1970, when only a week separated the Super Bowl from the two league championship games.

There was more. Transportation troubles erupted on game day. The pregame festivities were a near disaster, a situation aggravated by the wretched weather. And in the midst of trying to recover from the fiasco, the public address announcer blithely told the crowd of 80,000 that a tornado warning had been issued because a twister had been spotted not far from the stadium.

Yes, the NFL was officially welcoming fans to the "Fourth Annual Super Bowl," but "Stupor Bowl" would have been more apropos. There may be no better testament to Murphy's Law.

If all that weren't enough, the world championship game we were presenting looked like another mismatch: the all-powerful NFL Minnesota Vikings and their ferocious "Purple People-Eaters" defense were 12-point favorites over the AFL Kansas City Chiefs. Not as heavily favored as Baltimore had been the year before, but lopsided enough.

The game turned out to be a mismatch, all right. But not the one everyone anticipated. Nor could we anticipate a stunning postscript that was delivered the morning after.

Super Bowl IV has never enjoyed the acclaim or significance of Super Bowl III, perhaps because it lacked Joe Namath or a New York team. It's a pity.

As sports historians contend, the fourth championship game was as pivotal as the Jets' victory in Miami had been. It attracted a record crowd of 80,562, generated record receipts of almost $3.82 million, and produced what may have been an even more dramatic upset: The decidedly underdog AFL champions from Kansas City handed the Vikings a thorough 23–7 whipping. Never seriously threatened, the Chiefs marched to a 16–0 halftime lead and never looked back. The Chiefs, in fact, had more trouble defeating the Oakland Raiders in the AFL championship game one week earlier, winning 17–7 on the West Coast.

The irony was that Kansas City wouldn't even have qualified for postseason play had it not been for a one-season change in the AFL playoff format. Because the NFL's four-division structure created an extra week of divisional playoff games to sell to CBS television at the end of the 1969 season, we prodded the AFL to expand its playoff format to provide NBC with a similar opportunity. As a result, the Chiefs, who had finished second in the AFL West behind Oakland, won a spot in that league's title game by beating East Division champion New York, while Oakland beat Houston, the second-place team in the AFL East.

It had been quite a show of strength by virtually the same Chiefs team that Green Bay had humbled in 1967. But this time even NFL blue bloods applauded with enthusiasm, for we all realized we were in the midst of something exciting.

Kansas City's convincing victory did more than ratify the Jets' victory and the quality of AFL football. It gave credence to the new structure of pro football and single-league play that were coming in September. Four Super Bowls had been played, and each league had won twice. Having won the last two games gave the American Football League a fitting finale to its farewell season; a month later it dissolved as its 10 teams joined the NFL. Fans' tongues were wagging. Interest among the television networks was soaring, especially at ABC: Its daring, roll-the-dice decision to present 13 weeks of NFL football on Monday nights suddenly looked like a masterstroke. We couldn't have had it any better if we had written a script.

Nine months earlier I thought we were on the verge of writing a horror story. No one had given much thought to the condition of Tulane Stadium when the leagues' owners awarded the fourth Super Bowl to New Orleans at their 1969 annual meeting in March in Palm Springs (the same gathering, incidentally, that triggered the endless realignment debate). Even if we had voiced a concern, the city's vast delegation, led by gregarious *New Orleans Times-Picayune* publisher George Healy, would have overwhelmed it with its unbridled enthusiasm and hospitality. Everybody who was anybody in New Orleans, including legendary trumpeter Al Hirt, attended the meeting. That's how determined the city was to wrest the Super Bowl away from Miami and Los Angeles, both eager to host another game.

It was really the first time cities had made serious pitches to the NFL, whose Joint Committee still shouldered the majority of the negotiating and selection. It's one more reason why the fourth world championship game is significant. The cities' presentations mandated our initiating a new procedure to select Super Bowl host sites. Within a few years, we were awarding two games at a time and ultimately three or four.

New Orleans set quite a standard for hoopla in its first bid for the Super Bowl. Its jovial boosters held court practically from dusk to dawn in a designated press cottage on the hotel grounds. It was a real sideshow. Nothing was wrong with Miami, of course, but New Orleans convinced the league to give the Big Easy a try. The city's Tulane Stadium was already the home of the NFL Saints and the Sugar Bowl, and its 80,000 seats were appealing. So, what could go wrong?

Plenty, as I was about to find out. Once the 1969 NFL meetings adjourned, I went directly to New Orleans, where I spent about a week working on hotel arrangements and assorted details. My first look at empty Tulane Stadium was unforgettable and astonishing. Once the urge to cry subsided, I was inclined to ask, "Where do you go to plug it in?"

In gaping at this cavernous, ugly, rusty bowl and its sea of 80,000 bleacher seats, I wondered why it hadn't collapsed under the force of Saints fans stomping their feet on the metal floor of the stands, then a favorite activity of those boisterous throngs.

Tulane Stadium was built from the remains of U.S. Navy warships decommissioned after World War I (yes, *one*). They might have been better off scrapping the boats. The place creaked of old age. Everything was rusted, to the point that I wondered if even a single coat of paint had ever been applied.

Nothing had changed in many, many years. The only access to the stands was via ramps. The stadium's lone elevator went only to the press box and broke down often. Next to the old football press box in Chicago's Wrigley Field, Tulane had the worst facility in the league, with an upper level that was just plain junky; it leaked, to boot. The concessions and rest room facilities were equally miserable. The locker rooms were unsuitable for a professional football team and required us to erect a new building outside the stadium, like the locker room that had been built for the Saints' first year in 1967. We also had to erect a tent for staging postgame interviews, since the only usable room underneath the stands was a Tulane University weight room. Access ways between the stands, used to get teams on and off the field, were really too narrow. And wherever you looked, it was dingy, dirty, and rusty.

The grass field was very soft and surrounded by hedges that adorned many college stadiums in the South. By the end of the year, the field usually was in bad shape and almost devoid of grass at mid-field because Tulane still played and practiced there, along with the Saints. The stadium tarp was as inadequate as the rest of the place. Punctured and held together by tape, it leaked, too. Parking was minimal because the stadium was surrounded by both the university and the beautiful residential neighborhoods of New Orleans's fashionable Garden District. Getting to the stadium via one of the famed St. Charles Avenue streetcars was a pleasant alternative but not terribly practical for 80,000 people headed to a Super Bowl.

Stadium lighting would prove to be most challenging of all. With CBS planning to televise the game in color, candlepower had to be bolstered substantially a few days beforehand to bring lighting up to network standards. To supplement the power system, CBS ran all sorts of cables along the floor of the press box photo deck, a late development that NFL broadcast coordinator Bob Cochran neglected to tell me about. The instant I saw them, I knew we had to cover the wires with plywood, for safety's sake: If we didn't, they would be at the feet of scores of photographers and might also interfere with camera mounts. But in laying the plywood, we raised the floor of the photo deck so much that you couldn't walk erect without crashing into bare lightbulb fixtures in the ceiling.

I discovered that firsthand during my walk-through the day before the game, when I checked all the press box positions. With me was

George Mandich, an FBI agent from Chicago who worked for us during the game. I was familiar with the situation and knew when to duck. But George didn't, and as he made notes while we walked along on our inspection, I periodically heard a "plunk"—the sound of George smacking his head into a lightbulb.

With credentials distributed and press box positions long since mapped out, about all we could do was issue a warning—along with the other one we needed to issue: The small, welded metal loops that you'd see on the edges of the main decks of navy battleships were still part of the floor of the press box! Nobody had bothered to cut them off before shipping the scrap steel to the stadium site. Tripping over them—quite likely—could cause serious injury.

Other than its 80,000 seats, in fact, Tulane Stadium was totally inadequate and helped form my lasting impression of our first Super Bowl in New Orleans: walking in the rain, wet feet, mud . . . and rust. But there wasn't time for grumbling. No sooner had we unpacked our bags than we were confronting a full-blown crisis.

The story broke on the Tuesday before the game and was first reported by Chet Huntley on NBC's evening news broadcast: Kansas City's Len Dawson was being linked to Donald "Dice" Dawson—no relation, just a well-known gambler type from Detroit who had been under surveillance by the FBI and was now the subject of a full-blown investigation. The turmoil that Huntley's report unleashed dominated the entire week. It was a terrible distraction and much ado about nothing, as it turned out.

After both the NFL and FBI conducted extensive interviews over a two- to three-day period, it was clear that Len Dawson was innocent. He acknowledged knowing the gambler slightly and having spoken briefly with him on occasion during the past few years. But none of the conversations were remotely connected with gambling. In fact, we were more than a little chagrined that NBC had broken the story with as little basis in fact as it had and later expressed our feelings to the network. NBC merely had subpoenaed and examined phone records, and Len Dawson's name had come up. But so had the names of other players. With the Super Bowl approaching, however, the focus was on the Chiefs' quarterback. Essentially, NBC said that Len

Dawson was under investigation by the FBI in light of some suspicious phone contacts with Detroit figures. The furor the report triggered took us completely out of our routine.

Compounding our dilemma was the fact that Pete Rozelle had taken a short break after the NFL championship game and was on his boat in the Caribbean near Bimini when the story broke. Pete loved to fish, and whenever he got the chance he'd shove off in his boat. So, before we could fully react, we needed about 24 hours to get Rozelle into New Orleans.

In his absence, Jim Kensil initially led our investigation. But I was involved, too, along with our security director, Bill Hundley, whom Rozelle had hired a few years earlier. Pete felt that the game's integrity was so important that he created a full-time security department reporting directly to the Commissioner and usually manned by those with FBI experience of some kind. They kept pretty close tabs on the odds of NFL games, to see if any unusual fluctuations were developing. They also had assembled a security network incorporating franchise cities, Las Vegas, and other relevant points. So, at least we were prepared to react.

The Chiefs already were in town, of course, so we first talked with them, especially with Len Dawson himself and head coach Hank Stram. Naturally, federal authorities needed to question Dawson, too, and did so extensively behind the scenes. But with 1,200-odd writers in town for the game, arranging those conversations was extremely difficult, and all the writers were intent on talking to Dawson about the gambling story, too. It was one of the few times when we regretted the media's massive presence. Under the circumstances, we felt strongly that Len shouldn't say a word. Other than issuing a brief statement, he didn't.

Toward the end of the week, we became convinced of Dawson's innocence and concluded that we had no reason to keep him out of the Super Bowl game. Rozelle held a press conference, hastily formed in the registration area of the hospitality room of the Roosevelt Hotel, our New Orleans headquarters. We didn't have time to get a ballroom and set up a podium, or anything like that. Pete just walked into the room, stood amid a semicircle of desks, and started speaking. He exonerated Dawson and cleared him to play. Pete was joined by FBI representatives, who also stated that the allegations first reported by NBC were without any foundation.

But while the press conference settled one issue, it provoked another. For some unknown reason, two veteran football writers, Pat Livingston, of the *Pittsburgh Post-Gazette*, and Mo Siegel, of the *Washington Star*, began pushing and shoving each other after exchanging some harsh words. In addition, Will Grimsley of the Associated Press, a former colleague of mine and a real bulldog of a reporter in an era when aggressive sports writers were rare, raised a second ruckus trying to get to a telephone to call in his story. We had embargoed the phones in the hospitality room until the press conference ended, fearing chaos would erupt if we didn't. Chaos almost erupted anyway. Will's attitude and anger reflected the contentious, circuslike atmosphere prevalent in a hospitality room that at the moment wasn't hospitable at all.

Perhaps it was only fitting that the zany week preceding Super Bowl IV also marked my personal introduction to a James Snyder, officially a sports columnist for a Las Vegas newspaper. He was born Demetrios Synodinos. He was more commonly known as Jimmy the Greek, *the* sports oddsmaker in Vegas. Jimmy had matter-of-factly applied for and received credentials under the name of James Snyder. But under the circumstances, we felt it was inappropriate for him to be in the pressroom, as Jim Kensil and I quietly explained when we introduced ourselves to him. Cordial and polite, Jimmy departed willingly, saying he understood completely. He didn't exit New Orleans, though, and was more often an interviewee than an interviewer, making us feel like we still had egg on our face.

By then we had grown accustomed to operating in crisis mode in New Orleans. We had lots of practice, beginning the preceding August, when on a steamy, rainy night our most harrowing episode of all ignited—literally.

Bill "Granny" Granholm and I had planned to spend 10 days or so in New Orleans reviewing details and finalizing arrangements. With the Roosevelt Hotel already designated as our headquarters hotel for the game, we made it our headquarters for this trip, too, and shared a two-bedroom suite on one of the hotel's upper floors. I brought along a healthy pile of documents, figuring our lengthy stay would give me ample spare time to process credentials requests and routine paperwork.

Our visit happened to coincide with the premier of *QB 1*, a football movie starring Charlton Heston and featuring some New Orleans Saints players in cameo appearances. Knowing Granny and I were in town, Saints owner John Mecom Jr. invited us to attend the premier showing at a downtown theater around the corner on Canal Street. Heston, who played the Saints' quarterback in the movie, was on hand, along with the customary spotlights, crowds of people, and all the excitement you'd expect.

The real excitement came later, though. It had been a typical August day in New Orleans: humid and very hot. It was raining as Granny and I came out of the theater, accompanied by *New Orleans Times-Picayune* sports columnist Bob Roesler and his wife, Chloe. Our casual pace suddenly turned to a frantic gallop when we looked up and saw the top floor of the Roosevelt Hotel—our hotel—on fire! Fire engines were all over the place and the hotel lobby was in total chaos.

Granny and I had two things on our minds: our clothing and our files, which represented 98 percent of all the documents pertaining to the game. Our distress soared when we learned the fire was on the floor right above our suite. We had two saviors that night, Bob Roesler and Father Peter Rogers, the fire department chaplain, whom Bob knew. Bob and I both spoke with him, explaining the importance of the papers. Somehow, Father Rogers got permission for Granny, Bob, and me to use one of the emergency elevators still operating to go up to our rooms and retrieve what we could.

The scene greeting us when we reached our floor was dark and eerie: no lights at all, very soggy carpets, lots of smoke, and water all over the place. The mail slot alongside the elevator was so full of water that it looked like a mill race. Within two or three minutes after we rushed into our suite, firefighters appeared, saying, "You'd better get the hell out of here. We've got to go up through the ceiling." I continued stuffing into my briefcase the papers I had spread out on a desk earlier that day, then grabbed as many of my personal belongings as I could, most of them, as it turned out. In the other bedroom, Granny was doing the same thing. Meanwhile, the firefighters, who were getting rather urgent, started knocking holes in the ceiling. We splashed out of our suite into the hallway, scrambled into the elevator, pressed the "down" button with authority, and descended to the lobby—too slowly, it seemed. But we made it without incident.

When we reached the lobby, Father Rogers was there to greet us. He had declined to accompany us, which should have been a sign that we were courting even more danger than we suspected. We salvaged enough to finish our work but had to change hotels and cut short our trip. And, I don't think we ever again wore much of the clothing we had salvaged.

The fire had been set deliberately by a disgruntled hotel employee. While the blaze itself had been confined to the Roosevelt's top floor and seemed to mostly affect only a new section of the building, firefighters had poured untold gallons of water onto the flames to extinguish them. Because the fire was on the top floor, many of those gallons had flowed downward, causing a great deal of water damage, plus serious structural damage.

The next day, we met with the Roosevelt's general manager, Dan Mikulak, who assured us that the 200 or so damaged rooms would be ready in time for the January game. They weren't. We never did get a straight story from the Roosevelt about the situation, and an already bad hotel situation became downright dire.

I've said over the years that New Orleans has brought out the best and the worst in the Super Bowl, and this first year was easily the worst. After the fire in August, only a few of the damaged rooms at the Roosevelt Hotel were back in business in time for the game—and barely, at that—triggering a litany of complaints: "I've got this lovely room, but there's no dresser in it." "There's no place to put my clothes." "There's no television set." "There's no telephone." "There's no this or that . . ." In addition, we were forced to walk a bunch of media people to other hotels at the last minute because the rooms that the Roosevelt had assured us would be ready weren't available.

Had we had two weeks between the Super Bowl and the league championship games that we also were running, we might have had time to resolve the mess. But we had only one week, and in those days New Orleans didn't have enough hotels to really alleviate the shortage. Many of the Chiefs' fans had to stay in Biloxi and Gulfport, Mississippi, and commute the 100 miles back and forth to New Orleans.

We had known about the hotel shortage early on. But it had been another detail no one had given much thought to when the city had been awarded the game back in March. Of the hotels available, not many were first grade, either. As we had done in Miami, we did our best to gain control of as many rooms as we could, both to minimize rate gouging and to distribute available rooms in a sound, organized fashion. A little NFL-inspired confusion added to the challenge, which Granny and I discovered during one visit with Royal Sonesta managing director Jimmy Nassikas.

"Well, how 'bout the other guy I talked with last week?" Jimmy asked during our meeting. "He's from the National Football League, too, and he wants my whole hotel." The "other guy" turned out to be one of our dear friends from NFL Properties, which was trying to snap up hotel rooms, just like we were. "You make the deal with us," I said in a pleasant but firm voice, explaining that Properties would gain access to the Royal Sonesta, or any other hotel, only with our blessing. Although we cleared up such confusion, it didn't alleviate the shortage of rooms.

As long as we were running short of hotels, it figured that we would run short of shuttle buses, too. Getting to Tulane Stadium became almost as much of a headache as the stadium itself. We thought we had set up an efficient shuttle system with 10 buses operating in what would amount to a continual loop. We even appointed dispatchers to help direct traffic. Consistent with Murphy's Law, some of those buses made just one trip, then went off somewhere and parked, leaving lots of folks stranded, particularly writers who weren't eager to get to the stadium early, since there wasn't any place to go once they got there.

The street scene in front of the Roosevelt the day of the game was wild. And, of course, it had been raining. Members of our staff commandeered cabs all over the place, piling people into them and paying the drivers in advance because the drivers weren't going to budge unless they were sure of collecting their fare. We were handing them $20 bills like drunken sailors, saying, "Here, take these guys! Then come back for another load!"

We later found out that the bus drivers we counted on didn't receive the right instructions, which shouldn't have been surprising. Transportation is a perpetual problem, and you're never certain it's all going to work out. Drivers are frequently brought in from other cities and thus are often unfamiliar with exactly where they are going and unsure of what to do once they arrive.

Those who did get to the stadium on time saw an unforgettable show. Unfortunately, it wasn't the one we had planned.

Prior to the pregame show, a huge float slipped off its plywood tracks while being moved onto the field. It sank into the mud up to its wheels and held up the pregame show for what seemed like forever, and had to be pulled out by a tractor, which, of course, made a mess of its own.

The pregame show was an out-and-out disaster. We had two hot air balloons, both piloted by professionals. One was dressed up as a Chief, the other as a Viking. A nice touch, we thought. The balloons were supposed to take off and float into the sky just before the singing of the National Anthem. The Chiefs' balloon lifted off exactly as planned. The Vikings' never really got off the ground.

It started moving, but when released it headed straight toward the stands, with its burners ignited. As film clips of the sorry episode show, people were running all over the place trying to get out of the way as the balloon sailed across the field. One of them was Granny. He was running backward and ultimately fell head over heels when he smacked into a rolled-up tarp that had been used to cover the field during a pregame shower.

The Vikings' balloon finally crashed into the stands at about the goal line on the far left-hand side of the stadium, opposite the press box. Fortunately, the pilot had the foresight to extinguish the burners, or it really could have caused some problems. As it was, the balloon hit a group of young ladies dressed as southern belles, who were going to be participants in the halftime show. One of them suffered a broken leg, the most serious injury that occurred. Considering what was about to happen to the Minnesota Vikings, the balloon adventure was prophetic.

A feature of the pregame show was the War of 1812 and proved to be more aptly named than anyone planned: One guy lost a couple of fingers because he got too close to the blank charge that came out of the cannon that was used in the show. When it fired, a couple of people fell off their horses because the horses reared at the sound. It was a horrible mess . . . only to be followed by the dreadful declaration from the stadium public address announcer.

For the first time, the public address announcer was not sitting in the same booth with me but in a separate booth, along a mezzanine situated between the first and second levels of stands. We had a phone link, but the guy pretty much operated on his own, as he did for the Saints' games during those years. All of a sudden, I hear him tell 80,000 spectators that a tornado warning has been issued for the area around the stadium and that a twister could be heading our way! He had received the tornado warning from the weather bureau and simply passed it on, never once thinking about first conferring with anyone from the NFL. It marked the last time any stadium public address announcer uttered so much as a word without our first knowing exactly what he was going to say.

Yes, about anything that could have gone wrong that day did— even the weather. I awoke on the morning of the game, peered out my window, and saw a steady stream of water and garbage running down an alleyway below. After all we had put up with, it was like getting kicked in the stomach.

Amid the chaos, though, a few things went right, too. The demand for tickets, for instance, soared, particularly among fans of the participating teams. Both Kansas City and Minnesota were limited to 5,000 tickets apiece, but it caused the Chiefs untold grief. Kansas City could have sold 35,000 tickets, at least according to them. They almost went crazy, trying to meet the demand of their wildly enthusiastic fans.

Interest was soaring everywhere, though, to the point that we had to allocate tickets to virtually all our constituencies: NFL clubs, participating television networks, you name it. We also began allocating a certain number to writers covering the game, to purchase for their spouses. A broader distribution of tickets was hampered by our policy that allowed the Saints' season ticket holders to buy Super Bowl tickets on a one-for-one basis, as we had done in Los Angeles and Miami. The Saints, in fact, built their season ticket list primarily through Super Bowl IV, selling around 55,000 tickets, leaving us only about 17,000 to play with.

The experience prompted us to rethink this policy, and today the host city usually gets only 10 percent of its stadium's capacity. Super Bowl IV also marked the first time we went to a single price throughout the stadium: $15.

The name "Super Bowl" became official, too. Pete Rozelle had relented at last, and even started his annual press conference by saying, "This is officially Super Bowl IV. You've heard me say I don't like the term. . . ."

And as embarrassing as the snafus had been, we learned from the experiences, and our weekend checklist soon grew to include far more than just hotels.

To dress up drab Tulane Stadium, we worked out a deal with IBM and brought in a large portable scoreboard that greeted fans with "Welcome to the Fourth Super Bowl Game." We decided to bring our own tarp as well to the Super Bowl, seeing that the tarps available in most of the stadiums we used were lacking or leaking. Locker room facilities attracted our attention, too, and workout sites generated a checklist of their own because we had two teams to accommodate for a week and some of the locations we were considering just didn't have the hotels or the workout facilities that we required. Finally, our first experiences on the field for Super Bowl IV were such that we went back to New Orleans for Super Bowl VI under the condition that artificial turf would be in place when we returned. It was.

In spite of the lousy conditions, Super Bowl IV also launched the practice of developing special designs on the field. We had had the end zones painted in Miami but extended the practice to include the playing field, beginning the next year. In short order, designing the field almost became an art form.

Perhaps the most memorable and enduring development, though, was presenting Super Bowl IV in a way that has not been equaled since: NFL Films affixed a microphone to Kansas City coach Hank Stram, who narrated the game as only he could. If the ill-fated Viking balloon was prophetic, so was the decision by NFL Films to wire Stram. The 30-minute highlight film that resulted remains a classic.

Dapper, quick-witted, excitable, and boastful, Stram was absolutely perfect in the role and even seemed to sense what it could mean to him. Throughout the game, Hank had something rolled up in his hand, a depth chart or a game program, and waved it around constantly. From experience, NFL Films knew what a colorful guy the talkative Stram could be on the sidelines. But what he delivered exceeded their wildest expectations: Comments like "Way to go, boys! Just keep matriculatin' that ball right down the field!" soon followed by "Just keep negotiatin' that ball down the field!" will live forever in pro football lore.

Two portions of the film are especially memorable: In one instance, a Minnesota Vikings defender looks over to coach Bud Grant with a shrug, suggesting the Vikings have no clue about what to do, while Stram is heard to quip, "Look at 'em, boys. They're running around out there like it's a Chinese fire drill!" Later, after calling for a run by Mike Garrett, Stram says to those standing with him on the sideline, "We're going to call 65 toss power trap. Watch this now, boys! Watch this now! This thing just might bust wide open." Predictably, of course, the play unfolds, and bursts wide open. Garrett scoots into the end zone, giving the Chiefs their 16–0 lead and giving Stram the chance to add, "How 'bout that, boys? Huh? How 'bout it?"

Such slices of football life, along with the banter about the officials—"Oh, you marked it all wrong!" coupled with "Great job! These officials are really calling a great game!"—made Stram larger than life. More important, they gave weight to the claim that the Jets' 1969 Super Bowl victory hadn't been a fluke and that AFL teams would be worthy competitors in the new expanded league.

What you may find surprising is that after the game, Stram was gracious, a posture that could be difficult for my longtime friend to strike. I always associated the word *peacock* with Stram. He loves clothes, is an impeccable dresser with quite a wardrobe, and always traveled "heavy," as we described it. Hank *always* wore a shirt and tie on the sidelines, many times complemented by a red vest and a blue blazer with the Chiefs' insignia on the pocket.

We should have been suspicious of the Chiefs' underdog status all along, notwithstanding the distractions swirling about Len Dawson. This was essentially the same team that had played in Super Bowl I, except it was three years older, more experienced, and led by guys who were being recognized as truly dominant players, such as Dawson, Buck Buchanan, Bobby Bell, Willie Lanier, Curtis McClinton, and Otis Taylor, the star receiver whom an AFL "hand-holder" had pulled out of a motel window in late 1965. The Chiefs' line was first rate, Mike Garrett was an elusive back, and Jan Stenerud was one of pro football's better kickers. He demonstrated as much by kicking three first-half field goals.

While the New York Jets won Super Bowl III in part because Baltimore squandered so many scoring chances, the Chiefs in Super Bowl IV just flat out beat up the Vikings. Dawson played a near-flawless game, winning most valuable player honors after completing 12 of 17 passes, for 142 yards, and one touchdown of 46 yards to Taylor. In light of his tumultuous week, Len had the last laugh after all, and part of his reward was a phone call from President Richard Nixon, yet another tradition begun at Super Bowl IV.

Kansas City's defense, meanwhile, held Minnesota to 67 yards rushing, intercepted three passes, and recovered two fumbles. Joe Kapp, Minnesota's quarterback and team leader, who had coined the "40 for 60" slogan ("40 guys coming at you for 60 minutes"), took a horrible beating. He really got smacked by a train against the Chiefs. Play after play, I can see Kapp dragging himself up off the turf.

At times that year in New Orleans, we all felt as battered as Kapp had been during the game. Yet, what we had endured suddenly seemed well worth it the morning after.

In addition to holding the Commissioner's press conference on Friday, it was Rozelle's practice to meet with writers still in town for some postmortems on the Monday morning after the game. What Pete said in New Orleans was concise but startling: "More people watched yesterday's Super Bowl game than watched Neil Armstrong walk on the moon last July."

It was true. By the time of the press conference, we had received the overnight television ratings of the game televised by CBS. When I first saw the numbers, my mouth just dropped: we drew 69 percent of the television sets in use, which represented more than 23 million U.S. households.

People have long been asking us when we first felt that the Super Bowl was something special, something more than a championship football game. That morning may have been the first time. We've always said the Super Bowl just started growing and never stopped, but here was a piece of concrete evidence. Not even Rozelle, who had an incomparable grasp of television's importance to sports, could have anticipated this expression of popularity.

Although it didn't happen overnight, the Super Bowl had a stunning impact on the city of New Orleans, too. Dazzling new hotels sprang up, convention business took off, and, of course, the Louisiana Superdome was built. The Super Bowl launched it all. In fact, odd as it may sound, given our initial experience there, New Orleans became my favorite game site. Not only was it a fun city with the French Quarter, jazz clubs, and excellent restaurants, but it also was a compact venue for us. It's the one place where the media and many fans can walk to the game from their hotel rooms. That alone makes a difference.

Yet, our first experience there sparked an idea that still is discussed on occasion: build our own Super Bowl stadium and create a permanent home for it. A pipe dream? No doubt, but it was still a notion that Jim Kensil, Bill Granholm, and I, plus a few others, kicked around now and then. We even envisioned a "Super City" near, say, Augusta, Georgia, home of the Masters, so that the facility might be used for other events. It would have been in a warm-weather, neutral site, just like Rozelle originally envisioned. We visualized a stadium with a retractable roof, in case it rained, and workout facilities and team hotels built to our own specifications—such as seven-foot beds for the players. A place such as Branson, Missouri, served as our model, due to all its hotels and restaurants. The overwhelming shortcoming, of course, was what to do with it the rest of the year. Play a bowl game in it, someone always suggested, or use it as some kind of Olympic facility. We were more serious than you might imagine.

But on our returning to Miami a few times, where hotels were plentiful, or to California, our dream would fade away. Wherever we took the Super Bowl, its spiraling growth demanded more and more of our waking hours, and took on a life of its own that was quite real.

The following year in Miami, the Roman numerals became official, and Earl Morrall won redemption when Baltimore beat Dallas 16–13. The year after that, Don Shula won redemption, too, guiding the Miami Dolphins to their magical undefeated season. By then, the Super Bowl was the sports event of the year.

Much of the Super Bowl's momentum came together in New Orleans, just when it seemed like it was coming apart.

THIRTEEN

HALFTIME

The caller at the other end of the telephone identified himself as Bob Jani. I didn't know him at all, but I knew all about his employer: Walt Disney.

So, when Jani called out of the blue during that summer of 1976, I listened. The eagerness in his voice was appealing and put a smile on my face. And when he all but insisted that we meet to consider his idea for a halftime show the next time I was on the West Coast, I readily agreed.

It may have been the most pivotal Super Bowl decision I ever made. Bob Jani was Disney's director of entertainment, whose presentation a few weeks after his call was one of the most memorable that Bill Granholm and I had ever experienced. All Jani had was an easel and a cassette tape recorder, but that's all he needed because he also had his arms and his eyes . . . and most of all, his *enthusiasm*. It was absolutely infectious. I've lost count of the sophisticated multimedia presentations I've sat through, but none of them can touch what Bob Jani rolled out for Granny and me that afternoon in his office in Anaheim, California.

To say he had a remarkable ability to combine his voice and his gestures with samples of music on the tape recorder would be an understatement. It was a true gift of a man whom I came to regard as a true genius and one of the most expressive persons I have ever met. He was a multimedia presentation all by himself. Jani became totally absorbed in what he was doing, darting from easel to tape recorder and back again, then to another part of his office, then back to the easel . . . all to demonstrate a halftime show that he had conceived in his mind and which was now bursting to life before us. Jani's arms never stopped moving. His eyes literally rolled as he spoke and danced with delight.

"We'll open this way!" he began in a bubbly tone. "Then we'll do this! . . . Then we'll do that! . . . And then these colors will appear . . . and here's the music we'll play. . . ." He was conductor, choreographer, sound technician, and fabulous salesman rolled into one, and he never stopped moving as he described one portion of the show after another. Granny and I were mesmerized.

It was an incredible and inspired performance from a dapper, dynamic fellow who stood no more than 5 feet 8 inches tall but was a giant in his field. It was easy to see why he was so successful, especially in an organization such as Disney. Jani got us so excited that Granny started imitating him, an endorsement in itself, for Granny only imitated people of substance and significance. Halftime at the Super Bowl has never been the same since, even if I was a nervous wreck before it was all over.

The wellspring of Bob Jani's inspiration was the decision by the powers that be in Pasadena that the National Football League was at last welcome to play the Super Bowl in the Rose Bowl. Recalling the decade-old snub, we were thrilled. But Jani had been positively ecstatic, for unbeknownst to us he had developed his own fascination with the cavernous stadium.

With Disney about to open theme parks in Japan and France, Jani found himself on lots of flights, particularly to and from Tokyo. Invariably, all of them glided over the Rose Bowl on their way into or out of the Los Angeles airport, and as he kept peering into the big bowl from above, he couldn't get over its almost perfect symmetry. His observations sparked an idea, and playing Super Bowl XI in Pasadena was the perfect occasion to launch it.

The Rose Bowl, Bob exclaimed, was the *ideal* venue to stage a massive card show as part of the halftime festivities that Disney was proposing to arrange and direct on our behalf. What Jani envisioned wasn't just a display by a card section (such as the ones he himself had once produced for USC games in the Los Angeles Coliseum) but a grand spectacle that would involve every fan in the stands: 103,438 fans, to be exact. At different times during the show, which he called "It's a Small World," fans would hold up different portions of the four-color cards that they would find waiting for them when they reached their seats. They'd be directed by Disney personnel, who would be strategically positioned throughout the giant stadium. Complemented by a cast of 1,500 energized performers, "It's a Small World" would create more pageantry than we could hope to imagine.

Pageantry. The word and the idea struck more of a chord than Jani might have intended. By 1976, the Super Bowl was well established as a blockbuster event. The demand for tickets was insatiable, and television ratings were off the charts. Jani's idea was ideal because it offered a halftime concept in keeping with the game. We got excited about it quickly.

To be sure, Disney's own interests were fueling part of this enthusiasm. Given our promotional instincts, we could discern that in the blink of an eye. Presenting its first overseas theme parks to a Super Bowl television audience of hundreds of millions around the world was also an ideal way to promote their respective merits. In addition, Disney had some new cartoon characters to introduce. But those considerations didn't dampen our interest one bit.

What did dampen our excitement, however, was reality. "It's a Small World" was a massive challenge and fraught with uncertainty. That's what made me nervous. Designing a halftime show for USC, featuring one card section, performed by a bunch of college kids who could rehearse on campus for hours on end was one thing. What Jani was insisting on with Billy Sunday–like fervor was something entirely different.

To begin with, *would* 103,000-plus fans want to participate? The majority of Super Bowl spectators were not college kids but well-heeled captains of industry and corporate types. What they spend on this game was two to four times more than what any other sports crowd in the world spends. We couldn't know if they were even interested in the idea until they got in their seats. Then we had to convince them not to leave their seats at halftime—a challenge in itself—and to pay attention to and follow the directions of what amounted to a corps of Disney cheerleaders toting megaphones. Most important, assuming we could get the crowd to participate, we still couldn't know *how well* they would participate or, more to the point, how their performance would look on hundreds of millions of television screens around the globe. What's more, plenty of card shows had been staged in the Los Angeles Coliseum but nary a one in the Rose Bowl.

What Jani and his pals were proposing, then, was as ambitious as it was inspired, which might be one reason why we decided to go for it. A second reason was the idea's dramatic potential. In addition, we felt we had a good enough grasp of Super Bowl demographics to roll the dice. If our resolve ever faltered, Jani was always there to shore it up with his unbridled enthusiasm. It was as if he were foreshadowing the television commercial that ends with "Yeah, we can do that!"

Our hunches didn't let us down. And maybe fate was on our side, too. The crowd accepted our instructions without hesitation, helped along by our own carefully coordinated promotion of the event.

The multicolored cards placed at each seat were a courtesy of United Way, a longtime NFL partner, which had inscribed a promotional message on them. Also printed on the cards were specific instructions. We made pointed public address announcements before and during the game, urging fans to stay in their seats at halftime and be part of an unprecedented experience. To help drive home the idea, we conducted short but focused rehearsals during the television timeouts throughout the first half. We used the scoreboard to flash cues, section by section, at the same time Disney directors were instructing the crowd. "On the count of four, you'll hold up a card," they'd say, "and it will be yellow!" or whatever color was called for in a given section.

By the end of the first quarter, everybody was on the bandwagon, and during the break before the second quarter, we conducted what you could call one final dress rehearsal that involved the entire stadium. It worked. Something else worked, too: raw peer pressure.

None of the captains of industry and corporate types in the stands wanted to be embarrassed on national television. How could they face their friends or vie for bragging rights at cocktail parties? Afterward, then, we heard plenty of tales of fans saying to other fans next to them, "Hey! Not the red card! The *blue* card! . . . Hold it *this* way!" and similar directives.

Besides, after the near-disasters in New Orleans at Super Bowl IV, maybe we had earned some good fortune. I still felt like an expectant father, though. After all, I was the guy who had approved this idea. I can't begin to count the hours spent on it, and I've forgotten how many trips I made to the West Coast on its behalf. The record books say Oakland won Super Bowl XI, whipping Minnesota, 32–14. You couldn't prove it by me. All I was thinking about in the control booth that day in the Rose Bowl was halftime.

Bob Jani's creation rocketed the Super Bowl into another league as an entertainment experience. Halftime became a blockbuster production all its own. It afforded us an opportunity to develop new sponsorships dedicated to our new attraction and enabled television networks to sell targeted advertising time around the show.

The audience-participation extravaganza was such a hit that we repeated it when the Super Bowl returned to the Rose Bowl, as it did on four occasions. As we gained experience, the shows' complexities increased. One show, "KaleidoSUPERscope," called for the cards to move almost continuously. Up With People was part of that Disney-produced show, too. These encores were just as successful, save for one hitch in 1980, when the Pittsburgh Steelers played the Los Angeles Rams in Super Bowl XIV.

On the strength of a fourth-quarter surge, the Steelers beat the Rams, 31–19, for their fourth Super Bowl triumph. But the Rams led both at halftime and at the end of three quarters, a state of affairs that understandably annoyed Pittsburgh's coach Chuck Noll. Intensifying Noll's annoyance was the fact that we had given some 104,000 fans in the Rose Bowl cards coated with shiny Mylar material, which reflected Southern California sunlight with mirrorlike intensity. It did indeed give the halftime show an incredible sparkle. Unfortunately, the fans discovered that incredible sparkle long before halftime, and a number of them started flashing the cards during the first quarter, accidentally reflecting the sun's rays into the eyes of the football players. It played havoc with pass receivers and kick return specialists. Noll became irate and demanded we do something to stop it.

We acted immediately, making public address announcements that appealed to the crowd's "sense of sportsmanship and fair play." By mixing in a dash of flattery and thanking fans in advance for not using the cards until cued, we solved the problem without much difficulty. That about half of the crowd were Steelers fans helped.

Even with this miscue, the card shows—the first one in particular—were as enjoyable and memorable as any Super Bowl halftime show I've ever seen. When he died in 1989, Bob Jani was hailed as "a master of the art of celebration" and properly so. His successes included the fireworks spectacular in New York harbor during the bicentennial celebration and the 1984 presidential inauguration.

What Jani's 1976 telephone call inspired was part of the second stage of halftime's evolution, which began with Super Bowl X. The first stage of halftime entertainment had begun with presentations that were standard fare at almost every football game: marching band shows. They were great shows, too, featuring some of the best college bands in the country and produced by capable, experienced people, all hired expressly for the occasion, since no one in the NFL office had any halftime production expertise to speak of. We'd never needed it.

For the first game, which was played in the Los Angeles Coliseum, Pete Rozelle turned to Tommy Walker, a veteran of West Coast stadium shows whom Pete knew from his days in the 1950s when he was the Los Angeles Rams' general manager. Tommy arranged for a performance that featured the combined college marching bands from the University of Arizona, Grambling College, and the University of Michigan. Over the next decade, Walker also produced a second show in the Coliseum, plus the three halftime shows in Tulane Stadium when New Orleans hosted the game.

For the early Super Bowls played in Miami, we used Earnie Seiler, who had been producing the halftime shows for the Orange Bowl. Once the Orange Bowl game became a New Year's night affair in 1965, its halftime shows became increasingly lavish. Earnie applied the same touch to the Super Bowls in Miami, accented by up-tempo tunes and lightning-quick formations performed by nationally known bands from Grambling and Florida A&M.

Along with top-quality bands, most of our early halftime shows included some pageantry and star quality. In the Orange Bowl, for example, Seiler brought the Grambling band onto the field through a huge cornucopia crafted especially for Super Bowl II. It was a good 30 to 40 yards long. Carol Channing was a featured performer at Super Bowl IV in New Orleans, appearing on the float that got stuck in the mud, while Al Hirt and Doc Severinsen staged a "Battle of the Horns" during pregame festivities. Channing and Hirt were back for halftime in New Orleans two years later, joined by Ella Fitzgerald and a Marine Corps drill team.

In the early years, the only halftime show not produced by Tommy or Earnie was Super Bowl VIII, played in Houston's Rice Stadium, where it was Miami's turn to beat Minnesota. Halfway through the Dolphins' 24–7 victory, the massive University of Texas band staged a huge show. Regaled in their distinctive burnt orange uniforms, band members literally covered the field, making for a dramatic sight. They also may have helped solidify our nagging concern about halftime.

As entertaining as the musicians were, these were still essentially band shows, and they all had one unavoidable shortcoming: The bands faced the side of the stadium where the television cameras were mounted and, in effect, played to that portion of the crowd, which meant fans sitting on the opposite side of the field missed most of the performance. And that didn't sit well with us. After all, this was the Super Bowl, and as part of Pete Rozelle's original vision, we felt the halftime show should be just as special as the game. So, we began looking for something more dramatic with as much pageantry as we could find.

Although Jani's brainstorm gave what we called "people shows" their real momentum, we were blessed with other timely assistance, too, starting with the Bicentennial Commission headed by John Warner, the future senator from Virginia.

Stage two of halftime's evolution first appeared at Super Bowl X, played in Miami on January 18, 1976. The game enjoyed the distinction of being the official kickoff of the nation's bicentennial celebration, one more indication of how big the Super Bowl had become in the public's mind. A bicentennial coin was minted for the kickoff, the official bicentennial logo was posted all over the Orange Bowl, and the design of our own Super Bowl X logo reflected the nation's approaching two hundredth birthday.

Naturally, we all but insisted on a halftime show befitting the occasion. Once again, thanks in part to some of Pete Rozelle's contacts, we created a show featuring Up With People, the internationally known musical troupe of young singers and dancers. Their presentation filled practically every corner of the field with activity, which was exactly what we were looking for. By the time Up With People danced off the field, halftime was marching in a different direction.

Up With People would go on to provide terrific halftime entertainment at four Super Bowls, in part because I personally became involved with the organization as one of its board members. For its inaugural performance at the bicentennial game in Miami, Up With People also gave us a moving pregame event: One of its members was a blind singer named Tom Sullivan, whose rendition of the National Anthem was incredibly memorable. It brought tears to your eyes and put a lump in your throat, that's how special it was.

Virtually on the heels of Up With People's first show came Bob Jani's phone call and his dazzling idea. More than a coincidence? I've wondered.

Yet, I'm not sure the card shows were our most ambitious halftime productions. For my money, that title hangs over the halftime show presented at Super Bowl XXII, our first visit to what was then called Jack Murphy Stadium in San Diego.

In the 1980s, Bob Jani left Disney and joined Radio City Music Hall in New York, which at the time needed the kind of revitalizing that only Jani's talent could provide. Initially, Radio City may have wondered what it was getting into. One of Bob's first directives was to tell the Rockettes they all needed to lose 20 pounds! Fortunately, that wasn't any of our business.

What *was* our business was the halftime show Radio City brought us in 1988. "Something Grand" featured the Rockettes dancing on a giant stage crafted to look like a grand piano. We had no problem there, since we had long mastered the challenge of getting a stage set up at midfield in five minutes or less and taking it down after the halftime show in another five minutes or less. Sharing the spotlight with the dancers was Chubby Checker, who had brought the "twist" into the world in the early 1960s, plus 88 white grand pianos, which were to ring the field during the performance. Finding 88 white grand pianos might have been a problem, but at least it was somebody else's. Our problem was what to do with them once they arrived. It presented a stiff logistical challenge: how to conveniently store 88 grand pianos until halftime, then get them on and off the field in the prescribed amount of time. Somehow, we managed. As photos show, most of the pianos were placed under wraps on the field. But we also found room in the stands to stash a few of them, odd as it sounds.

Like Jani's motivation to involve Disney with the Super Bowl, Radio City had a motive for bringing the Rockettes and all those pianos to the Super Bowl: use our game to promote the revival of Radio City, much as Jani had promoted Disney's new theme parks and characters. This, too, proved to be a win-win partnership, and Radio City remains a valuable NFL Super Bowl partner to this day.

Another win-win partnership has been the one with George Toma. Throughout the years, he has been an unsung hero of halftime, too. You almost could call George Bob Jani's alter ego. Toma serves as our Super Bowl groundskeeper, as he has throughout the game's 36-year history. He's achieved a little fame in recent years by being featured in a promotional television message produced for ESPN. George is the guy throwing dirt and sprinkling water on the carpet of the sports network's offices, all the while wearing a T-shirt proclaiming him to be the "Marquis de Sod."

That he is. George has earned any number of accolades for the tender loving care he has applied to the Super Bowl gridiron, including the Gladiator Award from the Pro Football Hall of Fame. He's earned another salute from me because, along with delivering manicured game fields and workout sites, George has been asked to solve myriad hassles and crises created by our zeal for unmatched halftime pageantry. I'm sure some of the shows left him muttering and wondering about our collective sanity. But he's always come through.

And, we've tried to help. At the very beginning, in 1967, we promised George that we would never allow halftime shows to tamper with or damage the playing field in any way. We've kept that promise, even if on occasion we had to remind producers and coordinators that we would never tolerate their leaving six-inch ruts in the middle of a grass field after a show or putting too much weight on an artificial surface. We also decreed that the halftime show would be performed from the sidelines should a field become sloppy due to inclement weather. Fortunately, that's never really been an issue. Perhaps the closest we ever came was at Super Bowl IV in New Orleans. It would have been in keeping with everything else that happened there.

Preparation and rehearsals have posed another challenge. We never really get the chance to work closely with halftime performers until the Thursday or Friday before the game, which doesn't give us much time to see the way everything is coming together. Consequently, we may discover that a float or some other prop is too heavy or too big, as we found out after the fact in New Orleans, when the oversized float that was to carry Carol Channing got stuck in 18 to 20 inches of mud as it was rolled out onto the field.

We learned from that mishap, just as we settled into halftime routines as part of planning the game itself and the more than 100 related activities. One of our practices became tying the theme of the halftime show into the annual Friday night Commissioner's party and having the entertainers on hand for it, too. For example, the "A Salute to the Big Band Era" theme of Super Bowl XIV's halftime show in Pasadena in 1980 (the year the Mylar episode glowed) was also the theme of the party.

The halftime show itself consumes all of 12 minutes and is to run without any interruption for television commercials. I shudder to think of all the hours that have been spent planning, preparing, and rehearsing over the past 36 years. We used to like all halftime activities to last no more than 24 or 25 minutes from the time the teams leave the field at the end of the first half until they return for the second-half kickoff. It might be a bit longer these days. We allocated no more than five of those minutes for setup and another four or five minutes for teardown after the performance. At Super Bowl XXXVI in New Orleans, for instance, teardown took almost exactly four minutes.

The challenge to meet these parameters became stiffer when the Super Bowl halftime show evolved into its third and current stage— featured headline performers.

We might well have continued with "people shows" and "audience-participation" halftimes to this day, although like any genre of entertainment, they might have run their course. In their heyday they were successful and comparatively inexpensive to present. Virtually all of the thousands of halftime performers volunteered their time and considerable talents. So did the college marching bands in the early years. Everyone was just thrilled to be part of a Super Bowl experience, and other than basic expenses and travel costs, the price of the halftime show was modest. In those very early years, in fact, we budgeted a mere $50,000 for the show.

Bringing in headliners changed all that. Now Super Bowl halftime is a multimillion-dollar production all its own. What the NFL today spends on halftime is close to twice what it cost to present the Super Bowl in its entirety in each of the first three years, including the winners' and losers' shares paid to the players and coaches. Ironically, a key factor in our decision to alter our halftime concept was an old ally: television.

The Super Bowl itself is unmatched as a television program. Competing networks simply can't touch it and have learned not to bother to try. But as the 1980s moved along, we began to notice that the networks not carrying the game were making concerted efforts to air programs designed to woo away Super Bowl audiences during halftime. Their underlying strategy may have been pinned in part on the hope that, if the game itself was one-sided and a competing program was especially appealing, it just might be able to pull away a portion of our audience and hold onto it. All the networks—CBS, ABC, NBC, and later FOX and cable channels such as TNT and MTV—wielded this strategy. And, of course, a number of games were one-sided contests, pretty much decided by halftime.

In turn, we felt we had to respond by putting more emphasis on the halftime show itself. Enter the headliners, beginning with none other than Michael Jackson.

Jackson performed at Super Bowl XXVII, which was played in the Rose Bowl in January 1993, and caused exactly the kind of stir we were after. The press conference we held during the week prior to the game was mobbed, attracting many more writers than several press conferences devoted to the game itself did. Jackson never said much, but he didn't need to. His presence had the desired effect, and his "Heal the World" performance was a huge hit.

Our timing wasn't bad, either, on two counts: Jackson took the stage that year with Dallas enjoying a commanding 28–10 halftime lead over Buffalo en route to a 52–17 walloping. That the Bills would suffer their third consecutive Super Bowl defeat was obvious by halftime. The Jackson show also made the logistical challenges it presented worth the effort. The show opened with Jackson being raised slowly from beneath the stage that was erected and wheeled into position by a hydraulic crane that also had to be wheeled in. Once he was lifted into position, he was to strike a pose and hold it for a few seconds. On his first move, the show would begin. For whatever reason, Jackson held that pose for what seemed like an eternity. He looked frozen, while the television guys, who think in terms of tenths of seconds, were getting antsy and irritated. At last, though, Jackson moved and fears vanished.

Appearing as extras were about 3,500 Southern California young-sters, plus one more tried-and-true card stunt, again courtesy of our affable fans in the Rose Bowl stands. In keeping with our desire for pageantry, we've continued to encircle headline performers with legions of cheering extras. Even so, we can still clear the field after the show in less than five minutes, in part because the stage, what-ever its configuration, is built in sections that are on rollers.

Our roster of halftime performers reads like an entertainment who's who and represents a spectrum of musical talents and tastes. Early on, we seemed to be partial to trumpeters: Al Hirt, Doc Sev-erinsen, Wynton Marsalis, and Herb Alpert all performed at halftime or before the game. Our first years also featured the likes of Woody Herman and Pete Fountain, Pearl Bailey, Diana Ross and James Brown, the Blues Brothers, Patti LaBelle, and Tony Bennett. Phil Collins and Gloria Estefan & Miami Sound Machine made appear-ances, too, while country stars Wynonna and Naomi Judd, Clint Black, Travis Tritt, and Tanya Tucker headlined Super Bowl XXVIII in 1994, the first year the game was played in Atlanta. Most recently, the focus has been on rock stars such as Aerosmith, 'N Sync, U2, and Britney Spears.

Pregame festivities have evolved much like halftime and have become shows of their own. Initially, the pregame program consisted solely of player introductions and the singing of the National Anthem. In 1969, we added the Apollo astronauts leading the Pledge of Allegiance, a feature that continued for several years, almost always in cooperation with NASA. A rendition of "America the Beau-tiful" by Vikki Carr helped give pregame a patriotic theme, as did military flyovers. We've featured flyovers at outdoor venues on seven or eight occasions. They provide a great climax to the National Anthem, which remains the focal point of pregame ceremonies. Rehearsals of the song can be exhausting. For one thing, it's a chal-lenging song to sing. And, we always want to sign off on the rendition.

"It's not a National Anthem until Don's heard it," declares Lesslee Fitzmorris, a talented choreographer and one of two longtime pregame producers. The senior member of the duo is Bob Best, a former public relations director at Tampa Bay, whom we hired many years ago to produce both pregame and postgame and also help coordinate halftime.

The pregame show that Bob and Lesslee produce is now 20 to 25 minutes of multimedia entertainment that begins once the teams finish warming up and leave the field, and leads into the coin toss, player introductions, and the singing of the National Anthem. In our minds, it's time and effort well spent because pregame delivers more than pure entertainment. It helps attract fans to the game early and thus spreads out the inevitable traffic jams around the stadium. And because the majority of fans are walking into an unfamiliar stadium, pulling them in early helps them get properly seated with less hassle.

As the years have gone by, pregame has taken on more and more of the trappings of the halftime pageantry, to the point that we have as many headliners before the game as we do at halftime. Watching them all at Super Bowl XXXVI in New Orleans inspired a question. "How do you think Rozelle would have reacted," I asked a longtime colleague, "if I had ever suggested bringing the Boston Pops Orchestra to the Super Bowl?" All we could do was chuckle.

No matter who participates, halftime entertainment always has produced adventures all its own. For one thing, it has offered gatecrashers an opportunity to talk their way into the stadium by claiming to be a part of the halftime show. More characters than I can count have dressed up as Santa Claus, and in the game's formative period several of them wearing the disguise managed to bluff their way past security guards.

An episode in Miami's Orange Bowl at Super Bowl XIII sent a bunch of my colleagues scrambling. The theme of the halftime show was a "Caribbean carnival" and called for a huge blue canvas to be spread across the field, on which were painted all the nations of the Caribbean Islands. A float designed as a big boat was to roll across the canvas and visit each of the islands, accompanied by a musical number at each stop. We recruited 500 youngsters to roll out the canvas, but in the rush, part of it got stuck around one of the goalposts. The harder the kids tried to pull it free, the more entwined the canvas became. Finally, George Toma decided that the only solution was to cut the canvas loose with a knife. He shouted desperately, "Has anyone got a knife?" No sooner had the words flown out of George's mouth than about 10 knives flew out of the stands.

Toma thus was able to cut the canvas free, but the show's troubles persisted. The motor in the float failed, and the big boat had to be pushed off the field. It was the first real dilemma to confront Jim Steeg, who succeeded me as Super Bowl coordinator when he was hired as NFL director of special events in the fall of 1978. A halftime scheduled to last 23 minutes took 31 minutes instead, and Steelers coach Chuck Noll was not amused. In fact, he was pretty steamed, unusual for Noll because he took most other Super Bowl distractions in stride. Up in the NBC broadcasting booth, Curt Gowdy and Merlin Olsen weren't pleased either. They suddenly had extra minutes of airtime to fill while Steeg and his helpers tried to get the ailing boat off of the field.

Super Bowl XVIII, played in Tampa in 1984, produced a snafu that escaped many people's attention, much to our relief. With the Los Angeles Raiders cruising to a 38–9 whipping of Washington, one would have thought fans would have been more observant of distractions. For the halftime finale, performers carried lighted torches from the end zone onto the field. The torches were sitting in a rack, and when they were lit, they set fire to the big banners flapping behind them. Firefighters had to rush in with extinguishers to put them out. Nobody seemed to notice. "The media just thought it was part of the act," Steeg later said. I don't know that we told them any differently, either.

Looking at Super Bowl halftimes on television today, you might think the NFL would save itself headaches by turning back the clock and relying on the bands. I'm not so sure. It was a band, in fact, that taught us that halftime shows are really never over until the game is. And maybe not even then.

The lesson came courtesy of the University of Michigan band, after its performance in the Los Angeles Coliseum, at Super Bowl VII. It was the second appearance of the band, which also participated in pregame festivities that saluted Apollo 17, NASA's final moon mission. The Apollo crew was there to lead the Pledge of Allegiance, and

Woody Herman joined the Michigan musicians for the halftime show titled "Happiness Is." It was, too. But the postgame was decidedly unhappy.

A single tunnel leads to the Coliseum's playing field, and the one and only entry to the teams' lockers rooms is off that tunnel. In fact, other than passageways in the stands, the tunnel is the only way into or out of the stadium. A record number of media turned out for the game, and we installed a series of television monitors with sound along the tunnel walls so that the writers who couldn't squeeze into the locker rooms could still hear postgame interviews and take notes while standing in the tunnel.

The Michigan band had planned to play a couple of numbers after the game before leaving, a tradition in college football and one we adopted. Postgame music helps "play the crowd out," as we say. Since some fans linger and listen to the music, it establishes a better crowd flow out of the stadium.

But the band was forced to cancel its plans at the last minute. Late in the fourth quarter, the Coliseum's exit gates were opened, creating a temptation that several hundred youth standing outside couldn't resist. They rushed through the gates and began working their way into the stadium at its peristyle end, close to where the Michigan band had formed on the field. After first filling the aisles, the youngsters made their way onto the field itself, practically filling that portion of it and mingling with the band.

Security personnel rushed onto the field to try to clear out the gate-crashers, but it was impossible. Surveying the scene, the Michigan band director marched his musicians into the tunnel, intending to take them to the buses and depart. But by now a crush of media were pouring into the tunnel, and the band was suddenly stuck. At one end of this mass of humanity was my buddy Bill Granholm, who had gotten into the mess when he first led security to round up the young intruders.

Just as the postgame interviews started, the band director decided that as long as the band was standing there in the tunnel, it might as well make itself useful and play the music it had planned to play on the field. The timing was incredible. We couldn't have orchestrated it any worse. As Miami's Don Shula received the Lombardi Trophy from Pete Rozelle to cap his undefeated season, the writers who were jammed in the tunnel heard an unforgettable flourish as the director struck up the band. Ever hear a 400-member band play in a tunnel? Take my word for it. It's deafening. Trying to monitor the press conference taking place on the television screens mounted in the tunnel was fruitless, of course.

It took Granny a good 12 minutes to make his way through the mob to the band director and get him to stop the impromptu performance. By then the initial interviews were over, and the writers were in a rage. One of the writers standing in the tunnel, besieged by trumpets and trombones, happened to be Edwin Pope, of the *Miami Herald*, and, more important, the then-reigning president of the Pro Football Writers Association. I don't recall what Ed wrote about the game or about his Super Bowl champion Dolphins. What I can't forget is the four-page, single-spaced letter he wrote to the NFL the next day. It was powerful. Beginning the very next year, we initiated our policy of conducting postgame interviews in a separate area outside the locker rooms, where no other traffic is permitted—especially bands.

We also adjusted another policy: Band leaders were not to play unless instructed to.

FOURTEEN

CELEBRITIES, MOTORCADES, COACHES . . . AND *BLACK SUNDAY*

As if we needed it, one more reliable indicator proved to us that we had a hit on our hands. The instant the Super Bowl's drawing power became clear, celestial personalities swarmed around the game like moths lured to a dazzling light: entertainers, media moguls, corporate moguls, scions from the advertising world, sports heroes, and "groupies" of every persuasion. Every time we turned around, people were clamoring to be part of our great January celebration.

Swelling the steady stream of calls from aspiring advertisers and sponsors were calls from agents who wanted to involve their singers, their clients, their companies. Not so long ago, *we* were the ones placing the calls, trying to prime the pump and willing to risk assorted miscues in the process. All of a sudden we had a blistering-hot property that was climbing to heights even Pete Rozelle himself couldn't have envisioned. At times we just sat back and grinned; it was that hard to fathom.

The Super Bowl was more than a sports event. It was more than a media event. It was one big party. And everyone wanted to be there, even if some of them didn't have game tickets. Every Super Bowl city now lures a good 25,000 to 35,000 people who come without a thought of ever trying to see the game. They're just around and content to go somewhere and watch the game on television, soak up the atmosphere, and be part of it all.

I won't dare say we didn't enjoy the flattering attention. We did, and we still do. We also had built-in reality checks, for our relations with the celebrities, leading lights, owners, and coaches weren't always what you'd call celebrations.

The most nerve-racking episode I ever endured at any Super Bowl involved country star Garth Brooks. He was to sing the National Anthem at Super Bowl XXVII in the Rose Bowl, the same game that featured Michael Jackson's landmark performance at halftime. Michael didn't know it at the time, but he came precariously close to being upstaged because Garth came within a whisker of refusing to sing the Anthem.

Because Garth himself seemed like a nice guy, I've always sensed the source of that pregame furor in 1993 was his agent. NBC did the telecast that year, and someone at the network promised Garth's entourage that his latest video would be aired during the pregame show in exchange for an interview with Brooks during the same show. The understanding was that Garth's video was to be delivered to NBC's production truck before the program went on the air at 12:30 P.M. But when 12:30 arrived, no video was there. Since NBC had scheduled the video to run at 12:50 P.M., it and the interview were scratched by the pregame show's producer.

The video finally arrived about 45 minutes later. Too late, snapped the producer, holding firm and instructing someone to so inform Garth's agent. No one thought any more about the cancellation until about an hour before Garth was to sing the Anthem, when the country star suddenly appeared and told NFL special events director Jim Steeg that he wouldn't sing unless NBC kept its promise to air his video. The threat quickly rushed NBC executive producer Terry O'Neill into the dilemma. He promised to call Brooks as soon as possible and did, but nothing was resolved.

With the pregame show rolling toward its conclusion, time was critical. Player introductions and other official ceremonies were to follow immediately. Worse, because Brooks had earlier refused to prerecord the Anthem, we were left without any kind of backup rendition if the singer left the stadium, which he was now threatening to do.

The stalemate dragged on, punctuated by Brooks's changing into, then out of, his star-spangled-banner costume. Whenever Garth peeled it off, he was left standing in the middle of the ongoing debate in flaming red long underwear. This ritual was repeated four times, as Jim Steeg duly apprised me while reporting progress—or lack thereof—via walkie-talkie. I was in my customary perch in our control booth and couldn't leave, not even for a mounting crisis like this one. At one point, Steeg became so exasperated that he barked, "If I see Brooks in his goddamn red underwear one more time, I'm going to personally throw him out of here."

Yet, it appeared more and more likely that Brooks would leave under his own power. After his fourth costume change, Garth disappeared into the Rose Bowl tunnel to await his limo and depart the stadium. With each tick of the clock becoming more ominous, NBC's O'Neill finally agreed to air at least a portion of the video *if* we would agree to roll back the kickoff three minutes. Putting everybody under a three-minute hold may not sound like much, but it meant alerting the game officials, the teams, television and radio crews, and NFL and stadium coordinators and technicians scattered around the Rose Bowl, plus additional coordinators outside the stadium directing the scheduled pregame flyover. Disruptions notwithstanding, we said OK.

The most critical contact we had to make was intercepting Garth Brooks himself, still in the tunnel awaiting his limo. Eddie McGuire, of our staff, caught up with him literally as the star was climbing into the backseat of his limo. He handed Brooks his walkie-talkie, saying that I wanted to speak with him.

"Garth, this is Don Weiss, of the NFL," I began, then quickly recounted our getting acquainted at a game-related press conference a few days earlier, in the hope he would recall it. Garth had helped launch one of our outreach programs in south-central Los Angeles and in fact donated concert proceeds of nearly $1 million to the cause.

"Garth, we really need you to sing and really want you to sing," I continued, stressing that it wouldn't be in anybody's best interest if he didn't. If that's not exactly what I said, it was close enough, and evidently it struck a chord. Brooks couldn't have been more agreeable and cooperative, leading me to suspect it was his agent who had really provoked the dispute. Brooks climbed out of the car and into his costume for the fifth and last time. His rendition of the National Anthem was music to my ears.

Ever since that episode, we've insisted on prerecording the Anthem. We had prerecorded it on occasion in earlier years, but, beginning in 1993, we took no more chances. Frankly, the networks prefer it that way because they know exactly how long it's going to take, their timing is that precise. Many performers prefer it, too, because some of them get incredibly nervous.

Helen O'Connell was a classic case of nerves before she sang the Anthem at Super Bowl XV. Played in New Orleans in 1981 just five days after the Iran hostages were released, it was to be an extra-special occasion. Her nervousness surprised me. O'Connell was a most accomplished and experienced band singer who over the years might well have appeared before more people than anyone else who ever performed the Anthem. She was completely at ease in New Orleans until someone casually remarked that her performance would be seen by more than 100 million people watching in the United States alone. The comment really shook her. Helen did a beautiful job but remained a bundle of nerves until the last notes of the song left her lips.

A vast television audience wasn't about to upset Diana Ross. Already a world-famous superstar when she sang the Anthem the following year at Super Bowl XVI, she also was in familiar surroundings. That year, for the first time, we played the game in Michigan in the Pontiac Silverdome, less than an hour away from the singer's Detroit home where she had launched her career as lead singer of the Supremes. Unfortunately, Diana's familiarity with Michigan didn't extend to the structural details of the Silverdome, and that lack of information literally blew trouble her way.

It was an oversight on everyone's part, and thankfully nothing came of it. The Silverdome's Teflon roof is held up principally by air pressure, so the design of the big indoor stadium includes large revolving doors to help maintain the proper pressure. If a door is ever locked in the open position without a second door in front of or behind it being closed, the escaping air creates quite a force. Amid the usual hoopla that always erupts after the singing of the National Anthem, we overlooked that little detail when Diana departed shortly thereafter.

Had Diana and her group left by one of the Silverdome's revolving doors, no mishap would have occurred to recount. But a crush of pregame performers and lots of props in the area around the logical exit point made it necessary for her to be escorted through an access way that led to a freight door. As soon as that large door was opened, the escaping blast of air gave Diana the kind of shove that a linebacker might cheer. The rush practically blew Diana into the frigid Michigan night. She was caught completely off guard and was lucky she didn't go into orbit. Fortunately, she wasn't injured, and neither was anyone else.

And then there was the traffic mess. Saying traffic was snarled around the Silverdome doesn't do justice to the reality of the situation. The traffic jam was the worst of any Super Bowl in memory. It's always been assumed that the source of that mess was the icy January weather. Not entirely.

Temperatures in south-central Michigan that Sunday were undeniably bone-chilling, and a terrible ice storm that had raged on the Friday before the game left many reserved parking spaces unusable and some highway signs unreadable. The windchill was between 23 and 26 degrees below zero, and the icy gusts felt like a knife as they slashed at your skin. Yet, the source of the monumental traffic jam wasn't only Jack Frost. He had ample assistance from Vice President George Bush's 16-car motorcade. It caused untold anguish and disrupted the plans of thousands of fans, hundreds of writers, even some of the San Francisco 49ers themselves.

Much of the mess could have been avoided if only one of Mr. Bush's chief aides (one of them wore western boots and a hat, which prompted us to nickname him Tex) had accepted our recommendations. But the Bush staff, including Tex, ignored every suggestion we offered.

The vice president had been invited to the Super Bowl by Detroit Lions owner William Clay Ford, who had been one of Mr. Bush's college pals at Yale. As you'd expect, we had the requisite meeting or two with members of the vice president's staff, assorted details and security arrangements to review, and numerous phone calls. Time and again during these discussions, we urged—we pleaded—with the vice president's staff to bring Mr. Bush to the game either very early or just a few moments prior to kickoff. Arriving at almost any other time would inevitably bring traffic to an absolute standstill and wreck our best-laid plans to control the heavy flow of cars and buses to the Silverdome.

I probably don't have to tell you when the Bush caravan showed up: right when the crush at the stadium was at its worst and precisely when we asked them not to. Don't ask me why. It was a disaster. Access to the Silverdome is limited to begin with. Interstate 75 runs nearby, but only one major highway leads from that expressway to the stadium, which sits in a predominantly rural area (at least it was in January 1982). To accommodate the Bush entourage, all other traffic heading to the stadium was halted. Predictably, the consequences were just awful, worse than you can imagine. If hell ever does freeze over, I can tell you what it might look like.

A number of cars stalled or slid off the slick pavement, and their drivers simply parked them along the highways and side roads and trudged across fields through the snow. Some walked a mile or more to the Silverdome. Included in their numbers were scores of writers. They abandoned media buses snarled in traffic for fear they would miss the kickoff and part of the first quarter. Many of these media folks were traipsing through the snow in the frigid temperatures without their overcoats. With the game being played indoors and buses providing door-to-door service, the writers had left their coats in their hotel rooms, figuring they wouldn't need them. For these scribes, then, the conditions were downright dangerous. A close family friend of mine was also among the walkers, and I was scared to death he wasn't going to survive. He was so short of breath from his frigid walk that he couldn't really enjoy the game.

At one point as I sat in the Silverdome control booth getting updates, I even thought about delaying the kickoff because one of the buses caught in traffic was carrying some of the 49ers' players, including head coach Bill Walsh. San Francisco's first bus had left early and wasn't affected. But the second bus was caught cold, although it arrived in time for the players to dress and warm up. Along the way, Walsh tried to make light of the matter.

"I have good news and bad news," Walsh told his players as the bus inched its way toward the Silverdome. "The bad news is that the game has already started, the equipment manager is playing right tackle, and the trainer is playing left tackle. The good news is we're only down 7–0 in the first quarter." Walsh rates a salute for his demeanor. I was furious.

The vice president's staff had ignored one other detail. For our efforts in arranging his visit, several of us were promised opportunities to meet Mr. Bush. We certainly appreciated the thought, of course, but also explained that we might have a narrow window of time. As the kickoff of any Super Bowl nears, timing is ever so critical and is measured in seconds if not tenths of seconds. It's a countdown that virtually rivals a space shuttle launch because so many events involving so many people take place in such a short time. When the clock hits the three-minute mark prior to kickoff, we don't even allow radio traffic on the walkie-talkies. Everybody shuts up and everything stops so that we can focus entirely on getting the Anthem sung, getting guys off the field, getting players on the field, flipping the coin, and on and on. And I was ultimately responsible for keeping everything on schedule.

Naturally, then, we heard a tap on the door of our control booth about three minutes before kickoff. Our security man responded, then walked over and tapped me on the shoulder and said, "A gentleman wants to see you."

It was Tex, of course, who said, "George Bush would like to meet with you now."

"Sorry," I replied as politely as I could. "I can't leave my post now."

I guess this experience makes for an interesting career note: Before Super Bowl III, I had to tell Vice President Elect Spiro Agnew he had to leave the field. Before Super Bowl XVI, I had to tell Vice President George Bush I was too busy to shake his hand.

Six years earlier I had been worrying about the prospects of another horror story erupting during Super Bowl X, in 1976, the year we helped the country kick off the bicentennial. By and large, we averted trouble. But with Hollywood standing along the sidelines, I held my breath.

If you think scenes from the movie *Black Sunday* look too real to be staged, you're right. A number of them, including one of the movie's climactic action scenes, were filmed during Pittsburgh's 21–17 victory over Dallas, the Steelers' second Super Bowl victory. The movie producers, in fact, hired Steve Sabol and NFL Films to help supervise the shooting of action sequences during the game.

Frankly, agreeing to the idea in the first place created some apprehension. We spent huge amounts of time on it and had to arrange for additional camera locations in the Orange Bowl. But it was Pete's call, and he said OK, in part as a gesture to Carroll Rosenbloom, who sat on the board of Warner Brothers pictures and who by that time had acquired the Los Angeles Rams' franchise from Bob Irsay in exchange for the Baltimore Colts. Pete's willingness to cooperate surprised me a little because Rosenbloom could be one of Rozelle's severest critics. In any event, Pete said we'd do it, so we did.

But not to the extent that the production crew of *Black Sunday* requested. The movie's script called for the hero, played by British actor Robert Shaw, to leap out of the stands at one end of the stadium at the critical moment in the story and race to the television production truck at the open end of the Orange Bowl: He's discovered that the Goodyear blimp has been commandeered by terrorists and is approaching the stadium carrying a bomb. Since Shaw's character has only moments to warn the production truck of approaching

The officiating crew and alternates for Super Bowl I, in the uniforms designed expressly for the game. Standing are Art McNally (left), Bernie Ulman, Burl Toler, Harry Kessel, Norm Schachter (referee), Herman Rohrig, and George Young. Kneeling are Al Sabato (left), Mike Lisetski, Paul Trepinski, Charlie Musser, and Jack Reader. Six officials were chosen from each league.
Copyright © Vernon Biever/NFL Photos

Pete Rozelle presents the first Super Bowl trophy to Green Bay coach Vince Lombardi in Los Angeles, January 15, 1967. The scene was more chaotic than the photo suggests; I was clinging to the rafters overhead to hear what was said.
Copyright © NFL Photos

Pregame in the Super Bowl's early years now looks pretty mundane.
Accompanied by bands, two giant figures representing Oakland and Green Bay
met and shook hands at midfield before Super Bowl II, played at the Orange
Bowl in 1968.

The NFL's support of Nancy Reagan's antidrug campaign in the 1980s took me to the White House and a meeting with President Reagan.

At Super Bowl XX in New Orleans, we honored all the game's MVPs: On the platform are (from left) Bart Starr, Marcus Allen, Joe Namath (in white shoes), Joe Montana, Harvey Martin, Lynn Swann, Larry Csonka, Jim Plunkett, Terry Bradshaw, Randy White, Fred Biletnikoff, Franco Harris, Jake Scott, and Chuck Howley. Roger Staubach has just left the platform behind John Riggins, while Len Dawson is walking with Super Bowl pregame coordinator Lesslee Fitzmorris.

Streamers and cards made of Mylar looked great during the halftime show of Super Bowl XIV, played in the Rose Bowl in 1980. But some eager fans flashed the cards from their seats during the first half, distracting Steelers and Rams receivers by the reflections.

Super Bowl XIV's pregame show included the largest Terrible Towel this side of Pittsburgh. Evidently it was effective: The Steelers wiped up the Rams to win their fourth Super Bowl, under Chuck Noll.

Red Grange, standing next to me at Super Bowl XII in New Orleans, was the first football celebrity we invited to toss the coin before the game. Grange was an ideal choice.

By the time Pete Rozelle posed for this promotional photo in the late 1970s, the trophy awarded to the Super Bowl champion was called the Lombardi Trophy. This is one of my favorite photos.
Copyright © NFL PHOTOS

Kansas City's convincing victory in Super Bowl IV deserves more attention than it has received. On the heels of the Jets' win in Super Bowl III, it affirmed that the AFL could compete in an expanded NFL and established coach Hank Stram as a personality all his own. Copyright © ROD HANNA/NFL PHOTOS

Super Bowl XI marked the first time we played in the Rose Bowl, in 1977, and made me a nervous wreck because we didn't know if 103,438 fans would participate in the card stunts designed by Disney's Bob Jani as part of halftime. I needn't have worried. The idea worked to perfection.

Now a collector's item, the official scroll of the Royal Order of Realignment Recorders was bestowed on writers who dutifully covered the interminable realignment talks in 1969 and 1970. Dick Forbes was the pro football writer for the *Cincinnati Enquirer*. My dad, a commercial artist, designed the graphics and lettering.

Joe Namath on the sidelines of Super Bowl III. We loved the headlines that his presence guaranteed but still couldn't believe the 16–7 upset of Baltimore that he engineered. Copyright © NFL PHOTOS

What a well-organized Super Bowl looks like from the air. This was Super Bowl XXII, played in San Diego. As well-organized as our game plan was, Washington's was better: Doug Williams threw a record four touchdown passes in the second quarter alone.

The pregame show of Super Bowl XXII featured Bob Hope, as reflected by the giant caricature positioned on the star adorning the 50-yard line.

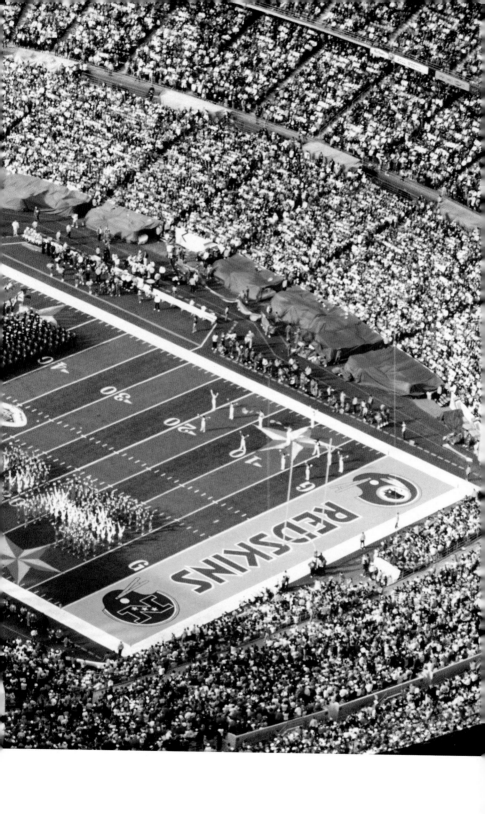

Standing next to Pete Rozelle (center) and NFL director of public relations Joe Browne, I had reason to be glum: Pete is about to announce his "resignation" as Commissioner. That was always the word he used.

Pete's surprise announcement of his resignation began with the words, "I'm today resigning my position as Commissioner, subject to a search committee identifying my successor."

Joe Browne (left), Jim Kensil, Pete Rozelle, me, and Jim Heffernan were all smiles at Rozelle's retirement dinner in July 1989 at the Regency Hotel in New York. The smiles belied our true feelings.

The 1990 NFL Competition Committee at its meeting at Saddlebrook Resort near Tampa, Florida. Standing are the Giants' George Young (left); Seattle's Tom Flores; Buffalo's Bill Polian; me; Jan Van Duser, of the NFL office; and the NCAA's Davey Nelson. Seated are Art McNally, of the NFL office (left); Kansas City's Marty Schottenheimer; New Orleans's Jim Finks; Miami's Don Shula; and Cincinnati's Paul Brown. Four months earlier Finks had been passed over as Rozelle's successor.

The only time we ever removed a goalpost for a halftime show was to get this replica of the Delta Queen onto the field at Super Bowl XXIV. Those are "Peanuts" characters riding on top of the float.

As it turned out, it was easier getting this red-white-and-blue map of the United States onto the field before Super Bowl XXVII than it was getting Garth Brooks to sing the National Anthem.

As much effort as Natalie Cole put into singing the National Anthem at Super Bowl XXVIII in Atlanta, the people who held up pieces of the American flag behind her labored just as mightily.

doom, he has to take the shortest route possible: *right down the middle of the field during the Super Bowl game itself!*

I don't recall our actually saying, "Are you guys nuts?" But that's
what we thought.

"Absolutely not. Not a chance!" I replied when some colleagues
and I heard the proposal. I couldn't get the words out of my mouth
fast enough. A few pleas and a bit of haggling were forthcoming, but
we held firm and forced the action to be shot according to these
ground rules: During the second quarter, Shaw's character would race
down the aisle at the northwest corner of the Orange Bowl and leap
onto the field, as the original script called for. But instead of charg-
ing down the middle of the field, Shaw was to run between the stands
and the team bench on the north side of the stadium until he reached
the back of the east end zone, then tear across the back of the end
zone where the film crew had erected a dummy production truck. The
real CBS truck was in a different location, outside on the Orange
Bowl's south side.

One take and one take only is all they would get, and we insisted
that the director and producer agree to our instructions in writing,
just so we would have no misunderstanding. Even then, I decided not
to take any chances. Hollywood being Hollywood, I could envision
the director telling Shaw to ignore our decree. After all, what could
we do if he did? I had a response all prepared: Jim Kensil's robust son
Mike was as strapping as his 6-foot-4 dad, and with the film crew's
knowledge I hired him to tail Shaw along the actor's entire route. "If
Shaw takes so much as one step onto the playing field," I told Mike,
"tackle him, just like you would anyone else trying a stunt like that."

Mike was ready to follow my instructions to the letter and also
knew to stay out of camera range. I needn't have worried. Shaw, who
was really a nice guy to work with, kept his promise and followed the
agreed-upon route. The game was not disrupted at all. Shaw all but
blended into the crowd, belying the fame he had earned from his starring role in *Jaws*, released the preceding summer. Afterward, I'm told,
the actor admitted that when he got within 30 yards of the east end
zone, he had been tempted to run across that portion of the field. "It

would be the logical thing to do under the circumstances," Shaw said. But recalling his "tail" and his promise to us, he decided not to. A wise choice.

Near the end of his frantic run along the back of the end zone, Shaw was spotted by veteran Super Bowl photographer Tony Tomsic. As robust Tony likes to tell his buddies, he shouted to Shaw, "What are you doing here? There're no sharks in the Orange Bowl." And no actors on the playing field, either.

While not as dramatic as this incident, Super Bowl X foreshadowed another bit of pageantry. John Warner, the bicentennial administrator, who was to become one of Virginia's senators and one of Elizabeth Taylor's husbands, provided us with a bicentennial medal to use for the coin toss, so we invited him to join us on the field to flip the coin as part of the celebration's kickoff.

It was a nice touch, we concluded, and two years later in New Orleans, when we played in the Superdome for the first time, we launched the tradition of inviting a celebrity to toss the coin before the game. Legendary Red Grange was our first invitee, and for the most part top sports figures have done the flipping ever since. George Halas followed Grange, in 1979 in Miami, the last year the Orange Bowl hosted the Super Bowl. He nearly made it more eventful than it needed to be.

Being as close to a patriarch as the NFL had and the legendary coach of the Chicago Bears, Halas was riding in a vintage 1920 convertible for the coin toss of Super Bowl XIII. At 83 years of age and after two hip operations, George wasn't very mobile, and with split-second timing paramount, we decided to have him flip the coin from the backseat of the car. As the car was rolling to the 50-yard line, however, I heard over my walkie-talkie that George wanted to get out of the car.

"Tell him he can't," I shot back. "It'll take too long."

As the car stopped, Halas started to stand up and wave. And I started muttering softly, "Stay in that car." Still uneasy, I asked to speak to him via the walkie-talkie.

"George, this is Don Weiss," I said quickly. "Please stay in the car!"

Halas stayed put, thank goodness, and as the car pulled away after the coin toss, I heard my assitant, Joe Browne, mutter, "Weiss 7, Halas 0."

With Halas, you never could be sure. He was a character's character, with a vocabulary that would make a sailor blush and an occasional mean streak: The Bears went to Minnesota in 1961 for the Vikings' NFL debut and somehow managed to get trounced 37–13. Fran Tarkenton, the Vikings' quarterback, ran all over the place. Afterward, Halas was so angry at his team that he couldn't talk—not even swear—and refused to give his players anything to drink on the flight back to Chicago, out of sheer spite.

For the record, one coin toss wasn't flipped in the stadium where the Super Bowl was being played. In 1985, President Ronald Reagan did the flipping for Super Bowl XIX from the Blue Room of the White House as television cameras beamed it back to Stanford Stadium and around the world. Hugh McElhenny, the Hall of Famer and former 49ers great, stood in for the president at the 50-yard line. As his thank-you letter details, Reagan got such a kick out of participating that he asked us if he could keep the coin. We obliged, of course.

One coin has also been tossed by a woman: Marie Lombardi, Vince's widow, did the honors at Super Bowl XV in New Orleans. Asked what her late husband would have thought, Marie quipped, "He'd probably wonder what the hell a woman was doing on the football field."

Vince might have tolerated a female's presence, but begrudgingly. As uptight as he was preceding his two Super Bowls, that's how he usually reacted to our requests—begrudgingly. In that respect, Lombardi wasn't unique.

Coaches are a class of Super Bowl celebrities all their own. They have lots of distractions and demands on their time and their players' time. It's all the hoopla, the people in the hotel lobbies, the hordes of media. By now, most NFL coaches have had sufficient experience with what goes on and accept it, while we've gotten better at managing the week's activities. Still, some coaches handle it better than others, a skill that is pretty much reflected by their results on the field. It's a conclusion I've quietly related to many participating teams, to help them better prepare.

Of all those who have endured the meat grinder of pressures that the Super Bowl represents, Pittsburgh's Chuck Noll and Minnesota's Bud Grant stand out in my mind as representing each end of the spectrum.

Noll approached the Super Bowl better than anyone else I know. He did whatever we asked him to do and enjoyed himself. He rarely complained and generally made do with the facilities we provided. Chuck also was very good at letting us know in advance what he wanted in the way of equipment to work with, items like blocking sleds, for instance. We never got too many surprises from Chuck. Moreover, he was very good about meeting all the media requirements and issuing marching orders to his players.

"Here's what's going to happen, and here's where you'll be," Noll would say. "You *will* be there, too. You *will* stay there for 45 minutes, and you'll enjoy it! This is the approach we're going to take. We've got a time when we can practice, and when we do practice we'll do things as we've always done them. But if we have to do something special, we'll do it. That's part of the game and one of the reasons we all make the big bucks we make."

The Steelers' players, in turn, were unfailingly loosey-goosey. And it showed. Under Noll, the Steelers' Super Bowl record was 4–0. No other NFL coach has matched it.

Other than Lombardi's being so uptight, I saw a great deal of similarity between the Packers in Super Bowls I and II and the Steelers in the four Super Bowls they won over a six-year span in the 1970s. Most of the guys on both teams were solid professionals who were used to winning, knew how to handle the media attention, and handled it well. But credit Chuck Noll for his deft approach and for his contribution to Pittsburgh's four victories.

At the other extreme was Bud Grant. Grant really was not the stoic he often appeared to be on camera and let things bother him that really shouldn't have. He just never seemed to accept all that went on at the Super Bowl. At least that's how it appeared to us.

We bent over backward trying to do things for Bud that people who worked for him told us he wanted, only to have Bud later complain that he hadn't wanted that at all, much to the surprise of his aide who had made the initial request. He was uptight about all kinds of little things. I guess it was just his nature. He was a big believer in team concepts as a coach, as his teams demonstrated. As a person, though, he didn't take direction too well.

For example, if we told Bud that he was to be someplace between 10 and 11 in the morning and that his AFC counterpart would follow him from 11 to noon, invariably he'd ask, "Why am I first? Why can't I be second?" If we explained our rationale for scheduling press conferences in the morning and team workouts in the afternoon to help the writers meet their daily deadlines, Bud would always ask why, implying he didn't like the time and wanted it changed.

Purely due to the luck of the draw, Miami used the Oilers' workout facility leading up to Super Bowl VIII, played in Houston's Rice Stadium. Minnesota used a high school facility on the edge of town, but it was still a nice, modern workout facility, with access to both natural grass and artificial turf. When Bud first arrived, a sparrow had somehow found its way into the locker room. Grant immediately told the press that the NFL had put him in a bird sanctuary. Bill Granholm, who had put tons of effort into making the arrangements, was irate over the remark. The rest of us weren't very pleased either.

In the end, of course, neither was Bud. When his Vikings played Miami at the end of the week, the Dolphins scored the first two times they had the ball, on long, sustained drives, and that was about it. The final score was 24–7. In fact, the Vikings did not play very well in any of their four Super Bowl appearances. The Chiefs manhandled them in Super Bowl IV, 23–7; and Oakland beat them handily in Super Bowl XI, in the Rose Bowl, 32–14. They played tough against Pittsburgh in Super Bowl IX but still lost, 16–6, in New Orleans's Tulane Stadium.

Bud never said too much about his defeats. Nor did he reveal the secret behind the headsets he became famous for wearing: Most of the time the headset wasn't hooked up to anything. The wire never went anywhere and just dragged along the ground. I never knew why.

George Allen, who coached the Redskins to Super Bowl VII, against undefeated Miami, wasn't any more comfortable in the Super Bowl spotlight than Bud Grant. It showed, too. Washington was matched against Don Shula's unbeaten Miami team in the Los Angeles Coliseum, and Allen was so uptight that, as soon as he verified what time the game was going to be played, he sent his people to the Coliseum to see what the shadows were like at 4:00 and 5:00 and 6:00.

Allen just never let his team enjoy its conference championship (Washington beat Dallas, 26–3) or its Super Bowl experience. It was all much too serious.

"If we could have played the Super Bowl the Sunday after we won the NFC championship game, we could have beaten anybody," Redskins tight end Jerry Smith later told me. "But by the second Sunday we were so sick of each other and so sick of the whole situation, it wasn't fun. We dreaded what we were having to do. We were poorly prepared and way overprepared."

Smith is a sharp guy and a player I got to know well because he did a lot of public service stuff for us. And I've concluded that what he said is probably true. The Redskins were simply past their peak and just too wound up when they got to the Super Bowl, a consequence of Allen's being too uptight. George just never relaxed, not once. Even if he had, though, it doesn't mean the Redskins would have upset the undefeated Dolphins.

Don Shula, the man across the field from Allen that day, is among the coaches who had a good grasp of what the Super Bowl was all about. Although Don lost more championship games than he won, he still won back-to-back Super Bowls in 1973 and 1974, and the victory in Super Bowl VII in 1973 capped a perfect 17–0 season. No other NFL coach has matched it.

Tom Landry of Dallas and Bill Parcells of the Giants, who both won two Super Bowls, were able to take the hoopla in stride, too. And while you might think he would have been overwhelmed by the excitement, John Madden was also very good to work with. John won just one Super Bowl for the Raiders, against Bud Grant in Super Bowl XI. But I guess John also passed on some pointers to his successor, Tom Flores, along with a solid football team. Flores, too, was easy to

work with and has the distinction of being the only person to participate in a Super Bowl as a player (with Kansas City in 1970), as an
assistant coach (with Oakland in 1977), and twice as a head coach
(with the Raiders in 1981 and 1984).

San Francisco's Bill Walsh was somewhat of an exception. He has
the distinction of being one of the Super Bowl's three-time winners,
along with Joe Gibbs of Washington. But in his first Super Bowl in
Pontiac, Michigan, Walsh was frequently fussing about the eastern
time zone. If he were asked today what time he worked out that week
in Pontiac, he's liable to say six o'clock in the morning because, while
it was 9:00 A.M. in Detroit, it was 6:00 A.M. in California. Bill often
moaned that Super Bowl XVI was conducted entirely in the wee
hours of the morning and was forever replying, "I'd rather go second," on seeing a schedule of morning events. His laments usually
prompted coin tosses to determine which coach went first.

We had a really tough time with both coaches that year. Walsh's
opposite, Forrest Gregg of Cincinnati, really seemed to let the pressure get to him. Even though he had been through the Super Bowl
twice as a player in Green Bay and once in Dallas, Super Bowl XVI
was his only game as a coach, and he gave us quite a challenge. He
was very difficult, in a game that itself was very contentious throughout. Its being our first Super Bowl up north probably didn't help. It
was different in many respects: the vice president's visit, for one thing,
and the weather, for another. It forced us to use the Silverdome as the
workout facility, as well as the game site. That alone required delicate coordination. What's more, Rozelle was ill during the week of
the game, forcing cancellation of his annual Friday morning press
conference, and the ice storm that night badly disrupted the Commissioner's party, held in suburban Dearborn.

One thing was different about Super Bowl XVII, too: a horrible decision rendered jointly by the Washington Redskins' owner, Jack Kent
Cooke, and the Miami Dolphins' owner, Joe Robbie. In their wisdom,
they decided to stage one combined postgame party and put the
winning and losing teams in the same room after the 1983 game, in
the Rose Bowl, just to save money. It was a bad idea, and I said so as

soon as I heard about it. In response, Cooke darned near had me for lunch.

"I've been putting on parties since before you were born," he barked over the telephone, in as haughty a tone as I've ever heard. "Don't you tell me how to put on a party!" Cooke was the most arrogant man I have ever encountered. Nobody else came close.

Bobby Beathard, the Redskins' general manager at the time, was sitting with Cooke when I called. He heard every word of the conversation and recounted it from his vantage point the next time I saw him.

"Heard you had a little conversation with the boss," Bobby began with that impish grin of his. It was classic.

I *was* right, too. The Dolphins were crestfallen, as it was, after losing to the Redskins, 27–17, largely on the strength of John Riggins's record 166-yard rushing performance. To have to attend Cooke's party later at the Beverly Hilton Hotel was needless humiliation. I'm surprised they even showed up, but they did—briefly—before departing for their own gathering.

In a manner of speaking, I settled the score the next year at Super Bowl XVIII in Tampa, a host city that didn't have a lot of great team hotels available in 1984. We booked the Redskins into a Holiday Inn—an upscale Holiday Inn, to be sure, with well-appointed rooms and a presidential suite—perfectly acceptable, but still unworthy to a Jack Kent Cooke.

The sight of the owner of the Chrysler Building (and who knows how much else) standing in line to check into a Holiday Inn struck *Washington Star* writer Mo Siegel as utterly hilarious. "A sight I'll never forget," Mo said. "I don't think it had happened ever before in his life."

It wasn't especially funny to Cooke, however. The next time he saw me, he bellowed, "*You're* the one who put me at the Holiday Inn!"

Among my own Super Bowl celebrities are the writers and photographers who have covered all 36 games. They compose a true fraternity that suddenly seems to have dwindled.

Beginning with Super Bowl X, we saluted those with "perfect attendance" every five years. We've made just one accommodation, for legendary *Los Angeles Times* columnist Jim Murray. He was at Miami in one of the early years, when something ruptured in his eye on the morning of the game. Jim, who had been there all week, was taken to a hospital and wasn't released in time to get to the game. He later petitioned me at some point, once we initiated our salutes, and we decided to include him, as we should have.

The group was never as large as you might think—about 166 at first—because a number of writers who covered as many as 30 Super Bowls didn't cover the first one. Their papers chose not to send them. Our last big get-together was Super Bowl XXXV, in Tampa, what we called the "Super 35 Club." A lot of the guys who have retired continue to come to the game to maintain their record, but the number still is down to 14: writers Jerry Green of the *Detroit News*, Jerry Izenberg and Dave Klein of the *Newark Star Ledger*, Will McDonough of the *Boston Globe*, Bob Oates of the *Los Angeles Times*, and Edwin Pope of the *Miami Herald*; photographers John Biever of the *Green Bay Press-Gazette* (his father, Vern, missed Super Bowl XXXVI), Walter Ioos of *Sports Illustrated*, Mickey Palmer, Dick Raphael, and Tony Tomsic; Steve Sabol of NFL Films; Lee Remmel of the Green Bay Packers; and me.

Our 30th reunion at Super Bowl XXX, played in Tempe, Arizona, in 1996, was especially memorable. Pete Rozelle was still alive but in failing health with a brain tumor and unable to travel to the game. So, we got Pete hooked up on a speakerphone from his home in California, and he spoke individually to each of the guys after I introduced them—one after another—for more than two hours. Even though he was in ill health, something would trigger some memory and then a story or two. It was an unforgettable night for all of us and for Pete's dear wife, Carrie. That night, she said, Pete was the happiest he had been in years. He died that December.

For all their grumbling, football writers, for the most part, are like the rest of us. And like the celebrities, they love the Super Bowl, too.

FIFTEEN

MY FAVORITE YEARS

I should have been in Tampa. Super Bowl XXV, our silver anniversary game, was now only 11 days away, and preparations were intensifying. But I was nowhere near Tampa. Instead, I was huddled in wintry Washington, D.C., with Warren Welsh, the NFL's security director, and William Baker, assistant director of the FBI.

Our meeting in Baker's office was part of a daylong agenda, arranged with the help of our lawyers, to appraise in detail the likelihood of the Super Bowl being threatened by terrorists. It was mid-January 1991, and while Baker briefed us about what the Bureau knew of suspicious activity and the whereabouts of people most likely to cause trouble, the rest of the nation was bracing for war with Iraq.

"As we speak," Baker noted during the afternoon, "the decision is being made as to when we might launch an attack."

A short time later, the news that Desert Storm had begun flashed across television screens while I sat in Washington National Airport, waiting to fly back to Tampa. Soon after I landed in Florida, my colleagues and I resumed debating another issue: whether or not Super Bowl XXV should be played.

Fifteen years earlier we had confronted a mock threat from the producers of *Black Sunday*. Now, as a milestone Super Bowl approached, we confronted a very real threat. It's a big reason why the silver anniversary game remains my most memorable and my favorite of all played so far. It remains the only Super Bowl that's ever faced a legitimate threat of being canceled.

We kicked off as scheduled on January 27, and given our discussions beforehand and my own recollections, I don't think we ever really came that close to not playing. Paul Tagliabue, who had succeeded Pete Rozelle as Commissioner in late 1989, spoke to President Bush, who said he very much wanted to see the game played. So did General Norman Schwartzkopf, who, in addition to directing the war with General Colin Powell, had family ties in Tampa.

Baker's report concluded that the odds of a violent disruption were small, and the FBI had assured us that no known troublemakers were in the area. Even so, we were in constant contact with federal authorities. From the start, the majority of us felt we should go ahead with as "normal" a Super Bowl as possible.

Once the decision to play was affirmed, the next question was: How much ceremony and pageantry should we present? This topic dominated discussions for days during the week that Desert Storm was launched, the week prior to the arrival of the teams in Tampa. Two schools of thought were presented: One group contended that the Super Bowl should be a subdued and patriotic affair, without most of the celebratory pomp and circumstance, and with just a marching band at halftime. The other group (including me) felt strongly that the fans coming to the game were still paying top dollar and were thus entitled to experience the Super Bowl in its entirety—at least as much of it as made sense under the circumstances. I had to express most of my thoughts in phone conversations because I was in Tampa for final preparations while others were still in New York and elsewhere.

Befitting the 25th-anniversary game, we had made grand plans: the unveiling of an all-time Super Bowl team, special pregame festivities, and many nostalgic touches. In press releases, we called attention to what was popular when the Super Bowl debuted in 1967—songs such as "Windy," "Never My Love," and "Along Comes Mary" and movies such as *Camelot*, *Wait Until Dark*, and *Bonnie and Clyde*. We also had lined up the cast from the show *Beatlemania* to sing cuts from *Sgt. Pepper's Lonely Hearts Club Band* and other favorites of that era.

In the end, many of the activities surrounding the game were minimized. The Friday night party was scratched, and the halftime show, featuring New Kids on the Block and a salute to 25 years of Super Bowl halftime shows, was toned down and not as spectacular as it might have been. Our focus became the in-stadium entertainment and tribute to our soldiers. It turned out to be not only appropriate but also every bit as emotional and unforgettable as we could have hoped.

A dramatic and thundering flyover was provided by a tactical training wing from nearby MacDill Air Force Base, and Pete Rozelle, ending his first year of retirement, tossed the coin as planned. Then came the most dramatic moment of all, Whitney Houston's singing of the National Anthem.

A debate had ensued about that, too, a few folks arguing that the Anthem should be performed by a band or an opera star instead of a celebrity. Whitney's rendition, which literally became a hit song when subsequently released by Arista records, was one of the most dramatic I have ever heard. Actually, it was her second rendition that was aired in the stadium and around the world, while Whitney lip-synched the words on camera. Either her father or her manager (I forget who) didn't care for the first one she had recorded about two weeks earlier. So, she had done it again.

It was a powerful performance. ABC, which did the telecast, had arranged for live camera shots of troops watching the game in Iraq and Saudi Arabia, and mixed scenes of military personnel watching Whitney sing, frequently with tears coming down her face, and shots of people in the stadium waving American flags. It was a very special moment.

Adding to the atmosphere were the Blackhawk attack helicopters that circled the stadium in full view. They, too, presented a powerful and menacing sight. For me, it was also an ironic sight, for it reflected an old fight I had been waging for years with the Federal Aviation Administration.

I had been concerned about random, unrestricted aircraft flying over Super Bowl stadiums, fearing that something might happen. The skies were getting downright cluttered. What once had been a single

Goodyear blimp was now almost a squadron of aircraft: two or three blimps, plus assorted low-flying planes, touting the virtues of somebody's sports saloon or hardware store. I thought it was high time to make the skies more orderly and went to the wall with my concern several times. My plea was routinely ignored. "The air is free," the FAA kept replying, at times scornfully. Meanwhile, commercial aviators aware of my lonely campaign became aroused, to the point that "Down with Don Weiss" banners were flown periodically above some of the stadiums. This all came to a head in Tampa, yet even then the FAA dismissed my concern. It finally altered its stance . . . after September 11, 2001.

On the ground in Tampa, however, security was incredibly tight. The security game plan was humongous. Anybody and anything coming into the stadium had to undergo a search. We used metal detectors, wands, random searches, the whole nine yards, no exceptions. We urged fans to come a couple of hours early. NFL Director of Special Events Jim Steeg and I were among the first to arrive, in separate cars, seven to eight hours before kickoff, and security strip-searched the whole doggone car. Each vehicle got as thorough an inspection as I've ever seen—inside, outside, the trunk, the hood—they even pulled out the seat cushions.

Inside, we set up extra first aid stations throughout the stadium, just in case, and each one of them had a special hot line phone. My telephone console in the control booth was larger than it's ever been before or since. All kinds of preparations were made.

Fortunately, nothing happened, and that was what made it so memorable. Nor was any evidence uncovered that anything had been planned. All we had was a fantastic football game.

The game played in Super Bowl XXV was one of the best Super Bowl battles ever and featured perhaps the most exciting finale until Super Bowl XXXVI, when the New England Patriots won in a last-second victory over the St. Louis Rams. Both games ended the same way, too. The difference was that the Patriots' Adam Vinatieri made his 48-yard field goal as time expired in Super Bowl XXXVI, while Buffalo's Scott Norwood missed his 47-yard field goal attempt in Super Bowl XXV, preserving the New York Giants' 20–19 victory.

Norwood had had enough leg, but the ball sailed to the right of the goalpost. As the ball floated, Buffalo quarterback Jim Kelly was almost praying, "Please go through," but the ball never did.

"It was moving," Norwood said. "It just wasn't being drawn in."

Generally, it was a well-played game, especially by New York. The Giants controlled the ball for 40 minutes, 33 seconds, a Super Bowl record. They took the second-half kickoff and held the football for 9:29 (another record) in lumbering ever so methodically to the end zone, covering 73 yards on 14 plays. Quarterback Jeff Hostetler, substituting for the injured Phil Simms, converted on three third-down situations, with clutch passes of 14, 11, and 9 yards, before Ottis Anderson scored the touchdown on a 1-yard run. The Giants controlled the ball so effectively that the Bills had it for less than eight minutes in the second half. But they still had the chance to win at the end.

It was the kind of game you hope the Super Bowl always will be. Coming on the Super Bowl's 25th anniversary amid all that swirled around it made it unforgettable.

World affairs had made Super Bowl XV almost as memorable because giant yellow ribbons adorned the New Orleans Superdome. It was 1981, just days after the Iran hostages were freed. Out of the blue, I got a call from the owner of CPS Industries in Franklin, Tennessee. He offered to make a huge yellow ribbon to hang over the Superdome's main entrance, a task that would take several days. "Come on down," I replied quickly. The company used miles of yellow satin ribbon to make a bow several stories high and didn't charge us a dime. CPS also made two other big ribbons that hung above each end zone inside the Superdome. Consider it a patriotic gesture, the owner said.

There was more: under the owner's direction, three or four CPS workers also made 80,000 yellow ribbon corsages—assembling them in the back of the truck as it transported the three large ribbons from Tennessee to New Orleans. Each person attending the game received a corsage upon entering the Superdome. In the spirit of the occasion, we also affixed yellow ribbons to the helmets of the participating teams, the Oakland Raiders and Philadelphia Eagles. Having heard that the hostages themselves were eager to watch a Super Bowl after more than a year in captivity, the players seemed genuinely happy to oblige.

Other years have been memorable, too, such as Super Bowl IX in 1975, the year of Pittsburgh's first championship. More important, it was Art Rooney's first championship of any kind.

The sight of the man whom I always called Mr. Rooney clutching the Lombardi Trophy in New Orleans's Tulane Stadium is forever etched in my mind and in others'. More people than I can count were emotionally attached to Mr. Rooney as a person, solely because he was such a beloved, likeable, and wonderful man. Because he came into the NFL in the 1930s, Mr. Rooney wasn't regarded as a patriarch of pro football like, say, George Halas, and it's too bad. He devoted all of his life to the Steelers and endured decades of losing. At last, he was finally being rewarded. Seeing him reach the pinnacle at the Super Bowl was really special. I know Pete Rozelle felt the same way.

Without fail, Mr. Rooney always made you feel welcome. He was among the first NFL owners I got to know during my Associated Press days, in part because he had a fondness for the writers he called "my boys." He'd just as soon let his oldest son, Dan, attend owners' meetings so that he could spend time with the writers. Mr. Rooney lived so close to Three Rivers Stadium that, if we were in Pittsburgh, he invited us to park in his driveway and walk to the game or ride with him.

The gesture reflected his heart. The only complaint we ever fielded from the Steelers during any of their Super Bowls (other than Noll's yelling about a couple of game situations) came from Dan Rooney. "My dad's giving away too many tickets," he said. "I need you to help me control him."

Pittsburgh's first Super Bowl victory wasn't a particularly outstanding game. It led only 2–0 at halftime, after Dwight White sacked Minnesota quarterback Fran Tarkenton in the end zone, midway through the second quarter. Pittsburgh's "Steel Curtain" defense completely stifled the Vikings, who were trying for the third time to win a Super Bowl. Minnesota's only touchdown came on a blocked punt, with Terry Brown covering the football in the Steelers' end zone. Pittsburgh answered by taking the kickoff 66 yards in 11 plays to seal the victory. Franco Harris gained what was then a record 158 yards on 34 carries, while the entire Minnesota team managed but 17 yards rushing—also a Super Bowl record.

For my money, that Steelers team was the best of that generation and maybe of any generation. It took time to jell, as it took Terry Bradshaw several seasons to mature. He even lost his starting quarterback job to both Terry Hanratty and Joe Gilliam before he fully developed. His teammates were ready when he was. Pittsburgh played in four Super Bowls in a six-year stretch, won all four, and had supreme talent on both sides of the ball. I think it would have had a winning record against any of the other Super Bowl champions, including Don Shula's undefeated Dolphins team. In some respects, the Steelers of the 1970s were like the Packers of the 1960s. Both stayed virtually intact for many seasons.

Mr. Rooney tossed the coin before Super Bowl XIV in the Rose Bowl. It was a fitting tribute. So was the game. The Steelers beat the Rams, 31–19, for their fourth championship.

Super Bowl X in the Orange Bowl, the game that officially kicked off our nation's bicentennial, also makes my list. It was gratifying to have our game selected as the official kickoff for the nation's birthday celebration, and the tribute made the week even more festive than usual. Special logos and bunting were placed around the stadium, and we had a special coin toss.

In the spirit of it all, we sponsored an essay contest in connection with the bicentennial, asking students to write about the NFL's contribution to American history. A few historians, including the eminent Henry Steele Commager, chided us no end for the idea (it was one of mine), but we still received lots of entries. The winner, 16-year-old Anna Jane Leider, from Alexandria, Virginia, received a $10,000 scholarship and a trip to the game with her parents. Her essay, by the way, challenged Dr. Commager's dismissal of the NFL as having any significant role in American history.

The bicentennial alone would have kept us busy. But that also was the year of the filming of the movie *Black Sunday*. That we managed to deal with both extra events so successfully accounts for some of my appreciation for this Super Bowl.

The Steelers won this game, too, beating Dallas, 21–17. The final moments did justice to both the movie and a bicentennial celebration. Pittsburgh had overcome a 10–7 Dallas lead at halftime, scoring 14 second-half points on a safety, two field goals, and a 64-yard touchdown pass from Terry Bradshaw to Lynn Swann. But Pittsburgh failed to convert a fourth down, handing the Cowboys the ball deep in their territory with 1:22 left. But Dallas's desperation bid ended with an interception in the end zone on the game's final play.

While the Steelers rejoiced over winning back-to-back Super Bowls, I breathed a sigh of relief. The filming of *Black Sunday*, which I had been dead set against, had transpired without incident. I even had a hand in it myself.

The shooting of one of the key scenes during the game began on my command. That was part of our understanding with the producers. Since actor Robert Shaw was to run down the aisle before jumping onto the field and racing toward the open end of the Orange Bowl, I didn't want to authorize action at any point in the game where a lot of concession traffic or fans in the aisles would unduly disrupt Shaw. So, I watched the game more carefully than I might otherwise have, looking for the ideal situation. I found it early in the second quarter, when the teams were playing in the Orange Bowl's closed end.

"Get ready," I told the film crew. A few plays later, I said simply, "OK, go now," which was the cue for action to begin. For all I know, it entitles me to add "movie direction" to my career vitae. At least I can appreciate how a director feels.

After my cue, I still crossed my fingers that an interception and runback toward the other end of the field wouldn't occur while Shaw was running behind the bench. It didn't.

A sequel of sorts came weeks later. I got a letter from Warner Brothers, plus a check for $8,500, payment for my services. I showed it to Rozelle.

"Send it back," Pete said quickly. I raised no objection. Most of the time, under Pete Rozelle, the NFL was a benevolent democracy. Every once in a while, though, it was a benevolent dictatorship, where decisions were made unilaterally. That was one of them. I could say the experience itself was worth $8,500. But I'm still wondering.

I wonder, too, how we managed to maintain control over all that we did during Super Bowl XX. We were back in New Orleans, where the heavily favored Chicago Bears throttled New England, 46–10. It was an unfortunate season finale for Patriots coach Raymond Berry, for the former Colts standout receiver had done a terrific job getting an overachieving team into the Superdome.

But my lasting memories of this milestone don't come from the game. We invited the most valuable players from the first 19 games to come and be honored in a special pregame ceremony. It was a wonderful experience, with Green Bay's Bart Starr serving as emcee at some functions and Joe Namath arriving for the ceremony in white shoes.

It wasn't without its other moments, either. Finding all the MVPs and getting them to New Orleans was a task in itself. Miami's Jake Scott, for example, was off in the Colorado mountains someplace and tough to track down. Pittsburgh's Bradshaw was almost as tough. In fact, I occasionally wonder how FOX gets Terry to Los Angeles for the studio show he's part of during the football season.

And then there was John Riggins. Riggins was a free spirit who set the Super Bowl single-game rushing record of 166 yards in helping the Redskins pull away from Miami in Super Bowl XVII in 1983. I like to say that nothing was very practical about John. He wasn't irresponsible. We just never could be sure where he was going to be. At the same time, you couldn't help but like John.

We planned to bring the players onto the field for the ceremony in vintage roadsters loaned from a museum and ideal for the occasion. Then they were to climb out of their vehicles, mount a revolving stage, and accept the accolades from the cheering crowd. Donna Montana, then my assistant and now Paul Tagliabue's assistant, was in charge of shepherding these former players into the cars and the caravan onto the field. As the procession was set to begin, I heard Donna's distinctive voice crackle, "Don Weiss! Don Weiss!" over the walkie-talkie. "It's Donna," she said when I acknowledged. "I've lost Riggins."

Somehow, he had vanished. Being the MVP of Super Bowl XVII, he was pretty far down the line. While he waited, he'd gotten thirsty, he later told us with an impish shrug, so he had sauntered off looking for a six-pack.

Riggins caused me more grief per square inch than any other former player ever, probably without ever realizing it. As John departed, he flashed his big grin and expressed thanks. "It's been great. Best time I've had in a long time," he said. "I can't wait until we do it again."

I thought to myself, "It'll be a while, John."

Ten years, to be exact. We did another salute to the MVPs at Super Bowl XXX in Tempe, Arizona, after hosting a special lunch for them during the week. Riggins was in town, appearing on behalf of a corporate sponsor. He didn't make the lunch or the game. Don't ask why.

Super Bowl XIII, played in Miami on January 21, 1979, marked the last time the game was played in the Orange Bowl stadium and the last time I planned and controlled it directly. I had become the executive director of the NFL in the summer of 1977, but for one more year we ran the Super Bowl out of the public relations department under my tutelage. With the game still growing, we created our special events department under Jim Steeg's direction a year later, in the fall of 1978. Starting with Super Bowl XIV, I worked closely with Steeg over the next five or six years, then gradually focused on advanced planning of activities. I also continued in charge of game-day operations, holding that responsibility until Super Bowl XXXVI.

Super Bowl XIII was an interesting swan song of sorts. Pittsburgh became the first three-time Super Bowl winner, defeating Dallas for the second time in three championship games, 35–31. As the score suggests, it was a wild game. Terry Bradshaw threw for 318 yards and four touchdowns as the Steelers took a commanding 35–17 lead late in the fourth quarter. The Cowboys didn't depart meekly, however. Roger Staubach threw two touchdown passes in the game's final 2:30, the second pass coming with 22 seconds left after Dallas recovered an onside kick. The Cowboys tried the tactic again, but Pittsburgh's Rocky Bleier scooped up the football to seal the victory.

Halftime was equally suspenseful. That was the year of the "Caribbean Carnival" mishaps that delayed the start of the second half. It was a good trial by fire for Jim Steeg. He had to round up the bodies required to push the show's main float off the field after its motor failed.

Along with individual Super Bowls, a few teams and players have stood the test of time. In addition to the Steelers of the 1970s and the Packers of the 1960s, I need to mention the 1972 Miami Dolphins, the only NFL team to complete an undefeated season. They capped that season in Super Bowl VII, beating Washington, 14–7. The game wasn't as close as the score suggested. Miami was a *team* in every sense of the word, like its "no-name defense" suggested. One of the no-names, safety Jake Scott, was named the game's MVP, and another, defensive tackle Manny Fernandez, might have been just as deserving. "It was the best game I ever saw Manny play," Don Shula said later.

While the Dolphins didn't go undefeated the following year, I thought that team, which whipped Minnesota, 24–7, in Super Bowl VIII in Houston, might have been stronger. They scored touchdowns on their first two possessions—both long drives—and were in complete control throughout.

As for truly memorable players, only a few come to mind, really. Dallas's defensive tackle Bob Lilly tops my list. He appeared in only two Super Bowls (V and VI), but it always seemed like he played in several more. Such was his presence. I never saw Lilly play a bad game. In the two memorable NFL championship losses to Green Bay in the 1960s, the Packers consistently ran away from Bob. I particularly enjoyed Dallas's winning Super Bowl VI. Lilly played a big part in the Cowboys' setting a Super Bowl record for fewest points allowed in the 24–3 victory over Miami, at one point sacking Bob Griese for a huge loss. Dallas's first Hall of Fame inductee was an intense competitor, too. The year before, in Super Bowl V in the

Orange Bowl, Dallas fell to Baltimore, 16–13, on the game's final play—a Jim O'Brien field goal after three late Cowboy passes were intercepted. While the Colts celebrated, Lilly slowly rose from the line of scrimmage and took off his helmet. After he took a few steps, he flung his helmet with his left hand. It traveled a good 35 yards down the field. It was nice to see Bob celebrate a Super Bowl the following year.

Jerry Rice and Joe Montana, of the San Francisco 49ers, stand out, too. Of course, they had numerous opportunities to shine. Rice was the consummate pro and always a factor in the three Super Bowls he played in. He was voted Super Bowl XXIII's MVP after catching 11 passes for 215 yards and one touchdown in a great game. The 49ers beat Cincinnati, 20–16, on a Montana touchdown pass to John Taylor with 34 seconds left.

Heroics like that put Joe Montana on my favorites list, as you'd expect. He's the only three-time Super Bowl MVP and an almost incomparable championship game performer. When Jim Breech's field goal gave the Bengals their 16–13 lead in Super Bowl XXIII, Cincinnati receiver Cris Collinsworth heard a teammate say, "We got 'em now!" No, they didn't, not even when the Bengals' kickoff left the 49ers on their own eight-yard line with 3:10 to play. How cool was Montana?

"I remember waiting for the start of that series feeling very uptight," San Francisco tackle Harris Barton recounted. "Joe came over and said, 'Hey, Harris, check it out. There's [actor] John Candy.' I looked and sure enough, there he was. We both laughed. Then the referee blew his whistle and Joe said, 'OK, guys, let's go.' He was totally cool, totally in command."

One other quarterback merits a nod, too: Denver's John Elway. I don't know about you, but coming back to win two straight Super Bowls after getting shellacked in three lopsided losses shows me character and class. In the 31–24 victory over Green Bay in Super Bowl XXXII, especially, Elway's determination was obvious and probably infectious. You could see him sense that this was at last his year, and he was not about to be denied. Terrell Davis was the game's MVP, but Elway was the Broncos' leader.

Pete Rozelle was not to be denied, either, in his desire to play a Super Bowl at Stanford Stadium. If Super Bowl XIX wasn't a favorite, it certainly was memorable. Pete always wanted to play the game there and finally got his wish in 1985.

When I first saw the place, I was wishing he hadn't. One of the lowest points of my NFL career was walking into that stadium in Palo Alto, California, and seeing tomato plants growing up between the seats. It looked like all the builders had done was dig a bowl out of a hill with some bulldozers and put down some planks. Whatever tears I had left after looking at Tulane Stadium in 1969 were ready to be shed as I surveyed Stanford in the early 1980s.

Like Tulane, another "Where do you go to plug it in?" moment was at hand. I could find no electrical outlets and no locker room facilities, either. We had to build them. On game day, even Pete may have had misgivings. On his way into the stadium, he got his pocket picked.

SIXTEEN

WHAT YOU PROBABLY DIDN'T SEE

No Super Bowl has ever been played in Philadelphia. But one almost was, outdoors in Veterans Stadium, no less. Ultimately, wiser heads prevailed, concluding a saga that offers a glimpse into pro football politics.

The Super Bowl had moved north to Detroit in 1982, as a reward of sorts to Ford and Chrysler for their many years of sponsoring pro football telecasts. In return, of course, we were handed a string of icy ordeals. The NFL must have set a record for the number of space heaters we rented to help keep our offices warm in our headquarters hotel, the Hyatt Regency Dearborn. The number of frozen car batteries we had to revive after the Commissioner's party that year may have set another record. How does 200 sound? Admittedly, the frigid weather had been a blessing, too. The deep freeze much of the country suffered during the winter of 1981–1982 helped Super Bowl XVI draw the second-largest television rating ever: 49.1. Only the final episode of $M*A*S*H$ attracted more viewers.

Chilling though the experience was, our trek north inadvertently sent a signal to many other cities, arousing their civic pride and ambitions. No fewer than 14 communities made pitches to host a Super

Bowl during an NFL owners' meeting held in Washington, D.C., in May 1984. We spent days listening to presentations that were as ambitious as our halftime shows. So ambitious, in fact, that Pete Rozelle hastily altered our host city bidding practice after the meeting. We had to do something, for at times our meeting looked more like a circus. The Minneapolis delegation, for example, staged a parade through the lobby of the L'Enfant Plaza Hotel, complete with a woman (fully clothed, thank heavens) riding a white horse

Yet, Philadelphia's massive presentation was the wildest of them all. It was orchestrated by Leonard Tose, then the Eagles' owner and a big promoter in his own right. Tose didn't bring a woman on a horse, but he and his henchman, Jimmy Murray, brought just about everyone else they could think of. The parade through the L'Enfant Plaza lobby included Pennsylvania governor Richard Thornburg and U.S. senator Arlen Specter, headed by a cadre of Mummers—those string musicians and clowns who march down Market Street in Philadelphia on New Year's Day outfitted in elaborate costumes that even Liberace might not have worn during his Las Vegas tours. I didn't count the number of Mummers on hand, but their flourishes were reminiscent of what the Michigan band had generated in the tunnel of the Los Angeles Coliseum after Super Bowl VII. The L'Enfant Plaza wasn't terribly annoyed, however, since the Mummers marched straight to the hotel bar, bringing hundreds of celebrants with them.

They had reason to celebrate. All of a sudden Philadelphia found itself on the verge of walking away with a Super Bowl date because its spectacle of a presentation had mustered far more support than we had anticipated. Those of us in the NFL office who would have done the work found the prospect downright frightening: Philadelphia in late January could be as wintry as Detroit but lacked a domed stadium. Veterans Stadium was essentially a baseball park with a comparatively modest 63,000 seating capacity and was carpeted with a notoriously bad artificial surface.

Fortunately, enough owners got concerned, too. They rallied to defer a decision and instead passed a resolution calling for a future Super Bowl to be played in a northern city *with a domed stadium* within "the next several years." That resolution eventually paved the way for Super Bowl XXVI to be awarded to Minneapolis. I always saw it as a compromise choice but, compared to Philadelphia and its great outdoors, even "Minny" looked appealing.

In the aftermath of this episode, we declared that henceforth presentations by aspiring Super Bowl host cities would be by invitation only from the NFL . . . and from a limited number of presenters.

Indianapolis, Detroit (Pontiac), and Seattle, cities with domed stadiums, also made pitches to host a game at that meeting, as did Jacksonville, Anaheim, Tampa, Phoenix, Houston, San Diego, Los Angeles (Rose Bowl), San Francisco (Stanford), Miami (Orange Bowl), and Dolphins owner Joe Robbie, on behalf of his proposed new stadium. I always thought Indianapolis, with what I call an "intimate" downtown area that would be good for staging a Super Bowl and a solid track record for organizing sports events, might do well as a host city someday—with a break in the weather.

Frankly, though, I still harbor doubts about the Super Bowl being played in any northern clime. The game was conceived to be a midwinter celebration at a neutral site in warm weather. Playing the Super Bowl in a freeze introduces myriad transportation and logistical challenges. We have to find quality indoor workout sites, for instance, or schedule workouts in the game venue itself, like we did reluctantly in Detroit and Minneapolis. Yet, doing that makes it more difficult for architect Jerry Anderson, George Toma, and others to properly prepare the stadium. We also have to battle the elements—and answer questions about the elements.

About six weeks before Super Bowl XVI was held in Pontiac, Michigan, writers started asking enough weather-related questions that we prepared a fact sheet to help ensure consistent responses. The questions turned out to be well considered. As part of its bid presentation, Detroit had cited a 20-year weather survey showing heavy snows being rare during the January weekend in question. Still, the area was battered by an ice storm on the Friday preceding the game.

Weather was not a factor during the Minneapolis Super Bowl in 1992, although a shortage of taxicabs following a Harry Connick Jr. concert one night forced many attendees to trek back to their hotels in bitterly cold weather. The chief disadvantage that year turned out to be the 60,000-seat Hubert Humphrey Metrodome. It was the smallest stadium ever to host a Super Bowl, and its undersized press box forced us to use unusually large numbers of seats in the stands to accommodate the media. That, in turn, created an even tighter allocation of tickets. Then again, staging Super Bowls in warm-weather locales produces trials and tribulations, too.

At first, it had sounded like a dynamite idea: stage our traditional Commissioner's party for Super Bowl VII in Los Angeles aboard the Queen Mary. Permanently anchored in Long Beach, California, the famous ocean liner was being renovated in late 1972 for use as a hotel and convention center. We thought it would be an absolutely perfect site and so did Rozelle. But we knew he would. Pete loved a great party almost as much as he loved pro football.

As long as it was a *great* party: varieties of food and drink in great abundance; plenty of food stations and plenty of bars; short lines and happy, smiling guests; superb entertainment and a festive atmosphere—first class in every respect. Those were Pete's standards. We were confident that a Super Bowl party aboard the Queen Mary would set new standards for merriment. We set a standard, all right—for embarrassment.

Our strategy was sound: serve food along buffet lines in the ship's two grand ballrooms and serve cocktails, beverages, and hors d'oeuvres elsewhere onboard so that people could circulate. A portion of the ship's engine room, being restored as an exhibition area, was at our disposal, too.

Trouble first loomed when we learned that one of the ballrooms being renovated wouldn't be ready, effectively cutting our seating capacity in half. Then, barely a week before the party, the company operating the Queen Mary abruptly replaced its entire corps of supervisors. When its new crew asked, "What's this about a party?" we sensed we had a problem.

Rozelle remained calm. With the party being in Long Beach and many NFL owners and other guests being housed a good 90 minutes away in places such as Century City and Beverly Hills, he reasoned that a good portion of our 2,500 guests wouldn't show up at all. Well, Pete was wrong. They all showed up . . . and they all brought a friend. As big as the Queen Mary is, it wasn't big enough for the National Football League on that Friday night.

The atmosphere on the decks of the ship was elegant. But the ballroom was a nightmare. VIP tables reserved for NFL owners' groups were being commandeered by others because available seats were scarce. That alone provoked quarrels that dominated much of my evening. More guests than I'd like to remember had to sit on the floor with plates of food between their legs. Don't ask me what was served. I couldn't tell you because I was too busy to even think about food. I never tasted a bite, which was just as well because food was in short supply. I never was so happy to see a party end in all my life.

As the last guests disembarked, I muttered to myself, "We're lucky we didn't sink the ship."

The irony was we had booked the Queen Mary to *escape* such mob scenes, for that's what the Commissioner's party was beginning to create. Hosting gala parties on the night before NFL championship games was a tradition the league had launched years earlier. At the Super Bowl, they became Friday night affairs, and as corporate involvement with the game soared, so did the party's appeal. Participating teams wouldn't bring their players, but they brought everybody else. Every other NFL team brought a delegation, too, as did television networks, major sponsors, and our other partners. Former players started showing up, too. And, of course, Rozelle was always there with his large entourage, befitting one of the NFL's major events of the year. Within about three years, in fact, an invitation to the Commissioner's party became a status symbol more prized than a ticket to the game itself.

Demand became so intense that it soon overwhelmed hotel ballrooms. I came to dread the last few days of any Super Bowl week. People could accept not getting a ticket to the game, but they wouldn't take no for an answer when it came to an invitation to the

Commissioner's party. Invariably, some guy holding one invitation would show up with a dozen of his closest friends. More than a few of them tested our patience.

For what became the last big affair we held in a hotel, at the old Roosevelt in New Orleans during Super Bowl VI, NFL Properties had designed framed plaquelike illustrations of every AFL and NFL team. They had to be about 8 feet by 10 feet in size, and we hung them on the mezzanine level, perhaps 18 feet above the ballroom's floor. Don't ask me how, but somebody marched off with one of the illustrations. It had to take five or six people to carry it away, but the place was so crowded that nobody noticed.

Centerpieces and glasses disappeared, too. Some items, champagne glasses, for instance, were meant to be taken as keepsakes but not the 20 or 30 specially engraved cocktail glasses people were carting away. We took the thefts as one more signal to find larger, more dramatic locations to accommodate crowds that were now swelling into the thousands.

Planning time and expense swelled right along with the crowds. We eventually turned party planning responsibilities over to Susan Minogue, and when she left the league office, Sue Robichek took over. Sue still handles the task today. With the guest list all but forcing us into convention centers, our forte has become intriguing varieties of food and a range of activities: jazz combos and music for dancing, plus celebrity entertainers, a number of whom also entertain at the Super Bowl itself.

We've hosted some memorable bashes in unique settings. In Miami we used Hialeah Race Track one year, and for Super Bowl XIII, the new multilevel international wing of the Miami airport. We had as many as 16 bands on hand that night, one from each of the locales represented by the Caribbean Tourism Council, our partner for that game's halftime show.

The Commissioner's party we hosted in Houston's Astrodome during Super Bowl VIII in 1974 may have been one of our most elaborate and ambitious—for good reason: it followed the Queen Mary episode. While not big enough for the game, the Astrodome was ideal for the party. We welcomed as many as five thousand guests but also had room to herd a few head of Texas cattle into a corral we built on the floor, which was covered with sawdust. We roasted pigs in huge barbecue pits, set up chuck wagons, covered the tables with red-and-white-checked cloths, had branding irons all over the place, and brought in country singer Charley Pride to entertain everyone. We urged people to come dressed in keeping with the party's western theme, so I was decked out in a red-checked shirt, denim trousers, boots, and cowboy hat on my head. Ever since, some staff members have called me "Tex."

"Ringmaster" might have fit me in 1984, the first year we held the Super Bowl in Tampa. We gave the party a circus theme and held it at the county fairgrounds. One of its featured events was a high-wire act performed above guests in the main dining room. Something different and exciting, we thought. Rozelle thought differently. Visions of an aerial artist falling off the wire and into the crowd made him nervous, so we cut the act short.

At various times over the years, we've tried to cut the guest list, too. Even though we were hosting parties in spacious settings, the demand for invitations kept outpacing the space. Of course, it wasn't easy keeping the lid on the number of party guests when your best effort is being sabotaged by a staff member.

Arriving early for the party we hosted in the Pasadena Civic Center one year, Bill Granholm and I noticed a large group of well-dressed people milling about the long walkway leading from the parking lot to the building's side entrance. We didn't give them much thought until we noticed them again a little later . . . inside the civic center enjoying the party. We knew they hadn't come in through the front door because that's where Granny and I had been standing. Our curiosity aroused, we discovered that the uninvited group of 150 had been ushered in through the side door by Jack Danahy, our own chief of security.

Jack was a former FBI agent who had built our extensive network of security agents. He loved a good party, too, and wanted to treat his pals to some NFL hospitality. We couldn't throw out all 150, but we surely could chat with Jack. He was too capable to dismiss, but his party duties were reassigned on the spot.

Parties with a cast of thousands invariably attract characters. One of my all-time favorites was Skipper McNally. A cynic might call him a professional party crasher. I'll just call Skipper a professional hanger-on, for he was an affable, white curly-haired, middle-aged chap from Los Angeles who built ties with NFL teams on the West Coast, particularly the Oakland Raiders and Al Davis. At times, he even flew on the Raiders' team plane. When he ran into bad luck late in life, Davis helped him out and later paid for Skipper's funeral.

Year after year, Skipper took special delight in crashing the Commissioner's party. His intent wasn't evil because he didn't have a malicious bone in his body. Skipper just loved to do it, while Jim Kensil took equal delight in personally "excusing" Skipper from the evening's festivities as soon as he became aware of his presence.

It got to be a Super Bowl ritual. I'd spot Skipper at the bar or mingling in the crowd, duly inform Jim, then watch Kensil's eyes dance with delight. "Ah, wonderful!" Jim would grin. "I'll see to it immediately."

Off he'd go. And out would go Skipper . . . for a few minutes. By the time Jim could boast to me that Skipper had been tossed, Skipper had found a way back in—except through the front door—and the ritual would begin anew. Skipper never caused any serious trouble. Why, some years he made it a point to come over and say hello. He could even finagle his way into the party's VIP section. We'd see him at the game, too. But it wasn't quite the same—Skipper usually had a ticket.

Other Super Bowl gate-crashers weren't nearly as endearing, but they were enterprising and often brazen, especially in Miami. Whoever made it inside the Orange Bowl wearing a Santa Claus suit and claiming to be part of the halftime show wielded that ruse three of the first four years the game was played there. It was quite effective, really, although the ruse was almost always exposed later on. One year, the guy made the mistake of sitting down in the auxiliary press section. I always made it a habit to check out that section before the game and spotted Santa sitting right in the middle of it. We sent him back to the North Pole or someplace. Another Miami sideline-crasher momentarily foiled security by wearing a simple Eastern Airlines baggage tag.

And at Super Bowl III, a gentleman appeared at the business office, near gate 14 of the Orange Bowl, seeking admission with very official-looking television credentials. As well done as they were, one telltale sign of fakery stood out: The credentials bore the "CBS eye" . . . Super Bowl III was televised by NBC.

Even those who get inside the stadium aren't always satisfied. At Super Bowl VI in New Orleans, some pickpockets grabbed the red satin vests that had been worn before the game by Ford supervisors of the pass, punt, and kick competition. At least four of the vests were torn into strips of red that exactly matched the red armbands we had issued to sideline photographers for easier sideline control. Four field-crashers were on the sidelines for nearly an entire half before they were discovered.

Each of the four years the Vikings were in the Super Bowl, they brought along their official mascot, who's dressed in Viking fur with horned helmet, shield, and sword. The garb inspired another enterprising sideline-crasher at Super Bowl VIII in Rice Stadium, where the Vikings met the Miami Dolphins. This fellow dressed up in a seedy fish outfit, and he nearly got to the bench area before he was tossed back into the sea of humanity . . . outside the stadium.

At Super Bowl VII in Los Angeles, we gave pregame credentials to 70 pigeon handlers. They were to release the birds and then leave because we had no room for them once the game kicked off. Two of them tried to use those credentials to sneak into the press box. "There aren't any pigeons in the press box that I know of," I said when I encountered them in an elevator. Then I called security.

While many of these characters prompt smiles today, I don't have any warm feelings about a more notorious Super Bowl gate-crasher. You may have read about him, at times in flattering and praiseworthy terms, or heard how he's managed periodically to get photographed with the winning Super Bowl coach. What you haven't read about is his checkered and unsavory past. He's no saint, nor is he a stranger to me. One year, I even sent pictures of him in several of his disguises to NFL team public relations directors as an alert. Anyone who has caused us so many headaches, I reasoned, might also try to sneak into regular-season games. He's very accomplished at what he does . . . but not accomplished enough to get his name in these pages.

Skipper McNally could be as helpful as he was affable. He provided valuable assistance in exposing ticket-scalping operations. Even with such assistance, Super Bowl ticket distribution, ticket scalping, and ticket scams are perennial problems. The problems are exacerbated when we have only one week between conference championship games and the Super Bowl: We have less time to ensure an orderly distribution of game tickets.

Ticket-scalping laws vary widely by state, which doesn't make it any easier to nab scalpers, and willing buyers are always in abundance. Depending on which game, Super Bowl tickets can be sold for up to 10 times their face value, or $3,500 for a $350 ticket. And we could sell each available ticket at least three or four times.

Unfortunately, one of the biggest sources of ticket troubles is the NFL's own players. The master union agreement provides two Super Bowl tickets to each player on a team roster. Today, that amounts to almost 3,400 tickets. Most teams have unofficial Super Bowl ticket "coordinators" who literally take orders for the unwanted tickets early in a season, then funnel the tickets into the hands of assorted agents and ticket brokers just before the game. Some of the channels used in this exchange are legitimate; others are not. It's not a pleasant situation, but it's virtually impossible to stop.

This underground network, in turn, also helps fuel ticket scams that have turned some Super Bowl tours into nightmares. Stories of groups showing up for a Super Bowl and finding they have no tickets or counterfeit tickets are all too real. We faced many unhappy fans through the years but couldn't do a thing for them.

The worst case of counterfeit tickets surfaced before Super Bowl XIX at Stanford Stadium in 1985. As many as 500 were in circulation. About a week before the game, police arrested a Honolulu man near San Francisco's airport after a guy bought 32 tickets from him, paying $250 a ticket, which each had a face value of $60. With the top price of tickets "on the street" estimated to be $350 that year, the buyer had become suspicious and contacted police.

It wasn't a very good counterfeit job, either. The fake tickets were duller and printed on thinner paper, and the typeface showing the stadium stairway, section, and seat number was oversized. Even so, Warren Welsh, our security director at the time, had to set up a ticket verification center to sort things out.

It wasn't the first such incident. At Super Bowl X in Miami, we ran into a similar case, but the number of tickets had been no more than three dozen. The following year, several people showed up at the Rose Bowl with bogus tickets, listing rows that, had they existed, would have placed their seats a good quarter of a mile *above* the rim of the stadium.

The Super Bowl's rampant popularity ignited other dilemmas, such as the demand for hotel rooms. In mustering corporate support for the Super Bowl, we never imagined that along with fans who had game tickets we also would lure upwards of 30,000 fans to the host city just to enjoy the festivities and the parties. Virtually all of these folks were well-heeled free spenders and not at all averse to tempting hotel sales managers with bundles of cash in exchange for hard-to-find rooms.

Nor was it uncommon for a maitre d' in a popular restaurant to be offered tidy sums for special favors. To combat this one year in New Orleans, the city's restaurant association gave us special "medallions" that we passed on to team owners and key associates. Flashing the medallions helped guarantee a table in popular restaurants.

Putting the brakes on private hotel room deals that overly ambitious sales managers tried to cut with the free spenders and panic-stricken tour group operators became another unending battle. For whatever reason, some innkeepers conveniently ignore the master agreement we sign with a host city that calls for rooms to be priced up to a certain amount. If we've heard "He's new and he didn't know about our agreement" once, we've heard it a hundred times, and we've spent hundreds of hours unscrambling these messes.

In New Orleans one year, a hotel tried to raise its rates by more than 60 percent during Super Bowl week, despite a written agreement signed six months earlier. The hotel's excuse was that it was under new management.

We heard the "new management" lament time and again, too, but often for good reason. Coping with turnover in the hotel world became a hurdle we learned to live with. One year in Miami, the entire catering department of our headquarters hotel turned over three times in the year before the game. We were forever initiating Super Bowl plans with one person and completing them with another. People would come and go in a heartbeat, without warning.

The same year we boarded the Queen Mary, we established our media headquarters at the Newporter Inn in Newport Beach, to be closer to the teams. Both Miami and Washington were staying in Orange County, where the workout facilities were better and the skies were free of smog. Shortly before we checked in, the Newporter Inn's general manager suddenly died. During his tenure he had adorned the lobby and public areas of his 300-room hotel with cuckoo clocks of every description, all of which worked. What the general manager had left behind was appropriate because the woefully inexperienced young man appointed to replace him just about drove us cuckoo.

Commitments simply weren't being kept. We had booked the entire hotel, but that didn't seem to matter. When Jim Kensil and I scheduled a meeting to discuss the situation, the hotel manager didn't show up. That he was ducking us soon became clear. At one point, he locked himself in his office and refused to come out. About the only good thing that did come out of this mess was a declaration that I finally uttered out of sheer frustration: "The next time this happens," I growled, "we'll just take this damn game out of here and put it where it belongs."

The threat proved so effective that it became part of my administrative repertoire. I never did divulge just where the game "belonged," but I never had to. Folks in Florida assumed I meant California, and folks in California figured I meant Florida or New Orleans. Truth be told, it was an empty threat in Newport Beach. By that time, we had nowhere else to go.

"Don't forget about the game" was another phrase that tumbled from my lips. It was more of a lament. The party atmosphere swirling about the Super Bowl could almost rage out of control at times and leave us virtually competing with corporate events and unrelated activities. One year, I even heard someone from NFL Properties quip, "Oh, no one cares anything about the game anymore, anyway." It wasn't true, but the perception was troubling and potentially dangerous. Then again, it could be easy to forget about the game, given all the gaffes that a Super Bowl can foment.

Perhaps the number one scene of Super Bowl mishaps was old Tulane Stadium, where we played three games before moving into the Louisiana Superdome for Super Bowl XII. The multitude of deficiencies in that dumpy, rusty bucket turned Super Bowl IX into almost as much of an adventure as Super Bowl IV had been.

One episode began the Friday before the game. The lack of usable space inside the stadium required us to erect a tent alongside the locker room building so that we could conduct postgame player interviews. The next day, we also put up a chain-link fence to screen off the tent and some nearby trailers that were being used as darkrooms by photographers and NFL Films. The fence went up while the Pittsburgh Steelers were having a team meeting prior to their final workout. Once the fence was up, the Steelers couldn't get out of the locker room . . . until we tore the fence down.

With the weather forecast calling for chilling temperatures and biting winds, we rented some kerosene heaters to use in the same tent after the game. But security guards who were in the tent the preceding Saturday night used up all the kerosene. The next morning, not so much as a drop was left, forcing Bill Granholm to dispatch a courier all over New Orleans to find kerosene. A supply arrived while the game was in progress.

Once it did, Granny confronted another crisis. He and my public relations successor, Joe Browne, led a posse of security officers and police who gave chase to a woman. Dashing onto the field as the half-time show was about to start, she had flung off her raincoat and, despite the cold weather, began dancing in a very well-filled bikini. Granny and Browne showed some deft moves themselves. They got to her quickly, picked her up while she laughed and struggled with them, and bodily tossed her over a fence that bordered the field.

The thrill of having thwarted this stripper with such dispatch was short-lived, however. In a conversation with New Orleans mayor Moon Landrieu the next morning, we discovered that the stripper not only was well known as one of the French Quarter's finest but also was rumored to be a female impersonator.

Tulane Stadium bedeviled Super Bowl groundskeeper George Toma, too. It rained so heavily the day and night before Super Bowl IX that Toma had to vacuum the water off the stadium's artificial surface with a modified Monsanto Zamboni machine. Renowned for its ability to resurface ice on a hockey rink, the modified Zamboni is a machine we always bring to stadiums that have outdoor synthetic surfaces. George sorely needed it in 1975. The field was so soaked that it was starting to flood. George vacuumed up more than water on that cold and windy morning, though: After he took a turn in the end zone and started back up the field, he started pulling up sections of turf, 20 to 30 yards of the stuff before he realized it.

The turf was replaced in time for the game, but the Zamboni performed an encore all by itself: As a 100-man New Orleans police unit was doing roll call on the field, a valve on the Zamboni broke, spraying the men in blue with gallons of ice-cold water. The entire unit had to go home and change clothes, blowing away half of our stadium security.

Inside the stadium, meanwhile, as part of our control system, we had installed a telephone in the walkway that led to the adjacent locker room building outside. Positioned about head high, the phone was put there for emergency use. It was common practice, since the media used this walkway to reach the postgame interview area as the

Super Bowl ended. But soon after the game began, some fan who was seated about four feet above the walkway discovered the phone. He reached down and pulled it up to where he was seated, apparently to make a call. But the phone had a direct ring to our control booth atop the stadium, and this setup was driving us crazy. We spent much of the first half trying to get this guy off the phone while we also deployed security personnel to locate him in the stands—to no avail, as it turned out. As our frustration grew, my FBI helper, George Mandich, joined in the search and finally nabbed the would-be caller.

"Just tear the phone wire loose," I told George when he reported in. But before George finally yanked the right wire, he yanked the wrong wire—to an electrical circuit in the tunnel.

Compounding our frustration was the fact that we weren't supposed to have played Super Bowl IX in Tulane Stadium. The game was supposed to be played in the Superdome, and Mayor Landrieu promised us it would be ready in time. It wasn't. In light of all our calamities in New Orleans, maybe we should have figured as much.

When we finally did get inside the Superdome for Super Bowl XII in 1978 (the first time the game was played indoors), we were getting ribbed by people wondering how we'd stage a pregame flyover. We managed, in a sense. Since its completion in mid-1975, the Superdome had been home to a pair of pigeons that had been trapped inside during construction and had survived quite nicely, thank you, feeding off peanuts and other stray morsels of food dropped by fans. Just before kickoff, the pigeons were startled by something, took off from their concealed perch, and circled the field at press box level for five minutes.

"Ladies and gentlemen," we proclaimed, "there's your flyover."

At Super Bowl XI, hundreds of balloons were to fly over the Rose Bowl, following the singing of "America the Beautiful." As we released them, however, a cluster of balloons got caught on the uprights of one of the goalposts. While George Toma went hunting for something long enough to pry them loose, a policeman told Bill

Granholm he'd just *shoot* them off with his revolver and actually started to go for his gun. Granny quickly grabbed his arm and told him that wouldn't be a good idea.

It didn't seem like a good idea for Green Bay's Max McGee to be out carousing the night before Super Bowl I, either. "I could barely stand up for the National Anthem," he later claimed. Max had reportedly sneaked out of his hotel room in Los Angeles the midnight before and beat a path to the Sunset Boulevard nightclubs. He rolled in at 7:30 A.M. In the twilight of his career, McGee never expected to play and wouldn't have, had Boyd Dowler not reinjured his shoulder in the first quarter against Kansas City.

When Vince Lombardi started yelling for McGee, Max figured he was about to be fined for his escapades the night before, but Lombardi was calling for him to get into the game. McGee was so wobbly that he hadn't even brought his helmet to the field. On the first series, he wore a lineman's helmet that was several sizes too big. No matter. McGee was the game's top receiver, catching seven passes for 138 yards and two touchdowns.

An Oakland defensive end, the late John Matuszak, made McGee look like a choirboy at Super Bowl XV in New Orleans. On arrival, Matuszak, a player synonymous with late-night high jinks, had vowed to behave himself and avoid the French Quarter. His vow lasted until midweek, when at 3:00 A.M. he found himself no longer able to resist the siren song of Bourbon Street. Off he went. While his Raiders teammates were enduring media interviews later that morning, the "Tooz" was AWOL in a French Quarter hotel—and not alone, according to reports. He tried to sneak into the interview sessions without being noticed. Not a chance.

Matuszak claimed he was patrolling Bourbon Street, making sure his teammates were behaving themselves. His performance won him $1,000 in fines from coach Tom Flores. Matuszak took it in stride.

And his stellar performance on Sunday helped Oakland beat Philadelphia, 27–10.

You didn't see Roman numerals until 1971 at Super Bowl V. While we've been chastised to no end for appearing pretentious, our sole intent was to avoid confusion between the year of the season played and the year in which its Super Bowl was played. Each Super Bowl is played early in the year following a chronological season. Super Bowl V, for instance, concluded the 1970 season but was played on January 17, 1971, just as Super Bowl XXXVI, played in February 2002, was the finale to the 2001 season.

Something else you never see, either, is the full impact of losing a Super Bowl. It's devastating, unlike any other defeat in sports, and it's compounded by the relentless grilling of 1,500 or more writers and broadcasters. Everyone hates to lose, of course, but after most games, players at least have the next week and a new opponent to look forward to. The Super Bowl's different: No next game and no new opponent await the vanquished. Unsuccessful teams almost can be relieved when a season ends. They can start thinking about a fresh start next year.

"Anyone who says that one loss cannot ruin a season," coach Dick Vermeil said after his Philadelphia team fell to Oakland in New Orleans, "never lost a Super Bowl."

SEVENTEEN

GAME DAY

What You Still Don't See

The Louisiana Superdome has 387 doors and 84 rooms. I know because I once spent the better part of a day before the first Super Bowl we played there in 1978 opening every door and looking in every room. My madness had a purpose.

To begin with, I am always looking for places to store stuff . . . and to uncover stuff already stored that shouldn't be. For example, behind one of those doors, in the building's uppermost reaches, I found a collection of trash and garbage that was a fire and health hazard, all rolled into one disgusting heap. It looked like it had been there since the building opened. Suppressing the urge to utter my most intimidating "Do what you promised or we'll take this damn game where it belongs" warning, I ordered the heap removed posthaste.

Equally important, I also had wanted to see where all those doors led. The Superdome's design is an apt reflection of its interior: It really *is* a big spaceship, the equivalent of a 20-story building, and I was both investigating the existence of any shortcuts we might be able to use in an emergency and making sure none of those doors opened onto any entryways that could be commandeered by gate-crashers. None could.

Wandering amid the stadium's nooks and crannies was among my pre–Super Bowl rituals, one I performed at every stadium where the game was played. I also inspected rest rooms, concessions, offices, and every space in between. I always wanted to reduce the odds of surprises when it matters most—on game day.

My Super Bowl always began a good six to eight hours before kick-off and up to four hours before the gates officially opened. I always had plenty to do.

The "nerve center" of our operation is what we call the NFL control booth. When we created it at Super Bowl II in Miami, it filled only a modest portion of the Orange Bowl's original mezzanine-level press box and had room for me, Jim Kensil, and Don Smith, our press box public address announcer. We equipped it with two manual typewriters and a single two-button telephone. One line connected us to Pete Rozelle, wherever he was sitting, and the other to an outside telephone line.

Until Super Bowl XXXVI (which ended 35 years of my presence in the NFL control booth), it was home to the public address and press box announcers (something we insisted on after we were shocked to hear the tornado alert from the P.A. announcer prior to Super Bowl IV), as well as our statistics crew, two officiating observers, a liaison person from the network televising the game, and five or six NFL colleagues who have specific game-operations duties. All of them are Super Bowl veterans who are intimately familiar with their tasks. For example, Kevin Coyle, who spends the rest of his year as the New York Jets' travel coordinator, worked alongside me for so long that I felt lost during the one year that a family illness forced his absence.

Linked to us was Jim Steeg, who succeeded me as Super Bowl coordinator and is the NFL's vice president of special events. A second control post is at field level, with its own staff. As long as I was involved in NFL control, Jim had always been on the field and said he was happier there because he was better able to move to wherever he might be needed, as the game's chief troubleshooter.

The 2-button telephone we first used in the Orange Bowl has grown into a collection of 32-button consoles that reflect the Super Bowl's complexity and link us with ticket and will-call operations, security, first aid, concessions, supply rooms, stadium management and operations, pregame coordinators, halftime coordinators, the Commissioner's booth, suites of the participating teams' owners, and anyone and everyone we could conceivably need to contact before, during, and after the game.

The consoles are part of our own telephone system that we literally create for each Super Bowl venue. A story probably goes with virtually every button we've added, the result of the experiences over the years of staff veterans such as Bill Granholm, Joe Browne, Val Pinchbeck, Jim Heffernan, Pete Abitante, Dick Maxwell, Greg Aiello, and Peter Hadhazy. In the wake of technological advances, telephone deregulation, and the enormous number of calls we make, it became far more advantageous to create our own phone system, linking our headquarters hotels, team hotels, media centers, and other venues. NFL Films also coordinates its extensive Super Bowl operation and schedule over a network that is part of this same system.

It's a far more efficient way to go because we're not continually having to reinvent the wheel each year. Larry Hodge, whom we met through GTE, serves as our communications specialist, along with a number of his former GTE colleagues, headed by Ken Wells. Larry and Ken know exactly what we need each year, so when we arrive everything is set up. If we were to rely on local telephone companies, we might have to negotiate with as many as three separate service providers in some cities and perhaps a fourth for long-distance service. That's a hassle we don't need.

From the control booth, we direct every facet of a Super Bowl involving the football game itself. We've established a countdown of activities and troubleshooting checks that begins more than six hours before kickoff. The following time frame is an example of a countdown for a game played on the West Coast.

9:00 A.M. (12:00 NOON ET)

- Troubleshoot for general game services.
- Install telephones.
- Distribute game programs to teams, officials, and media.
- Secure parking access.

- Prepare for team arrivals.
- Secure press and television areas.
- Check for field control, stadium security, transportation, catering, and other services.

All of our security services are provided by CSC, Contemporary Security Corporation. It owes much of its dramatic, nationwide growth to the Super Bowl. CSC was formed on the West Coast by Pete Kransky and Damon Zumwalt, a pair of former UCLA football players. They hired many former college football players to staff their events. CSC got its start by handling security for the Los Angeles Rams, who referred the young firm to me years ago. After meeting with its founders for a few hours, I was satisfied and hired CSC for Super Bowl XI, in the Rose Bowl. They've been with us ever since. Kransky says he about fell over at our first meeting when I stood up and said, "OK, we want you to do it. Bring us a plan, and good luck!"

Transportation is another critical concern, in part because we dispatch some of the departing media buses from our control center. Carol Constantine, of the NFL headquarters staff, has been our transportation coordinator for 20 years and always does a fantastic job. During much of the season, Carol attends to the minute details of pro football personnel procedures. For 10 days, though, she is at the Super Bowl. On game day, she's often connected to the control booth via a walkie-talkie, and without her we wouldn't operate as effectively as we do.

This is also the hour when we make sure the locker rooms are fully equipped and ready, as well as the camera repair areas that we have set up for photographers and videographers.

10:00 A.M.

- Continue to troubleshoot all of the same areas for problems and special needs.
- Check all press areas.
- Greet, set up, and coordinate early media arrivals, including television, radio, and club radio feeds and photographers.

Media accommodations are always high on our list, and we use several press box areas to squeeze in the 2,300 writers, broadcasters, and photographers who typically show up for a Super Bowl. Even in an ideal stadium, the main press box has room for only 300 or so writers, so we have to create auxiliary press areas elsewhere, including a large auxiliary section in the stands and workstations under the stands for those who come primarily to write sidebar stories and conduct postgame interviews. We appropriate about 1,000 seats in the outside stands, which can require special considerations such as being ready for rain when we're playing outdoors. We always had plastic raincoats and hats on hand in the Orange Bowl, prompting *New York Times* Pulitzer prize–winning columnist Arthur Daley to quip, "You guys think of everything."

We're sometimes *criticized* for doing that, too. But we'd much rather be chided for doing too much than for doing too little. Even then, we take heat. One early year, I wrote a pregame story that a wire service reporter picked up and filed verbatim . . . and then he complained about the quality of my effort.

Assisting the media hordes is a Super Bowl public relations staff that has grown from a handful to more than a hundred. Most of them are veterans from NFL teams who also manage our media center and various pressrooms. For instance, Gary Wright of the Seattle Seahawks oversees activities at the media center during Super Bowl week and at the working press box for the game. Technology has eased our task to a degree. We once had to provide hundreds of typewriters. Now it's computer connections and space for satellites: Outside any Super Bowl stadium are 300 to 400 satellite dishes, transmitting feeds all over the world, plus three or four NFL staffers on hand to attend to any of their needs.

11:00 A.M. (four and one-half hours before kickoff)

- Review credentials information and troubleshoot problems in all areas.
- Conduct systemwide phone check from the control booth to communications system installers, and check individual arrangements for

officials' and teams' locker rooms;
postgame interview areas;
security control;
regular and press will-call windows;
scoreboard control;
Jumbotron;
network, pregame, halftime, and postgame trucks;
main press box areas (left, center, and right);
auxiliary press locations;
concessions;
first aid and emergency services;
Commissioner's booth;
participating teams owners' suites;
NFL member club owners' suites;
all levels of stadium lobbies;
press gate;
press elevator;
console four (field-level backup to radios);
sideline phones;
tunnel phones (or other entryways);
pregame coordination;
player introductions; and
special ringdowns.

This checklist alone is reason enough to have our own telephone system in place. It also reflects all the details we need to attend to and why we like to have two weeks of preparation time between conference championship games and the Super Bowl. Many fans think we're merely trying to hype the game. In our early years, that was true. Not anymore.

While the number of credentials and tickets picked up at will-call windows is small, more tickets than you might think are distributed this way; even 1 percent represents a large number. Whatever has not been distributed by Saturday evening is routed to will-call.

And, in case we need it, we also have at our disposal the "blueprint" of seat locations that Jim Steeg has prepared, as Jim Kensil and I did before Jim. The blueprint tells us where blocks of seats are located so that we can pinpoint where different groups are sitting. It varies from year to year, but each participating team gets about 20 percent of the available seats, and the host city gets 10 percent. That leaves 50 percent for the league itself and the other 29 NFL clubs.

12:00 NOON

- Open gates and begin in-stadium entertainment.
- Check public address sound levels.
- Check credentials information and troubleshoot.
- Prepare for team arrivals.
- Conduct full-scale, systemwide phone check with game-assigned personnel.

A crush of people are always waiting at the gates when they open, and our security people naturally have to concentrate on official entry points. That makes "unofficial" entry points areas of concern that merit special attention.

The year we brought Super Bowl XI to the Rose Bowl, our first visit there in 1977, we happened on two large fellows literally tossing fans over a fence that ran along the roadway that encircles the stadium's entire perimeter. They had driven a van up to the fence and then climbed on top of the van and were hoisting their pals over the fence and into the stadium as fast as they could. Another bunch of gate-crashers in Tampa resorted to the same strategy to sneak into Super Bowl XVIII when we played the game there for the first time in 1984.

We expect the teams to arrive about three hours before kickoff, so we're continually in touch with transportation. About the only deviation from this timetable occurred in Pontiac, Michigan, when the second 49ers team bus didn't show up until about *one hour* before kickoff because of severe traffic tie-ups (thanks to Vice President Bush's motorcade and an ice storm). More often than not, we'll see a few players on the field by this hour trying to walk off pregame jitters. Other players spend time reading the program; that's why locker rooms are tops among the special program distribution points.

We used to issue credentials to pregame and halftime performers but found they often made their way into unauthorized hands and caused problems. Now all performers come through one designated gate.

12:30 P.M.

- Begin network television pregame show.
- Check facility-wide television monitors.
- Check time with television.
- Check final catering for media and other locations.
- Check security of VIP areas, including club box seats, suites, and special booths.
- Check for any problems with in-stadium parking and other parking areas.
- Troubleshoot.

Once television coverage begins, we're in almost constant contact with network producers so that every event is coordinated. The network frequently switches to live scenes of and at the stadium during its pregame show, so we need to be ready for them.

Plenty of tailgating always takes place near the stadium. We monitor those activities, too, and anticipate when these parties will make their way to the stadium. We were surprised at Super Bowl XIX in 1985 when huge groups of tailgaters suddenly descended on Stanford Stadium. That's the year Pete Rozelle had his pocket picked. He later got his wallet back, though. It was so crowded that even the thief couldn't get away.

1:45 P.M.

- Teams take the field for pregame warm-ups.

2:35 P.M.

- Teams clear the field.

As teams clear the field, we're busy getting a couple thousand pregame performers on the field, so I was always in touch with Bob Best, our longtime pregame show coordinator and producer. We continue to troubleshoot, of course, as we move closer to kickoff. For example, it was during the hour before the National Anthem that we were strenuously trying to resolve the snit between NBC and Garth Brooks over the airing of his video. If special television situations are going to arise, this is likely to be the time. We do what we can, but some situations are beyond our control.

At one of our outdoor venues, for instance, our pregame show included some parachutists who were to land at the 50-yard line. Of course, we had to cue the folks directing the airplane so that the jumpers would jump at the proper moment. An instant after the cue was given, veteran NBC producer Larry Cirillo called. The network was slightly behind schedule, he said, so could we delay the jump by a couple of minutes? "Sorry, Larry," I replied. "They're already out of the plane."

2:40 P.M.

• In-stadium pregame show begins.

Our chief concern at this point is a breakdown of equipment and any adjustments it might cause, plus any disturbances in and around the stadium. We always have to be ready to alter our plans, no matter what. We're also now starting to get everyone lined up for the National Anthem, player introductions, and the coin toss.

3:00 P.M.

• Network coverage of the Super Bowl goes on the air.

At this point, all conversations in the control booth cease, save for essential exchanges between game coordinators directing the singing of the Anthem, player introductions, and the coin toss. I was in direct contact with Bob Best and the network producer and director during this time.

3:18 P.M.

- Kickoff

Lord willing, the game finally begins! But we can't begin to relax. Now the control booth switches to a full-scale game operations center, and all my public relations colleagues swing into action, as they would for a regular-season game. Then again, this game is special.

Now our focus is game-related events, principally injury reports, statistical information, and play-by-play details. The Elias Sports Bureau people who we have with us (in my years, it was Seymour Siwoff and Steve Hirdt) are directly linked to computers at their New York headquarters so that they can pull up records for *everything* and relay that information to the media. Play-by-play detail is provided at every NFL game, but the Super Bowl receives extra attention. Don R. Smith of the Hall of Fame was our chief statistician for more than 30 years.

Throughout the game, of course, we continue to troubleshoot and maintain direct lines to television and radio feeds and all other key points in the stadium. I'm watching all the activities and rarely able to focus on what's going on between the sidelines.

4:00 P.M.

- Begin countdown to halftime and show coordination with Bob Best and network television.

With halftime being the production that it is, this task has a checklist all its own that Bob Best directs on the field from the sound booth.

4:45 P.M. (estimated)

- Halftime begins.

Our focus now is ensuring that teams get off the field easily while the halftime show is being set up and performers are moving onto the field. Normally, setup takes about five or six minutes, but we still have to monitor activities. Any delay requires us to alert the television network because its contractual agreement requires televising the 12-minute halftime show without a break or commercial interruption.

5:00 P.M. (estimated)

- Warnings are given to officials' and teams' locker rooms to get back on the playing field.

5:05 P.M. (estimated)

- Halftime ends.
- Coordinate second-half kickoff.

Here again, we have to be ready to adjust, as we did at Super Bowl XIII in Miami, the year the giant map of the Caribbean got tangled around the goalpost. It took us about 12 extra minutes, or twice the allotted time. The broadcasters took it in stride, but Steelers coach Chuck Noll had a tizzy. Like every head coach of a Super Bowl team, Noll had a time sheet showing the precise moment when the Steelers were expected back on the field. And since he'd gotten his warning from the officials while still in the locker room, Noll had his team sprint back onto the field, where they stood . . . waiting. We couldn't cut the show, either. Under our contract, it was mandatory for the show to run in its entirety. Noll wasn't happy, but the Steelers still won the game.

Second-half kickoff

- Maintain game operations.
- Conduct full-scale check of interview area and telephones.
- Coordinate media walk-down to interview area for postgame.
- Troubleshoot.

At last, that grand feeling of relief begins to envelop us . . . to a point. We're still pretty much in a troubleshooting mode. The big concern during the second half (besides doing our part to make sure the game runs smoothly) is to be certain that all of the postgame monitors are working and that the interview areas are ready. I'm also watching for potential problems. While the crowd watched the Minnesota Vikings march toward a touchdown one year in Tulane Stadium, my gaze was fixed on some Minnesota cheerleaders in the end zone. "Get them out of there," I snapped into a radio. "They're right where they might get hurt."

6:45 P.M. (estimated)

- Conclude game.
- Coordinate MVP announcement.
- Prepare for Lombardi Trophy presentation.
- Prepare for in-stadium televised coverage of interviews.
- Disseminate postgame media transportation information.

The postgame is typically a two- to three-hour stretch in itself. Here again, we depend on traffic control to give us a critical view of the exodus from the stadium, just in case.

9:00 P.M.

- Report any pertinent injury information to the Pro Bowl offices in Honolulu.
- Announce Monday's head coach and MVP interview schedule.
- Complete statistics, records, and performance data and transmit to press box, media workrooms in stadium, and media headquarters hotel.

Some of the players in the Super Bowl are headed straight to the Pro Bowl in Honolulu. If any of those players are injured during the Super Bowl, we have to notify the coaches and staffs so that they'll know to arrange for alternate players. It was always the last thing I did before I walked out of the stadium. Well, the next to the last. I never left the control booth until I was sure that cleanup functions were being performed, that special media transportation needs had been arranged, and that any stragglers were to be taken care of.

Most of the Super Bowl game action I've seen in 36 years has been at postgame media functions, where the replay is shown on giant screens in a hotel ballroom, or in my hotel room. In fact, I used to say, "I'm looking forward to my first Super Bowl game."

Having the early games blacked out was advantageous for me because a delayed telecast would be aired in the local area at midnight. I'd make it a point to leave the parties and other stuff, go back to my hotel room, climb into bed, and watch the replay of the game— so I could say that I'd seen all of it.

Truth be told, I didn't miss seeing the live game action as it unfolded below me. What I did miss was being on the field at the end of the game and in the locker rooms to get postgame quotes, as I was in the early years. I heard firsthand Vince Lombardi's memorable quote in 1967, in which he stated that several of the NFL teams were probably better than the Chiefs and his "There, I said it" addition. And I also heard Dallas's moody Duane Thomas break his self-imposed silence after Super Bowl VI and mutter, "If it's the ultimate game, how come they're playing it again next year?" I'd take the quotes back up to the press box for distribution to writers who were unable to get to the locker rooms because they were working against deadlines.

Looking over the long day and all that is packed into it, you can better understand why we might feel the urge to play the Super Bowl in the same city every year, as New Orleans once hoped for, or why we fantasized about building our own "Super City."

That notion remained a fantasy, of course, and probably always will. Although taking the Super Bowl to a new city or a new venue (as will happen when the game goes to Houston, Jacksonville, and

Detroit, respectively, in three consecutive years beginning in February 2004) invariably introduces new challenges, the change also enhances the Super Bowl's appeal.

I had a new venue myself at Super Bowl XXXVI in 2002 in New Orleans. It marked the first year I wasn't in the control booth. It felt strange at first, but watching the thriller between St. Louis and New England from the vantage point of a suite turned out to be a thrill in itself: Don Shula and Tex Schramm were sitting next to me, Miss America was right behind me, and nearby was Joey Harrington, the Oregon quarterback destined to be the Detroit Lions' number one draft choice.

With the game tied at 17 and the clock winding down to its climactic final seconds, we were doing what television broadcasters Pat Summerall and John Madden—and everybody else, too—were doing: debating whether the Patriots should kill the clock and take their chances in overtime or go for the victory. Shula never hesitated.

"You don't know if you'll even have the ball in an overtime," he said forcefully. "And you don't know if you'll ever have another chance to win a Super Bowl. You go for the victory!"

EIGHTEEN

WHAT REALLY MADE IT SUPER

The Lombardi Trophy isn't the only award presented after a Super Bowl. The lesser-known Rozelle Trophy is bestowed to the game's most valuable player. Few can describe what the trophy looks like, though, and its presentation is often overshadowed by the wild celebration ignited by the crowning of pro football's world champion, just like Pete Rozelle's contribution to the Super Bowl tends to be overlooked after all these years. It shouldn't be.

Many things powered the Super Bowl's meteoric rise, such as the eye-popping television ratings, best exemplified by Super Bowl IV, which commanded a wider audience than Neil Armstrong's walk on the moon. By 1970, we suspected that we had something very special, as the ratings confirmed.

We also could see that writers were coming to the game city earlier and earlier and staying later. Corporate executives, advertisers, and assorted celebrities weren't far behind. Ford's biggest dealer incentive program, for example, became a trip to the Super Bowl. Countless other companies followed suit, fueling an unprecedented weeklong party atmosphere. Eyeing these festivities, more cities began to appreciate what hosting a Super Bowl could do for their economies and prestige. That bandwagon has yet to stop rolling. As these words are being written, even the venerable Rose Bowl is mulling major improvements that may help that grand stadium to become a more appealing Super Bowl venue.

The calendar made a contribution to the popularity of the Super Bowl, as well. When we launched the Super Bowl, it faced virtually no serious competition from other sports events. Coming as it did in mid- to late January, it became a rationale for winter social gatherings all over the country. As its popularity grew, other events were planned around it. In fact, we argued for years that the Nielsen ratings, as high as they are, still never reflect the 22 to 24 percent of fans who watch the game away from their homes.

Yet, these are only indicators of popularity. The source of their inspiration was Pete Rozelle himself. It wasn't so much his crisp but powerful vision of staging the game at a neutral site in a warm-weather city before a huge crowd. Rather, it was his consummate, almost incomparable ability to bring people together and build cooperation. That is what really made the Super Bowl super.

Looking back, I don't think Pete has ever gotten the full credit he deserves for persuading pro football owners to pool their resources and interests. Given the levels of investment, debt loads, and leverage prevalent in pro sports today, I'm not sure that what Pete was able to achieve then could be duplicated today. People have changed, too. Moreover, he did it in the early 1960s, as a young, untested NFL Commissioner. His thinking made very rich men of most owners and others who followed them. It also made the NFL the role-model sports organization that it is today.

Convincing powerful personalities, such as the Giants' Jack and Well Mara, Chicago's George Halas, Cleveland's Paul Brown, Los Angeles's Dan Reeves, and Baltimore's Carroll Rosenbloom, that sharing all television revenues would enable them to create a larger revenue source than anything they could create on their own was an initial masterstroke. Most masterful of all was convincing them that it was to their advantage to support the fundamental concept that gave the NFL's smaller-market cities the wherewithal to compete so that they could survive and prosper, too.

It was this concept that ensured the success of the 1966 merger with the AFL and its numerous small-market cities, which, in turn, gave the Super Bowl its foundation and reason for being. Notably, each of those smaller-market teams—Buffalo, Cincinnati, Denver, Green Bay, Kansas City, Minnesota, and what is now the St. Louis Rams—has played in at least two Super Bowls. A coincidence? I doubt it.

What helped win the owners' deep and abiding respect was Pete's patience and sense of timing. A classic example of his use of these attributes is an exchange that took place during as contentious a meeting as the league ever convened. An owner who sat through it later recounted it to me. The subject of that session, comprising only the owners and Commissioner Rozelle, was Pete himself. Rosenbloom, who often was one of Pete's avowed antagonists and who could get quite emotional, was especially irate.

"I'm gonna have your job!" Carroll finally bellowed. "I don't want to be Commissioner. But I'm going to get you out of here!"

His tirade continued, creating a tension-filled atmosphere. Yet, when it subsided, Pete said calmly, "Anything else?" The room remained quiet. "OK, let's break for lunch," he concluded. The strength that Pete demonstrated in not lashing back that morning left an impression on everyone assembled and served them all well.

It served Joe Namath well, too, in the summer of 1969. Although he was the toast of the sports world, Broadway Joe had suddenly become embroiled in a dispute with the league when we learned that Bachelors III, a New York nightspot Namath owned with some partners, was being frequented by known gamblers and that some gambling activity was taking place on the premises. After Pete threatened Joe with suspension if he didn't dispose of his interest, Joe dramatically announced his retirement from pro football. It was a very emotional incident, especially for Namath. Yet, Pete waited patiently until Joe realized it was more important to him to continue his football career than maintain whatever misguided loyalties he had to his business partners. It was strictly a matter of timing.

Pete's ability to bring people together extended to sports writers and the media. He used to say his early career goal was to become the sports editor of the *Los Angeles Times*. It showed. Pete genuinely loved sports writers and relished subjecting himself to questions from 1,500 or so media guys on the Friday preceding the Super Bowl. He was a master at it, an absolute master, and his "state of the union" press conference helped transform the Super Bowl into the showcase event that advanced the NFL itself. It became far more than a championship football game.

To be sure, by nature Pete was a public relations guy. He broke into pro football by doing the programs for the Rams' games (he earned $50 per issue) as a student at Compton Junior College in Southern California, was the student athletic director at San Francisco, then became the Rams' public relations director in the 1950s. It was always very important to him to be dealing with the public.

Other than when he was at an NFL game, he was never more at home than in New York. Heading out from Park Avenue for one of our frequent meetings on Manhattan's West Side was an exciting adventure . . . and good exercise. Pete was 6 feet 3 inches, with long legs and an enormous stride. We rarely took a car or a cab. We walked. He'd go from here to there in a heartbeat. I'm 6 feet tall myself, but I had a tough time keeping up with him.

Pete never lost his common touch, however. Today, it's almost laughable to remember that he was concerned that the $10 and $12 ticket prices might have been too high for Super Bowl I and a reason it didn't sell out. But he was genuinely concerned. Heck, for years he fought my recommendation to raise the price of the Super Bowl game program. It even might have been costing us money to sell it at $5 or $6, but he still resisted.

Pete was very ill when I retired in mid-1994. He had barely settled in Rancho Santa Fe, California, when he underwent surgery for a brain tumor. Still, he prepared a videotape that lauded my role as the National Football League's unofficial historian of the last three decades. Everyone instinctively looked to me, he said, because I'd been a part of so much of everything that had happened, particularly regarding the Super Bowl. Those words meant more to me than I can express, in part because the tape was presented at my retirement dinner in New York.

In NFL circles, I've come to be regarded as the Super Bowl's architect. Or, maybe now, I'm grandfather to Jim Steeg's father. Yet, Pete Rozelle was its inspiration. Days after announcing the merger in 1966, Pete said he envisioned the Super Bowl's becoming the "sporting event of the century."

Has it ever.

PART III

PRIME TIME

NINETEEN

STICKING OUR TOES IN THE WATER

I can't recall a time when Pete Rozelle wasn't thinking about pro football being on prime time television. Without a doubt, it was on his agenda by the time I joined the NFL in mid-1965. The conversations we had that year and in the months approaching the merger in 1966 convinced me that Pete had been pondering it for a while, perhaps since the early 1960s, when he convinced NFL owners of the wisdom of negotiating a single network television contract covering all 14 NFL teams.

Pete had a better grasp of what pro football and television could do for each other than anyone else outside of broadcasting and, for that matter, better than many people *inside* television broadcasting, too. As soon as he understood how powerful this relationship could be, all sorts of ideas were running through his mind. Pro football in prime time was one of them. It was revolutionary thinking.

Television sports in the 1950s and early 1960s was fragmented. More often than not, programs were produced locally and almost always during the day, predominantly on weekends. NBC aired its *Friday*

Night Fight of the Week and ABC offered a *Wednesday Night Fight* for a time, while local television contracts of major league baseball teams provided for a smattering of night games to be telecast during the week. But these were the exceptions. The World Series was strictly a daytime affair. So were college bowl games.

Contrary to what you might think, pro football telecasts themselves were becoming more fragmented in 1960, too. The National Football League had made its television debut on October 22, 1939, when two just-patented RCA ionoscope cameras beamed the Brooklyn Dodgers' 23–14 victory over the Philadelphia Eagles at Ebbetts Field to the 370 television sets that existed in New York City. Alan "Skip" Walz described the action for W2XBS. Why the station that was to grow into WNBC selected this game remains a mystery. The Dodgers had lost their first five games, and across town that same afternoon the New York Giants and Chicago Bears were waging a more meaningful battle, before 58,000 fans at the Polo Grounds.

A decade later, a number of entities paid $75,000 for the rights to NFL games in the 1949 season (the amount the league got from the DuMont Network in 1951 for rights to its first nationally televised championship game, between Cleveland and Los Angeles). But this accord was the exception that proved the rule: Pro football television contracts in the early 1950s were decidedly local, modeled after the contract that the Rams had negotiated in 1950 to televise all their away games back to Los Angeles. The success of that deal wasn't lost on Commissioner Bert Bell and numerous NFL owners. Each club typically received about $100,000 per season from this emerging television strategy, setting the stage for CBS to start carrying the away games of most NFL teams on a regional basis in 1956. Most, but not all. That distinction became pivotal and contentious.

The Cleveland Browns' television rights had long been held by the Carling Brewing Company, which had negotiated a deal with the independent Sports Network to feed Browns games to stations all over the country. The venture's success prompted NBC to strike a similar deal with the two-time champion Baltimore Colts and the Pittsburgh Steelers for the 1960 season. That fall, NBC fed either a Colts or Steelers game to its affiliates.

Competing with two other packages of NFL games had the CBS eye seeing red: It was paying broadcasting rights to nine teams to reach a nationwide audience, while Sports Network and NBC were reaching the same audience by paying just one and two teams, respectively. In fact, CBS was intent on dropping some of the nine NFL teams from its package to focus on big markets such as New York, Chicago, Philadelphia, and Detroit.

Yet, the nine-team CBS package was the very vehicle Pete wanted to use to launch his leaguewide television strategy. And, he wasn't about to let it unravel. He first outlined his television strategy the morning after his election as Commissioner in January 1960. Following lengthy sessions at the owners' meeting a year later, Pete got authorization from member teams—including the Browns, Colts, and Steelers—to negotiate his long-sought-after deal with CBS. Getting owners in large markets to share television revenues with smaller markets was a true breakthrough, no doubt aided by the almost $400,000 per season each NFL team was to receive as part of the $4.65-million-per-year CBS contract.

But Pete's television strategy needed one more element: congressional legislation in order to avoid any antitrust challenges the deal might present. He eventually won that, too, and the irony is that the friendly sponsor of what became public law 87-331 was none other than the Brooklyn congressman who five years later would turn into the NFL's archenemy: Emanuel Celler!

Celler's bill was signed into law by President Kennedy in the fall of 1961, and the first leaguewide CBS contract took effect for the 1962 NFL season. From that two-year deal grew the role-model sports television alliance that most other sports entities came to emulate and the riches that went with it: When the contract was first renewed, beginning with the 1964 season, it took a $14.1-million-per-season offer from CBS to outbid NBC and ABC.

As lucrative as the relationship with CBS was becoming, it remained a Sundays-only alliance, plus a couple of Saturdays late in the year after the college football season ended. In fact, the only modern-day regular-season or postseason NFL game not played on a weekend had been the 1960 championship game: The Eagles edged Green Bay, 17–13, on a Monday afternoon in Philadelphia because the Sunday on which the teams would have met was December 25 and the league felt that playing on Christmas Day was inappropriate.

Yet, in watching pro football's popularity soar while television sports matured, Pete soon envisioned NFL games being televised in prime time during the week. At first, he talked of a Friday night prime-time package. I first heard of that idea before I joined the league. My reaction to Jim Kensil was crisp: "What in the world is he thinking of?"

Merely whispering the notion of NFL football on Friday night would outrage the entire high school coaching world. Friday nights *belonged* to high school football. Had Pete pressed his idea, opposition from high school football coaches and officials would have been so overwhelming that Congress might well have killed the vital antitrust protection amendment that the 1966 merger required. If you ever want to alienate Congress, just alienate the high schools.

As it was, the amendment protecting the merger from antitrust action also ensured that high schools would not face competition from the NFL on Friday nights, just as the 1961 television legislation that Pete had secured prohibited the NFL from playing on Saturdays until the end of the college football season. The fight might have been moot, anyway. Dallas played a Friday night game or two during its first season in 1960, and the sparse attendance confirmed the futility of challenging the high schools. The NFL does play preseason games on Fridays today but always in August before the scholastic season kicks off.

If Friday night was the sacred domain of high school football, Saturday was the equally sacred domain of college football, for identical reasons. The defense of Saturday was aided by the presence of ABC, then building its relationship with NCAA college football. Like the high schools, the colleges' reactions were understandable. Until the late 1950s, pro football had never represented a threat. But its explosive growth, triggered in large part by the 1958 NFL championship game between the Colts and the Giants, had suddenly made the NFL a force to be reckoned with and wary of: The NFL was competing for the loyalties of *all* football fans.

Because Thursday was judged to be competitively unfair for the teams who would be required to play, except in a rare instance, Pete was left to pursue his prime-time notions on Monday night, almost by default. That wasn't all bad, for Monday was best for the teams, a contention pro coaches had expressed repeatedly. NFL teams could play on Monday night and still adequately prepare game plans and do what was needed to be competitive the following Sunday.

Whether NFL games on Monday night in prime time would be attractive to audiences and advertisers was another matter, however. We simply didn't know. Saturation was a continuing concern of ours, and we discussed it frequently. As strange as it may sound today, nobody could say for sure that fans would follow the NFL on Monday nights in the same number and with the same enthusiasm as they did on Sundays. Nor did we know if pro football advertisers would maintain their interest, a far more pressing concern because boosting revenues from television was unquestionably our overriding objective.

What we did know was that prime-time television audiences were vastly different from weekend audiences. Advertising rates were much different, too, and more expensive. Accordingly, the network executives of the 1960s were extremely wary of disrupting viewing habits that might erode their audiences, and in those days the three networks absolutely ruled television. Network executives were especially sensitive about Monday nights. On the first night of the workweek, they reasoned, people were even more inclined to head home from the job and flip on the television set. CBS's powerful Monday night lineup boasted several blockbusters, headlined by Lucille Ball's *Here's Lucy*, one of her spin-offs from the legendary *I Love Lucy* show.

By 1965, however, CBS was the NFL's only viable option. NBC was now televising AFL games, while ABC was devoting its energies and dollars to college football. Lacking the alternatives he could leverage in 1963, Pete was having a tough time negotiating a new deal with CBS, so tough, in fact, that he considered launching the NFL's own sports network.

Pete Rozelle was never a greedy man. At the same time, whenever money was on the table, he was determined that no dollar would remain there. He saw plenty of money on the table for NFL football, including fresh dollars from the prime-time package he envisioned. By 1965, Pete also was perceptive enough to sense that player salaries might be poised to soar wildly and that the league needed to become more bottom-line oriented to shoulder the consequences without losing any financial momentum.

Just how serious Pete was about building his own network was never clear. Certainly, a precedent of sorts was being set for it at the time: 1965 was also the year Pete brought both NFL Films and NFL Properties into the league's organizational structure so that their respective promotional and revenue potentials could be tapped to the fullest. Start-up costs notwithstanding, a television sports network would not have been that much of an additional leap.

Moreover, Pete was serious enough to sound out owners and win their support. One of his key confidants became Art Modell, who had built a successful television advertising career before becoming the Cleveland Browns' principal owner in 1961. Pete tapped Modell's broadcasting knowledge extensively during this time. He also conferred with Elton Rule, a rising star in California broadcasting whom Pete had gotten to know during his days with the Rams. Rule, notably, would move to New York himself in 1968 to become president of ABC television, where he would meet Pete again a few years later.

Whatever Pete's true intentions were, CBS evidently took his threat seriously. At the eleventh hour, it reached a new television accord with the NFL, one that included a provision for a few Monday night games as experiments. Pete's advocate within the network was Bill MacPhail, head of CBS Sports. A pro football fan himself, and son of baseball magnate Larry MacPhail, Bill had built a close personal and pivotal relationship with Pete and was a tremendous influence for decades. Many of Pete's television ideas were shaped by their friendship. Tex Schramm was another key television confidant. Once the Rams' general manager, Tex had left the team during an owners' squabble in the late 1950s and joined CBS Sports, as one of

MacPhail's key lieutenants, before returning to pro football as the operating head of the expansion Dallas Cowboys.

With the new contract in place, CBS televised the debut of NFL football on Monday nights on October 31, 1966. That it was Halloween night was coincidental. That the game was played in St. Louis wasn't. With the networks starting to televise in color, a key factor to consider was the lighting capabilities of the stadiums we wanted to use for prime-time games. Busch Stadium was new, and its lights boasted the candlepower that color cameras required.

The Cardinals won that first game, beating the Chicago Bears, 24–17. The more important figure, though, was the television rating: 16.3. It was credible enough but not overwhelming. The average November and December ratings for *Family Affair*, one of the CBS programs preempted by the game, was higher, 21.1. Still, the game's performance and the performance of the four others that followed between 1966 and 1969 were strong enough that Rozelle, Modell, and other owners who constituted the league's new broadcast committee concluded that prime-time games would be successful enough to insert them into a regular-season schedule.

However, NFL owners as a whole seemed as indifferent about playing on Monday nights as they had been about playing a new championship game against the AFL when the merger was announced. They really didn't care much about the idea, as minutes from a league meeting held on December 1, 1966, indicate. "All member clubs were in accord with the scheduling of Monday night games," the minutes duly report, "*if such games were necessary.*"

They weren't necessary. But they surely were successful.

TWENTY

ARE YOU READY FOR SOME FOOTBALL?

Even in the dim light of the late hour, the face and voice of Howard Cosell were unmistakable. But his demeanor was startling. I had never before seen Howard more disconsolate. It might have been the lowest moment in his career.

The sixth telecast of ABC's *Monday Night Football* in that inaugural 1970 season had issued the traditional "Good night" and signed off the air from Bloomington, Minnesota, where the atmosphere was cheery and warm, even for a late October night. The Vikings had whipped the Los Angeles Rams, 13–3, in what had been another grand evening for the NFL. My chores as the league's public relations director done for the night, I returned to the hotel and strolled into the bar to wind down. Sitting there by himself, Cosell quickly recognized me and motioned for me to join him. Once I was seated, a thoroughly dejected Howard Cosell bared his soul.

"I don't have to take this stuff anymore. And I'm not," he muttered. The volumes of hate mail and derisive comments that had been hurled his way since the season's first telecast were finally taking their toll. "You know what I'm going to do?" Cosell declared. "I'm going to quit."

The longer Howard talked, the more upset he became. If he was exaggerating, it wasn't by much. That I knew. We, too, had been awash in hate mail and derisive comments about Cosell's performances and not just by fans and writers. William Clay Ford, who owned the Detroit Lions, had been so critical that he all but insisted that we summarily yank Cosell off the air. Other owners were almost as angry, but Ford's anger was harder to dismiss. Along with owning the Lions, Ford owned a good chunk of Ford Motor Company, one of the NFL's key advertisers.

Those harsh words drifted through my mind as Howard talked. I listened attentively, now and then offering a few words of encouragement, until he at last retired to his hotel room.

The significance of our impromptu meeting was locked in my mind when I flew back to New York early the next morning. The first thing I did on returning to my office was call Pete Rozelle to relate the late-night conversation. Pete promptly called Cosell and that afternoon made a trip to Howard's apartment in Manhattan. As much as anything, Pete's expressed support that day convinced him not to cave in. Cosell himself always said that Pete's intervention had a great deal to do with his decision to stay. Howard made a wise choice, at least in our collective opinion, as his network had 18 months earlier in choosing to broadcast football games in prime time.

Monday Night Football's robust and often raucous history makes it easy to forget why ABC televised the inaugural game played in Cleveland Stadium on September 21, 1970.

CBS didn't want to. Neither did NBC.

It's another of the ironies abounding in NFL history. Like the decision to play on Monday night itself, ABC gained the rights to the television package practically by default. It was a stroke of incredibly good fortune. Television coverage of pro football was influenced as never before by these ABC telecasts, an unexpected consequence that fuels the kind of "what if?" speculation usually reserved for coaching decisions on the field or dramatic, game-ending heroics.

For example, what kind of productions would CBS or NBC have developed had either one of them embraced Pete Rozelle's ambitious prime-time proposal, just extensions of their existing NFL coverage or something dramatically different, as ABC fashioned? How would the television history of pro football (indeed, of all sports) have been altered? And would *Monday Night Football* be enjoying its 33rd consecutive season, extending its longevity record for prime-time television? We can only imagine.

Hindsight being 20/20, the decisions made by CBS and NBC now look as short-sighted as ABC's willingness to take a chance on Monday night football telecasts looks like a brilliant masterstroke. But in late 1968 and early 1969, when the negotiations were in full swing, their decisions really were logical, at least from the networks' perspective.

Existing television commitments, particularly the AFL's obligations to NBC, effectively prevented Pete Rozelle from trying to assemble any substantial prime-time package of games until the 1970 season. Other reasons caused us to wait, too: The leagues would be realigned by then and a single-league schedule would be in place. And, more stadiums would be equipped with lighting powerful enough to accommodate the needs of color cameras.

Once Pete put his plan together and had it approved by league owners, he marched it to Bill MacPhail, at CBS Sports, almost as a matter of course. Yet, as close as Pete was to CBS and as enthusiastic as MacPhail was about football, they were unable to sell the idea to the network's top brass. Then again, no one could have sold it, not in 1969.

While CBS had been willing to televise one NFL game in prime time on one Monday night as a special event during the past four seasons, it had no interest in televising an NFL game for 13 consecutive Monday nights in the fall, just as a new prime-time television lineup was being launched. It would have been a huge roll of the dice. Within television's realm, Monday was one of the key nights of the week: People who tended to pass up weekend shows for other activities had now returned to work. Worn out after a typical "blue Monday," all they wanted to do when they got home was eat supper, flip on the set, sit back, and watch television. That was the premise, and plenty of numbers validated it.

Other numbers also had to be reckoned with: higher advertising rates, for one thing, with no assurance that our core advertisers would pay them, and larger audiences, for another, but audiences strikingly different from weekend television sports crowds.

Programming was markedly different, too. CBS was the prime-time leader in the late 1960s, and it all but *dominated* Monday night television with a powerful lineup: *Gunsmoke*, Lucille Ball's *Here's Lucy* comedy, Andy Griffith's *Mayberry R.F.D.*, a comedy starring Doris Day, and Carol Burnett's popular variety show. In the final analysis, CBS was not interested in tampering with success. Nor did it want to risk doing anything that might erode the good rating numbers that NFL games were generating on Sunday afternoons. "We just can't do it," the network's top executives concluded, despite MacPhail's strenuous efforts on our behalf.

Disappointed but undaunted, Pete then took his idea over to Rockefeller Center and NBC, which was televising AFL games. But NBC came to the same conclusion: Neither Carl Lindemann nor Chet Simmons, who then directed NBC Sports, could convince the network to take a chance on pro football in prime time and endanger the success of its hit show, *Laugh-In*, or its series of Monday night movies. Ironically, within a year or two, *Laugh-In*, which aired at 8:00 P.M. eastern time, was generating its best ratings ever because, as our television data suggested, it led right up to *Monday Night Football* at 9:00 P.M. eastern time, a switch of the dial away on ABC.

That left ABC, which was not only the third choice of the NFL but also the third choice of prime-time viewers. Though ABC was often characterized as network television's "energetic newcomer," the network's programming successes had been uneven in the 1950s and 1960s, while its finances were often strained or plagued by red ink, a dilemma ABC was confronting when Pete came knocking on Roone Arledge's door in early 1969. ABC also had the smallest number of exclusive affiliate stations, all of which meant it had the most to gain by striking a deal with the NFL.

ABC had been the first network to televise AFL games, starting with that league's initial 1960 season and continuing until 1965, when it lost those rights to NBC's eye-popping $36 million bid for five seasons. ABC also had bid on NFL games once before, in 1963. With the Super Bowl now fully established in the wake of the Jets' upset victory over Baltimore in January 1969 and pro football's popularity soaring in general, ABC was more eager than ever to grab a share of pro football.

To Arledge, who was in charge of sports at ABC, it was not a question of taking a chance, but seizing an opportunity. Ever the innovator, Roone was enthusiastic right from the get-go, and he had ample support from Elton Rule, among others. The same California broadcast executive who had huddled with Pete a few years earlier about an NFL-operated sports network had come east to take over at ABC in 1968. In fact, Rule would ultimately wield *Monday Night Football* and the network's Olympics coverage as key programming building blocks to lead ABC to prime-time supremacy by the late 1970s.

The network's overall programming philosophy also worked on behalf of Pete Rozelle's proposal. Leonard Goldenson, who had played a lead role in the network's reorganization in 1953 and had since risen to chairman and CEO of ABC Inc., believed in winning audiences by finding programming niches ignored by his rivals. Having backed innovative concepts such as Walt Disney's Disneyland (both the television program and the theme park), Goldenson was ready, willing, and able to endorse Arledge's plans to air *Monday Night Football*, especially since Arledge promised not merely a prime-time pro football game but a prime-time pro football *event*.

The original three-year agreement to televise 13 Monday night games each season was announced on May 26, 1969, in New York. Once the deal was done, Arledge certainly made good on his promise.

Prior to 1970, football telecasts used no more than a half dozen cameras and sometimes as few as four. *Monday Night Football* rolled at least nine of them into each venue. With our approval, it also strung extra microphones in the stadium, to better complement the sights on the field with the sounds of the game along the sidelines and in the stands. Arledge also made more use of the instant replay technique that ABC had pioneered in the 1960s. More technological concepts would follow. And every game was to be televised in color, a significant feature for the times.

More significant still were the innovations to take place in the broadcast booth: not two broadcasters but three. Handpicked by Arledge were Keith Jackson, former Cowboys quarterback Don Meredith, and, of course, Howard Cosell. A year later, Frank Gifford moved over from CBS, and while he had assumed the analyst's role when he had teamed with Pat Summerall at CBS, Gifford took over *Monday Night Football's* play-by-play duties from Jackson.

Although a sportscasting trio was unprecedented, Pete had no real reservations about it mainly because he had a great deal of respect for Arledge and he knew it was in keeping with the nature of the production ABC was crafting. Essentially, Pete's reaction was "More power to you if it works." Notably, he also specifically concurred with the choice of Cosell; in fact, he encouraged it, according to Howard.

Controversial? Without question. But it did work and immediately. Jackson was a solid professional in the single season he was part of the team before returning to what would be a highly successful career broadcasting college football. Gifford, a longtime friend and tennis pal of Pete's, didn't miss a beat in succeeding Jackson. Meredith, who had been part of a preseason ABC tour to promote the broadcasts, assumed his "down-home, aw shucks! Dan-deroo" analyst's role with ease. Putting him alongside Cosell was brilliant because Howard was . . . well, Howard.

I think the love-hate relationship between Howard Cosell and his television audience was established before the end of the season's first month. By the late 1970s, he was named as the most-loved and the most-hated sportscaster in the country—in the same poll. Meanwhile, sports writers had a field day reacting to Cosell's unique, bombastic, and often abrasive style.

Cleveland Press columnist Bob August was rather polite: "Howard Cosell," he wrote, "could equate a hangnail with the fall of the Roman Empire." Jimmy Cannon, the legendary New York columnist, simply responded in kind: "He changes his name from Cohen to Cosell, puts on his hairpiece, and then goes out and 'tells it like it is.' "

Cannon was correct. But Howard, who earned a law degree before entering broadcasting, had a ready rebuttal: His father's real name had been Kasell. U.S. immigration officials changed it to Cohen when he arrived at Ellis Island, and Howard then changed his last name to Cosell to honor his father. Howard well might have had a rationale for his hairpiece, too, but I never heard it. Whether or not he really did "tell it like it is," Cosell always had a wealth of outrageous things to say each week.

Like the fans and the writers, NFL owners formed opinions in a heartbeat. Some, like Bill Ford, demanded the instant fall of Howard Cosell. In retrospect, I think many who heard him simply weren't prepared for a dramatically different kind of sports commentary. It never bothered Pete, however. For as long as Cosell was part of *Monday Night Football*, Pete was very supportive of him.

Whatever misgivings I had about ABC's approach to NFL football had little to do with its choice of broadcasters. Almost from the moment our partnership began, we had the hardest time convincing the network that the game could carry itself. I sometimes thought its crew members were a little terrified of what they had gotten themselves into and were always looking for other things to enhance the broadcast. They cross-promoted the hell out of the game, too (and still do, for that matter). Everybody who's anybody seems to traipse into the broadcast booth and disrupt the flow of the telecast.

I remember well the meeting between Irv Brodsky, the *Monday Night Football* publicist throughout its first decade, and my NFL colleague Jim Heffernan and me before the first season began. Brodsky asked, "What do we have to do to make this work?"

More than slightly annoyed, my reply was brusque. "Just make sure the lights are turned on," I snapped. "Everything else will take care of itself."

And it did. The game's popularity took off from the start. All the fears about fans and advertisers and rates went right out the window.

Monday Night Football's popularity wasn't something that grew gradually; it started high and stayed there, at times cracking prime time's top 10 rankings, and earning audience shares of 40 percent or more. Being a new venture shrouded in such uncertainty, we wouldn't have been surprised had lots of viewers tuned in to the first few games out of curiosity only. But that didn't happen.

The first game gave us great momentum, too, and drew the largest crowd ever to see the Browns play in ancient Cleveland Stadium, more than 85,000 people. The matchup was ideal: The Browns were perennial contenders and had played in the 1968 and 1969 NFL championship games. The New York Jets had Joe Namath, of course, and some of the aura from their Super Bowl victory remained. The Browns jumped to an early lead, but Namath's arm brought New York back. Cleveland was hanging on to a 24–21 lead, with less than four minutes to play, but the Jets regained the football, sending a collective shudder through the stadium . . . until Namath threw an interception that the Browns returned for a touchdown, cementing their 31–21 victory. The game lasted past midnight in the East, but nobody cared.

We worked very closely with the ABC *Monday Night Football* crew throughout that first year. In addition to participating in scores of meetings, we made ourselves available all day Monday to help provide material for the telecast. Some weeks we were in the game city with the crew. At other times we conferred with their people from our New York office. We'd spend as much time as they wanted, keeping them abreast of football matters as the season progressed.

Frank Gifford was always very close to our office, and we fed a lot of information to him. Giff would call us from wherever the Monday night game was being played and get briefed on what was going on around the league, and much of that material got on the air. It became part of our Monday routine during a season. Of course, we'd do exactly the same thing for the other networks as often as they asked. Only they never asked as much as Gifford and ABC.

I find it incredible that the series is still going strong after 32 years. To the best of my knowledge, no serious consideration has ever been given to taking it to another network. Its ratings are lower today compared with what the numbers were in the 1970s, but so are all other network ratings in the wake of the rise of cable television and satellites.

More important are the other opportunities it spawned for pro football. The Sunday night package we launched with ESPN (and initially TNT) and the occasional Thursday night games we developed all came about because of the success of *Monday Night Football*.

ABC has benefited handsomely, too. To a certain extent, the network wasn't taken seriously until *Monday Night Football* debuted. ABC had gained a reputation as an innovator, partly due to its success with *Wide World of Sports*. But its lack of big sports properties had put it at a disadvantage. Frank, Don, and Howard and, to be sure, the football games, changed all that. In fact, the series and its personalities became such fixtures that, in the mid-1980s after ABC got into the Super Bowl television rotation for Super Bowl XIX in 1985, we started a countdown of sorts.

A staple of my speeches were declarations like, "It's 1 year, 11 months, and 14 days before Howard Cosell broadcasts his first Super Bowl" or "Only 361 days to go. If that doesn't mean anything to you, it does to us. That's when Howard Cosell is supposed to do his first Super Bowl."

I can't tell you how many times I mentioned it. Sometimes I'd put the words in the form of a question: "Do any of you here know the significance of 1 year, 10 months, 29 days, 3 hours, and 16 seconds?" Then I would explain that it was the countdown to the kickoff of the first Super Bowl that Cosell was to broadcast, except by the time San Francisco and Miami squared off in Super Bowl XIX, Howard had left *Monday Night Football*. I always found it ironic, for that game, played in Stanford Stadium, also marked Dan Marino's only appearance in a Super Bowl. But Cosell missed it entirely.

He had left the crew somewhat abruptly before the 1984 season. Apparently, he decided he had had enough of the travel and the late nights. And in the latter part of his life, he was battling Parkinson's disease.

A bitter man, he up and quit. But this time, nobody talked him back into the booth.

TWENTY-ONE

THE BLACKOUT BATTLES

With all due respect to the electrifying talents of players such as Jim Brown, Gale Sayers, Barry Sanders, or Emmitt Smith, one of the more memorable pieces of broken-field maneuvering I witnessed during my 29-year NFL career didn't take place on a football field. It took place in a ballroom at the Americana Hotel in Bal Harbor, Florida.

The man with the moves was Pete Rozelle. His pursuers on that Friday morning before Super Bowl V in 1971 were a process server from Florida's Broward County, and a deputy sheriff. But they were mere intermediaries.

Our real adversary was Ellis Rubin, an annoying southern Florida attorney with political ambitions, whose unending campaigns to lift the NFL's television blackout of the Super Bowl in Miami earned him more notoriety than he deserved. Rubin always insisted that it was everybody's "right" to see the Super Bowl. To us, it was an old, worn-out issue. Challenges to our blackouts of NFL championship games had been mounted several times, but courts repeatedly upheld our policy: Because we owned the rights to the games, we had every right to decide if, when, and where they would be televised. By and large, fans accepted the rulings.

Rubin persisted, however, and as the Super Bowl's popularity soared, his campaign intensified. By Super Bowl V, he was attracting considerable attention, which, of course, is exactly what he was after.

This time Rubin petitioned a circuit court, claiming that, because local tax money was being used to help stage a Super Bowl that was already sold out, southern Florida's 2.5 million television owners were entitled to watch it. In our opinion, Rubin's real objective was amassing political support in Ft. Lauderdale and Broward County because that area was within the 75-mile radius of the Orange Bowl that was subject to the blackout. With more than enough to do the week before the game, the last thing we needed was for Pete to have to show up in some courtroom . . . and as long as he could stay out of sight and avoid being served a summons, he wouldn't have to.

One factor working in our favor was Pete's decision not to stay at our headquarters hotel but rather on his boat, anchored in Miami's Biscayne Bay. Pete served on the board of directors of Chris-Craft in those days and had a very nice powerboat, which he often used for getaway fishing trips. It was the ideal haven, and throughout Super Bowl week his location in Miami remained a carefully guarded secret. Friday presented a dilemma, however, because Pete would preside at his traditional press conference, where we were absolutely certain a process server would show up and try to hand him a subpoena. So, we started plotting.

The press conference was scheduled to be held in an Americana Hotel ballroom that adjoined the hotel's kitchen. We did not permit filming or taping of the press conference in those days. Instead, we set up television and radio interview locations in an adjacent room so that once Pete concluded the press conference he could go directly there and do one-on-one interviews. The arrangement fit our plans perfectly: He would enter the ballroom through a rear door from the kitchen, meet with the press, and then move directly to the adjoining room for his television interviews. From there, we'd whisk him back into the kitchen, out of the hotel, and to the safety of his boat, all the while steering clear of anyone who might be bearing a summons.

As was standard procedure, I stationed two team public relations directors, Joe Blair of the Washington Redskins and Jan Van Duser of the Atlanta Falcons, at the glass doors of the ballroom's main entrance to ensure that only those with proper press credentials were admitted. Sure enough, a process server and a deputy showed up. After they were denied entry, they stood outside the doors, looked through the glass, and waited. I became aware of their presence about halfway through the press conference and tried to keep half an eye on them.

Once Pete had finished and moved to the next room, the two men realized he wouldn't be coming out through the main entrance. So, they decided to force their way in and confront him. As they literally blasted their way through the doors, Joe Blair, who probably weighed all of 135 pounds soaking wet, was knocked over. His fall triggered a brief scuffle, during which Van Duser "accidentally" tripped the process server. "You'll go to jail for that!" the deputy growled as he started running toward Pete.

Standing in the usual post–press conference crowd of reporters, Pete knew immediately what the commotion was all about. Although he never actually ran during the next few moments, he did a terrific slow-motion imitation of an NFL halfback on a broken-field jaunt. He ducked here, darted there, then moved around a post in the ballroom, in a bid to get to the door leading to the kitchen. But, as he was en route to the door, either the process server or the deputy was able to work his way through the crowd, most of whom were still totally unaware of this impromptu chase. Pete might have escaped even then, but something inside of him finally said this is silly. He stopped, walked toward the server, put out his hand, and let the guy serve him with the subpoena.

Pete appeared in a Broward County court in Ft. Lauderdale the next morning, a Saturday, the day before the game. Predictably, Circuit Court Judge Arthur Franza heard the case and declared that he had no authority to issue an injunction. But before he tossed it out, he couldn't resist offering his own personal opinion, calling the blackout "a transgression and a usurpation of the airwaves" and saying he would "applaud a decision by Pete Rozelle" to remove it.

Arrest warrants citing obstruction of justice were issued for Van Duser and Blair, although the official complaint referred to "two unidentified security people from the NFL." Rubin lost that one, too. Jack Danahy, our security chief, got both warrants quashed.

More than 30 years later, it's an amusing tale. But it shows just how seriously we defended what has sparked mountains of controversy: the NFL blackout policy.

Certainly it is both flattering and gratifying to know that millions of fans are so attached to the Super Bowl and to NFL football that they feel they have a "right" to see every game that's played on television, no matter what. However, such expressions of loyalty remain at odds with a long-standing axiom of any business: *You don't give away what you're trying to sell. If you do, sooner or later people stop buying.*

That was Pete Rozelle's enduring sentiment for as long as he was Commissioner, notwithstanding the law Congress hurriedly passed in September 1973 that lifted blackouts of home games sold out 72 hours before kickoff. Bert Bell, Rozelle's predecessor, felt exactly the same way as Pete. Both men strongly believed that televising a team's home games in its own market was very damaging to a team's long-term finances and unnecessary, given the NFL's long-standing insistence that every team's road games were to be televised back to that team's home market without fail. That obligation was part and parcel of every league television contract the NFL ever signed.

It was part of a fundamental philosophy: To be guaranteed of seeing your team's home games, you needed to purchase a ticket or, ideally, season tickets. In return, the NFL's television policy guaranteed that you would see every one of your team's road games. The same philosophy extended to all NFL postseason playoff and championship games and, once it began, the Super Bowl.

The origins of our thinking date back to 1950, when games were beginning to be televised on a regular basis. The same agreement that the Los Angeles Rams reached with television maker Admiral to televise the team's road games back to the region's 690,000 homes with television sets also provided for home games to be shown throughout Los Angeles, as an experiment, with the stipulation that Admiral would make up the difference for any lost ticket revenues, based on the gate sales of the preceding season's six games. The Rams were a powerhouse in 1950 and played in the NFL title game. Still, attendance tumbled sharply, to the point that the agreement cost Admiral $307,000. It was a staggering sum in its day and cost several Admiral executives their jobs.

The experience offered a precedent-setting lesson that neither the Rams nor any other NFL clubs ever forgot. By the late 1950s, the policy of promoting pro football by televising all of a team's road games back home but none of its home games was well established. Owners felt so strongly about it, in fact, that they also declared that no other NFL games would be shown in any team's market when it played at home.

In his attacks on the NFL, Rubin liked to claim that by the late 1960s "most NFL games" were sellouts. Many were, as pro football's popularity mushroomed. But to us, the sellout was due to the fact that you needed to buy a ticket if you wanted to see the game.

A few fans occasionally bemoaned the situation, but many more set a precedent of their own: traveling in caravans just beyond the 75-mile blackout radius to watch their team's home games in the comfort of a motel, bar, or restaurant. Many innkeepers in Connecticut hosted throngs of New York Giants fans, all the while rejoicing over their geographic good fortune.

But, starting in 1965, NBC began telecasting rival American Football League games into every market every Sunday. If, say, the Packers were playing at home, another station in Green Bay or Milwaukee would be showing an AFL game. Confronting the competition, the NFL modified its policy a year or so later and began beaming another NFL game into markets of teams playing at home, usually after the home team's game had concluded. Doubleheader games were added to the television schedule, too.

Modifying the blackout policy made all kinds of competitive sense. For one thing, no one wanted a televised AFL game to go unchallenged. Why, we asked ourselves, should we concede certain markets to the AFL and let it boost its ratings at the NFL's expense? If an NFL team playing at home had to compete with pro football on television, better it be with another NFL game, to maintain interest in the league . . . and hope that gate receipts didn't suffer too much. With more games selling out and most teams blessed with a solid base of season ticket holders, the majority of owners felt the change was a risk worth taking.

Ticket sales were impacted but not as much as a handful of faint-hearted owners feared. And through it all, the league's fundamental philosophy never changed. Still, it was a delicate situation, with discussions punctuated by howls of protest from those predicting doom. "You're going to televise *against* us?" they asked incredulously. A couple of owners really screamed.

They were to have lots more to scream about a few years later. However, the source of that brouhaha was a force from within: the astonishing rise of the Washington Redskins.

As soon as new head coach George Allen arrived in Washington in 1971, he quickly put together a Redskins team that reached the NFL postseason for the first time since 1945. A year later, the Redskins marched all the way to the Super Bowl. Led by retread quarterback Billy Kilmer and a collection of grizzled veterans, dubbed the "Over the Hill Gang," Allen's team had Capitol Hill and everyplace else in and around D.C. going crazy. Declaring, "The future is now!" the Redskins attracted fans from around the nation.

We had only one problem: Cozy, 55,000-seat Robert F. Kennedy Stadium couldn't begin to squeeze in the multitudes who wanted to see Washington's rise to glory. The demand for tickets was overwhelming. But rather than motor 75 miles out of town to escape the blackout, senators, congressmen, their staffs, and the bureaucrats did what came naturally: They talked, they expressed deep concern, they issued statements, and finally they introduced legislation. Never mind the Cold War, Vietnam, and other pressing affairs of state. This was important stuff, absolutely vital to the nation's well-being.

The outcome of this federal assault on the NFL's blackout policy was inevitable and never in doubt. Pete did his best to stem the tide. He talked, too, and issued a detailed position paper that explained the blackout's history and rationale. He pointed out how mere expectations of local television coverage had depressed attendance at the first Super Bowl in Los Angeles. It didn't matter. As potent as Pete's powers of persuasion were, he was no match for the people's duly elected representatives.

Jack Kemp, who was elected to Congress in 1970 after a solid career as a quarterback for San Diego and Buffalo, was stunned and still chuckles when he talks about it. In all his 18 years in the House, he often said, he never saw any bill race through Congress as fast as that one did in September 1973.

When the pro football season opened later that month, it was the law of the land: Any NFL game that was sold out 72 hours before kickoff had to be offered to local television. We even had to file reports with the Federal Communications Commission to verify our compliance with the law. Labeled an experiment, the statute was in force for only three seasons, expiring on December 31, 1975. But the NFL has honored its provisions ever since, principally because Pete and the owners assumed that if they didn't, Congress would pass another law even faster and one that might be more onerous.

A cynical reaction? Not when you consider an idea that floated in Minnesota some years later. As city and state officials considered using public funding for a new domed stadium for the Vikings, someone in the state legislature proposed that the team be required to televise its home games in the Twin Cities once 60 percent of the tickets had been sold, whenever that occurred, be it 72 or 2 hours in advance.

The proposal begged a question: Which 60 percent of the Vikings' fans should purchase tickets to the game so that everyone else could see the game on television for free? According to that logic, a theater should give away its tickets once 60 percent of the seats to a production are sold, or a supermarket should give away its steaks once 60 percent of a day's cuts have been purchased.

It's all moot, though. In the three decades since the 1973 law was passed, the league and its teams have learned to live with it as a necessary evil.

At least one consequence was unintended, however. Teams whose home games rarely sell out have almost no chance of hosting *Monday Night Football*. ABC doesn't want to risk the advertising and broadcasting hassles associated with televising a game that has a good chance of being blacked out in some portion of the country.

Make no mistake. The NFL draws up the season schedule as it sees fit, including the designation of Monday night games. Yet, ABC gets to see the schedule in advance. Occasionally, it suggests an adjustment, and the league tries to accommodate its needs. Still, this factor has eliminated games from consideration that otherwise would be attractive prime-time matchups and, in turn, prevented cities from enjoying the many civic perks that come with hosting *Monday Night Football*.

The irony of it all is that Pete Rozelle always insisted that NFL telecasts "be over the air." More owners than you might imagine would have been willing to move all NFL games to cable channels or some other form of subscription television. In fact, the prospect of generating riches from pay television was one of the reasons why Al Davis fought so hard to move the Raiders from Oakland to Los Angeles in 1982 (and why Walter O'Malley took the Dodgers west to Los Angeles in 1958).

The NFL now uses cable television, of course, but very judiciously. Our ESPN contracts always specified that fans without cable service in the markets of the teams playing the games still would be able to see them on over-the-air channels. (Notably, the Sunday night and Thursday night games became tremendous promotions for ESPN because its number of subscribing households grew significantly in the years immediately following the time that it signed its first contract with the NFL).

Pete's insistence on this issue reflected his abiding concern for not only the league's best long-term interests but also the fans' best long-term interests. We'll never know how he and NFL owners might have addressed the blackout question had Congress not forced legislation on them. By the early 1970s, the issue could not be ignored, yet the league never had any opportunity to shape its own proposals that might have served everybody's best interests. The fact is that nine months before Congress acted, Pete had lifted the blackout voluntarily, as an experiment. He chose the Super Bowl VII in Los Angeles.

Deep down, Pete Rozelle really did want fans everywhere to enjoy what he envisioned long before anyone else as the "sporting event of the century."

PART IV

MEN WHO MADE A DIFFERENCE

TWENTY-TWO

PETE ROZELLE

A Man for His Time

I first met Pete Rozelle when I was assigned to cover a National Football League meeting at the Warwick Hotel in New York City in January 1961. I was a member of the sports department of the Associated Press's New York office at Fifty Rockefeller Plaza in midtown Manhattan. It was an ideal locale. From our fourth-floor newsroom, we looked down across 50th Street to Rockefeller Center's famous skating rink and, to the right, to what was then called the RCA Building.

The NFL had recently become a neighbor of sorts. One of the first decisions Rozelle had made after being elected Commissioner in 1960 was to move NFL headquarters to New York from the Philadelphia suburb of Bala Cynwyd, where Bert Bell had presided since World War II. Rozelle and his tiny staff wound up in a suite of offices at One Rockefeller Plaza. From the 23rd floor, they, too, looked down at the skating rink; to the left, to the RCA Building that had housed the National Broadcasting Company since its opening in 1940; and, to the right, the AP building where I had toiled since 1951.

It was more by design than coincidence. The move also put the NFL only a block and a half from Madison Avenue, and within easy walking distance of CBS and ABC, the two other television networks that enriched NFL clubs through rights fees during the next four decades. With the 33-year-old Rozelle standing 6-foot-3, with extra-long legs and a stride to match, the walk was even easier. It wasn't far to Toots Shor's saloon, while 21, Manuche's, and Gallagher's were also within easy reach. And, if you wanted to mingle with the Rockettes having a bite between shows at Radio City Music Hall, there was P. J. Moriarity's joint directly across the street from the stage entrance. Obviously, this was no Bala Cynwyd!

The NFL meeting at the Warwick was in its second day, and the writers were doing what was expected of them, lounging in the overstuffed mezzanine chairs, smoking their cigarettes and cigars, and talking to whoever would listen—mostly each other. On that morning, though, we all were listening to Art Rooney. Then in his fourth decade as owner of the Pittsburgh Steelers, Art enjoyed nothing more than ducking out of the meeting room for a fresh cigar and a chat with the guys he referred to as "my boys" while his son, Dan, tended to league business on the other side of the door.

Which meant I was sitting among the "boys" listening to Art Rooney's wonderful stories when this tall, lanky man suddenly appeared and asked, "Anyone here from AP?" I introduced myself, wondering why Pete Rozelle was singling me out.

He flashed that infectious grin of his, making me even more curious, but then asked, "Do you know this fellow Jim Kensil?" I did, I replied quickly. In fact, I said, Jim was my best buddy at AP and I his, and we lived in the same Long Island town of Massapequa, often commuted together either by car or on the Long Island Railroad, and shared a very strong interest in the National Football League, although our lack of seniority on the AP sports staff didn't give us many opportunities to write about pro football. I think I had gotten to about the point where Kensil and I commuted together when Rozelle smiled again and said, "Ask him to call me, please." Then he excused himself and went back into the meeting room.

It turned out that Pete wanted to talk to Kensil about his plans for a leaguewide television contract. Something Jim had said in the radio and TV column he wrote in his spare time had provoked Pete. Within a couple of days, they met for lunch, and the next thing I knew, Pete had hired my best buddy to be the NFL's new public relations director. It was a perfect match. It wasn't long before Pete and Jim were working so closely together that many considered them inseparable. Kensil became Rozelle's right-hand man, with total access to him night and day. When Jim resigned from the NFL office 16 years later, in 1977, to become president and chief executive officer of the New York Jets—a job Rozelle recommended him for to Jets owner Leon Hess—Pete said he was losing "my offensive and defensive coordinator."

As for me, I hung around the AP for another couple years, eventually building a bit of a national reputation as a golf and college basketball writer (I covered five Final Fours long before they acquired that name), covered the 1962 and 1963 World Series and NFL championships, and worked with the great Will Grimsley in covering numerous golf tournaments, including the Masters, PGA, and U.S. Open. I finally left the AP at Joe Dey's invitation to take charge of golf publications and public relations at the United States Golf Association. I'll never forget my first week on the new job—on that Friday, President John F. Kennedy was assassinated.

Something remained constant, however. Kensil and I, though working apart, remained neighbors and talked constantly on the phone. And although Rozelle and I seldom saw each other professionally, we were each aware of what the other was doing.

It was in the aftermath of the suspensions of Paul Hornung and Alex Karras in 1963 that *Sports Illustrated* named the young Rozelle its "Sportsman of the Year," a public-recognition breakthrough for him. By then, he had his league television contract with CBS and had convinced all NFL clubs to share the revenues equally. The NFL's television revenues were climbing, and attendance was escalating, but so was the league's war for talent with the upstart American Football League. Finally, in the summer of 1965, Rozelle told Kensil to find someone else to run the public relations department so that he could spend more time with Rozelle. Jim called me for advice and offered me a short list of names. I said I would be interested myself.

Next thing I knew, Rozelle had talked with Joe Dey (tampering rules, you know), I had met with Rozelle, and I was on my way to the NFL. Rozelle later wrote to me that "kensil certainly did a great job in the league office, but as far as i'm concerned his biggest contribution was in recommending his 'buddy from ap' to me for our organization. i can't remember a single assignment you were ever given that you didn't execute perfectly. but beyond that were the many significant things you initiated on your own that contributed so greatly to our success when we worked together." (Pete typed every personal letter he wrote throughout his career in lowercase letters on his manual typewriter.)

If Rozelle had a left-hand man, I guess it was me, although the size of our staff was such that everyone—there were fewer than 10 regulars at the start—had a hand in virtually everything we did. Titles didn't matter, except for one. You knew who that was when pizzas were delivered to the conference room for lunch and half of each pizza was covered with anchovies, complemented by a chocolate milkshake. Strange eating habits aside, you knew at once who was number one.

No one I knew ever bettered Pete Rozelle's hands-on management style. We used to say he was like Johnny Carson's Carnac—he gave you the answer before you even asked the question. He knew what needed to be done and what should be done before he went through the formality of asking you what you thought. But he was considerate enough to let you get there by yourself, or, at least, that's what you always thought. He loved to think on his typewriter, the way anyone who ever wanted to be a writer in those days had to do. And nothing pleased him more than to talk about the days when he was the Rams' public relations guy shepherding a group of writers from game to game and city to city. His goal as a kid, he said, was to become the sports editor of the *Los Angeles Times*. When he didn't, he adopted most of the traits of a writer, including hustling off to his manual typewriter when we had problems, creating just the right language for an important statement. Of the different versions we considered, his was usually the best and the one we used.

Pete was a master of the art of persuasion. Ask the owners who knew him at his peak. In the late 1970s, we were convinced that we needed to adopt a 16-game regular-season schedule, with 4 preseason games, instead of 6 preseason games and 14 regular-season games. Eddie DeBartolo Jr. had just taken over as owner of the San Francisco 49ers, and when the debate over a 16-and-4 versus a 14-and-6 schedule got testy, Rozelle took a break and quietly moseyed over to DeBartolo. Tex Schramm, who favored retaining the 14-and-6 schedule, said later, "You S.O.B. I saw you, picking on the newest, most naive guy in the room." The 16-and-4 proposal was adopted, with the 49ers casting a "yes" vote.

Rozelle knew more about television and how to use it than anyone else alive. What he didn't know or wasn't sure of he extracted from his close associates in the business. To them, though, it seemed pointless. "Why's he asking me that?" Bill MacPhail, head of CBS Sports, once said to me. "He knows the answer." I replied, "Just to be sure, I guess." Pete never once doubted that *Monday Night Football* would succeed, just as he believed from the beginning that the Super Bowl would grow into the number one sports event of the year.

That genius invigorated the various promotions and marketing projects in which the league was involved. By 1965, Ed Sabol's mom-and-pop outfit that was shooting footage of the NFL championship games on a shoestring had become NFL Films, owned by each of the NFL member clubs. So had NFL Properties, which had begun with bobble-head dolls as a West Coast sideline operation of Roy Rogers Enterprises. Pete took a personal interest in all of NFL Properties' early planning, with only one lament: "Be sure you come to lunch with me when we entertain those Properties guys," he'd say to Kensil and me. "They never remember what I tell them and what they agreed to do."

Rozelle ran a meeting unlike anything *Robert's Rules of Order* ever could have contemplated. Most meetings were informal, to the point of casualness, mainly because he wanted everyone who wanted to be heard to be heard and because often he knew beforehand how things were going to come out anyway. His straw polls were infamous: Pete just wanted to be sure his lobbying the night before hadn't been unraveled. He suffered few defeats in the meeting room mainly because his premeeting routines—including countless one-on-one conversations—were so persuasive. If a measure did go down, it was often because he himself wasn't convinced it should be adopted, although he would rarely say that to those who proposed it.

When his passes no longer had a tight spiral (and it happened at a time in the 1980s when messy legal entanglements, many of them internal, dominated his waking hours), it became painful for those of us who had marveled at that steel-trap mind for so many years. He never complained. He just said it wasn't as much fun as it had been.

When he retired in 1989, he had earned every accolade that was to come and had affirmed what his buddy Tex Schramm had said on Rozelle's induction into the Pro Football Hall of Fame in 1985: "he was more than anything else a man for his time."

he was indeed, and make that lowercase, no caps.

JIM KENSIL

A Tough Act to Follow

Jim Kensil and I lived two blocks from each other in the Long Island community of Massapequa, so it was only natural that, when my family's home was destroyed by fire on a Saturday during Memorial Day weekend in 1977, Jim was among the first to volunteer to help. The following Tuesday, amid arguments with the insurance adjusters, Kensil and I got a long two-by-four to use as a wedge to close the half-melted door of our refrigerator, which had been packed with foodstuffs and was now giving our neighbors something else to smell besides smoke and waterlogged debris.

"By the way," Jim said as we worked, "Pete wants to talk to you when you feel up to it. I'm leaving to become president of the Jets, and he wants to talk with you about taking over my job. You want it, don't you?"

That's how Kensil left the NFL office, after 16 years, and how I succeeded him as executive director, just as I had succeeded Jim as the league's public relations director 9 years earlier.

Jim Kensil always was a tough act to follow because he was one of the brightest persons I have ever met. He was born in Philadelphia, the son of a Pennsylvania Railroad employee, and went to the University of Pennsylvania on a scholarship given to children of the railroad's employees, by earning the then highest score ever posted on the exam given to scholarship applicants. During one summer break from the university, Jim got a job working at the New York office of the Associated Press, a little advance training for a full-time position with Associated Press Sports in the future. First, however, came a stint in the army, serving in Europe (most of it spent writing for *Stars and Stripes*). Once discharged, Jim joined the Associated Press bureau in Columbus, Ohio, where he was working when a job opened up with Associated Press Sports in New York. My job, he thought. Instead, it went to some guy already working in New York for Associated Press radio sports, which is how Jim Kensil first heard of Don Weiss.

"I was prepared to hate you," he later said. Instead, we became best friends and very soon Associated Press buddies. The next job opening did bring Jim to New York, where we worked side by side for six years until he left for the NFL in the spring of 1961.

Among our achievements was teaching Ted Smits, the general sports editor for the Associated Press, about professional football and the National Football League. That's putting it mildly. Football to Ted meant *college football*, so our Associated Press staff was routinely dispatched to cover seven or eight college games each Saturday throughout the East and as far west as Pennsylvania: the Ivy League, Army, Navy, Penn State, Pitt, and Syracuse. By comparison, the NFL (and the AFL when it debuted in 1960) got short shrift on the Associated Press wires. Sunday coverage of the New York Giants and eventually the AFL New York Titans was an afterthought. The first time Ted and his wife, Pam, hosted a Christmas party in their apartment for the sports staff was on the same Sunday, at the same time, that the Giants played the Chicago Bears for the NFL championship at Yankee Stadium in 1956. Kensil and I had to sneak into the kitchen to listen to the game on the radio with the caterers but eventually had to give that up because our wives complained that our frequent absences were getting embarrassing. The Giants won in a rout, and we weren't even able to listen to it.

In 1958, we would have given almost anything to have covered the Giants' championship game against the Baltimore Colts, which *Sports*

Illustrated's Tex Maule called "the greatest football game ever played." As it was, Kensil and I wrote a major portion of the pregame stories that week, without ever stepping foot out of our Associated Press offices in Manhattan. But despite our insatiable interest in what has been called the one single event that made pro football, we were assigned desk duty, putting the commas and periods where they belonged in someone else's copy.

It wasn't until Kensil became Rozelle's public relations director in 1961 that Associated Press Sports came of age in covering this exciting brand of football, which was pushing its way into the sports world's public consciousness. To the wire service's credit, its leading football writer became Jack Hand; no one was better. After Jim and I were both in the NFL, we took turns accompanying Jack on preseason training camp tours, affording him access to owners, coaches, and players who would help him do his job better and indirectly help us promote the NFL. Our guided tours weren't reserved for Jack alone. Others could come, too, and some did, including Tex Maule.

Almost as significant as Hand's appointment was the fresh enthusiasm that other major Associated Press bureaus were bringing to their pro football coverage. It rivaled New York's budding interest. Kensil, meanwhile, spent his first few years as the league's public relations director initiating programs that would help revolutionize pro football coverage, which is exactly why Rozelle had hired him.

For years at the Associated Press, Kensil and I railed at the lack of assistance we (and most writers) received from the NFL's public relations office. Once Jim was in a position to do something about it, he did—in spades. He initiated capsule pregame reports of each of the Sunday games—summaries that highlighted interesting facts about the two teams that were meeting, what had happened in previous games, and what to look for—presented in such a manner that they could stand alone in a newspaper (many of these releases were printed verbatim) or could trigger ideas in a writer's mind for feature stories that could accompany the pregame data. By the time I joined the staff in 1965, Jim had established a pattern of releases unlike anything newspaper sports departments had ever seen before. He was the first person to develop the weekly NFL injury report, which is still a league staple. He also wrote what we called a "tease" release in advance of every league meeting and the annual NFL draft.

Those efforts, coupled with Rozelle's willingness—eagerness, even—to meet and talk with the press, quickly doubled, then tripled, the number of writers and media personnel assigned to follow NFL teams and the league itself. One of Jim's and Pete's first acts was to schedule an annual off-season meeting of all club public relations personnel. Almost overnight, these public relations people gained a status throughout the league they had never enjoyed before, while the telephone became the most-used instrument in the NFL office. If you asked a question, you got an answer—and more. High school students were hired to clip everything that was written about the NFL in the hundred-odd daily papers to which the NFL subscribed. The clips were used to build hundreds of files on players, coaches, and every conceivable football topic. The best—and occasionally the worst—were distributed throughout the league to keep clubs apprised of what various writers were thinking. When the tone of a columnist indicated that some friendly guidance was needed, he'd get a phone call offering it. A West Coast columnist once wrote, "You guys seem to know what I need before I discover I need it." Even the inimitable Beano Cook, ever the champion of college football, said simply, "You're the best." Whatever it was, Jim Kensil had a hand in it.

After he became the league's first executive director in 1968, he was the person Pete Rozelle called on to come up with one solution after another, in matters ranging from scheduling patterns to legal and congressional issues and, certainly, the league's varied business affairs. Jim was tireless, and you could count on one hand the number of workdays he missed because of illness. Like Rozelle, he didn't care much for doctors. If something was bothering him or one of his children, he'd simply visit his local pharmacist, tell him what was wrong, and ask him to deliver something to his house for when he returned. Jim's workday didn't end at the office, either. It was a rare night when he didn't speak with Rozelle or me, and he often spoke with both of us.

When Kensil left for the Jets in 1977, Rozelle called him "my offensive and defensive coordinator." Our contact with Jim was somewhat reduced after his departure due to the nature of our respective daily responsibilities, but both Pete and I talked with him by phone several times each week until illness forced his retirement from the Jets in June 1988.

Jim and I remained neighbors throughout, beginning when we helped the Kensils look at houses when they wanted to move to Massapequa in the mid-1950s and continuing until my retirement in 1994. In a rare coincidence (although it wasn't when you really think about it), word of Jim's death, on January 16, 1997, reached my wife and me at the moment we were in a Manhattan church attending a memorial service for Pete Rozelle.

Jim had never changed. If he wasn't well enough to work a full schedule, he still was able to pick up a phone and challenge a sports talk show host about a statement he had made. He had an opinion about everything and freely expressed it. Debating Jim was fruitless; he was never wrong. Most of the time he wasn't, either.

He was an insatiable reader of history, and war stories intrigued him. He didn't just read them; he practically memorized them, to the point that he was able to insert himself comfortably into history even when he hadn't been a part of it. He once told a fellow Long Island Railroad passenger—a total stranger he had met in the bar car—a fascinating first-person tale about General George Patton's final World War II assault on the Germans. A couple of weeks later, Jim told the same passenger about an equally dramatic encounter that he had been part of in the Pacific, which had occurred about the same time Patton was attacking the Germans. That it was impossible for Kensil to have been in both places at the same time never occurred to his spellbound listener. The fellow hung on every word, right to the last stop of the train.

Jim had a caustic wit, too. During the flower-child era, we had a young writer working for NFL Properties who wore hippie garb in the office: flowing robe, sandals, beard, and granny glasses. During the holiday season, the young man passed Jim in the hall, smiled, and said cheerfully, "Merry Christmas." Without breaking stride or changing expression, Jim replied, "Happy birthday."

And he was ever frugal. In the early years of riding the Long Island, Jim would get off the train at Jamaica Station, 30 minutes from Penn Station, and get on the subway two long blocks away because it ran close to our office, too, and a subway token cost but a fraction of what it cost to stay on the train. If we had a beer after work, we'd never stop in the city. Instead, we'd wait the hour or so until we got to Massapequa, where a draft at Gannon's was eight cents. Jim and his family lived comfortably and never wanted, of course, but even three decades later he was exhibiting the same traits. Shortly before I retired and left Massapequa for Florida, I saw Jim out for a walk as I drove to the train station to make my commute to New York.

"Going up to the library," Jim said. "I can read three daily papers there without spending a dime." Then he added, "I'm a pensioner now, you know."

TWENTY-FOUR

TEX SCHRAMM

One Brilliant "Bullmoose"

It was during the third round of the 1987 NFL draft, and the Denver Broncos, drafting 27th that year after losing in the Super Bowl to the New York Giants, were on the clock. As their allotted five minutes wound down, those of us at the podium in the Marriott Marquis ballroom in New York became aware that Denver was talking with Dallas about trading its pick to the Cowboys. The phone conversations between the two teams eventually hit a snag, and before it could be unraveled the five minutes had expired. Under long-established draft rules, that became an automatic pass for Denver and immediately bounced rights to the next selection to the Giants.

Without hesitation, the Giants selected Stephen Baker, a quick, little receiver from Fresno State, affectionately known as "Baker the Touchdown Maker." As soon as we announced the pick, Tex Schramm of the Cowboys was on the phone from the team's draft room in Dallas.

"What the hell's going on up there?" Tex demanded of me in his booming voice.

"You didn't get your trade done in time," I said, "and since Denver hadn't picked, it was the Giants' turn and they picked Baker."

Schramm bellowed back, "Who was involved in the decision?"

"The usual," I replied. "Joel Bussert and Jan Van Duser, and I was part of it, too."

"You're all assholes!" Tex roared.

We all took Schramm's outburst in stride. As league office liaisons to the NFL Competition Committee that Schramm chaired for years, Bussert, Van Duser, and I probably had the closest workday relationship with Tex of all the people at NFL headquarters. He frequently called on us to develop data for his committee to study when contemplating rules changes. The three of us set the agenda and ran the committee's annual two-week meeting, usually on Maui in Hawaii. We were regularly on the phone and spent hours and hours each year discussing the competitive issues the committee would study. A common bond of confidence and, we thought, respect had been forged from the close and ongoing contact. And now we were all assholes.

"We were only doing our jobs," I reminded Tex. "You'd be the last one to expect us to bend the rules. It's the only way the draft can be run in an orderly fashion."

"Well, . . . damn it, we wanted Baker and were just about to complete the deal when you guys put New York on the clock!" Tex shouted. Silence followed, then the hint of a chuckle. "Well, I guess I was too strong in calling you what I did. Tell them they aren't assholes," he said, before briefly heating up again as he thought about what happened. Because the Cowboys hadn't completed the trade in time, Baker—a coveted selection—now belonged to the Giants, one of Dallas's chief NFC Eastern Division rivals and the reigning Super Bowl champions.

"Tell them they're nothings," he finally laughed, "or at least half-nothings!" I didn't ask where I stood at that moment, but we all knew how blustery Tex Schramm could be when he was upset, so we tended to give him the benefit of the doubt when he resorted to name-calling. He was so famous for it that even Pete Rozelle, probably Tex's closest friend in the league, appealed to him a couple of times to tone down his temper.

During a Dallas game that I attended, several close officiating calls went against the Cowboys. Schramm never let out a peep, and I got concerned. I walked over to behind where he was sitting and asked,

"Tex, are you all right?" "Yeah," he said, "just trying to behave myself."

A short time later, yet another call went against Dallas, and this time Tex had had enough. "You . . . damn blind bastards," he screamed, loud enough for everyone in the press box to hear. I said to my companion, "He's OK now."

With the exception of Pete Rozelle, no one else meant more to the National Football League during the time I was around than Texas E. Schramm. He, too, started out as a newspaperman, in Austin, Texas, before becoming an assistant to Los Angeles Rams owner Dan Reeves and later his general manager. Their relationship began in the late 1940s, and by the time Schramm left the team during an owner-ship squabble in the mid-1950s, Reeves was referring to Tex as "the most competent executive in the NFL." Before his departure, Tex hired and worked with the Rams' young publicity man, Pete Rozelle, and it was Rozelle who became general manager when Tex joined CBS Sports in New York. Three years later, Schramm and Rozelle were reunited in the NFL: Pete was elected to succeed the late Bert Bell as Commissioner at the tender age of 33, and Tex came on board as Clint Murchison's first and only president and general manager of the Dallas Cowboys.

Here they were, the two protégés of Dan Reeves, guiding the NFL into its glory years. While Rozelle was Commissioner from 1960 to 1989, Schramm and coach Tom Landry were steering the Cowboys from a scrambling expansion team to a team of dominance. "America's team," Tex liked to call it.

In those three decades, Dallas became the prototype professional sports organization. Just as the Rams had built football's foremost scouting system under Reeves and Schramm, the Cowboys developed a program second to none: the first team to use computers and the first team to supplement its draft choices with a supply of undrafted free agents, many of whom had outstanding careers. As Dallas pros-pered, Tex became chairman of the most powerful body in the NFL, the Competition Committee. He was a key figure in virtually every NFL activity, starting with the agreement to merge with the Ameri-can Football League in 1966 and ending when Jerry Jones bought the

Cowboys in 1989. Under Schramm's leadership, the Competition Committee kept the NFL's growth spiraling upward on the playing field on the strength of a series of significant playing rules changes and innovative measures that made each NFL game a special event.

The uniform marking of the playing field with its six-foot white border, for instance, was Tex's idea. So were the single standard goalposts, painted a uniform yellow.

When defense began to dominate NFL games in the 1970s, it was Tex's committee that decided offensive linemen would be allowed to block with their hands open and arms extended. When defensive backs started taking too much excitement out of the games by smothering gifted wide receivers, Tex's committee gave them three yards and only one opportunity for the defense to contact or "chuck" receivers coming off the line of scrimmage. The committee's moves extended to player safety by redefining what acts of aggression defenders could administer to players who were in vulnerable positions. The basic structure of the game remained the same—"No dresses on quarterbacks," as Steelers linebacker Jack Lambert once sneered—but if tweaking was called for, Tex and his committee were there to apply the tweaks.

He didn't do it alone, of course. Some of the best football minds worked alongside him: Don Shula, Paul Brown, Marty Schottenheimer, Eddie LeBaron, and, yes, Al Davis, too, for a while. In his own special way, though, Tex directed their efforts, and the game benefited enormously.

Some knew him as "Bullmoose." Others scoffed at his meeting room antics that tended to brush aside objectors. But as much as his tactics differed from Rozelle's, they still delivered the same results. Together, Tex and Pete presided over the renaissance of pro football by fashioning a pair of remarkable careers so similar that historians will find it hard to believe: They started together in the late 1940s, and they both ended their NFL careers in 1989. "Out together," Pete said. Along the way, they presented each other for induction into the Pro Football Hall of Fame, Tex introducing Pete in 1985, Pete returning the honor in 1991.

Pete Rozelle was "a man for his time," said Tex during Pete's induction ceremony. "If I was," Pete said many times, "it was because of people like Tex helping me."

Tex helped us all. I worked with him on the Competition Committee early on, then again on a regular basis, starting in 1977, when I became the league's executive director. The task had its rewards.

One day in 1978 we discovered a new Westin Hotel property at Wailea Beach on Maui, featuring a two-story beachfront facility that couldn't have suited the committee better had it been built for us. We pounced on it, and for most of the next 13 years Wailea Beach was the committee's home. We reserved the same rooms each year and operated in the same section for offices and hospitality so consistently that we installed phone and cable lines for our use year after year. The hotel employees were like relatives, all known by their first names. We laughed and hugged when we arrived, and embraced and shed real tears when we departed.

It was there that many of the key rules proposals and competitive changes were discussed and formulated. A short walk from our rooms was a Jacuzzi where we took our glasses of wine (and Tex his bullshots or Scotches) and reconvened discussions that lasted far into the night. Our merriment had method, however. Those of us from the league didn't dare leave the committee alone, or by morning it would have dramatically changed decisions that we had reached the preceding afternoon. In the Jacuzzi, at least, we had input.

On many evenings we'd assemble at the Wailea Steak House for something to eat (and drink), then drift back to the hospitality room, where someone would try to stay the course with Tex and his wonderful wife, Marty, who served as the barkeep. Yet, promptly every morning at 9:00—at times with Tex on his hands and knees—we'd be back at the table on the grounds near the ocean to tackle that day's agenda.

If it included a new definition of offensive holding, hotel guests were treated to a display of five or six middle-aged men grappling with each other on the plush lawn near the beach units. The year we first talked about helmet radios, to enable quarterbacks and receivers to hear each other amid the bedlam of noisy stadiums, everyone wore a regulation helmet adorned with his team's logo on the outside and a Telex radio or transmitting device on the inside. Eddie LeBaron would fling passes to Don Shula after telling him where to run. Paul Brown would be in a Bengals helmet kibitzing from a lawn chair. And Tex would take it all in, confident that the league's crowd-noise problem had been solved.

Much of it worked. Receivers don't have radios in their helmets, but quarterbacks do, and coaches call plays to them from the sidelines, which, in turn, allows 40-second and 25-second play clocks that accelerate the pace of the game. Using television instant replays to review officials' decisions wasn't Tex's idea alone, but as soon as the concept became practical he took it and ran, developing the first system that the NFL tried, between 1986 and 1991, and the forerunner to the modified coaches' challenge system now in place. Walk into an NFL stadium—any NFL stadium—and you'll see a uniform look. The official time is kept on the stadium clock for all to see. Every halftime lasts 12 minutes. Officiating signals are clear and understandable— at least when the referee uses his microphone properly, as Tex envisioned. At season's end, in the playoff system, the teams who square off qualify under a uniform tiebreaker procedure that everyone accepts, even if some of them don't fully understand it. And, of course, the Dallas Cowboys cheerleaders were Tex's idea and among the countless reasons the National Football League owes him many, many thanks.

TWENTY-FIVE

GEORGE HALAS

A Picture of Irascibility

When she was a little girl, Anne Marie Rozelle used to play in the NFL offices while her dad, the NFL Commissioner, caught up on some important paperwork. Occasionally, she would be in the care of Peter Hadhazy, then a teenager, who was hired to work in our mailroom and whose main task in those days was to clip news and comments about pro football and other major sports from the one hundred or so daily newspapers to which we subscribed.

Peter loved to play games with the little girl he called Annie. Their favorite was hide-and-seek, not a revolutionary concept, but one that Peter played with a distinctive twist: He'd tell Annie to run and hide in a place where no one could find her; then he'd go back to his scissors and paste pot and clip more stories from the newspapers, often waiting 10 or 15 minutes before setting out to track her down. Eventually, Annie would be found, of course, and Peter would have her hide again and return to his clippings.

A couple of times, Annie hid under my desk while I was working. She'd been there only a moment or two one day, when she poked her head out, looked up, and asked, "Why is that man's picture under here?"

The man whose picture was under my desk—not framed, just stuck to the backside of the front of the desk with Scotch tape—was George Halas. *The* George Halas, the founder and patriarch of what became the National Football League.

George's photo was there for two reasons: First, at that particular time in the mid-1960s, George and his Chicago Bears organization had aroused our concern in the league office because they didn't always accept what *we* (and I use the term very loosely) decided the Bears and the rest of the teams ought to do. Pete Rozelle wanted our clubs to have strong, active public relations and media relations programs. He was also a strong believer in something for which I was personally responsible for many years, the NFL's weekly injury report. Rozelle wanted a report that was prompt, accurate, detailed, and complete. Besides good, clean competition on the field, Pete said, it was the best way to show everyone that the NFL stood for integrity—integrity that he felt was at the very heart of the game. If we ever lose that, he said, we have no game; we must have the confidence of the public and the media.

I'm sure George Halas felt just as strongly about integrity as Pete did. He just didn't necessarily agree with how it was demonstrated. To him, as well as some other owners and coaches, our weekly injury report—even in the informal way we did it—was just plain wrong. Publicizing such matters, they contended, only called the enemies' attention to a team's potential weaknesses and put it at a disadvantage come Sunday's game. Their opposition created a prolonged stalemate, frustrating me no end. In desperation, I carefully positioned George's photo under my desk, as an occasional object of my frustration.

Almost as frustrating to me was the fact that George's public relations department was a seasonal operation. It took me a while to realize it, but once a season was over, the Bears' public relations man, Dan Desmond, no longer came into the office. After taking some time off, Desmond turned his attention to publicizing hockey and basketball. NFL training camps didn't resume until the next summer, at which time I would get an answer to the letter I had sent to Dan four or five months before.

George's photo hung where it did for a second reason, I liked to declare. Because I grew up near Chicago, I'd always had a soft spot in my heart for Mr. Halas and the Bears, and since I now was toiling in behalf of all 15 NFL clubs but couldn't very well put 15 pictures on my desk, I decided to offer my own little tribute to Papa Bear in a way that wouldn't seem too obvious or partisan. Sure, I did!

Anyway, the second reason is the one I recited when Annie Rozelle asked why that man's picture was under my desk. She seemed to accept it, too, especially since she had more pressing matters to consider: Peter might be searching for her.

Annie's father eventually faced these differences with the Bears head-on. He ordered the venerable league founder to travel from Chicago to our New York office for a private chat, on virtually the eve of one of the Bears' most important games and while owner Halas was also the Bears' head coach. George got Rozelle's message.

People often ask me to describe George Halas. The first word I think of is *irascible*, the second is usually *cantankerous*, and the third probably would be *frugal*, except that it's off the mark. Doug Atkins, one of the Bears' Hall of Famers, told me at the 1966 Pro Bowl that Papa Bear "used to throw around nickels like they were manhole covers." Yet, nothing could be further from the truth. You can check the records to see how many players George helped get started in business or how many players he helped put through medical school. At one time, he said, 19 NFL alumni were practicing physicians, and 9 of them were former Chicago Bears. Or check out how he helped establish the Brian Piccolo Cancer Fund, in honor of the running back who died all too young at the height of his career.

The first time I visited their training camp to prepare my preseason prospectus, the Bears were at Rensselaer College, in Indiana. After a long, hot drive through the cornfields to get there, I was somewhat uneasy about the reception I might receive. The next thing I knew, I was seated beside Papa Bear in a golf cart, and we were wheeling down to practice, where he drove right up and introduced me to Gale Sayers and Rudy Bukich, plus a couple of the team's assistant coaches. Then George said, "All right, what do you want to know?" He didn't stop talking for an hour, and I had more than enough material for my press release.

George didn't coach too much longer after that. I always felt he stayed an extra year or two to coach the remarkable Sayers, the most exciting pro football runner I ever saw. George was suffering from deteriorating hips and spent considerable time in England undergoing a method of replacement surgery that was not yet accepted in this country. I think it's safe to say we became friends over the years and until he passed away during the 1983 season, at the age of 88.

George had moved the Decatur Staleys, the pro team he started after leaving the University of Illinois, to Chicago in 1921. Once settled, he coached the team on four different occasions, for 40 years, winning a record 324 games before retiring after the 1967 season. He and his son, Mugs, operated the franchise until the McCaskey family took over after their deaths. Of the immediate Halas family, only daughter Virginia (Papa called her "Gin") survived to celebrate the Bears' and Refrigerator Perry's victory over the Patriots in Super Bowl XX in 1986. More's the pity because Gin's husband, the redoubtable Ed McCaskey, and their oldest son, Michael, were just starting to get their feet wet as the organization's chairman of the board and club president, respectively, in what would have been George Halas's 67th season in his beloved National Football League.

We all regretted that.

TWENTY-SIX

JIM FINKS

"Football Man"

He was a better-than-average quarterback.

He wanted to go to Illinois, but Tulsa offered him a scholarship.

He played six years for the Pittsburgh Steelers.

He never stopped wearing saddle shoes.

He became an assistant coach at Notre Dame.

He had very simple tastes.

He was a successful executive in Canada.

He was a better tennis player than a golfer because he never lost his "banana" ball.

He was a very successful executive in the National Football League.

He smoked too much and his voice often sounded more like a growl.

He came within three votes of succeeding Pete Rozelle as NFL Commissioner.

He went into the Pro Football Hall of Fame on the first ballot.

Jim Finks was all of the above and more, the person whom I would say knew more about football than anyone else I ever worked with. Jim had a nickname for everyone. Don Shula was "Jaw," Paul Brown was the "Wily Mentor," Marty Schottenheimer was "Kraut," Jim Kensil was "Curly," Bill McGrane, his assistant in Minnesota for many years, was "Trophy Head," and Rozelle was "Czar." My nickname was relatively mild: "Herr Veiss." He had nicknames for more people, mostly unprintable. If I were to give Jim a nickname, it would be "Football Man." He was one, through and through.

I first became aware of Jimmy—as many called him then—when he was quarterbacking the Steelers in the 1950s. Hall of Famer Ernie Stautner played on that team, too, along with a kick returner–receiver named Lynn Chandnois, who had played at Michigan State, and a rangy receiver named Elbie Nickel. Pittsburgh's games were often televised into New York in those days, and one of them caught my eye. A less-than-formidable Steelers team happened to hand the New York Giants a 63–7 drubbing at old Forbes Field, the worst defeat the Giants ever suffered, and Jimmy Finks was at the controls. He was still at the controls two weeks later when the Steelers returned to form and lost to the Rams in Los Angeles, 28–14. But the score wasn't terribly important, at least not to owner Art Rooney. He was used to losing. What was important were the 75,000 paying customers in the Los Angeles Coliseum that day, the most ever to watch a Pittsburgh team. The visitors' share to Rooney's Steelers was $42,000, by far his biggest gate on the road up to that point. "Can you imagine," said Rooney, "what would have happened if we'd only beaten the Giants 23–7?"

Finks played for three more years with the Steelers, who kept him as their quarterback over a youngster from the University of Louisville named Johnny Unitas. After the 1955 season, Finks decided to take a job coaching at Notre Dame, under Terry Brennan. Jim always had football administration in the back of his mind and shortly thereafter migrated to Canada. He spent the next decade as general manager at Calgary, while a coach named Bud Grant won four Grey Cup championships at Winnipeg, thus setting the stage for the eventual marriage of the two with the Minnesota Vikings in the mid-1960s. Ten divisional titles and three Super Bowl appearances later (Grant himself was in four), Finks moved on to build a Chicago Bears team that eventually won Super Bowl XX.

He then took a short break but spent part of that time getting the Chicago Cubs baseball organization on track. Next, Finks moved to New Orleans and produced the first playoff team in the Saints' history. When he succumbed to lung cancer in 1994, he had clearly established himself as one of the top administrators in football history. His achievements were honored by his induction into the Hall of Fame the following year. Yet, his career might have concluded differently.

That he didn't serve as the NFL's third Commissioner of modern times resulted from a minirevolt by a group of league owners who became known as the Chicago 11, so named because of the meeting's location and the number of owners involved. When Pete Rozelle announced his retirement as Commissioner in March 1989 (subject to the owners' selecting a successor), a six-man search committee was named. The two conference presidents, Lamar Hunt of the AFC Kansas City Chiefs and Wellington Mara of the NFC New York Giants, were cochairs. Other members were Dan Rooney of Pittsburgh, Art Modell of Cleveland, Judge Robert Parins of Green Bay, and Ralph Wilson of Buffalo.

At a May owners' meeting, the committee reported that it had developed a list of 11 prospects and was in the process of identifying the best candidates among them. On July 6 at the Hyatt Regency O'Hare Hotel, near Chicago's airport, cochairman Hunt presented Finks as the committee's unanimous recommendation for Commissioner. Rozelle then called for other nominees. Hearing none, he called for a vote. Finks needed a two-thirds majority, or 19 votes, to be elected. But in secret balloting, Finks received only 16 votes. Eleven abstentions were recorded—the Chicago 11.

In the weeks that followed, Modell and Rooney resigned from the search committee, and a new committee was formed. Hunt and Mara remained as cochairs and were joined by Ken Behring of Seattle, Mike Lynn of Minnesota, John Kent Cook (Jack's son) of Washington, and Al Davis of the Raiders. Four more votes were taken during an October 10 meeting at Dallas–Fort Worth Airport, and Paul Tagliabue emerged as a strong challenger to Finks. Five more failed ballots ensued at a subsequent meeting in Cleveland in late October before

Tagliabue was chosen by acclamation on the sixth ballot, conducted after yet another committee, composed of Rooney, Mara, Modell, Lynn, and Pat Bowlen of Denver, now made Paul their unanimous overnight recommendation.

I felt somewhat responsible for the anguish that Finks underwent during those contentious months. After one session, Finks said in exasperation to me that he was pulling out as a candidate. Our chance conversation took place away from the meeting room, and I urged Jim to stay in the race because he owed it to himself and to the owners in the league who had made him the early favorite. To his credit, Jim stayed the course, and although he was the loser, he remained a contributing member of the league until his illness cut short his career.

Appointed by Tagliabue, he served as Competition Committee chairman, starting in 1990, after longtime chairman Tex Schramm left the Cowboys to become president of the NFL's newly formed spring league, the World League of American Football. In turn, Jim and I worked closely on a day-to-day basis for the rest of our careers, dealing with the competitive aspects of the game, with college relations, and with the other football parts he knew so well.

You always knew where you stood with Jim. After holding meetings for one year in Florida at Tagliabue's request, Finks successfully lobbied for the Competition Committee's return to Maui. On arrival, we thought we'd have a midmeeting celebration, so we persuaded one of the hotel's employees to find us a backcountry restaurant where we could "raise a little hell," as Finks put it, without jeopardizing our impeccable standing with the folks at Wailea Beach (and the local police). The place was located off a country road, partway up the slopes of Haleakala, a dormant volcano that dominates the western Maui landscape. We took off in several caravans, and most of us arrived without incident, except Finks and his wife, Maxine, who were riding with Joel Bussert of the NFL office and doubtlessly arguing over the league's intricate waiver system or some other distraction.

He, Maxine, and Joel never did make it. It was a long night, and we didn't see our missing companions until breakfast the next morning. "What happened to you guys?" I asked. "There's no way to get there from here," Finks grumbled. "We went to McDonald's," he said, adding sarcastically, "It was the best meal I've had since I've been here."

After Rozelle decided to retire, his close associate Thelma Elkjer stayed on in New York to get his files in order and to prepare the way for Tagliabue before setting up Pete's office near his retirement home in Rancho Santa Fe, California.

Days dragged into weeks, and every time I talked to Finks, he wanted to know why Thelma was still around. In fact, she was around as long as her then-favorite dog (ill and somewhat crippled) was still alive. She knew the dog would never survive the trip to the West Coast and didn't want to abandon him. Finks found this more amusing than most because (1) he wasn't Thelma's biggest fan, (2) she wasn't Jim's either, and (3) dogs did not exactly rank high on Jim's list of favorites.

I always knew when Finks had made an effort to talk to the Commissioner before Thelma transferred him to me—no doubt reluctantly. He never identified himself when I picked up the phone. He didn't have to. He'd just say, "I guess the damn dog's still alive."

TWENTY-SEVEN

DON SHULA AND PAUL BROWN

Master and "Wily Mentor"

Charlene and I and another couple had been invited to spend a long weekend with Don and Mary Anne Shula at the Shulas' summer home in the Carolinas. Naturally, several golf games were on the agenda. We'd gotten as far as the 11th hole, and Don and I, as partners, were winning the bet, but barely.

As the cart we were riding in approached the tee, I began to step out of the passenger's side. But when my spikes hit the surface of the railroad ties bordering the tee, I slipped and took a nasty spill. One of my legs was caught between the ties and the cart. My other leg was buckled underneath me. My initial thought was that I had broken something. As I lay there, afraid to move, I heard the unmistakable voice of my partner.

"Hey, get the hell up and tee off," it said. I tried to protest weakly, but his voice was decidedly unsympathetic. "Hell, anybody can play when they're healthy," Shula declared.

Yes, sir! was my body's response. I struggled up, limped over to the markers, swung bravely, and hit the ball off the tee—fairly well, too, as it turned out. We continued on, we won our bet, and although it was nearly two weeks before my severely sprained ankle would allow me to play again, I guess I fulfilled my obligation to the Master.

Don Shula and I played golf many times during our long relationship mostly because our work on the NFL Competition Committee—he as a key member for 21 years and I as the committee's liaison to the league office—took us to Maui in Hawaii 13 times, where excellent golfing weather tends to prevail. If, as it is said, one learns much about one's fellow man during times spent together on a golf course, then I learned plenty about Shula. Our matches, often involving Paul Brown and Eddie LeBaron, and sometimes Marty Schottenheimer and Tex Schramm (when his back wasn't hurting), were classic.

"You play it like a man," Brown would say, which meant, "You play it like I say you play it." No mulligans. No gimme putts. And you play it as it lies. "Rollovers are for IRAs," he'd say.

PB, as we knew him, was well into his seventies by then and always kept score. The man that Jim Finks called "Wily Mentor" would choose his partners well, and by the time the two weeks of committee meetings were ending, the tally on the blackboard usually showed the old coach in the lead. And the chalkboard was never erased until all debts had been settled. It became a ritual that included PB's reminding everyone that we'd convene at the same time, same place, next year.

Shula played his college ball at John Carroll University, in Cleveland, about the same time Paul Brown was finishing off his remarkable accomplishment with the Cleveland Browns of the All-America Football Conference—the first post–World War II rival of the National Football League. When Cleveland was merged into the NFL, Shula and his running-back partner at John Carroll, Carl Taseff, were both drafted by the Browns—Shula in the 9th round and Taseff, who led the nation in scoring as a senior at John Carroll, in the 22nd round. The two played together as pros for 5 years, then coached together over 20 years more—Shula always as the head coach and Taseff as one of his trusted lieutenants.

I once asked Brown what he saw in Shula as a player. "Smart," he told me, pointing to his head. "Had to be," he added. "He was one of the slowest players I ever saw."

Brown, as a charter member of the Competition Committee, and Shula, as a 21-year member beginning in 1975, were as unalike as any two men could be as committee members. Shula was always looking for something different and was receptive to new ideas, a perfect complement to Schramm and his many innovations. Brown, one of the great innovators as a coach and organizer, with many firsts to his name, now served us as the committee's caution light. As an owner, as well as a general manager, he was cognizant of how much Schramm's ideas could cost to implement. We often went to the floor of the main owners' meeting with PB as the lone dissenter to a proposal the rest of the committee endorsed.

I used to prepare the so-called prompting sheets, to which Schramm, as committee chairman, could refer when he was presenting a measure for discussion and voting. If I typed it once, I typed it 50 times: "Committee favors 6–1, Paul Brown will speak in opposition."

But that was good. With all his energy, Tex tended to run away with ideas sometimes. His enthusiasm was contagious (hell, you could support almost anything on the lush green lawn at Maui), but PB would eventually slow him down, often to Tex's displeasure. This made it an effective committee, with good, balanced consideration given to each issue. If it was worthwhile, it would eventually get adopted, maybe next year, maybe the year after.

What Shula brought to the table was a keen interest in all phases of the committee's work. For most coaching members of the group, that often meant just the playing rules. If the agenda shifted away from those rules and focused instead on waiver procedures, drafting procedures, tampering regulations, player transactions and trades, and the like, some of our coaching members lost interest. Not Shula. He was as well-rounded a thinker as we had, and when he talked, everyone listened without fail, for he would have something worthwhile to say.

A devout Catholic, Shula went to mass every morning, even in Maui. And when Dorothy, his first wife and mother of their five children, passed away, it was as much of a loss to the parish in Maui as it was to their church at home. The first year we returned to Maui after Dorothy had died, the priest from Lahaina insisted on conducting a memorial service for her in the rocks above Wailea Beach. I can still see the wreaths of flowers floating out to sea.

PB always stayed in an upper room of the two-story beach unit that had a railed patio where he could feed the birds and, as an early riser, could preside over the day's first activities long before the meeting would convene. Below his room was our hospitality area, and as our group began to gather for the daily buffet breakfast, Paul would appear on his balcony for everyone to see. He liked to imitate Mussolini, and he'd strike the Il Duce pose and make his declarations. I remember the first time I told my daughters about this. They were amazed: "But, Dad, he looks so serious on the sideline when he's coaching," they said. "And when he's not, no one wants to talk while he's in his box watching the game for fear he'll get angry!"

As Brown's balcony appearances became a ritual, he adopted "a joke of the day," which he would tell with grand gestures. I wish I still had those notes from the Maui meetings; I usually jotted down his tales so that I could tell those who had missed them because they were off jogging or snorkeling or, like Tex, still sleeping.

At one time or another, we had 12 Super Bowl champions on the committee: Chuck Noll, who won four; three-time winners Bill Walsh, Jerry Jones, and Al Davis; and two-time winners Vince Lombardi, Well Mara, George Young, Schramm, Shula, George Seifert, Tom Flores, and Bart Starr.

But for my money, Don Shula and Paul Brown were members of the strongest committee we ever had. Serving with them were Tex Schramm, Eddie LeBaron, and, later, Marty Schottenheimer. I had Joel Bussert, Jan Van Duser, and Art McNally to work with me, plus a terrific young lady named Donna Montana, who made it all go. Donna tells everyone these days that she worked "18 years at hard labor" with me. Appropriately, she is now Paul Tagliabue's executive assistant.

Schramm left after the 1989 meeting when the Cowboys were sold to Jerry Jones, Paul Brown died in 1991 at the age of 82, and Shula retired from the committee the first year after Jimmy Johnson succeeded him as coach of the Miami Dolphins. Eddie LeBaron, a remarkable fellow whom we'll talk about later in these pages, left football in 1989 to go into private law practice, and Marty Schottenheimer's last year on the committee was 1994.

From its inception, the Competition Committee always accomplished a great deal, but this was the period in which its contributions kept the game soaring to new heights year after year. Had you been party to the discussions, you would have wondered. But when you summed it up, what this group did was a plus under any kind of scrutiny. The game had become wildly successful and together these men made it more so.

The last year we were in Maui, we arranged for a Hawaiian tribute to Paul Brown. He was aging and his health was failing. The wife of one of the hotel employees was an accomplished dancer, often appearing at luaus. So, one night, unbeknownst to Paul, we invited her and a couple of her friends to do some special dances for PB. We put him in a robe; gave him a scepter that looked surprisingly like a broomstick; and read a tribute to the Great Kahuna, one of the legendary figures of Hawaiian lore. Our featured performer danced a frenzied hula to the beat of the drums so close to Paul that her costume brushed his face. Shula read part of the tribute. So did Jim Finks, who had assumed Schramm's leadership of the committee. I, too, addressed the group at the end as Paul giggled in delight.

And what did the Great Kahuna have to say to his subjects? I asked. Said Paul, "That's the closest I've ever been to a backfield in motion."

TWENTY-EIGHT

BILL GRANHOLM
Unsung Super Bowl Hero

One night during the final prepara-
tions for a Super Bowl at Tulane Stadium, eight of us slipped out of
New Orleans for a late-evening supper at a place called Mosca's. Our
two-car caravan had embarked to fulfill a promise to introduce three
of our secretaries to what we considered an undiscovered gem of a
restaurant—which looked more, in fact, like the kind of place where
you might stop only in an emergency to ask for directions. When the
girls gazed on Mosca's for the first time, they looked disappointed.
But because the rest of us had been there several times over the years,
we assured them of treasures to come.

We seated ourselves and for the next couple of hours ate and drank
under the guidance of a Mosca family member (we later learned the
same family had provided the chefs for the celebrated Commander's
Palace restaurant). It was close to 11:00 when we asked for the check,
but when one of us dropped an American Express card on the tray,
we discovered that Mosca's had instituted a cash-only policy since
our last visit. The women had no money to speak of, so that left it to
the five of us to try to come up with the scratch, which as I remember amounted to close to $400, not including tip. Even in the late
1970s, $400 cash was a hefty amount, especially during the heart of
the age of plastic and long before anyone thought of an ATM.

We didn't have anywhere near $400 in cash. So, for the next 20 minutes we did our best imitation of concealing panic while trying to convince our hosts that our faces were indeed honest, that our intentions were honorable, and that at dawn's early light we'd have some pink-cheeked gofer at Mosca's door bearing a bundle of cash. Finally, our hosts accepted a small deposit, and we were allowed to leave after quietly fighting off one of our colleagues who was still begging for a nightcap.

Bill Granholm and the three secretaries were in the car I drove. Naturally, the conversation turned to our escape and how long, if ever, it had been since we carried anything near that amount of cash when we traveled—and we did plenty of traveling. We were on a bridge that signaled our approach to downtown New Orleans and our headquarters hotel when Granny (as everyone called him) got this impish look and asked the women, "Did you ever see one of these?"

From the recesses of his wallet, he pulled out a $1,000 bill.

Granny was unlike anyone I ever met, twice over. The contributions he made to pro football were unlike anyone else's, too. Most fans have never heard of him, but pro football teams swore by him. We all laughed with him.

The first meeting of all the NFL club public relations directors at the Pro Football Hall of Fame in Canton, Ohio, began with a number of guys waiting impatiently at the airport for their luggage to appear on the circling carousel. Granny went prowling through a storage area and discovered a candelabra someone had left behind. Moments later, once the carousel began to move, here came Granny through the rubber flaps stretched out flat on his back on the conveyor belt, his eyes closed and the candelabra on his chest.

He never discarded an expired credit card. He cut them up and used them for stays in his shirt collars. When he died, we found hundreds of them in his apartment. He rarely bought a new shirt, yet he always dressed well, and most of his shirts bore monograms. A close inspection revealed that the initials were not his. He'd buy the shirts for a pittance from among leftovers at a laundry near his apartment.

He once showed me a Diner's Club card that he said was one of the first ever issued, back in the 1940s. He'd never used it.

As I planned one of my first visits to Los Angeles after joining the NFL office, Jim Kensil urged me to take Granholm, who then worked for the Rams, to dinner. "You'll have a great time. He's a great guy," I remember Jim promising. But I remember more clearly Jim expressly saying "take" him to dinner. He knew Granny's spending habits.

So did I, sort of. During my Associated Press days, I once had visited the Rams' locker room on an assignment and, without thinking, innocently picked up a soft drink. "Those are for the players," Granny told me curtly. "Twenty-five cents!"

But nobody contributed more to the image of the NFL and the lore of the Super Bowl than Bill Granholm. Pete Rozelle brought Granny to league headquarters in New York after he had spent 18 years as the do-everything equipment manager for the Rams. His principal assignment was to work in the player relations department with the legendary Buddy Young, but that was just part of his duties. As Rozelle's special assistant, Granny filled a number of positions in the league office, almost all of them player and game related.

He was a key coordinator of the Pro Bowl from its inception in 1951 and continued in that capacity after joining us in New York. He worked with planners for the overseas American Bowl series that began in 1986 and with the organizers of the World League, the forerunner of NFL Europe, in 1989 and 1990.

He was perhaps best known for the USO–Department of Defense goodwill tours that took nearly 200 players to military installations in the Far East and Europe. Between 1967 and 1988, Granny and his "men" helicoptered into remote firebases in Vietnam and onto aircraft carriers in the Indian Ocean. They made other goodwill stops in Korea, the Philippines, and Japan and also visited bases in Germany, Austria, France, and Turkey. The roster of players and football figures who he accompanied reads like a who's who of the NFL. The first group included Frank Gifford, Sam Huff, Willie Davis, and Johnny Unitas. They were later followed by other Hall of Famers such as Joe Namath, Bart Starr, Lance Alworth, Franco Harris, Bobby Bell, Jack Lambert, Bob Lilly, Dick Butkus, Gene Upshaw, and Larry Csonka. In 1985, the Department of Defense honored Granny with the highest award it can bestow on a civilian, the Secretary of Defense Award for Outstanding Public Service to troops overseas.

Granny's versatility and people skills very quickly made him our dependable right arm in Super Bowl planning. He knew what was good and what was not good about a team hotel. He knew just what was needed to prepare for a game, particularly when a Super Bowl team was asked to spend the last full week before the big game away from home. He knew how many towels teams would use, what they would eat and how much, where the buses should go, and how long it would take them to get there, especially—as happened in Miami a few times—where a drawbridge had to be crossed en route. If a team needed a special blocking sled, it would be ready and waiting in the morning. If the coaches decided to dress in the same room as the players, Granny would make the change. If a portion of a practice field needed resodding, it would be done.

Such were his responsibilities. But Granny's ability to shoulder them was only a part of what he contributed to pro football, something his old boss, Rams owner Dan Reeves, discovered long before we did.

Granny was a graduate of the University of Wisconsin, a lifelong buddy of Elroy "Crazy Legs" Hirsch, and even a summertime carnival hawker when he wasn't fighting in George Patton's Third Army (and winning a Bronze Star with clusters). A confirmed bachelor, he remained the Rams' equipment manager for many years, by choice. Soon after he arrived in Los Angeles in 1950 with Hirsch, he became Reeves's confidant and frequent companion during most of the years Reeves owned the Rams.

In Los Angeles, Granny owned a piece of a restaurant, a piece of a bar, and with Reeves a piece of real estate that cuddled up to what became Sun City, Arizona. After Granny moved to New York, he was the first person Reeves contacted when business or other functions brought him to the big city. If you were in midtown past 10:00 P.M.

and Dan and Granny were in town, you'd likely find them at Clarke's on Third Avenue—P. J. Clarke's to nonregulars. He was the best guy to be with and the best sounding board imaginable to guide you, whether it was how something looked, how it sounded . . . or even how it smelled.

"The whole idea smells," he said at Super Bowl XV in New Orleans, where we had planned a parade of elephants to complement the circus theme we created for pregame and halftime festivities. "It'll be delightful," I said confidently, expressing special pride in our plans to paint a baby elephant pink and put her at the end of the parade. "The crowd will love it," I added enthusiastically.

"Can't trust elephants, especially around people," Granny retorted, harking back to his carnival experiences in Wisconsin.

As you might surmise, Granny lost the argument, and the parade went on as planned. And just as the little pink elephant waddled into the middle of our beautifully decorated end zone, she let loose with as large and messy a bowel movement as any of us could imagine. We had just begun the tedious cleanup and deodorizing effort (the lack of a single drain on the Superdome floor made the task that much more difficult) when Granny's voice crackled over our walkie-talkies, "Told you so."

I dearly wish his voice still crackled. Together he and I made it through Super Bowl XXVI before colon cancer overtook him. The Super Bowl hasn't been quite the same without him.

TWENTY-NINE

EDDIE LEBARON

A Big Little Man

For those who dabble in pro football history, Eddie LeBaron has a reputation as being one of the game's best little men. Yet, the first time I saw Eddie I was amazed at how big he was. He stood about 5-foot-7, but the only thing short about him were his legs. Put his upper body on average-length legs, and he would have been 6-foot-1 or 6-foot-2.

And, boy, was he coordinated. He was both the tennis and golf champion at his club back home. When he joined the NFL's Competition Committee, he was in his fifties and the general manager of the Atlanta Falcons. On the golf course in Maui, he'd carry a jug of wine of excellent vintage produced on his family's winery in California's Napa Valley. Complementing the wine was an aromatic stogie, often from the renowned cigar factories of Tampa or perhaps farther south and east in Cuba. Provisions notwithstanding, Eddie still would shoot around par. He could be the most gifted all-around athlete I've ever known.

On the tennis court at Competition Committee meetings, he and Don Shula would meet at about 6:30 in the morning, and, whether he wanted it or not, Shula would get the workout of his life. For the next hour or so, LeBaron would run the heavy-legged Shula from courtside to courtside, from end line to net and back again, while he barely worked up a sweat. One year, Shula had his youngest son, Michael, with him. Michael was about 14 at the time and a few years away from becoming the starting quarterback for Alabama's Crimson Tide. The Shula tandem often would play doubles against Eddie, and by the time the meeting was over, Mike Shula was in the best shape of his life. His dad was just plain tired.

Eddie LeBaron had other claims to fame. He was a fine college quarterback at the College of the Pacific, and he played quarterback in the NFL with the Washington Redskins and then for the Dallas Cowboys when they started as an expansion team in 1960. Despite his size, he led the NFL in passing in 1958. In between, he excelled in the Canadian Football League and found time to serve with the U.S. Marines in Korea, where he gained the reputation as the "best thrower of a grenade" the Marine Corps ever saw. LeBaron also got a law degree and was a practicing attorney when the Falcons tapped him for their front office and Pete Rozelle tapped him for Tex Schramm's powerful Competition Committee. After he left the Falcons, the NFL Management Council benefited handsomely from Eddie's labor relations expertise.

Still, LeBaron made his greatest contributions to the Competition Committee. Eddie was there during the committee's Maui years, most of the 13 years between 1978 and 1992 that the committee bunkered at Wailea Beach, and devised, produced, and polished measures that helped take the NFL to unbelievable heights. He would sit in a chair at a table set up outside the beach units at Wailea and flip a pen end over end constantly while he and his committee colleagues tackled its agenda. Talk about coordination. He never once looked at the pen, at least not that I can remember, and not once did he drop it. Add that to his Guinness record for grenade throwing.

LeBaron never got angry. If he was frustrated about the long and tedious deliberations, he didn't show it. Always a twinkle in his eyes, always a grin on his face, and when you asked him his opinion on a subject, he was ready in an instant with an analytical response that cut its way through the subject with ease.

Tex Schramm chaired the committee in those days, and Paul Brown, Don Shula, and Eddie served as members, later joined by

Marty Schottenheimer and, for a few years, Chuck Noll and Bill Walsh. En route to Maui, Don and Eddie would meet Tex Schramm in Dallas, and, with their wives, they would fly Braniff Airlines non-stop from Dallas to Kahului Airport in Maui. They flew first class, of course, and by the time the 10- or 11-hour flight reached Kahului they were something to behold. Use your imagination.

We used to rent cars for each committee member. For their convenience, we'd have the cars at the airport ready for them on arrival so that as soon as they got their luggage they were on their way to the "other" part of the island of Maui, where the Wailea Beach Hotel was located. The route became familiar: Haleakala to the left, sugarcane fields on both sides of the little two-lane road, the old whaling capital of Lahaina straight ahead, the roads to Kanapaali to the right. It really was a fun drive of about 30 to 35 minutes . . . *after* you'd done it a couple of times. But the first time was the last time for this Braniff trio and their wives.

You can press me for the details, but suffice it to say that, in the interest of their future health and well-being, we changed our strategy thereafter. We ferried the rental cars to the hotel parking lot while we transported the "Dallas Six," as we called them, to the hotel in a professionally driven van.

We don't go to Wailea anymore, and that's a pity. For us, Wailea was the only place to hold a meeting like ours. And, in our own way, we left a lasting impression not only on the hotel management and employees, who as I've noted were like family to us, but also on the little Hawaiian gentleman who was in charge of cleaning up the tennis courts and getting them ready for play each morning.

Every day, just after the break of dawn, LeBaron and Shula would appear on the tennis court, and Eddie would start to toy with the coach in his special way—Shula plodding from side to side, from backcourt to net, until his clothes were soaked in sweat. Off to the side, the diminutive Hawaiian would be raking and repositioning tables and chairs. Every so often, he'd take a break to watch the tennis players.

This episode was repeated every morning throughout our stays on Maui, which usually lasted two weeks. On most mornings, Eddie and

Don would offer a hello or good-bye to the Hawaiian without any acknowledgment from him whatsoever.

But one year, on the last morning of our stay, the attendant looked up, grinned a great big grin, and exclaimed to Shula, "I know you! I know you!" Shula's chest swelled in anticipation. Finally, this fellow had recognized the man who was on his way to becoming the winningest coach in NFL history. Still grinning, the Hawaiian looked proudly at Shula and declared: "You're . . . you're . . . *Earl Campbell!*"

THIRTY

MARA, ROONEY, HUNT, AND MODELL

A Historic Quartet

A few years ago, the city of New York paid tribute to Wellington Mara, the venerable owner of the New York Giants. "Every organization needs a Wellington Mara," it was said during the festivities. Fortunately, the National Football League has him.

Describe Wellington Mara any way you like: elder statesman, patriarch, spokesman for the integrity of the game, loyal to the core, as stubborn as he is Irish, practitioner of the "league think" philosophy, an active monument to the Bert Bell/Pete Rozelle era. They all fit.

A league in transition (more than half of the NFL clubs today are led by persons who came aboard after Paul Tagliabue became Commissioner in November 1989) needs a traditional base on which to continue to build. Well Mara anchors that base. Together with three others, he represents a quartet of historic quality as the NFL moves into the 21st century.

The others? Dan Rooney of the Pittsburgh Steelers, Lamar Hunt of the Kansas City Chiefs, and—hold on, fans along Lake Erie's southern shore—Art Modell of the Baltimore Ravens are all quite unalike, but each has made a distinctive contribution to pro football.

Mara and Rooney both trace their roots back to a time when the National Football League was getting to know itself. As the second son of the Giants' founder, Wellington was an active participant in the team's organization from the time he was barely into long pants. At age 86, he remains a regular attendee at NFL meetings and has a hand in the consideration of every important issue that comes before the league. Beyond that, Well has done yeoman's work as a major part of the league committee system that was put in place in the late 1960s to help implement the merger of the NFL and the *fledgling*—as we called it—American Football League.

The Jim Finks philosophy of sports organizations holds that "owners own, coaches coach, and players play." Here's another proviso: Owners either participate or passively stand by while a league goes about its business. Whether it was labor, playing rules, litigation, operational matters, or policy issues, Wellington has played a major role in all of them and more during the eight decades that have passed since his father bought the Giants in 1925. The NFL took its greatest step forward when it adopted the revolutionary system of revenue sharing more than 40 years ago. The Giants and Mara were in the forefront of the revolution, representing as they did the number one market in the United States.

If anyone has spent more time than Wellington Mara in committee work in behalf of the league, it is Dan Rooney. Whatever the task—labor, scheduling, league alignment, administration and operations, competitive matters—Dan's been involved in its vital details and, like Mara, from the time he was old enough to walk into a meeting room.

It is rumored that Dan learned to fly his own plane primarily because he was spending so much time commuting between Pittsburgh and Manhattan on league business. More than anyone, he added "street smarts" to NFL deliberations over the years. When Dan speaks, he sounds like everyman, and all who hear him understand immediately where he stands and where he's coming from. I had the wonderful good fortune of working with both Dan Rooney and Art Rooney, his legendary father, from the minute I joined the league in 1965. When the Steelers won their first Super Bowl championship in 1975, Pete Rozelle and I were ecstatic.

The first time I worked closely with Lamar Hunt was when we, as NFL staffers, began attending and helping run AFL meetings during the implementation of the merger in the late 1960s. We've worked together in many ways since then.

Lamar was—and is—a great idea man. For me, one of life's little wonders is how a grown man could make so many indecipherable scribbles on the back of an envelope while flying from one place to another, usually cramped in a seat in coach. History has well recorded Lamar's premier role in the start and finish of the AFL, and in the expanded NFL that resulted from the merger of the two leagues. I often wondered how many other contributions he might have made if his handwriting had been a little clearer! A regular occurrence in the 1970s and 1980s was Pete Rozelle and his trusted assistant Thelma Elkjer trying to figure out what Lamar's latest epistle that had arrived that morning actually said. Inevitably, the scrap of paper would get to me via a routing slip with the notation "Please handle." If I could read it, I did as ordered because tackling ideas from Lamar often produced good results.

Art Modell, for all his possible faults as a businessman, deserves to be part of this historic quartet, too. For more than four decades, he made the meeting room bearable—even under the worst of situations—with his unmatchable wit.

Sure, Art knew plenty about the world of television and helped Pete Rozelle immeasurably during those growing years that followed the marriage between television and pro football. His hand was there with Pete's in crafting a pattern of broadcasting practices that helped make the NFL number one in national appeal through a medium that seemed as if it were made for the NFL and the NFL alone. But his expertise paled in comparison with his wit.

"Nothing's so serious that you can't have a little fun with it," Art once said. "Why, we'd grow into the ground if we tried to deliberate without a light moment now and then."

Can I cite an example of his wit? That's the dilemma. Modell flashed it so often and with such timing that no one or two instances stand out. I'll just say that Art was there when he was needed, and his contributions were nothing to laugh at.

APPENDIX A

Super Bowl Data

Super Bowl I

Green Bay Packers (NFL) 35, Kansas City Chiefs (AFL) 10
Location: Memorial Coliseum, Los Angeles, California
Date: January 15, 1967
Attendance: 61,946   **Ticket prices:** $12, $10, $6

Scoring Summary
Kansas City   0   10   0   0—10
Green Bay   7   7   14   7—35
GB—McGee 37 pass from Starr (Chandler kick), 8:56 1st
KC—McClinton 7 pass from Dawson (Mercer kick), 4:20 2nd
GB—Taylor 14 run (Chandler kick), 10:23 2nd
KC—FG Mercer 31, 14:06 2nd
GB—Pitts 5 run (Chandler kick), 2:27 3rd
GB—McGee 13 pass from Starr (Chandler kick), 14:09 3rd
GB—Pitts 1 run (Chandler kick), 8:25 4th
Most valuable player: Bart Starr, quarterback, Green Bay
Winners' shares: $15,000   **Losers' shares:** $7,500
Head coaches: Vince Lombardi, Green Bay; Hank Stram, Kansas
    City
Referee: Norm Schachter
Televised by: CBS, NBC   **Advertising rates (per 30 seconds):**
                $42,500
Rating: 22.6 (CBS); 18.5 (NBC)   **Share:** 43 (CBS); 36 (NBC)

Entertainment
Pregame: University of Michigan Band, University of Arizona Band
National Anthem: University of Michigan Band, University of
    Arizona Band, Grambling College Band
Coin toss: Game official
Halftime: University of Michigan Band, University of Arizona
    Band
Commissioner's party site: Los Angeles Hilton Hotel

Super Bowl II

Green Bay Packers (NFL) 33, Oakland Raiders (AFL) 14

Location: Orange Bowl, Miami, Florida
Date: January 14, 1968
Attendance: 75,546   **Ticket prices:** $12, $8, $6

Scoring Summary

Green Bay   3   13   10   7—33
Oakland   0   7   0   7—14

GB—FG Chandler 39, 5:07 1st
GB—FG Chandler 20, 3:08 2nd
GB—Dowler 62 pass from Starr (Chandler kick), 4:10 2nd
OAK—Miller 23 pass from Lamonica (Blanda kick), 8:45 2nd
GB—FG Chandler 43, 14:59 2nd
GB—Anderson 2 run (Chandler kick), 9:06 3rd
GB—FG Chandler 31, 14:58 3rd
GB—Adderley 60 interception return (Chandler kick), 3:57 4th
OAK—Miller 23 pass from Lamonica (Blanda kick), 5:47 4th

Most valuable player: Bart Starr, quarterback, Green Bay
Winners' shares: $15,000   **Losers' shares:** $7,500
Head coaches: Vince Lombardi, Green Bay; John Rauch, Oakland
Referee: Jack Vest
Televised by: CBS   **Advertising rates (per 30 seconds):** $54,000
Rating: 36.8   **Share:** 68

Entertainment

Pregame: AFL and NFL giant figures; U.S. Air Force flyover
National Anthem: Grambling University Band
Coin toss: Game official
Halftime: Grambling University Band
Commissioner's party site: Doral-on-Beach, Miami Beach

Super Bowl III

New York Jets (AFL) 16, Baltimore Colts (NFL) 7

Location: Orange Bowl, Miami, Florida
Date: January 12, 1969
Attendance: 75,389   Ticket prices: $12, $8, $6

Scoring Summary

New York   0   7   6   3—16
Baltimore   0   0   0   7—7
NY—Snell 4 run (J. Turner kick), 5:57 2nd
NY—FG J. Turner 32, 4:52 3rd
NY—FG J. Turner 30, 11:02 3rd
NY—FG J. Turner 9, 1:34 4th
BAL—Hill 1 run (Michaels kick), 11:41 4th
Most valuable player: Joe Namath, quarterback, New York
Winners' shares: $15,000   Losers' shares: $7,500
Head coaches: Weeb Ewbank, New York; Don Shula, Baltimore
Referee: Tom Bell
Televised by: NBC   Advertising rates (per 30 seconds): $55,000
Rating: 36   Share: 71

Entertainment

Pregame: Tribute to Apollo 8 astronauts, with Bob Hope
National Anthem: Anita Bryant, Pledge of Allegiance by Apollo 8
   astronauts
Coin toss: Game official
Halftime: "America Thanks," with Florida A&M Marching Band
Commissioner's party site: Jackie O'Hearts, Miami Beach Hilton

Super Bowl IV

Kansas City Chiefs (AFL) 23, Minnesota Vikings (NFL) 7

Location: Tulane Stadium, New Orleans, Louisiana
Date: January 11, 1970
Attendance: 80,562   Ticket price: $15

Scoring Summary

Minnesota	0	0	7	0—	7
Kansas City	3	13	7	0—	23

KC—FG Stenerud 48, 8:08 1st
KC—FG Stenerud 32, 1:40 2nd
KC—FG Stenerud 25, 7:08 2nd
KC—Garrett 5 run (Stenerud kick), 9:26 2nd
MIN—Osborn 4 run (Cox kick), 10:28 3rd
KC—Taylor 46 pass from Dawson (Stenerud kick), 13:38 3rd
Most valuable player: Len Dawson, quarterback, Kansas City
Winners' shares: $15,000   Losers' shares: $7,500
Head coaches: Hank Stram, Kansas City; Bud Grant, Minnesota
Referee: John McDonough
Televised by: CBS   Advertising rates (per 30 seconds): $78,000
Rating: 39.4   Share: 69

Entertainment

Pregame: "Battle of the Horns," with Al Hirt and Doc Severinsen
National Anthem: Al Hirt, Pledge of Allegiance by Apollo 11
  astronauts
Coin toss: Game official
Halftime: "Mardi Gras," with Carol Channing
Commissioner's party site: Roosevelt Hotel

Super Bowl V

Baltimore Colts (AFC) 16, Dallas Cowboys (NFC) 13

Location: Orange Bowl, Miami, Florida
Date: January 17, 1971
Attendance: 79,204   Ticket price: $15

Scoring Summary

Baltimore	0	6	0	10—16
Dallas	3	10	0	0—13

DAL—FG Clark 14, 9:28 1st
DAL—FG Clark 30, 0:08 2nd
BAL—Mackey 75 pass from Unitas (kick blocked), 0:50 2nd
DAL—Thomas 7 pass from Morton (Clark kick), 7:07 2nd
BAL—Nowatzke 2 run (O'Brien kick), 7:25 4th
BAL—FG O'Brien 32, 14:55 4th
Most valuable player: Chuck Howley, linebacker, Dallas
Winners' shares: $15,000   Losers' shares: $7,500
Head coaches: Don McCafferty, Baltimore; Tom Landry, Dallas
Referee: Norm Schachter
Televised by: NBC   Advertising rates (per 30 seconds): $72,000
Rating: 39.9   Share: 75

Entertainment

Pregame: Southern University Band, Northeast Missouri College
    Band
National Anthem: Tommy Loy, trumpeter
Coin toss: Game official
Halftime: Florida A&M Band
Commissioner's party site: Americana Hotel, Bal Harbor, Florida

Super Bowl VI

Dallas Cowboys (NFC) 24, Miami Dolphins (AFC) 3

Location: Tulane Stadium, New Orleans, Louisiana
Date: January 16, 1972
Attendance: 81,023   Ticket price: $15

Scoring Summary

Dallas	3	7	7	7—24
Miami	0	3	0	0—3

DAL—FG Clark 9, 13:37 1st
DAL—Alworth 7 pass from Staubach (Clark kick), 13:45 2nd
MIA—FG Yepremian 31, 14:56 2nd
DAL—D. Thomas 3 run (Clark kick), 5:17 3rd
DAL—Ditka 7 pass from Staubach (Clark kick), 3:18 4th
Most valuable player: Roger Staubach, quarterback, Dallas
Winners' shares: $15,000   **Losers' shares:** $7,500
Head coaches: Tom Landry, Dallas; Don Shula, Miami
Referee: Jim Tunney
Televised by: CBS   Advertising rates (per 30 seconds): $86,000
Rating: 44.2   **Share:** 74

Entertainment
Pregame: Kilgore Junior College Rangerettes, U.S. Air Force flyover
National Anthem: U.S. Air Force Academy Chorale
Coin toss: Game official
Halftime: "Salute to Louis Armstrong," with Ella Fitzgerald, Carol
    Channing, Al Hirt, and U.S. Marine Corps Drill Team
Commissioner's party site: Fairmont (Roosevelt) Hotel

Super Bowl VII

Miami Dolphins (AFC) 14, Washington Redskins (NFC) 7

Location: Memorial Coliseum, Los Angeles, California
Date: January 14, 1973
Attendance: 90,182   Ticket price: $15

Scoring Summary

Miami	7	7	0	0—14
Washington	0	0	0	7—7

MIA—Twilley 28 pass from Griese (Yepremian kick), 14:59 1st
MIA—Kiick 1 run (Yepremian kick), 14:42 2nd
WAS—Bass 49 fumble recovery return (Knight kick), 12:53 4th
Most valuable player: Jake Scott, safety, Miami
Winners' shares: $15,000   Losers' shares: $7,500
Head coaches: Don Shula, Miami; George Allen, Washington
Referee: Tom Bell
Televised by: NBC   Advertising rates (per 30 seconds): $88,000
Rating: 42.7   Share: 72

Entertainment

Pregame: Tribute to Apollo 17 astronauts, with the University of
    Michigan Band
National Anthem: Andy Williams and Little Angels of Chicago's
    Angels Church, Pledge of Allegiance by Apollo 17 astronauts
Coin toss: Game official
Halftime: "Happiness Is," with the University of Michigan Band
    and Woody Herman
Commissioner's party site: Queen Mary, Long Beach, California

Super Bowl VIII

Miami Dolphins (AFC) 24, Minnesota Vikings (NFC) 7
Location: Rice Stadium, Houston, Texas
Date: January 13, 1974
Attendance: 71,882   **Ticket price:** $15

Scoring Summary
Minnesota	0	0	0	7—7	
Miami	14	3	7	0—24	

MIA—Csonka 5 run (Yepremian kick), 9:33 1st
MIA—Kiick 1 run (Yepremian kick), 13:38 1st
MIA—FG Yepremian 28, 8:58 2nd
MIA—Csonka 2 run (Yepremian kick), 6:16 3rd
MIN—Tarkenton 4 run (Cox kick), 1:35 4th
Most valuable player: Larry Csonka, fullback, Miami
Winners' shares: $15,000   **Losers' shares:** $7,500
Head coaches: Don Shula, Miami; Bud Grant, Minnesota
Referee: Ben Dreith
Televised by: CBS   **Advertising rates (per 30 seconds):** $103,000
Rating: 41.6   **Share:** 73

Entertainment
Pregame: University of Texas Marching Band
National Anthem: Charley Pride
Coin toss: Game official
Halftime: "A Musical America," with the University of Texas
    Marching Band
Commissioner's party site: Astrodome

Super Bowl IX

Pittsburgh Steelers (AFC) 16, Minnesota Vikings (NFC) 6

Location: Tulane Stadium, New Orleans, Louisiana
Date: January 12, 1975
Attendance: 80,997   **Ticket price:** $20

Scoring Summary

Pittsburgh	0	2	7	7—16
Minnesota	0	0	0	6—6

PIT—Safety White tackled Tarkenton in end zone, 7:49 2nd
PIT—Harris 9 run (Gerela kick), 1:35 3rd
MIN—T. Brown recovered blocked punt in end zone (kick failed), 4:27 4th
PIT—Brown 4 pass from Bradshaw (Gerela kick), 11:29 4th
Most valuable player: Franco Harris, running back, Pittsburgh
Winners' shares: $15,000   **Losers' shares:** $7,500
Head coaches: Chuck Noll, Pittsburgh; Bud Grant, Minnesota
Referee: Bernie Ulman
Televised by: NBC   **Advertising rates (per 30 seconds):** $107,000
Rating: 42.4   **Share:** 72

Entertainment

Pregame: Grambling University Band
National Anthem: Grambling University Band, with Mardi Gras Chorus
Coin toss: Game official
Halftime: "Tribute to Duke Ellington," with Mercer Ellington Band and Grambling University Band
Commissioner's party site: Rivergate

Super Bowl X

Pittsburgh Steelers (AFC) 21, Dallas Cowboys (NFC) 17

Location: Orange Bowl, Miami, Florida
Date: January 18, 1976
Attendance: 80,187   Ticket price: $20

Scoring Summary

Dallas	7	3	0	7—17
Pittsburgh	7	0	0	14—21

DAL—D. Pearson 29 pass from Staubach (Fritsch kick), 4:36 1st
PIT—Grossman 7 pass from Bradshaw (Gerela kick), 9:03 1st
DAL—FG Fritsch 36, 0:15 2nd
PIT—Safety Harrison blocked Hoopes punt through end zone,
    3:32 4th
PIT—FG Gerela 36, 6:19 4th
PIT—FG Gerela 18, 8:23 4th
PIT—Swann 64 pass from Bradshaw (kick failed), 11:58 4th
DAL—P. Howard 34 pass from Staubach (Fritsch kick), 13:12 4th
Most valuable player: Lynn Swann, wide receiver, Pittsburgh
Winners' shares: $15,000   Losers' shares: $7,500
Head coaches: Chuck Noll, Pittsburgh; Tom Landry, Dallas
Referee: Norm Schachter
Televised by: CBS   Advertising rates (per 30 seconds): $110,000
Rating: 42.3   Share: 78

Entertainment

Pregame: Up With People
National Anthem: Tom Sullivan
Coin toss: Game official
Halftime: "Two Hundred Years and Just a Baby," tribute to
    America's bicentennial, featuring Up With People
Commissioner's party site: Hialeah Race Track

Super Bowl XI

Oakland Raiders (AFC) 32, Minnesota Vikings (NFC) 14
Location: Rose Bowl, Pasadena, California
Date: January 9, 1977
Attendance: 103,438   Ticket price: $20

Scoring Summary
Oakland   0 16   3 13—32
Minnesota   0   0   7   7—14
OAK—FG Mann 24, 0:48 2nd
OAK—Casper 1 pass from Stabler (Mann kick), 7:50 2nd
OAK—Banaszak 1 run (kick failed), 11:27 2nd
OAK—FG Mann 40, 9:44 3rd
MIN—S. White 8 pass from Tarkenton (Cox kick), 14:13 3rd
OAK—Banaszak 2 run (Mann kick), 7:21 4th
OAK—Brown 75 interception return (kick failed), 9:17 4th
MIN—Voigt 13 pass from Lee (Cox kick), 14:35 4th
Most valuable player: Fred Biletnikoff, wide receiver, Oakland
Winners' shares: $15,000   Losers' shares: $7,500
Head coaches: John Madden, Oakland; Bud Grant, Minnesota
Referee: Jim Tunney
Televised by: NBC   Advertising rates (per 30 seconds): $125,000
Rating: 44.4   Share: 73

Entertainment
Pregame: Los Angeles School District All-City Band and Ashley
    Whippet
National Anthem: Vikki Carr ("America the Beautiful")
Coin toss: Game official
Halftime: "It's a Small World," including crowd participation for
    the first time, with spectators waving colored placards on cue
    from Walt Disney personnel
Commissioner's party site: Pasadena Civic Center

Super Bowl XII

Dallas Cowboys (NFC) 27, Denver Broncos (AFC) 10

Location: Louisiana Superdome, New Orleans, Louisiana
Date: January 15, 1978
Attendance: 75,583   **Ticket price:** $30

Scoring Summary

Dallas	10	3	7	7—27
Denver	0	0	10	0—10

DAL—Dorsett 3 run (Herrera kick), 10:31 1st
DAL—FG Herrera 35, 13:29 1st
DAL—FG Herrera 43, 3:44 2nd
DEN—FG Turner 47, 2:28 3rd
DAL—Johnson 45 pass from Staubach (Herrera kick), 8:01 3rd
DEN—Lytle 1 run (Turner kick), 9:21 3rd
DAL—Richards 29 pass from Newhouse (Herrera kick), 7:56 4th

Most valuable players: Randy White, defensive tackle, and Harvey Martin, defensive end, Dallas
Winners' shares: $18,000   **Losers' shares:** $9,000
Head coaches: Tom Landry, Dallas; Robert "Red" Miller, Denver
Referee: Jim Tunney
Televised by: CBS   **Advertising rates (per 30 seconds):** $162,000
Rating: 47.2   **Share:** 67

Entertainment

Pregame: Southern University Band, Dallas Cowboys, and Denver Broncos cheerleaders
National Anthem: Phyllis Kelly, Northeast Louisiana State University
Coin toss: Red Grange
Halftime: Tyler Apache Belles, Pete Fountain, and Al Hirt
Commissioner's party site: Rivergate

Super Bowl XIII

Pittsburgh Steelers (AFC) 35, Dallas Cowboys (NFC) 31

Location: Orange Bowl, Miami, Florida
Date: January 21, 1979
Attendance: 79,484   Ticket price: $30

Scoring Summary

Pittsburgh	7	14	0	14—35
Dallas	7	7	3	14—31

PIT—Stallworth 28 pass from Bradshaw (Gerela kick), 5:13 1st
DAL—Hill 39 pass from Staubach (Septien kick), 15:00 1st
DAL—Hegman 37 fumble recovery return (Septien kick), 2:52 2nd
PIT—Stallworth 75 pass from Bradshaw (Gerela kick), 4:35 2nd
PIT—Bleier 7 pass from Bradshaw (Gerela kick), 14:34 2nd
DAL—FG Septien 27, 12:24 3rd
PIT—Harris 22 run (Gerela kick), 7:50 4th
PIT—Swann 18 pass from Bradshaw (Gerela kick), 8:09 4th
DAL—DuPree 7 pass from Staubach (Septien kick), 12:37 4th
DAL—Johnson 4 pass from Staubach (Septien kick), 14:38 4th
Most valuable player: Terry Bradshaw, quarterback, Pittsburgh
Winners' shares: $18,000   Losers' shares: $9,000
Head coaches: Chuck Noll, Pittsburgh; Tom Landry, Dallas
Referee: Pat Haggerty
Televised by: NBC   Advertising rates (per 30 seconds): $185,000
Rating: 47.1   Share: 74

Entertainment

Pregame: Dallas Cowboys cheerleaders and military bands
National Anthem: Colgate Seven
Coin toss: George Halas
Halftime: "Super Bowl XIII Carnival," salute to the Caribbean,
    with Ken Hamilton and bands of the Caribbean Islands
Commissioner's party site: Miami International Airport—
    "Caribbean Carnival"

Super Bowl XIV

Pittsburgh Steelers (AFC) 31, Los Angeles Rams (NFC) 19

Location: Rose Bowl, Pasadena, California
Date: January 20, 1980
Attendance: 103,985   Ticket price: $30

Scoring Summary

Los Angeles   7   6   6   0—19
Pittsburgh   3   7   7   14—31
PIT—FG Bahr 41, 7:29 1st
LA—Bryant 1 run (Corral kick), 12:16 1st
PIT—Harris 1 run (Bahr kick), 2:08 2nd
LA—FG Corral 31, 7:39 2nd
LA—FG Corral 45, 14:46 2nd
PIT—Swann 47 pass from Bradshaw (Bahr kick), 2:48 3rd
LA—R. Smith 24 pass from McCutcheon (kick failed), 4:45 3rd
PIT—Stallworth 73 pass from Bradshaw (Bahr kick), 2:56 4th
PIT—Harris 1 run (Bahr kick), 13:11 4th
Most valuable player: Terry Bradshaw, quarterback, Pittsburgh
Winners' shares: $18,000   Losers' shares: $9,000
Head coaches: Chuck Noll, Pittsburgh; Ray Malavasi, Los Angeles
Referee: Fred Silva
Televised by: CBS   Advertising rates (per 30 seconds): $222,000
Rating: 46.3   Share: 67

Entertainment

Pregame: Los Angeles School District All-City Band
National Anthem: Cheryl Ladd, Golden Knights Parachute Team
Coin toss: Art Rooney
Halftime: "A Salute to the Big Band Era," featuring Up With People
Commissioner's party site: Pasadena Civic Center

Super Bowl XV

Oakland Raiders (AFC) 27, Philadelphia Eagles (NFC) 10

Location: Louisiana Superdome, New Orleans, Louisiana
Date: January 25, 1981
Attendance: 76,135   Ticket price: $40

Scoring Summary

Oakland	14	0	10	3—27
Philadelphia	0	3	0	7—10

OAK—Branch 2 pass from Plunkett (Bahr kick), 6:04 1st
OAK—King 80 pass from Plunkett (Bahr kick), 14:51 1st
PHI—FG Franklin 30, 4:32 2nd
OAK—Branch 29 pass from Plunkett (Bahr kick), 2:36 3rd
OAK—FG Bahr 46, 10:25 3rd
PHI—Krepfle 8 pass from Jaworski (Franklin kick), 1:01 4th
OAK—FG Bahr 35, 6:31 4th
Most valuable player: Jim Plunkett, quarterback, Oakland
Winners' shares: $18,000   Losers' shares: $9,000
Head coaches: Tom Flores, Oakland; Dick Vermeil, Philadelphia
Referee: Ben Dreith
Televised by: NBC   Advertising rates (per 30 seconds): $275,000
Rating: 44.4   Share: 63

Entertainment

Pregame: Southern University Band, featuring a yellow ribbon
    tribute to the just-released Iran hostages
National Anthem: Helen O'Connell
Coin toss: Marie Lombardi
Halftime: "Mardi Gras Festival," featuring Pete Fountain
Commissioner's party site: Rivergate

Super Bowl XVI

San Francisco 49ers (NFC) 26, Cincinnati Bengals (AFC) 21

Location: Pontiac Silverdome, Pontiac, Michigan
Date: January 24, 1982
Attendance: 81,270   Ticket price: $40

Scoring Summary

San Francisco   7   13   0   6—26
Cincinnati   0   0   7   14—21

SF—Montana 1 run (Wersching kick), 9:08 1st
SF—E. Cooper 11 pass from Montana (Wersching kick), 8:07 2nd
SF—FG Wersching 22, 14:45 2nd
SF—FG Wersching 26, 14:58 2nd
CIN—Anderson 5 run (Breech kick), 3:35 3rd
CIN—Ross 4 pass from Anderson (Breech kick), 4:54 4th
SF—FG Wersching 40, 9:35 4th
SF—FG Wersching 23, 13:03 4th
CIN—Ross 3 pass from Anderson (Breech kick), 14:44 4th
Most valuable player: Joe Montana, quarterback, San Francisco
Winners' shares: $18,000   **Losers' shares:** $9,000
Head coaches: Bill Walsh, San Francisco; Forrest Gregg, Cincinnati
Referee: Pat Haggerty
Televised by: CBS   **Advertising rates (per 30 seconds):** $324,000
Rating: 49.1   **Share:** 73

Entertainment

Pregame: University of Michigan Band
National Anthem: Diana Ross
Coin toss: Bobby Layne
Halftime: "A Salute to the Sixties and Motown," featuring Up With People
Commissioner's party site: Fairlane Club, Dearborn, Michigan— "America on Wheels"

Super Bowl XVII

Washington Redskins (NFC) 27, Miami Dolphins (AFC) 17
Location: Rose Bowl, Pasadena, California
Date: January 30, 1983
Attendance: 103,667   Ticket price: $40

Scoring Summary
Miami   7 10   0   0—17
Washington   0 10   3   14—27
MIA—Cefalo 76 pass from Woodley (von Schamann kick), 6:49 1st
WAS—FG Moseley 31, 0:21 2nd
MIA—FG von Schamann 20, 9:00 2nd
WAS—Garrett 4 pass from Theismann (Moseley kick), 13:09 2nd
MIA—Walker 98 kickoff return (von Schamann kick), 13:22 2nd
WAS—FG Moseley 20, 6:51 3rd
WAS—Riggins 43 run (Moseley kick), 4:59 4th
WAS—Brown 6 pass from Theismann (Moseley kick), 13:05 4th
Most valuable player: John Riggins, running back, Washington
Winners' shares: $36,000   **Losers' shares:** $18,000
Head coaches: Joe Gibbs, Washington; Don Shula, Miami
Referee: Jerry Markbreit
Televised by: NBC   Advertising rates (per 30 seconds): $400,000
Rating: 48.6   Share: 69

Entertainment
Pregame: Los Angeles School District All-City Band
National Anthem: Leslie Easterbrook
Coin toss: Elroy Hirsch
Halftime: "KaleidoSUPERscope," a kaleidoscope of color and
   sound
Commissioner's party site: None

Super Bowl XVIII

Los Angeles Raiders (AFC) 38, Washington Redskins (NFC) 9
Location: Tampa Stadium, Tampa, Florida
Date: January 22, 1984
Attendance: 72,920　　Ticket price: $60

Scoring Summary
Washington　　　　0　3　6　0—9
Los Angeles　　　　7　14　14　3—38
LA—Jensen recovered blocked punt in end zone (Bahr kick), 4:52
　1st
LA—Branch 12 pass from Plunkett (Bahr kick), 5:46 2nd
WAS—FG Moseley 24, 11:55 2nd
LA—Squirek 5 interception return (Bahr kick), 14:53 2nd
WAS—Riggins 1 run (kick blocked), 4:08 3rd
LA—Allen 5 run (Bahr kick), 7:54 3rd
LA—Allen 74 run (Bahr kick), 15:00 3rd
LA—FG Bahr 21, 12:36 4th
Most valuable player: Marcus Allen, running back, Los Angeles
Winners' shares: $36,000　　**Losers' shares:** $18,000
Head coaches: Tom Flores, Los Angeles; Joe Gibbs, Washington
Referee: Gene Barth
Televised by: CBS　　**Advertising rates (per 30 seconds):** $368,000
Rating: 46.4　　**Share:** 71

Entertainment
Pregame: Florida State and University of Florida bands, MacDill
　U.S. Air Force Base flyover
National Anthem: Barry Manilow
Coin toss: Bronko Nagurski
Halftime: "Super Bowl XVIII's Salute to the Superstars of the
　Silver Screen"
Commissioner's party site: Florida State Fairgrounds—"Come to
　the Circus"

Super Bowl XIX

San Francisco 49ers (NFC) 38, Miami Dolphins (AFC) 16

Location: Stanford Stadium, Palo Alto, California
Date: January 20, 1985
Attendance: 84,059   Ticket price: $60

Scoring Summary

Miami	10	6	0	0—16
San Francisco	7	21	10	0—38

MIA—FG von Schamann 37, 7:36 1st
SF—Monroe 33 pass from Montana (Wersching kick), 11:48 1st
MIA—D. Johnson 2 pass from Marino (von Schamann kick), 14:15
  1st
SF—Craig 8 pass from Montana (Wersching kick), 3:26 2nd
SF—Montana 6 run (Wersching kick), 8:02 2nd
SF—Craig 2 run (Wersching kick), 12:55 2nd
MIA—FG von Schamann 31, 14:48 2nd
MIA—FG von Schamann 30, 15:00 2nd
SF—FG Wersching 27, 4:48 3rd
SF—Craig 16 pass from Montana (Wersching kick), 8:42 3rd
Most valuable player: Joe Montana, quarterback, San Francisco
Winners' shares: $36,000   **Losers' shares:** $18,000
Head coaches: Bill Walsh, San Francisco; Don Shula, Miami
Referee: Pat Haggerty
Televised by: ABC   **Advertising rates (per 30 seconds):** $525,000
Rating: 46.4   **Share:** 63

Entertainment

Pregame: Tribute with the NFL Huddles team mascots
National Anthem: Children's Choir of San Francisco
Coin toss: President Ronald Reagan (from White House) and Hugh
  McElhenny
Halftime: "A World of Children's Dreams," featuring the U.S. Air
  Force's "Tops in Blue"
Commissioner's party site: Moscone Center, San Francisco—
  "Super Bowl Salute to the Bay Area"

Super Bowl XX

Chicago Bears (NFC) 46, New England Patriots (AFC) 10

Location: Louisiana Superdome, New Orleans, Louisiana
Date: January 26, 1986
Attendance: 73,818   **Ticket price:** $75

Scoring Summary

Chicago	13	10	21	2—46
New England	3	0	0	7—10

NE—FG Franklin 36, 1:19 1st
CHI—FG Butler 28, 5:40 1st
CHI—FG Butler 24, 13:34 1st
CHI—Suhey 11 run (Butler kick), 14:37 1st
CHI—McMahon 2 run (Butler kick), 7:36 2nd
CHI—FG Butler 24, 15:00 2nd
CHI—McMahon 1 run (Butler kick), 7:38 3rd
CHI—Phillips 28 interception return (Butler kick), 8:44 3rd
CHI—Perry 1 run (Butler kick), 11:38 3rd
NE—Fryar 8 pass from Grogan (Franklin kick), 1:46 4th
CHI—Safety Waechter tackled Grogan in end zone, 9:24 4th
Most valuable player: Richard Dent, defensive end, Chicago
Winners' shares: $36,000   **Losers' shares:** $18,000
Head coaches: Mike Ditka, Chicago; Raymond Berry, New
    England
Referee: Red Cashion
Televised by: NBC   **Advertising rates (per 30 seconds):** $550,000
Rating: 48.3   **Share:** 70

Entertainment

Pregame: Salute to Super Bowl MVPs
National Anthem: Wynton Marsalis
Coin toss: Bart Starr, representing 17 Super Bowl MVPs
Halftime: "Beat of the Future," featuring Up With People
Commissioner's party site: New Orleans Convention Center—
    "Jazz 'n' Jive"

Super Bowl XXI

New York Giants (NFC) 39, Denver Broncos (AFC) 20

Location: Rose Bowl, Pasadena, California
Date: January 25, 1987
Attendance: 101,063   Ticket price: $75

Scoring Summary

Denver	10	0	0	10—20
New York	7	2	17	13—39

DEN—FG Karlis 48, 4:09 1st
NY—Mowatt 6 pass from Simms (Allegre kick), 9:33 1st
DEN—Elway 4 run (Karlis kick), 12:54 1st
NY—Safety Martin tackled Elway in end zone, 12:14 2nd
NY—Bavaro 13 pass from Simms (Allegre kick), 4:52 3rd
NY—FG Allegre 21, 11:06 3rd
NY—Morris 1 run (Allegre kick), 14:36 3rd
NY—McConkey 6 pass from Simms (Allegre kick), 4:04 4th
DEN—FG Karlis 28, 8:59 4th
NY—Anderson 2 run (kick failed), 11:42 4th
DEN—Johnson 47 pass from Elway (Karlis kick), 12:54 4th
Most valuable player: Phil Simms, quarterback, New York
Winners' shares: $36,000   Losers' shares: $18,000
Head coaches: Bill Parcells, New York; Dan Reeves, Denver
Referee: Jerry Markbreit
Televised by: CBS   Advertising rates (per 30 seconds): $600,000
Rating: 45.8   Share: 66

Entertainment
Pregame: Salute to California, with the Beach Boys
National Anthem: Neil Diamond
Coin toss: Willie Davis
Halftime: Disney's "Salute to Hollywood's 100th Anniversary"
Commissioner's party site: Universal Studios—"Hooray for Hollywood"

Super Bowl XXII

Washington Redskins (NFC) 42, Denver Broncos (AFC) 10

Location: Jack Murphy Stadium, San Diego, California
Date: January 31, 1988
Attendance: 73,302   **Ticket price:** $100

Scoring Summary

Washington	0	35	0	7—42
Denver	10	0	0	0—10

DEN—Nattiel 56 pass from Elway (Karlis kick), 1:57 1st
DEN—FG Karlis 24, 5:51 1st
WAS—Sanders 80 pass from D. Williams (Haji-Sheikh kick), 0:53 2nd
WAS—Clark 27 pass from D. Williams (Haji-Sheikh kick), 4:45 2nd
WAS—Smith 58 run (Haji-Sheikh kick), 8:33 2nd
WAS—Sanders 50 pass from D. Williams (Haji-Sheikh kick), 11:18 2nd
WAS—Didier 8 pass from D. Williams (Haji-Sheikh kick), 13:56 2nd
WAS—Smith 4 run (Haji-Sheikh kick), 1:51 4th
Most valuable player: Doug Williams, quarterback, Washington
Winners' shares: $36,000   **Losers' shares:** $18,000
Head coaches: Joe Gibbs, Washington; Dan Reeves, Denver
Referee: Bob McElwee
Televised by: ABC   **Advertising rates (per 30 seconds):** $645,000
Rating: 41.9   **Share:** 62

Entertainment

Pregame: Salute to Bob Hope, with flyover by U.S. Navy Blue Angels
National Anthem: Herb Alpert
Coin toss: Don Hutson
Halftime: "Something Grand," featuring 88 grand pianos, Radio City Music Hall Rockettes, and Chubby Checker
Commissioner's party site: North Island Naval Air Station, Coronado, California—"Hit Parade"

Super Bowl XXIII

San Francisco 49ers (NFC) 20, Cincinnati Bengals (AFC) 16
Location: Joe Robbie Stadium, Miami, Florida
Date: January 22, 1989
Attendance: 75,129   Ticket price: $100

Scoring Summary
Cincinnati	0	3	10	3—16
San Francisco	3	0	3	14—20

SF—FG Cofer 41, 11:46 1st
CIN—FG Breech 34, 13:45 2nd
CIN—FG Breech 43, 9:21 3rd
SF—FG Cofer 32, 14:10 3rd
CIN—Jennings 93 kickoff return (Breech kick), 14:26 3rd
SF— Rice 14 pass from Montana (Cofer kick), 0:57 4th
CIN—FG Breech 40, 11:40 4th
SF—Taylor 10 pass from Montana (Cofer kick), 14:26 4th
Most valuable player: Jerry Rice, wide receiver, San Francisco
Winners' shares: $36,000   **Losers' shares:** $18,000
Head coaches: George Seifert, San Francisco; Sam Wyche,
    Cincinnati
Referee: Jerry Seeman
Televised by: NBC   **Advertising rates (per 30 seconds):** $675,000
Rating: 43.5   **Share:** 68

Entertainment
Pregame: Salute to southern Florida and NASA program, and
    Homestead U.S. Air Force Base flyover
National Anthem: Billy Joel
Coin toss: Nick Buoniconti, Bob Griese (tossed coin), and Larry
    Little
Halftime: "Be Bop Bamboozled," featuring 3-D effects and
    southern Florida dancers
Commissioner's party site: Stephen Muss Convention Center—
    "Salsa 'n' Spice"

Super Bowl XXIV

San Francisco 49ers (NFC) 55, Denver Broncos (AFC) 10

Location: Louisiana Superdome, New Orleans, Louisiana
Date: January 28, 1990
Attendance: 72,919   **Ticket price:** $125

Scoring Summary

San Francisco   13   14   14   14—55
Denver   3   0   7   0—10

SF—Rice 20 pass from Montana (Cofer kick), 4:54 1st
DEN—FG Treadwell 42, 8:13 1st
SF—Jones 7 pass from Montana (kick failed), 14:57 1st
SF—Rathman 1 run (Cofer kick), 7:45 2nd
SF—Rice 38 pass from Montana (Cofer kick), 14:26 2nd
SF—Rice 28 pass from Montana (Cofer kick), 2:12 3rd
SF—Taylor 35 pass from Montana (Cofer kick), 5:16 3rd
DEN—Elway 3 run (Treadwell kick), 8:07 3rd
SF—Rathman 3 run (Cofer kick), 0:03 4th
SF—Craig 1 run (Cofer kick), 1:13 4th

Most valuable player: Joe Montana, quarterback, San Francisco
Winners' shares: $36,000   **Losers' shares:** $18,000
Head coaches: George Seifert, San Francisco; Dan Reeves, Denver
Referee: Dick Jorgensen
Televised by: CBS   **Advertising rates (per 30 seconds):** $700,000
Rating: 39.0   **Share:** 63

Entertainment

Pregame: "Super Mardi Gras Comes to New Orleans," featuring
  David Clayton Thomas and Archie Manning
National Anthem: Aaron Neville
Coin toss: Mel Blount, Terry Bradshaw, Art Shell, and Willie Wood
  (tossed coin)
Halftime: "Salute to New Orleans" and 40th anniversary of
  "Peanuts" characters, featuring Pete Fountain
Commissioner's party site: New Orleans Convention Center—"La
  Fete New Orleans"

Super Bowl XXV

New York Giants (NFC) 20, Buffalo Bills (AFC) 19
Location: Tampa Stadium, Tampa, Florida
Date: January 27, 1991
Attendance: 73,813   Ticket price: $150

Scoring Summary
Buffalo   3   9   0   7—19
New York   3   7   7   3—20
NY—FG Bahr 28, 7:46 1st
BUF—FG Norwood 23, 9:09 1st
BUF—D. Smith 1 run (Norwood kick), 2:30 2nd
BUF—Safety B. Smith tackled Hostetler in end zone, 6:33 2nd
NY—Baker 14 pass from Hostetler (Bahr kick), 14:35 2nd
NY—Anderson 1 run (Bahr kick), 9:29 3rd
BUF—Thomas 31 run (Norwood kick), 0:08 4th
NY—FG Bahr 21, 7:40 4th
Most valuable player: Ottis Anderson, running back, New York
Winners' shares: $36,000   Losers' shares: $18,000
Head coaches: Bill Parcells, New York; Marv Levy, Buffalo
Referee: Jerry Seeman
Televised by: ABC   Advertising rates (per 30 seconds): $700,000
Rating: 41.8   Share: 63

Entertainment
Pregame: "Super Show XXV," featuring flyover by 56th Tactical
    Training Wing, U.S. Central Command and U.S. Special
    Operations Command, MacDill U.S. Air Force Base, Tampa
National Anthem: Whitney Houston
Coin toss: Pete Rozelle
Halftime: "A Small World Salute to 25 Years of the Super Bowl,"
    featuring New Kids on the Block
Commissioner's party site: None (canceled due to Desert Storm)

Super Bowl XXVI

Washington Redskins (NFC) 37, Buffalo Bills (AFC) 24

Location: Hubert Humphrey Metrodome, Minneapolis, Minnesota
Date: January 26, 1992
Attendance: 63,130   Ticket price: $150

Scoring Summary

Washington	0	17	14	6—37
Buffalo	0	0	10	14—24

WAS—FG Lohmiller 34, 1:58 2nd
WAS—Byner 10 pass from Rypien (Lohmiller kick), 5:06 2nd
WAS—Riggs 1 run (Lohmiller kick), 7:43 2nd
WAS—Riggs 2 run (Lohmiller kick), 0:16 3rd
BUF—FG Norwood 21, 3:01 3rd
BUF—Thomas 1 run (Norwood kick), 9:02 3rd
WAS—Clark 30 pass from Rypien (Lohmiller kick), 13:36 3rd
WAS—FG Lohmiller 25, 0:06 4th
WAS—FG Lohmiller 39, 3:24 4th
BUF—Metzelaars 2 pass from Kelly (Norwood kick), 9:01 4th
BUF—Beebe 4 pass from Kelly (Norwood kick), 11:05 4th
Most valuable player: Mark Rypien, quarterback, Washington
Winners' shares: $36,000   **Losers' shares:** $18,000
Head coaches: Joe Gibbs, Washington; Marv Levy, Buffalo
Referee: Jerry Markbreit
Televised by: CBS   **Advertising rates (per 30 seconds):** $800,000
Rating: 40.3   **Share:** 61

Entertainment

Pregame: Showcase of Minnesota youth, including Metropolitan
  Boys Choir, Twin Cities Youth Symphonies, marching bands, and
  jazz group Moore by Four
National Anthem: Harry Connick Jr.
Coin toss: Chuck Noll
Halftime: "Winter Magic," including a salute to the winter season
  and Winter Olympics, featuring Gloria Estefan, Brian Boitano,
  and Dorothy Hamill
Commissioner's party site: Private party

Super Bowl XXVII

Dallas Cowboys (NFC) 52, Buffalo Bills (AFC) 17
Location: Rose Bowl, Pasadena, California
Date: January 31, 1993
Attendance: 98,374   **Ticket price:** $175

Scoring Summary
Buffalo	7	3	7	0—17
Dallas	14	14	3	21—52

BUF—T. Thomas 2 run (Christie kick), 5:00 1st
DAL—Novacek 23 pass from Aikman (Elliott kick), 13:24 1st
DAL—J. Jones 2 fumble recovery return (Elliott kick), 13:39 1st
BUF—FG Christie 21, 11:36 2nd
DAL—Irvin 19 pass from Aikman (Elliott kick), 13:06 2nd
DAL—Irvin 18 pass from Aikman (Elliott kick), 13:24 2nd
DAL—FG Elliott 20, 6:39 3rd
BUF—Beebe 40 pass from Reich (Christie kick), 15:00 3rd
DAL—Harper 45 pass from Aikman (Elliott kick), 4:56 4th
DAL—E. Smith 10 run (Elliott kick), 6:48 4th
DAL—Norton 9 fumble recovery return (Elliott kick), 7:29 4th
Most valuable player: Troy Aikman, quarterback, Dallas
Winners' shares: $36,000   **Losers' shares:** $18,000
Head coaches: Jimmy Johnson, Dallas; Marv Levy, Buffalo
Referee: Dick Hantak
Televised by: NBC   **Advertising rates (per 30 seconds):** $850,000
Rating: 45.1   **Share:** 66

Entertainment
Pregame: "Movies, Music, Hollywood," tribute featuring the Radio
    City Rockettes and flyover by U.S. Navy Strike Fighter Squadron
    from USS Nimitz
National Anthem: Garth Brooks
Coin toss: O. J. Simpson
Halftime: "Heal the World," featuring Michael Jackson and 3,500
    local children; finale included spectators' card stunt
Commissioner's party site: Los Angeles Equestrian Center—
    "Mane Event"

Super Bowl XXVIII

Dallas Cowboys (NFC) 30, Buffalo Bills (AFC) 13

Location: Georgia Dome, Atlanta, Georgia
Date: January 30, 1994
Attendance: 72,817   **Ticket price:** $175

Scoring Summary

Dallas   6   0   14   10—30
Buffalo   3   10   0   0—13

DAL—FG Murray 41, 2:19 1st
BUF—FG Christie 54, 4:41 1st
DAL—FG Murray 24, 11:05 1st
BUF—Thomas 4 run (Christie kick), 2:34 2nd
BUF—FG Christie 28, 15:00 2nd
DAL—Washington 46 fumble recovery return (Murray kick),
    0:55 3rd
DAL—E. Smith 15 run (Murray kick), 6:18 3rd
DAL—E. Smith 1 run (Murray kick), 5:10 4th
DAL—FG Murray 20, 12:10 4th
Most valuable player: Emmitt Smith, running back, Dallas
Winners' shares: $38,000   **Losers' shares:** $23,500
Head coaches: Jimmy Johnson, Dallas; Marv Levy, Buffalo
Referee: Bob McElwee
Televised by: NBC   **Advertising rates (per 30 seconds):** $900,000
Rating: 45.5   **Share:** 66

Entertainment

Pregame: "Georgia Music Makers," featuring Kris Kross, Georgia
    Satellites, Morehouse College Marching Band, and Charlie
    Daniels
National Anthem: Natalie Cole, with Atlanta University Center
    Chorus
Coin toss: Joe Namath
Halftime: "Rockin' Country Sunday," featuring Clint Black, Tanya
    Tucker, Travis Tritt, and Wynonna and Naomi Judd; finale
    included spectators participating in a flashlight stunt
Commissioner's party site: World Congress Center—"Hot Spots"

Super Bowl XXIX

San Francisco 49ers (NFC) 49, San Diego Chargers (AFC) 26
Location: Joe Robbie Stadium, Miami, Florida
Date: January 29, 1995
Attendance: 74,107   Ticket price: $200

Scoring Summary
San Diego   7   3   8   8—26
San Francisco   14   14   14   7—49
SF—Rice 44 pass from S. Young (Brien kick), 1:24 1st
SF—Watters 51 pass from S. Young (Brien kick), 4:55 1st
SD—Means 1 run (Carney kick), 12:16 1st
SF—Floyd 5 pass from S. Young (Brien kick), 1:58 2nd
SF—Watters 8 pass from S. Young (Brien kick), 10:16 2nd
SD—FG Carney 31, 13:16 2nd
SF—Watters 9 run (Brien kick), 5:25 3rd
SF—Rice 15 pass from S. Young (Brien kick), 11:42 3rd
SD—Coleman 98 kickoff return (Seay pass from Humphries), 11:59 3rd
SF—Rice 7 pass from S. Young (Brien kick), 1:11 4th
SD—Martin 30 pass from Humphries (Pupunu pass from Humphries), 12:35 4th
Most valuable player: Steve Young, quarterback, San Francisco
Winners' shares: $42,000   Losers' shares: $26,000
Head coaches: George Seifert, San Francisco; Bobby Ross, San Diego
Referee: Jerry Markbreit
Televised by: ABC   Advertising rates (per 30 seconds): $1,150,000
Rating: 41.3   Share: 63

Entertainment
Pregame: "Let's Celebrate," tribute to Florida's 150th anniversary, 75th anniversary of the NFL, and 25th anniversary of ABC *Monday Night Football*, featuring Sergio Mendes and Hank

Williams Jr., flyover by 93rd Fighter Squadron, U.S. Air Force Reserve Base, Homestead, Florida

National Anthem: Kathie Lee Gifford

Coin toss: Otto Graham (tossed coin), Joe Greene, Ray Nitschke, and Gale Sayers

Halftime: "Indiana Jones and the Temple of the Forbidden Eye," featuring Tony Bennett, Patti LaBelle, Arturo Sandoval, Miami Sound Machine, plus fire and skydivers stunts; finale included spectators' participation with light sticks

Commissioner's party site: Miami Beach Convention Center— "Razz Matazz"

Super Bowl XXX

Dallas Cowboys (NFC) 27, Pittsburgh Steelers (AFC) 17

Location: Sun Devil Stadium, Tempe, Arizona
Date: January 28, 1996
Attendance: 76,347   Ticket prices: $350, $250, $200

Scoring Summary

Dallas   10   3   7   7—27
Pittsburgh   0   7   0   10—17

DAL—FG Boniol 42, 2:55 1st
DAL—Novacek 3 pass from Aikman (Boniol kick), 9:37 1st
DAL—FG Boniol 35, 8:57 2nd
PIT—Thigpen 6 pass from O'Donnell (N. Johnson kick), 14:47 2nd
DAL—E. Smith 1 run (Boniol kick), 8:18 3rd
PIT—FG N. Johnson 46, 3:40 4th
PIT—Morris 1 run (N. Johnson kick), 8:24 4th
DAL—E. Smith 4 run (Boniol kick), 11:17 4th
Most valuable player: Larry Brown, cornerback, Dallas
Winners' shares: $42,000   Losers' shares: $26,000
Head coaches: Barry Switzer, Dallas; Bill Cowher, Pittsburgh
Referee: Red Cashion
Televised by: NBC   Advertising rates (per 30 seconds):
                      $1,085,000
Rating: 46.0   Share: 68

Entertainment

Pregame: Arizona theme celebrating Native American culture, Wild
    West traditions, and the great outdoors
National Anthem: Vanessa Williams
Coin toss: Joe Montana, representing 25 MVPs present
Halftime: Diana Ross and the one-thousand-member World Choir,
    celebrating 30 years of the Super Bowl, with special effects,
    pyrotechnics, and stadium card stunt; finale featured Ms. Ross
    departing stadium in a helicopter
Commissioner's party site: Phoenix Civic Plaza—"Good
    Vibrations—an NFL Happening"

Super Bowl XXXI

Green Bay Packers (NFC) 35, New England Patriots (AFC) 21
Location: Louisiana Superdome, New Orleans, Louisiana
Date: January 26, 1997
Attendance: 72,301   **Ticket price:** $275

Scoring Summary
New England   14   0   7   0—21
Green Bay   10   17   8   0—35
GB—Rison 54 pass from Favre (Jacke kick), 3:32 1st
GB—FG Jacke 37, 6:18 1st
NE—Byars 1 pass from Bledsoe (Vinatieri kick), 8:25 1st
NE—Coates 4 pass from Bledsoe (Vinatieri kick), 12:27 1st
GB—Freeman 81 pass from Favre (Jacke kick), 0:56 2nd
GB—FG Jacke 31, 6:45 2nd
GB—Favre 2 run (Jacke kick), 13:49 2nd
NE—Martin 18 run (Vinatieri kick), 11:33 3rd
GB—Howard 99 kickoff return (Chmura pass from Favre),
    11:50 3rd
Most valuable player: Desmond Howard, kick returner, Green Bay
Winners' shares: $48,000   **Losers' shares:** $29,000
Head coaches: Mike Holmgren, Green Bay; Bill Parcells, New
    England
Referee: Gerry Austin
Televised by: FOX   **Advertising rates (per 30 seconds):**
    $1,200,000
Rating: 43.3   **Share:** 65

Entertainment
Pregame: Los Del Rio performing the "Macarena"; country-rock
    star Mary Chapin Carpenter; and Cajun band Beausoleil
National Anthem: Luther Vandross
Coin toss: Mike Ditka, Tom Flores, Tom Landry, Chuck Noll,
    George Seifert, and Hank Stram (tossed coin)
Halftime: "Blues Brothers Bash," with Dan Aykroyd, John
    Goodman, and James Belushi; James Brown; and ZZ Top
Commissioner's party site: New Orleans Convention Center—
    "Bayou Bon Temps"

Super Bowl XXXII

Denver Broncos (AFC) 31, Green Bay Packers (NFC) 24

Location: Qualcomm Stadium, San Diego, California
Date: January 26, 1998
Attendance: 68,912   **Ticket price:** $275

Scoring Summary

Green Bay	7	7	3	7—24
Denver	7	10	7	7—31

GB—Freeman 22 pass from Favre (Longwell kick), 4:02 1st
DEN—Davis 1 run (Elam kick), 9:21 1st
DEN—Elway 1 run (Elam kick), 0:05 2nd
DEN—FG Elam 51, 2:39 2nd
GB—Chmura 6 pass from Favre (Longwell kick), 14:48 2nd
GB—FG Longwell 27, 3:01 3rd
DEN—Davis 1 run (Elam kick), 14:26 3rd
GB—Freeman 13 pass from Favre (Longwell kick), 1:28 4th
DEN—Davis 1 run (Elam kick), 13:15 4th
Most valuable player: Terrell Davis, running back, Denver
Winners' shares: $48,000   **Losers' shares:** $29,000
Head coaches: Mike Shanahan, Denver; Mike Holmgren,
   Green Bay
Referee: Ed Hochuli
Televised by: NBC   **Advertising rates (per 30 seconds):**
             $1,300,000
Rating: 44.5   **Share:** 67

Entertainment

Pregame: Fifth Dimension, Lee Greenwood, and Beach Boys
National Anthem: Jewel, with narration by Phil Hartman
Coin toss: Joe Gibbs (tossed coin), Eddie Robinson, and Doug
   Williams
Halftime: "A Tribute to Motown's 40th Anniversary," including
   Boyz II Men, Smokey Robinson, Queen Latifah, Martha Reeves,
   and the Temptations
Commissioner's party site: San Diego Convention Center—"Go
   West—a State of Mind"

Super Bowl XXXIII

Denver Broncos (AFC) 31, Atlanta Falcons (NFC) 19

Location: Pro Player Stadium, Miami, Florida
Date: January 31, 1999
Attendance: 74,803   Ticket price: $325

Scoring Summary

Denver   7   10   0   17—34
Atlanta   3   3   0   13—19

ATL—FG Andersen 32, 5:25 1st
DEN—Griffith 1 run (Elam kick), 11:05 1st
DEN—FG Elam 26, 5:43 2nd
DEN—R. Smith 80 pass from Elway (Elam kick), 10:06 2nd
ATL—FG Andersen 28, 12:35 2nd
DEN—Griffith 1 run (Elam kick), 0:04 4th
DEN—Elway 3 run (Elam kick), 3:40 4th
ATL—Dwight 94 kickoff return (Andersen kick), 3:59 4th
DEN—FG Elam 37, 7:52 4th
ATL—Mathis 3 pass from Chandler (kick failed), 12:56 4th
Most valuable player: John Elway, quarterback, Denver
Winners' shares: $53,000   **Losers' shares:** $32,500
Head coaches: Mike Shanahan, Denver; Dan Reeves, Atlanta
Referee: Bernie Kukar
Televised by: FOX   **Advertising rates (per 30 seconds):**
        $1,600,000
Rating: 40.2   **Share:** 61

Entertainment

Pregame: A Caribbean cruise theme, featuring the rock band Kiss
National Anthem: Cher
Coin toss: Raymond Berry, Roosevelt Brown, Art Donovan, Frank
    Gifford, Sam Huff, Tom Landry, Gino Marchetti (tossed coin),
    Don Maynard, Lenny Moore, Jim Parker, and Andy Robustelli
Halftime: "Celebration of Soul, Salsa, and Swing," featuring Stevie
    Wonder, Gloria Estefan, Big Bad Voodoo Daddy, Savion Glover
Commissioner's party site: Miami Beach Convention Center—
    "Aqua Odyssey"

Super Bowl XXXIV

St. Louis Rams (NFC) 23, Tennessee Titans (AFC) 16

Location: Georgia Dome, Atlanta, Georgia
Date: January 30, 2000
Attendance: 72,625   **Ticket price:** $325

Scoring Summary

St. Louis	3	6	7	7—23
Tennessee	0	0	6	10—16

STL—FG Wilkins 27, 12:00 1st
STL—FG Wilkins 29, 10:44 2nd
STL—FG Wilkins 28, 14:45 2nd
STL— Holt 9 pass from Warner (Wilkins kick), 7:40 3rd
TEN— George 1 run (kick failed), 14:46 3rd
TEN— George 2 run (Del Greco kick), 7:39 4th
TEN—FG Del Greco 43, 12:45 4th
STL— Bruce 73 pass from Warner (Wilkins kick), 13:06 4th
Most valuable player: Kurt Warner, quarterback, St. Louis
Winners' shares: $58,000   **Losers' shares:** $33,000
Head coaches: Dick Vermeil, St. Louis; Jeff Fisher, Tennessee
Referee: Bob McElwee
Televised by: ABC   **Advertising rates (per 30 seconds):**
$1,900,000
Rating: 43.3   **Share:** 63

Entertainment

Pregame: A salute to the great American music of the 20th century, featuring Tina Turner, Travis Tritt, the Georgia Tech Marching Band, and the Georgia Mass Choir
National Anthem: Narration by the Smothers Brothers, sung by Faith Hill
Coin toss: Bobby Bell, Bud Grant, Lamar Hunt (tossed coin), Paul Krause, Willie Lanier, Alan Page, Jan Stenerud
Halftime: "A Tapestry of Nations," with Phil Collins, Christina Aguilera, Enrique Iglesias, Toni Braxton, and 80-voice choir
Commissioner's party site: Cobb Galleria Center—"Art of the Ages"

Super Bowl XXXV

Baltimore Ravens (AFC) 34, New York Giants (NFC) 7

Location: Raymond James Stadium, Tampa, Florida
Date: January 28, 2001
Attendance: 71,921   **Ticket price:** $325

Scoring Summary

Baltimore	7	3	14	10—34
New York	0	0	7	0—7

BAL—Stokley 38 pass from Dilfer (Stover kick), 8:10 1st
BAL—FG Stover 47, 13:19 2nd
BAL—Starks 49 interception return (Stover kick), 11:11 3rd
NY—Dixon 97 kickoff return (Daluiso kick), 11:29 3rd
BAL—Je. Lewis 84 kickoff return (Stover kick), 11:47 3rd
BAL—Ja. Lewis 3 run (Stover kick), 6:15 4th
BAL—FG Stover 34, 9:33 4th
Most valuable player: Ray Lewis, linebacker, Baltimore
Winners' shares: $58,000   **Losers' shares:** $33,000
Head coaches: Brian Billick, Baltimore; Jim Fassel, New York
Referee: Gerry Austin
Televised by: CBS   **Advertising rates (per 30 seconds):**
$2,100,000
Rating: 40.4   **Share:** 61

Entertainment

Pregame: Sting, joined by Styx
National Anthem: Backstreet Boys, following "America the
Beautiful" by Ray Charles
Coin toss: Marcus Allen, Ottis Anderson, Tom Flores (tossed coin),
and Bill Parcells
Halftime: Aerosmith, 'N Sync, Britney Spears, and Mary J. Blige
Commissioner's party site: Tampa Convention Center—"Star
Gaze"

Super Bowl XXXVI

New England Patriots (AFC) 20, St. Louis Rams (NFC) 17
Location: Louisiana Superdome, New Orleans, Louisiana
Date: February 3, 2002
Attendance: 72,922   Ticket price: $400

Scoring Summary
St. Louis   3   0   0   14—17
New England   0   14   3   3—20
STL—FG Wilkins 50, 11:50 1st
NE—Law 47 pass interception (Vinatieri kick), 6:11 2nd
NE—Patten 8 pass from Brady (Vinatieri kick), 14:29 2nd
NE—FG Vinatieri 37, 13:42 3rd
STL—Warner 2 run (Wilkins kick), 5:29 4th
STL—Proehl 26 pass from Warner (Wilkins kick), 13:30 4th
NE—FG Vinatieri 48, 15:00 4th
Most valuable player: Tom Brady, quarterback, New England
Winners' shares: $63,000   Losers' shares: $34,500
Head coaches: Bill Belichick, New England; Mike Martz, St. Louis
Referee: Bernie Kukar
Televised by: FOX   Advertising rates (per 30 seconds):
                $1,900,000–$2,300,000
Rating: 40.4   Share: 61

Entertainment
Pregame: Boston Pops orchestra, "Lincoln Portrait" narrated by
    former presidents Gerald Ford, Jimmy Carter, George Bush, and
    Bill Clinton and former first lady Nancy Reagan, plus
    performances by Marc Anthony, Barry Manilow, Patti LaBelle,
    James Ingram, Mary J. Blige, Yolanda Adams, and Paul
    McCartney
National Anthem: Mariah Carey, accompanied by the Boston Pops
Coin toss: George H. W. Bush (tossed coin) and Roger Staubach
Halftime: U2 and a tribute to victims of September 11 terrorist
    attack
Commissioner's party site: None (canceled in respect for victims of
    September 11 terrorist attacks)

APPENDIX B

Bulls, Bears, and Super Bowls

Wall Street watches the Super Bowl as intently as anybody and for good reason. In 29 of 35 years since the game's 1967 debut, the Super Bowl's outcome has correctly predicted the direction of the Dow Jones Industrial Average for that year. According to "Super Bowl Theory," the Dow rises in years when the winner is an NFC team or an original NFL team and falls in years when the winner is from the AFC or the original AFL. Of late, however, the theory has looked increasingly suspect: Although the AFC Denver Broncos won the Super Bowl in 1998 and 1999, the Dow nonetheless advanced in both years, then declined in 2000 after a victory by the NFC St. Louis Rams.

Theory champions and critics alike could claim vindication in 2001 when the Baltimore Ravens' Super Bowl victory preceded the Dow's 700-plus decline. While officially a new franchise in the NFL's eyes and a member of the AFC, the Ravens and the city of Baltimore also have extensive ties to the original NFL. Baltimore was home to the Colts for more than 30 years, and the roots of the Ravens lie in Cleveland, home of the Browns. Moreover, both the Browns and the city of Cleveland have extensive ties to both the NFL and AFC, which is why 2002 is a far better test of the theory's viability. New England, the reigning Super Bowl champion as these words were written, has played exclusively in the AFL and AFC since its birth in Boston in 1960.

Super Bowl/Year	Winner	Dow Jones Close	Indicator
I/1967	Green Bay, NFL	905.11	Up
II/1968	Green Bay, NFL	943.75	Up
III/1969	New York Jets, AFL	800.36	Down
IV/1970	Kansas City, AFL	838.92	Up*
V/1971	Baltimore, AFC (old NFL)	890.20	Up
VI/1972	Dallas, NFC	1,020.02	Up
VII/1973	Miami, AFC	850.38	Down
VIII/1974	Miami, AFC	815.24	Down
IX/1975	Pittsburgh, AFC (old NFL)	852.41	Up
X/1976	Pittsburgh, AFC (old NFL)	1,004.65	Up
XI/1977	Oakland, AFC	831.17	Down
XII/1978	Dallas, NFC	805.01	Down*
XIII/1979	Pittsburgh, AFC (old NFL)	838.74	Up
XIV/1980	Pittsburgh, AFC (old NFL)	963.99	Up
XV/1981	Oakland, AFC	875.00	Down
XVI/1982	San Francisco, NFC	1,046.55	Up
XVII/1983	Washington, NFC	1,258.64	Up
XVIII/1984	Oakland, AFC	1,211.57	Down
XIX/1985	San Francisco, NFC	1,546.67	Up
XX/1986	Chicago, NFC	1,895.95	Up
XXI/1987	New York Giants, NFC	1,938.83	Up
XXII/1988	Washington, NFC	2,168.57	Up
XXIII/1989	San Francisco, NFC	2,753.20	Up
XXIV/1990	San Francisco, NFC	2,633.66	Down*
XXV/1991	New York Giants, NFC	3,168.83	Up
XXVI/1992	Washington, NFC	3,301.11	Up
XXVII/1993	Dallas, NFC	3,754.09	Up
XXVIII/1994	Dallas, NFC	3,834.44	Up
XXIX/1995	San Francisco, NFC	5,117.12	Up
XXX/1996	Dallas, NFC	6,448.27	Up
XXXI/1997	Green Bay, NFC	7,908.25	Up
XXXII/1998	Denver, AFC	9,181.43	Up*
XXXIII/1999	Denver, AFC	11,497.12	Up*
XXXIV/2000	St. Louis, NFC	10,786.85	Down*
XXXV/2001	Baltimore, AFC	10,021.50	Down
XXXVI/2002	New England, AFC	(year incomplete)	—

*Contradicts Super Bowl Theory

INDEX

Abitante, Pete, 253
Adams, Bud, 34
AFL. *See* American Football League (AFL)
Aiello, Greg, 253
Allen, George, 214, 295
Ameche, Alan, 10
American Football League (AFL), 3–4, 15. *See also* National Football League (NFL)
reconciling differences with NFL, 62–64
reconciling size of footballs and, 64–65
Anders, William, 158
Anderson, Donny, 66, 129, 142–43
Arledge, Roone, 284–85
August, Bob, 286

Baker, Stephen, 316
Baltimore Colts, 9–10, 20, 82
Super Bowl III, 149–54, 158–62
Baseball. *See* Pro baseball
Basketball. *See* Pro basketball
Beathard, Bobby, 216
Bell, Bert, 10, 13, 34, 153, 294
Bell, Bobby, 180
Berry, Raymond, 227
Best, Bob, 195–96
Beverly, Randy, 161
Bidwill, Bill, 41, 157
Biever, John, 217
Biggs, Verlon, 22, 161
Bisher, Furman, 162
Black Sunday, 208–10, 226
Blackout policies, 105–7. *See also* Television coverage
legal battles over, 291–96
Blair, Joe, 293

Bleier, Rocky, 229
Boeke, Jim, 110
Boggs, Hale, 55
Boozer, Emerson, 156, 161
Borman, Frank, 158
Bowen, Gabby, 9
Bowman, Ken, 143
Bradshaw, Terry, 225, 226, 228
Brady, Dave, 91
Breen, John, 27, 31
Brodie, John, 37
Brodsky, Irv, 287
Brooks, Garth, 202–4
Brown, Aaron, 48
Brown, Paul, 77, 78, 83, 332–35
Brown, Terry, 225
Browne, Joe, 73, 211, 253
Bruhn, Milt, 48
Buchanan, Buck, 180
Bush, George H. W., 205–8
Bussert, Joel, 316
Butkus, Dick, 26

Cannon, Jimmy, 286–87
Carothers, Hamilton, 50, 57
Cartwright, Seth, 27, 28–29
Cavanaugh, Mary, 18
Celler, Emanuel, 44, 50–58, 275
Chandler, Don, 127
Channing, Carol, 189
Chicago Bears, 6, 26
    Super Bowl XX, 227
Christman, Paul, 127

Chrysler, 136
Cleveland Browns, 82
Coaches, 211–15
Coca-Cola, 136
Cochran, Bob, 73, 80
Coin tosses, 210–11
Columnists, 217
Commissioner's parties
    demand for, 237–38
    gate crashers and, 240–42
    for Super Bowl VII, 236–37
    unique settings for, 238–40
Conerly, Charlie, 21
Considine, Bob, 10
Constantine, Carol, 254
Contemporary Security
    Corporation (CSC), 254
Control booths, 252–53
Cooke, Jack Kent, 215, 216
Cosell, Howard, 281–82, 286–87, 289
Coyle, Kevin, 252
Creamer, Robert, 56
Crisler, Fritz, 48
Cronin, Joe, 140
CSC (Contemporary Security
    Corporation), 254
Curtis, Mike, 24

Daley, Arthur, 48, 255
Dallas Cowboys, 12, 34, 182, 228, 229–30
Davis, Al, 29, 36–37, 45, 46, 56, 57, 63, 78, 83, 117, 146
Davis, Willie, 112

Dawson, Len, 64, 128, 166, 170–71, 180
DeBartolo, Eddie, Jr., 307
Denver Broncos, 26, 32
Dewveall, Willard, 36
Dey, Joe, 14, 305
Dirksen, Everett, 4, 55, 57, 58
Ditka, Mike, 37
Dowler, Boyd, 128, 147
Duncan, Mark, 18, 69, 73, 101, 125, 141, 144

Elkins, Lawrence, 35
Elkjer, Thelma, 18, 19, 89–90, 117, 329
Elliott, John, 161
Elway, John, 230
Ewbank, Weeb, 154, 155

Faulkner, Jack, 26
Fernandez, Manny, 229
Finks, Jim, 325–29
Fitzgerald, Ella, 189
Fitzmorris, Lesslee, 195–96
Flores, Tom, 214–15
Fong, Hiram, 58
Football. *See* Pro football
Footballs, reconciling size of, 64–65
Ford, Gerald R., 55
Ford Motor Company, 136, 145
Ford, William Clay, 206, 282, 287
Foss, Joe, 36
Fraley, Oscar, 10

Gabriel, Roman, 37
Garrett, Mike, 179–80
Gibbs, Joe, 215
Gifford, Frank, 286
Gilliam, Joe, 225
Gogolak, Pete, 40–41
Goldenson, Leonard, 285
Gowdy, Curt, 127
Grabowski, Jim, 36
Grange, Red, 210
Granholm, Bill, 80, 118–19, 144, 159, 172–74, 198, 213, 245, 253, 337–41
Grant, Arnold, 77, 214
Grant, Bud, 179, 212–13
Green Bay Packers, 5, 10, 229. *See also* Lombardi, Vince
Super Bowl I, 127–32
Super Bowl II, 144, 146–47
Green, Jerry, 5, 217
Gregg, Forrest, 215
Griese, Bob, 229
Grimsley, Will, 172, 305
Gunsel, Austin, 18

Hadhazy, Peter, 80, 253, 321
Halas, George, 6, 34, 78, 210–11, 321–24
Halftime shows, 183–84, 189–93. *See also* Super Bowls
performers at, 195
Super Bowl XI, 184–88
Halloran, Bob, 162
Hamilton, Tom, 98
Hand, Jack, 10, 112, 113, 311

Hanratty, Terry, 225
Harkins, Kenneth, 57
Harrington, Joey, 264
Harris, Franco, 225
Hart, Philip, 44, 50
Hayes, Bob, 142
Healy, George, 167
Heaton, Chuck, 143–44
Heffernan, Jim, 73, 253, 287
Hennigan, Charlie, 35
Herman, Dave, 156, 161
Herskowitz, Mickey, 113, 117
Hess, Leon, 164, 305
Hill, Winston, 156
Hilton, Barron, 34, 39
Hirt, Al, 167, 189
Hodge, Larry, 253
Hornung, Paul, 62, 131, 305
Houston Oilers, 26–27
Houston, Whitney, 221
Hruska, Roman, 5
Hudson, Jim, 162
Hundley, Bill, 73
Hunt, Lamar, 32, 33–34,
　　37–41, 43–45, 49, 50, 55,
　　57, 63, 78, 159, 347, 349

Ioos, Walter, 217
Isaacs, Stan, 162
Iselin, Phil, 164
Isenberg, Maxine, 113
Izenberg, Jerry, 217

Jackson, Keith, 286
Jackson, Michael, 194, 202
Jani, Bob, 183–84, 188, 191

Janoff, Murray, 162
Jimmy the Greek (James
　　Snyder), 172
Johnson, Lyndon B., 58
Joint Committee, 49–51. *See
　　also* National Football
　　League (NFL)
　　Super Bowl I and, 97–98
　　ruling on type of football by,
　　64

Kansas City Chiefs, 5, 24, 32,
　　179–81, 213
　　Super Bowl I, 127–31
　　Super Bowl IV, 166–67
Kapp, Joe, 181
Karras, Alex, 62, 69–70, 305
Kaze, Irv, 45, 117
Kemp, Jack, 297
Kensil, Jim, 8–11, 41, 117,
　　125, 144, 276
　　appointed executive director,
　　73
　　creation of Media Day, 109
　　hired by NFL, 12–14
　　as public relations director,
　　17
　　as Rozelle's right-hand man,
　　304–5
　　Don Weiss and, 309–14
Kensil, Mike, 209–10
Kent, Larry, 19
Kessel, Harry, 100
Kilmer, Billy, 296
King, Ed, 31
Kirby, John, 20

Klein, Dave, 217
Klein, George, 78, 91
Klosterman, Don, 24
Knox, Chuck, 24
Kramer, Jerry, 143, 146
Kransky, Pete, 254

Labrum, Joe, 13
Landry, Jack, 21, 24, 136
Landry, Tom, 140, 141, 142, 214
Lane, Chuck, 112, 117
Lang, Kay, 118
Lanier, Willie, 180
Leahy, Frank, 31
Leahy, Marshall, 11
LeBaron, Eddie, 320, 343–46
Lilly, Bob, 143, 229
Lindemann, Carl, 162, 284
Lisetski, Mike, 100
Livingston, Pat, 172
Lombardi, Vince, 10, 23, 41, 119, 134, 141, 146, 152, 248
    first Media Day and, 110–12
    redshirt draft and, 65–69
    at Super Bowl I, 129–30
Lombardi Trophy, 103
Long, Russell, 4, 55, 57, 58
Los Angeles Memorial Coliseum, 4–5, 121. *See also* Stadiums
    Super Bowl I and, 98–99
Los Angeles Rams, 20
Louisiana Superdome, 251–52
Lovell, James, 158

McClinton, Curtis, 180
McCormick, John, 56
McDonough, Will, 217
McElhenny, Hugh, 211
McGee, Max, 128, 147, 248
McGuire, Eddie, 203
McNally, Art, 100
McNally, Skipper, 240, 242
MacPhail, Bill, 278–79, 283, 284, 307
Madden, John, 214
Mandich, George, 170
Mara, Wellington, 38, 39, 40, 41, 53, 77, 78, 347–49
Marshall, George Preston, 34
Matte, Tom, 160
Matuszak, John, 248–49
Maule, Tex, 128, 311
Maxwell, Dick, 253
Maynard, Don, 156
Media Day, history of, 109–17
Medved, Ron, 31
Meredith, Don, 286
Miami Dolphins, 182, 213, 229
Michaels, Lou, 155, 160
Mikulak, Dan, 174
Mills, Wilbur, 58
Minnesota Vikings, 12, 20, 179–81, 212–13
    Super Bowl IV, 166
Mix, Ron, 20
Modell, Art, 41, 48, 79–80, 83, 106, 278, 347, 349–50
Monday Night Football, 276–79, 282–89
Montana, Donna, 227–28

Montana, Joe, 230
Morin, Milt, 31
Morrall, Earl, 149–50, 160,
    182
Morse, Arthur, 48
Murchison, Clint, 125
Murphy, Fido, 31
Murray, Jim, 217, 234
Musser, Charlie, 100

Namath, Joe, 27, 35, 154–57,
    161, 164, 227, 267,
    288
Nassikas, Jimmy, 175
National Football League
    (NFL), 3–4. *See also*
    American Football League
    (AFL); Joint Committee
    antitrust issues and merger,
    47–49
congressional approval for
    merger, 53–59
creating new divisions in,
    84–90
early staff of, 17–19
new headquarters of, 72
1967 championship game,
    139–43
Operation Baby-Sit, 19–32
public relations operations of,
    73
realignment process of,
    75–84
reasons for merging, 5–6
reconciling differences with
    AFL, 62–64

reconciling size of footballs
    and, 64–65
television debut of, 274
Neely, Ralph, 27
New England Patriots, 32, 227
New York Giants, 9, 38, 43
New York Jets, 22, 43, 164
    Super Bowl III, 150–51,
    158–62
NFL. *See* National Football
    League (NFL)
NFL Films, 18, 179, 307
NFL Properties, 18–19,
    137–38, 307
Nixon, Richard M., 180
Noll, Chuck, 187–88, 212
Norwood, Scott, 222–23
Nowatzke, Tom, 24
Nussbaum, Bob, 55

Oakland Raiders, 32, 43
    Super Bowl II, 145
Oates, Bob, 95, 217
O'Connell, Helen, 204
Office of the Commissioner,
    72–73
Officials, selecting, for first
    Super Bowl, 98–101
O'Neill, Terry, 202
Operation Baby-Sit, 19–32
Orr, Jimmy, 160
Outlar, Jesse, 55

Palmer, Mickey, 217
Parcells, Bill, 214
Peters, Jim, 162

Philadelphia Eagles, 10
Pinchbeck, Val, 45, 117, 253
Pitts, Elijah, 128
Pittsburgh Steelers, 82, 212,
    224–26, 228–29
Pollard, Dick, 24
Pool, Hampton, 29
Pope, Edwin, 199, 217
Press boxes, early, 71
Pro baseball, 6, 34, 49
Pro basketball, 34
Pro football
    college talent and, 17
    in 1950s, 6
    popularity of, 34–35
    television and, 12, 273–75
Pugh, Jethro, 143

Randle, Sonny, 48
Raphael, Dick, 217
Rauch, John, 29
Ray, Bill, 73
Reader, Jack, 100
Reagan, Ronald, 211
Redshirt draft, 65–69
Reed, Bill, 98
Reeves, Dan, 38, 42, 50, 118
Reichler, Joe, 10
Remmel, Lee, 217
Rentzel, Lance, 27
Rhome, Jerry, 26
Rice, Jerry, 230
Riedener, Oscar, 103–4
Riggins, John, 227–28
Robbie, Joe, 163, 215
Rochester, Paul, 161

Rohrig, Herman, 100
Rooney, Art, 12, 42, 79, 83,
    224, 304
Rooney, Dan, 42, 79, 83, 224,
    347, 348–49
Roosevelt Hotel, New Orleans,
    fire at, 172–74
Rose, Bert, 17–18, 20, 113,
    114, 117
Rosenbloom, Carroll, 34, 35,
    41, 50, 78, 79, 83, 152–53
    Colt's loss at Super Bowl III,
    162–64
Rosenthal, Harold, 73
Ross, Diana, 204–5
Royal Order of Realignment
    Recorders, 75, 91–92
Rozelle, Alvin Ray "Pete," 5,
    221, 303–8
    blackout policies and, 291–99
    elected NFL Commissioner,
    11–12, 34
    leadership qualities of, 19
    legacy of, 266–69
    merger with AFL and, 37–46
    obtaining congressional
    approval for merger,
    53–59
    redshirt draft and, 65–69
    role of television in sports
    and, 273–76
    television strategy of, 12–13
Rozelle Trophy, 265
Rubin, Ellis, 291–92, 295
Rule, Elton, 278
Ryan, Frank, 35

Sabato, Al, 100
Sabol, Ed, 18, 143, 307
Sabol, Steve, 121, 217
Salaries, player, for Super
    Bowl I, 101–2
Sample, Johnny, 161
San Francisco 49ers, 38, 43,
    230
Sauer, George, 22, 156, 161
Sayers, Gale, 25
Schaaf, Jim, 117
Schachter, Norm, 100, 127
Schleicher, Maury, 29, 30
Schottenheimer, Marty, 31
Schramm, Tex, 18, 25, 33, 36,
    37, 38–44, 49, 50, 57, 78,
    140, 141, 264, 278, 307,
    308, 314–20
Schuh, Harry, 27, 29–30, 32
Scott, Jake, 227, 229
Scott, Ray, 127
Seiler, Earnie, 145, 158, 189
Severinsen, Doc, 189
Sherrod, Blackie, 53
Shula, Don, 135, 151, 152,
    154, 161, 163, 182, 199,
    214, 229, 264, 320,
    331–35
Siegel, Mo, 172, 554
Simmons, Chet, 32, 162, 284
Smith, Bubba, 161
Smith, Don, 149–50, 159
Smith, Rankin, 37
Smits, Ted, 8, 9, 10, 310
Snell, Matt, 156, 161
Snow, Jack, 26

Snyder, Cameron, 91
Snyder, James (Jimmy the
    Greek), 172
Spadia, Lou, 38, 39, 41, 42, 67
Stadiums, 70–71, 86–87
    Los Angeles Memorial
        Coliseum, 4–5, 98–99,
        121
    pregame rituals at, 251–52
    press box accommodations
        in, 71
    selection of, for first Super
        Bowl, 98–99
    Stanford Stadium, 231
    Tulane Stadium, 168–70,
        245–47
    Veterans Stadium, 233
Standish, Harry, 18
Stanford Stadium, 231
Starr, Bart, 64, 100, 128, 143,
    147, 227
Staubach, Roger, 228
Steadman, John, 83
Steeg, Jim, 202, 203, 252
Stirling, Scotty, 29
Stram, Hank, 110, 113, 171,
    179
Sullivan, Billy, 32, 43, 50
Super Bowl I, 121–22, 127–32
    budget for, 102
    designing championship
        trophy for, 103–4
    hand falling off clock mishap
        at, 124–27
    organizing, 102–3
    player salaries for, 101–2

reasons for not selling out, 122–24

revenues, 122

television coverage for, 104–7

ticket sales for, 117–18, 134–39

Super Bowl II, 133–34, 189

success of, 147–48

Super Bowl III, 149–50, 158–62

Len Dawson affair, 170–71

Super Bowl IV, 165–66, 176–80, 213

effects of, 181–82

halftime show at, 189

New Orleans bid for, 167–68

Super Bowl V, 249

Super Bowl VII, 214, 229, 236

Super Bowl IX, 213, 224–25, 245–47

Super Bowl X, 188–89, 190, 208–10, 225

Super Bowl XI, 184–88, 213, 247–48, 254, 257

Super Bowl XIII, 228–29

Super Bowl XIV, 225, 228

Super Bowl XV, 204, 211, 223–24

Super Bowl XVI, 204–5, 215, 233

Super Bowl XVII, 215–17

Super Bowl XIX, 211, 231, 242–43

Super Bowl XX, 227

Super Bowl XXV, 219–23

Super Bowl XXVII, 194, 202, 235

Super Bowl XXXVI, 222, 228

Super Bowls, 95–97. *See also* Halftime shows

control booths for, 252–53

countdown example for, 253–64

demand for hotel rooms and, 243–45

impact of losing and, 249

postgame events, 263–64

security for, 254

selecting officials for, 99–101

statistic summaries for, 352–88

ticket scalping at, 252–53

transportation for, 254

use of Roman numerals for, 249

Wall Street and, 389–90

Swann, Lynn, 226

Tagliabue, Paul, 220, 227

Tarkenton, Fran, 224

Taylor, Otis, 27–29, 180

Teele, Jack, 113, 118

Television coverage

blackout policies and, 105–7, 291–96

Monday Night Football, 276–79, 282–87

pro football and, 12, 273–75

Super Bowl I and, 104–7

Thomas, Joe, 20

Ticket scalping, 242–43

Toler, Burt, 100
Toma, George, 191–92,
    196–97, 246
Tomsick Tony, 217
Tose, Leonard, 234
Trepinski, Paul, 100
Trophies, history of, 103–4,
    119–20
  Lombardy Trophy, 103
  Rozelle Trophy, 265
  at Super Bowl I, 130–31
Tulane Stadium, 168–70,
    245–47. *See also* Stadiums
Turner, Jim, 161
Twombly, Wells, 162
Two-point conversion rule, 63,
    101

Ulman, Bernie, 100
Unitas, Johnny, 10, 149, 162

Van Brocklin, Norm, 26
Van Duser, Jan, 293, 316
Vermeil, Dick, 249
Veterans Stadium, Philadelphia,
    233. *See also* Stadiums

Walker, Tommy, 188, 189
Wall Street, Super Bowls and,
    389–90
Walsh, Bill, 207, 215
Ward, Al, 116–17, 140, 141
Washington Redskins, 34, 214,
    229, 295
Weiss, Don
  appointed director of public
    relations, 73

early career of, 6–10
fire at Roosevelt Hotel and,
    172–74
hired by NFL, 14–15
Jim Kensil and, 309–14
job with U.S. Golf
    Association, 14
Monday Night Football and,
    287–89
Pete Rozelle and, 268–69,
    303–8
Super Bowl III and,
    159–62
Wells, Ken, 253
Wells, Lloyd, 27–28
Werblin, Sonny, 26–27,
    32, 35, 39, 106,
    156, 164
Whitaker, Jack, 127
White, Dwight, 224
Williams, Clarence "Clancy,"
    22–23
Williams, Fred, 128–29
Williams, Howie, 147
Wilson, Larry, 31, 50
Wilson, Ralph, 31, 34, 35,
    105
Wolf, Ron, 29, 30
Wood, Willie, 128
Woodard, Milt, 56, 57, 73
Wright, Gary, 255
Wynn, Jerry, 117

Young, Buddy, 18, 25
Young, George, 100

Zumwalt, Damon, 254